The Archaeology of East Oxford

The Archaeology of East Oxford

Archeox: the development of a community

Edited by

David Griffiths and Jane Harrison

with Olaf Bayer, Katie Hambrook and Leigh Mellor

Contributions by

Louise Bailey, Ruth Barber McLean, Mandy Bellamy, Paul Blinkhorn, Richard Bradley, Paul Booth, Anthea Boylston, Valeria Cambule, Helena Clennett, Stella Collier, Marcus Cooper, Nina Curtis, Peter Ditchfield, Pam England, Peter Finn, Christopher Franks, Sarah Franks, Nathalie Garfunkel, Nick Hedges, Will Hemmings, Janet Keene, Graham Jones, Jenni Laird, Tim Lee, Christopher Lewis, Swii Yii Lim, Thomas Matthews-Boehmer, Rob McLean, Gillian Mellor, Martin Murphy, Matt Nicholas, Steve Nicholson, Greg Owen, Adrian Parker, Gareth Preston, Phil Price, Roelie Reed, Joanne Robinson, Paul Rowland, Graeme Salmon, Philip Salmon, Andrew Smith, Julian Stern, Molly Storey, Chris Turley, Mark Viggers, Jeffrey Wallis, Leslie Wilkinson, William Wintle, Christopher Young.

Thames Valley Landscapes Monograph 43
Oxford University Department for Continuing Education
2020

Copyright © editors, 2020

Published by
Oxford University Department for Continuing Education

ISBN 978-1-905905-43-0

Designed by Charlie Webster at Production Line, Oxford
Printed in Great Britain by Short Run Press, Exeter, England

Contents

List of figures vii

Foreword: Professor Richard Bradley FBA xv

Heritage and Community: Rt. Hon. Andrew Smith xvii

Acknowledgements xix

Chapter 1 Introducing East Oxford 1

Features
    Alexander Montgomerie Bell, and the Bell Collection of stone tools 18
    A Neolithic axe from Chester Street, East Oxford 21
    The Leopold Street and Burgess's Meadow Bronze Age Hoards 22
    Early Medieval Weapons from the River Cherwell at Magdalen Bridge 26
    Two Stone Heads 30

Chapter 2 *Archeox*: the emergence of a community 33

Features
    The shared thrill of discovery 53
    Archeox at Boundary Brook Urban Nature Park 57

Chapter 3 Investigating a suburban landscape 59

Part 1: The test-pitting campaign 59

Features
    The Oxfordshire Roman Pottery Industry 86
    Medieval Pottery found in Oxford 88

Part 2: Geophysical Surveys in East Oxford 90

Feature
    South Park: interpretation of the earthworks 98

Part 3: Donnington Recreation Ground 2013: the excavation 103

Chapter 4 St Bartholomew's (Bartlemas) Chapel, surveys and excavations 111

Features
    Leper hospitals, lepers and leprosy 137
    Leprosy at Bartlemas 138
    Rickets at Bartlemas and anatomical dissection at Oxford 140
    Stable isotopic dietary analysis of the Bartlemas skeletons 142
    Bartlemas: its chapel, hospital and landscape 144

Chapter 5 Excavations at Minchery Paddock (Littlemore Priory) 2012 149

Features
    Excavation of the Priory Church, 2014 186
    The Littlemore Priory Book 188
    Nuns' Voices: Littlemore Priory 189

The patronage of SS Mary, Edmund and Nicholas at Littlemore Priory 193
Religion and rebuilding at St George's House, Cowley Road, Littlemore 195

Chapter 6 Place-names and the historic landscape of East Oxford 199

Features
The boundaries of Cowley in AD 1004 214
Domesday Book and the Normans in East Oxford 216
Improvement and enclosure in East Oxford 218
The Bath Street baths, St Clements, 1827–1879 222
Henry Taunt, a Victorian photographer in East Oxford 224

Chapter 7 A changing landscape and community 227

Meet some of the team
Chris Turley 232
Christopher Lewis 233
David Griffiths 233
Graham Jones 233
Greg Owen 234
Jane Harrison 235
Jeff Wallis 235
Jennifer Laird and Mark Viggers 236
Joanne Robinson 237
Katie Hambrook 239
Leigh and Gill Mellor 240
Leslie Wilkinson 240
Louise Bailey 241
Mandy Bellamy 241
Marcus Cooper with Charlie Cooper 242
Molly Storey with Leo and Nell 242
Northfield School (by Stella Collier) 243
Olaf Bayer 244
Peter Finn 244
Phil Price 245
Roelie Reed 245
Steve Nicholson 246
Tim Lee 246
Thomas Matthews-Boehmer 247
Valeria Cambule 247
Will Hemmings 248

Bibliography 249

Index 257

Project online research archive: https://doi.org/10.5287/bodleian:Am275j5p6
(Oxford University Research Archive - ORA; Dataset title: 'The Archaeology of East Oxford')

List of figures

Frontispiece

Excavations, test pits and geophysical surveys undertaken by *Archeox*, 2009–15
(contains Ordnance Survey data © Crown copyright and database right 2019) xiv

Location map

East Oxford in its local and regional context, with extent of project area (contains
Ordnance Survey data © Crown copyright and database right 2019) xvi

Foreword

1. (L-R), Hilary Lade, Jane Harrison, David Griffiths, Andrew Smith and Prof Jonathan
    Michie, Director of Continuing Education at Oxford, at the project launch xvii
2. Andrew Smith MP speaking at the Project Launch at 'Restore' in 2010, with (L) Prof
    Andrew Hamilton, Vice-Chancellor of Oxford University, and (R) Hilary Lade, SE
    Regional Board Member of Heritage Lottery Fund xvii

Chapter 1

Fig. 1.1.   Early Ordnance Survey Map, One inch to mile, 1830, source: Bodleian Libraries 2
Fig. 1.2.   The same area as Fig. 1.1 viewed from above today, © GetMapping plc 3
Fig. 1.3.   Geology and topography of East Oxford 5
Fig. 1.4.   Excavations in East Oxford under modern conditions by other organisations (contains
            Ordnance Survey data © Crown copyright and database right 2019) 7
Fig. 1.5.   Stone relief shield with *cross pattée* above the main door at Temple Farm, Sandford 13
Fig. 1.6.   Old St Clement's Church from south, prior to 1816, after Mallet (1924) 15

Chapter 1 features

Alexander Montgomerie Bell, and the Bell Collection of stone tools
1. A.M. Bell whilst studying at Balliol College, Oxford, in the late 1860s. Reproduced by
    kind permission of Master and Fellows of Balliol College, Bell AJM-26-5 18
2. Location of the Bell collections and Prehistoric finds from the Iffley Fields area. (Base
    mapping © Crown copyright/database right 2012. An Ordnance Survey/EDINA supplied
    service. Topography © Environment Agency copyright and/or database right 2019. All
    rights reserved). 19
3   Mesolithic, Neolithic and Early Bronze Age stone tools from the Bell collection, all
    © copyright Pitt Rivers Museum, University of Oxford. 20

A Neolithic axe from Chester Street, Oxford
1. Neolithic Axe from Chester Street in the Ashmolean Museum 21

The Leopold Street and Burgess's Meadow Bronze-Age hoards
1. Archive notes on the Leopold Street Hoard © Ashmolean Museum 23
2. Reproduction of the photograph of the Leopold Street Hoard in E.T. Leeds's report (1916) 23
3. Socketed, looped 'celt' from the Leopold Street Hoard 24
4. Palstaves from Burgess's Meadow (left) and Leopold Street (right) 24

Early Medieval weapons from the River Cherwell at Magdalen Bridge
1. The original shield boss in the Ashmolean Museum 26
2. The reconstructed shield boss 27

3.   The finished shield 27
4.   The stirrups © Ashmolean Museum 28
5.   Map of St Clements showing find-spots. Base Map 1900 Ordnance Survey 6 inch to the
          mile (© Crown Copyright and Landmark Information Group Limited 2014) 29

Two stone heads
1.   Small stone head from Hurst Street 31
2.   Paint traces on the small stone head 31
3.   Large stone head from St Clements 31

Chapter 2

Fig. 2.1.   Qualifications to degree level by area in Oxford ('LSOA', a statistical unit used by local
            government). Darker colours = higher, based on 2011 data © Oxford City Council 34
Fig. 2.2.   Numbers of people by area with less than five GCSE's or equivalent in Oxford. Darker
            colours = higher, based on 2011 data © Oxford City Council 35
Fig. 2.3.   Jane Harrison leads a guided walk in the early stages of the project 38
Fig. 2.4.   Jane Harrison teaches a student from Cheney School how to use survey equipment in
            South Park 38
Fig. 2.5.   David Griffiths and Nick Hedges with members of the public at *Archeox*'s stall at the
            2012 Cowley Carnival 39
Fig. 2.6.   Test pit 23 at Restore's Elder Stubbs gardens in Cowley 42
Fig. 2.7.   Test pit 29 at East Minchery Farm allotments 42
Fig. 2.8.   Earth resistance survey training 43
Fig. 2.9.   Swii Yii Lim operates the project's Leica GPS Smartrover 44
Fig. 2.10. Finds-sorting group at St Clement's Community Centre 45
Fig. 2.11. The 'Minchery', the surviving building of Littlemore Priory (from north), shortly after
            the closure of the pub in 2013. Minchery Paddock (Chapter 5) lies to right of the path 46
Fig. 2.12. Mark Viggers (left) allows children at the Cowley Carnival to play with a reconstructed
            Anglo-Saxon shield 48
Fig. 2.13. Gallery exhibition at Pitt Rivers Museum of Oxford Brookes students' art installations
            based on the project's finds. 48
Fig. 2.14. One of the Oxford Brookes art installations, featuring a piece of Medieval leaded stained
            glass (see Fig. 5.27) from the Minchery Paddock excavation 48
Fig. 2.15. Listening to the 'Matrix' sound art installation, conveying recorded sounds from the
            project's excavations 49
Fig. 2.16. Louise Bailey, an NVQ student, works on archaeobotanical material 49

Chapter 2 features

The shared thrill of discovery
1.   A group talk on place-names in a pub garden in Iffley 53
2.   Sorting and recording animal bone from the excavations 53
3.   A pottery workshop in Rewley House led by Paul Blinkhorn 53
4.   Rob McLean wet-sieving soil samples at Oxford Archaeology 54
5.   A GIS training session at Rewley House 54
6.   A drawing workshop 54
7.   Tea break at the Minchery Paddock excavation 55
8.   A visit to the Minchery Paddock excavation by Oxford University Vice-Chancellor
          Andrew Hamilton (right), talking to Will Hemmings (left) and David Griffiths (centre) 55
9.   Lucy Fletcher, discoverer of a Roman coin in Test Pit 12, Iffley Village 55
10.   Roman coin of Postumus, (Nick Hedges) 56
11.   Key from Temple Cowley Manor House in the Ashmolean Museum 56

***Archeox* at Boundary Brook Urban Nature Park**
1.   Some of the collection, Mrs Winslow's Soothing Syrup bottle on left 57
2.   A Victorian advertisement for Mrs Winslow's Soothing Syrup 57
3.   Test pit excavation at Boundary Brook Urban Nature Park 58

Chapter 3   Part 1: Test-pits

Fig. 3.1.   Map of East Oxford showing the numbered locations of all 72 test pits (contains
              Ordnance Survey data © Crown copyright and database right 2019) 60
Fig. 3.2.   All the finds from one context in Test Pit 72, after washing and sorting 61
Fig. 3.3.   Test pit 6 in the Ark-T Centre garden being recorded 62
Fig. 3.4.   Test pit distributions of Prehistoric lithics and pottery (Ceramic Phase 1) 64
Fig. 3.5.   Fragment of a Late Mesolithic flint arrowhead or barb: between 7500–4000 BC (L), and
              a flint from the mechanism of a flintlock gun, 17th–18th century (R) 65
Fig. 3.6.   Test pit distributions of pottery from Roman Period (Ceramic Phase 2) 66
Fig. 3.7.   Test pit distributions of pottery from the Early/Middle Anglo-Saxon Period (Ceramic
              Phase 3) 69
Fig. 3.8.   Test pit distributions of pottery from the Later Anglo-Saxon Period (Ceramic Phase 4) 71
Fig. 3.9.   Test pit distributions of pottery from the Medieval Period 1050–1400 (Ceramic Phase 5) 72
Fig. 3.10.   Test pit locations in and near Iffley Village. Base Map 1900 Ordnance Survey 6 inch to
              the mile (© Crown copyright and Landmark Information Group Limited 2014) 73
Fig. 3.11.   Test pit locations in and near Iffley Fields/Donnington. Base Map 1900 Ordnance Survey
              6 inch to the mile (© Crown copyright and Landmark Information Group Limited 2014) 74
Fig. 3.12.   Test pit locations in Littlemore. Base Map 1900 Ordnance Survey 6 inch to the mile
              (© Crown copyright and Landmark Information Group Limited 2014) 75
Fig. 3.13.   Test pit locations in Blackbird and Greater Leys. Base Map 1900 Ordnance Survey 6 inch
              to the mile (© Crown copyright and Landmark Information Group Limited 2014) 77
Fig. 3.14.   Test pit locations in Church Cowley. Base Map 1900 Ordnance Survey 6 inch to the
              mile (© Crown copyright and Landmark Information Group Limited 2014) 78
Fig. 3.15.   Test pit locations in and near Temple Cowley. Base Map 1900 Ordnance Survey 6 inch to
              the mile (© Crown copyright and Landmark Information Group Limited 2014) 79
Fig. 3.16.   Test pit distributions of pottery from the Later Medieval Period 1400–1550 (Ceramic
              Phase 6) 80
Fig. 3.17.   Test pit distributions of pottery from the Early Post-Medieval Period 1500–1700
              (Ceramic Phase 7) 82
Fig. 3.18.   Test pit distributions of pottery from the Later Post-Medieval Period 1650–1800
              (Ceramic Phase 8) 83
Fig. 3.19.   Test pit distributions of pottery from after 1750 (Ceramic Phase 9) 84

Chapter 3, Part 1, features

The Oxfordshire Roman pottery industry
1.   A Roman mortarium made in the Oxford potteries (C.J. Young) 86
2.   An excavated kiln at the Churchill Hospital site (C.J. Young) 86
3.   Map of Roman kiln sites 87

Medieval pottery found in Oxford
1.   St Neot's Ware (Maureen Mellor) 89
2.   Cotswold Ware (L) and Oxford Sandy Ware (R) (Maureen Mellor) 89
3.   East Wiltshire Ware (Maureen Mellor) 89
4.   Brill/Boarstall Ware (Maureen Mellor) 8

Chapter 3   Part 2: Geophysical and surface surveys

Fig. 3.20.   Locations of *Archeox* geophysical surveys (Contains Ordnance Survey data © Crown
              copyright and database right 2019) 91
Fig. 3.21.   Collecting data in the snow: South Park. The ground lines are visible either side of the
              surveyor, David Pinches 92
Fig. 3.22.   South Park: geophysical survey results and interpretation (Historic Mapping © Crown
              Copyright and Landmark Information Group Limited 2014) 93
Fig. 3.23.   Rose Hill: geophysical survey results and interpretation (Historic Mapping © Crown
              Copyright and Landmark Information Group Limited 2014) 94
Fig. 3.24.   Brasenose Wood: geophysical survey results and interpretation (Historic Mapping
              © Crown Copyright and Landmark Information Group Limited 2014) 95

Fig. 3.25. Donnington Recreation Ground: geophysical survey results and interpretation
           (Historic Mapping © Crown Copyright and Landmark Information Group Limited 2014) 96
Fig. 3.26. Donnington Recreation Ground static point gradiometer and earth resistance surveys 97
Fig. 3.27. Marking out features from the geophysical survey at Donnington Recreation Ground,
           prior to excavation 97

Chapter 3, Part 2, features

South Park: interpretation of earthworks

1.   Ridge and furrow in South Park, visually accentuated in light snow (David Griffiths) 98
2.   Lidar slope model of the lower end of South Park. The inset shows the data collected by
          the tractor-mounted GPS 99
3A.   A multidirectional hill-shade model of South Park derived from 1m resolution lidar
          Digital Terrain Model (© Environment Agency copyright and/or database right 2019.
          All rights reserved) 100
3B.   Interpretation of lidar data 100
4.   Eastern area excerpt from De Gomme's Map of Oxford's Civil War Defences, 1644/46
          © Bodleian Library, University of Oxford, with our annotation 102

Chapter 3   Part 3: Excavation at Donnington Recreation Ground, 2013

Fig. 3.28. Donnington Recreation Ground excavation: looking north 103
Fig. 3.29. Donnington Recreation Ground excavation: location map (Base mapping © Crown
           copyright/database right 2012. An Ordnance Survey/EDINA supplied service.
           Topography © Environment Agency copyright and/or database right 2019. All rights
           reserved) 104
Fig. 3.30. Plan of Trench, excavation completed, Plan 102 105
Fig. 3.31. Donnington Recreation Ground excavation: stratigraphic matrix 105
Fig. 3.32. Drawing of half-sectioned Neolithic pit [2028], section 1.02 106
Fig. 3.33. Drawing of half-sectioned tree-throw [2022], section 1.01 107
Fig. 3.34. Completed trench looking west 108
Fig. 3.35. Selection of the finds 109

Chapter 4

Fig. 4.1.   Bartlemas location map (Base mapping © Crown Copyright/database right 2012.
           An Ordnance Survey/EDINA supplied service. Topography © Environment Agency
           copyright and/or database right 2019. All rights reserved) 112
Fig. 4.2.   Bartlemas Farmhouse, east-facing frontage 113
Fig. 4.3.   Bartlemas House, south-facing frontage 113
Fig. 4.4.   Bartlemas (St. Bartholomew's) Chapel, from north-west 114
Fig. 4.5.   Chapel 3-D exterior scan, viewpoint from south-west, conducted by *Archeox* in
           conjunction with Mollenhauer Group, 2011 114
Fig. 4.6.   1840 Estate Map © Oriel College, Oxford, showing the chapel in its enclosure, the
           adjacent buildings and water feature (in blue) 115
Fig. 4.7.   Conjectured reconstruction of Bartlemas Chapel and it surroundings during the
           Leper Hospital period, from west. Artwork by Helen Ganly 116
Fig. 4.8.   Henry Taunt's photograph of the Chapel, circa 1900: HT3004 © OHC 117
Fig. 4.9.   Bartlemas test pit locations. Base Map 1900 Ordnance Survey 6 inch to the mile
           (© Crown Copyright and Landmark Information Group Limited 2014) 119
Fig. 4.10. Geophysical (earth resistance survey) results overview, by William Wintle. (Base mapping
           © Crown copyright/database right 2012. An Ordnance Survey/EDINA supplied service) 120
Fig. 4.11. Trench 2, working shot, from west 121
Fig. 4.12. Trenches, buildings and building phases 122
Fig. 4.13. Trench 1, surrounding the chapel, plan of early phase stone foundations 123
Fig. 4.14. Foundations of the earlier phase chapel protruding from under the current N wall,
           from west 124

Fig. 4.15. Wall foundations in Trench 3 125

Fig. 4.16. Medieval Oxford Ware OXY (SF 46) 125

Fig. 4.17. Trenches, burials and charnel pits 126

Fig. 4.18. Inhumation exposed in Test pit 72, east of the Chapel. North to right of image 127

Fig. 4.19. Trench 2, working shot, from south 128

Fig. 4.20. Relieving arch [1048] in southern wall of chapel 129

Fig. 4.21. Trench 1, Charnel pit (1015) (SK 3) to the south of the chapel 129

Fig. 4.22. Trench 1, SK 1, east of chapel, west at top of image 130

Fig. 4.23. Trench 1, SK and SK 12, intercut east of chapel 130

Fig. 4.24. Trench 2, Child burial SK 6-7 131

Fig. 4.25. Tudor Green pottery found with SK 5 131

Fig. 4.26. Three lead musket balls, probably manufactured on site 132

Fig. 4.27. Trench 1, working shot of charnel pit (1026) from east (bones collectively SK 4) 132

Fig. 4.28. Sketch of Bartlemas Farm, dated 1837, with smaller intermediate buildings since
           removed © Oriel College, Oxford 133

Fig. 4.29. Henry Taunt's photograph of Bartlemas © Historic England, taken from south in
           adjacent field (now allotments) showing ridge and furrow (foreground) and sheds
           behind precinct wall 133

Fig. 4.30. Finds from Bartlemas Chapel, 1 134

Fig. 4.31. Finds from Bartlemas Chapel, 2 135

Fig. 4.32. Silver coin of Henry III, Voided long cross, 1248-50 (SF 37) 135

Fig. 4.33. Copper-alloy jetton, probably from Nuremberg (SF 26) 135

Fig. 4.34. Turned bone cylinder with screw thread (SF 22) 135

Fig. 4.35. Copper-alloy cast crotal bell (SF 7) 135

Fig. 4.36. Decorated glass button with metal suspension loop (SF 29) 136

Chapter 4 features

Leprosy at Bartlemas

1.   Stone corbel in Lincoln Cathedral showing facial changes of leprosy, published by
        permission of Jo Buckberry 139

2.   Leprosy seen in an upper jaw bone from context (1016) 139

3.   Foot bones affected by leprosy from context (1015/5) 140

Rickets at Bartlemas and anatomical dissection at Oxford

1.   Rickets in both femora (thigh bones) of a female from context (1026) in charnel pit 1 141

2.   A drilled hole in bone from context (1026) 141

Stable Isotopic Dietary Analysis

1.   Carbon and Nitrogen stable isotope plot of the data obtained from the Bartlemas
        skeletons, with the data ranges of other comparative Oxford human collagen data sets 143

Chapter 5

Fig. 5.1.   Trench 3 from south-west, with the western façade of the surviving priory building
           (AerialCam) 149

Fig. 5.2.   Landscape map showing the surviving building and the Minchery Paddock excavation
           trenches of JMHS 2006/ 2014 and Archeox 2012 (Base mapping © Crown Copyright/
           database right 2012. An Ordnance Survey/EDINA supplied service. Topography
           © Environment Agency copyright and/or database right 2019. All rights reserved) 150

Fig. 5.3.   Site map showing locations of Trenches 2 and 3 with remaining priory building. 151

Fig. 5.4.   Barbed and tanged flint arrowhead of the Early Bronze Age, just after discovery 153

Fig. 5.5.   Roman white glass melon fluted bead (SF 111) 153

Fig. 5.6.   The former Priory pub, the last upstanding part of the priory, eastern façade 154

Fig. 5.7.   Locations of trenches and priory building with Pantin's (1970) proposed cloister plan
           superimposed 155

Fig. 5.8.   Excavation conditions in Trench 1 156

Fig. 5.9.   Peat layer exposed in south-facing section, Trench 1 156

Fig. 5.10.   Trench 1, south-facing section with locations of column samples marked 157
Fig. 5.11.   Monolith samples wrapped and ready to be taken for laboratory analysis 157
Fig. 5.12.   Trench 2, final plan 158
Fig. 5.13.   Trench 2, from south (AerialCam) 159
Fig. 5.14.   The hearth, working shot from north-east 161
Fig. 5.15.   Trench 2, southern area, from south showing cobbled yard 162
Fig. 5.16.   View across Building 2 later in excavation, from south-west 163
Fig. 5.17.   Wall [2030] from north 164
Fig. 5.18.   Elevation drawing of wall [2030] showing relieving arch built over pit [2058] 164
Fig. 5.19.   The bone tuning peg (SF 138) 165
Fig. 5.20.   Silver coin of Henry III, Voided long cross, 1248–50 (SF 85) 165
Fig. 5.21.   Silver coin, Henry II, Short cross, 1180–89 (SF 81) 166
Fig. 5.22.   Trench 2, silted water channel from south-east 166
Fig. 5.23.   Section dug across water channel (photograph) 167
Fig. 5.24.   Section dug across water channel (drawing) 168
Fig. 5.25.   Trench 3 at the end of excavation, from south (AerialCam) 170
Fig. 5.26.   Trench 3, final plan 171
Fig. 5.27.   Leaded window came with green glass (SF 38) 172
Fig. 5.28.   Green-glazed roof ridge tile fragments from Trench 3 172
Fig. 5.29.   Minchery Farm with ancillary buildings, 1876 Ordnance Survey 6 inch to the mile
            First Edition (© Crown Copyright and Landmark Information Group Limited 2014) 173
Fig. 5.30.   Conjectured reconstruction of life at Littlemore Priory, from west. Artwork by
            Helen Ganly 174
Fig. 5.31.   Blocked-up dormitory cinquefoil window, priory building, eastern façade 175
Fig. 5.32.   Flint barbed and tanged arrowhead, Early Bronze Age (SF 1); Flint leaf-shaped
            arrowhead, Neolithic (SF 142) 176
Fig. 5.33.   Lithic, bone and metal finds from Minchery Paddock, 2012 177
Fig. 5.34.   Pottery from Minchery Paddock, 2012 178
Fig. 5.35.   Pottery from Minchery Paddock, 2012 179
Fig. 5.36.   Decorated floor-tile of 'Stabbed Wessex' type, with Griffin facing right (SF 47) 181
Fig. 5.37.   Decorated floor-tile of 'Stabbed Wessex' type, with Griffin facing left, incomplete
            (SF 73) 181
Fig. 5.38.   Decorated floor-tile of 'Stabbed Wessex' type, with studded circle design, incomplete
            (SF 125) 182
Fig. 5.39.   Decorated floor-tile of 'Stabbed Wessex' type, with fleur-de-lys, incomplete (SF 95) 182
Fig. 5.40.   Fragment of gilded pewter bell (SF 129) 182
Fig. 5.41.   Clay pipe bowl, undecorated with part of stem. Date: 1700-1770 (SF 105) 183
Fig. 5.42.   'Tombac' button, brass alloy (SF 104) 183
Fig. 5.43.   (a) Flint barbed and tanged arrowhead, Early Bronze Age (SF 1); (b) Flint leaf-shaped
            arrowhead, Neolithic (SF 142) 184
Fig. 5.44.   Lead Civil War powder cap (SF 12) 184

Chapter 5 features

Excavation of the Priory Church 2014

1.   Plan of the church excavations © John Moore Heritage Services 187

The Littlemore Priory Book

1.   Calendar: July/August, man with scythe © Bodleian Libraries, Oxford 188
2.   Prayers of St Anselm: nun with a book kneeling before the Virgin and Child © Bodleian
          Libraries, Oxford 188

Nuns' voices: Littlemore Priory

1.   The Virgin holding a book (from the manuscript of St Anselm's prayers owned by
          Littlemore Priory) 189
2.   Priest celebrating mass and two female worshippers (from the manuscript of St Anselm's
          prayers owned by Littlemore Priory) 190

3.   St Anselm gives books to Countess Mathilda of Tuscany and to monks (from the manuscript of St Anselm's prayers owned by Littlemore Priory) 192

Religion and rebuilding at St George's House, Cowley Road, Littlemore
1.   St Georges House, Cowley Road, Littlemore, eastern range 196
2.   A late Tudor stained-glass window, allegedly signed by J. H. Newman (panel since removed) .. 196
3.   The rear wall of this inglenook contains fragments of a chamfered lintel and socketed stones 196
4.   Carved sandstone fragments from the rubble internal walls of an inglenook 197
5.   Shaped stone from an inglenook infill: possibly part of a slab used in a brass memorial 197
6.   Decorated upright or lintel from the rear rubble wall of an inglenook 197

Chapter 6

Fig 6.1.   Locations of place-names and field-names: Map 1 200
Fig 6.2.   Wood pasture (from the twelfth- century calendar owned by Littlemore Priory) © Bodleian Libraries, Oxford 201
Fig 6.3.   Lake Field and Catwell Field. Langdon map, Cowley, Corpus Christi College MS 533, 19 203
Fig 6.4.   Marshy land in Littlemore. Langdon map, Cowley, Corpus Christi College MS 533, 19 204
Fig 6.5.   Harvest (from the twelfth-century calendar owned by Littlemore Priory). © Bodleian Libraries, Oxford 205
Fig 6.6.   Magdalen Bridge. Langdon map, Cowley, Corpus Christi College MS 533, 19 205
Fig 6.7.   Harehedge. Langdon map, Cowley, Corpus Christi College MS 533, 19 206
Fig 6.8.   Locations of place-names and field-names: Map 2 207
Fig 6.9.   Open Fields in Littlemore. Langdon map, Cowley, Corpus Christi College MS 533, 19 208
Fig 6.10.   Shearing sheep (from the twelfth-century calendar owned by Littlemore Priory) © Bodleian Libraries, Oxford 209
Fig 6.11.   Routes leading east from Magdalen Bridge. Langdon map, Cowley, Corpus Christi College MS 533, 19 210

Chapter 6 features

The boundaries of Cowley in AD 1004
1.   Places referred to in text 215

East Oxford in Domesday Book
1.   Iffley Parish Church, from south-west 217

Improvement and enclosure in the East Oxford landscape
1.   View of Oxford from the East, 1669 by Pier Maria Baldi, reproduced with permission © Laurentian Library, Florence 218
2.   Magdalen Bridge photographed by Charles Dodgson, 1861 219
3.   Cowley open fields at enclosure in 1853. (Base Map: first edition Ordnance Survey 6 inch to the mile © Crown Copyright and Landmark Information Group Limited 2014) 221

St Clements Baths
1.   The Swimming School. Engraving by N. Whittock 223

Henry Taunt
1.   'Rivera', Henry Taunt's former home at 393 Cowley Road, East Oxford 224
2.   Henry Taunt, studio portrait, circa 1910 (CC56 743:© Historic England) 224
3.   The Blue Plaque to Henry Taunt on 393 Cowley Road 225
4.   A view looking north towards 'Rivera', taken by Taunt around 1901 (HT 8054: © Oxfordshire History Centre) 225

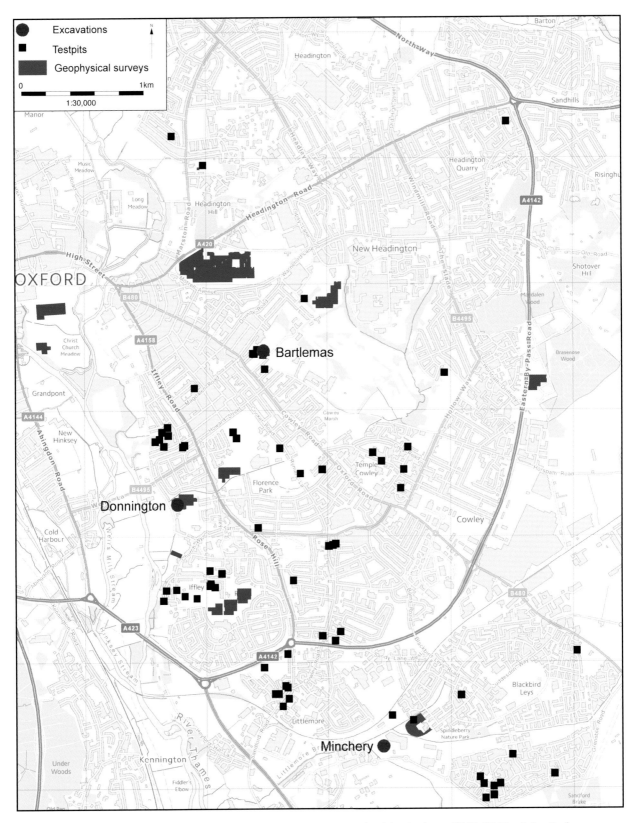

Excavations, test pits and geophysical surveys undertaken in East Oxford by *Archeox*, 2009-15 (Contains Ordnance Survey data © Crown copyright and database right 2019).

Foreword

I have lived in East Oxford for more than forty years and most of that time I taught archaeology at Reading University. Although I have done some research in the local area, much of the work took place in open landscapes – the Thames gravels and the Berkshire Downs. I never thought about the possibility of studying the archaeology of a suburban area. That was my loss.

This book teaches some important lessons. Field archaeology does not have to be restricted to farmland and gravel quarries, nor are large scale excavations necessarily the only way of working. *Archeox* has demonstrated how much can be learnt by methods that are better suited to urban areas: test pitting, geophysical survey, archival research, and the study of museum collections. The results have been a revelation and this book delivers on its aim to document *the development of a community*. While it does present the results of conventional excavations – thoroughly useful ones - it is this combination of methods, along with the skills of the participants, that really breaks new ground. The project asked important questions and it answered them convincingly. The result is a completely fresh understanding of East Oxford.

Many of its contents were unexpected, even though I knew the places where the work had taken place. I discovered even more about new ways of doing research. The involvement of the local community has been absolutely crucial, as the results of so much hard work show. The project was always an ambitious one and maintained a high standard from the beginning. Some of its findings are so intriguing that I have been visiting unfamiliar places in East

Oxford and seeing others with new eyes. That is what research is all about. We must thank the authors and other participants for conducting such a well organised and well-presented study. I hope that the initiatives recorded in this book will continue in the future. Now that their value has been shown, there can never be too many test pits!

Archaeologists – particularly those in English universities – have isolated themselves for far too long, conducting their projects without much contact with communities in the places where they work. *Archeox* offers another way of working, and a very good one. It has been an obvious success and the publication of such an attractive volume will teach that message to people who do not have the good fortune to live in this fascinating place.

Richard Bradley FBA
Aston Street, East Oxford.
Emeritus Professor of Archaeology,
University of Reading.

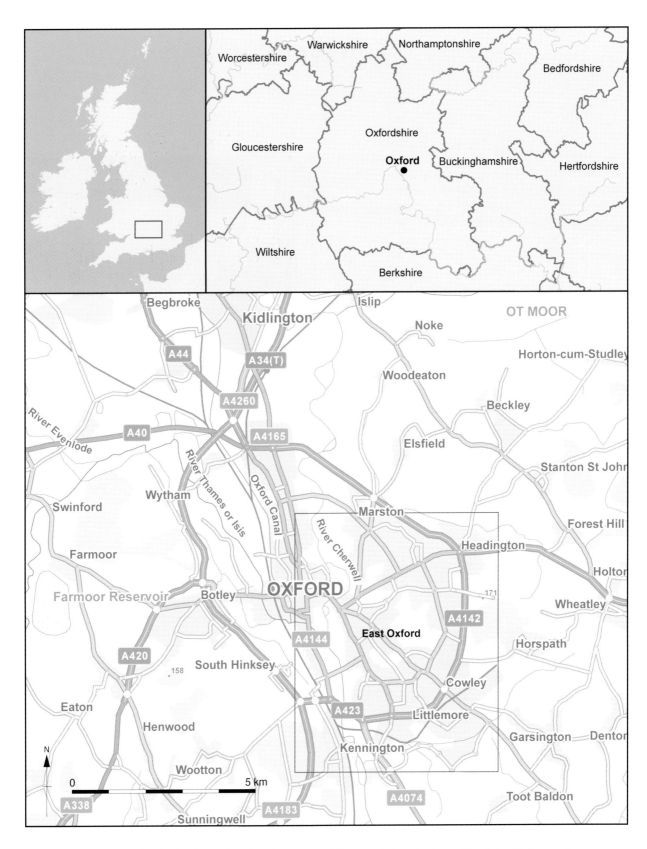

Location Map: East Oxford in its city and regional context, with extent of project area (Contains Ordnance Survey data, © Crown Copyright and database right 2019).

Heritage and Community in East Oxford

(L to R), Hilary Lade, Jane Harrison, David Griffiths, Andrew Smith MP and Prof Jonathan Michie, Director of Continuing Education at Oxford, at the project launch.

Andrew Smith MP speaking at the Project Launch at 'Restore' in 2010, with (L) Prof Andrew Hamilton, Vice-Chancellor of Oxford University, and (R) Hilary Lade, SE Regional Board Member of Heritage Lottery Fund

As a long standing member of Parliament, and as a local resident, I have been very pleased to support this project.

It was wonderful to see the scholarship of Oxford University allied so closely with the enthusiasm of local people of all ages keen to learn about what community archaeology could reveal about the past, and the lives of those who at different times also shared this space. This really was an initiative which brought town and gown together.

Community archaeology shows how our heritage is not a secret garden, but something we can all share in discovering and bringing to life.

It was great that the diversity of East Oxford was reflected in those who took part in the work. The success of the project has valuable lessons not only for the enormous potential for similar projects here and elsewhere, but more generally in how Continuing Education really can reach and engage the community.

Andrew Smith,
MP for Oxford East
(Labour Party) 1987–2017.

Acknowledgements

It is hard to know where to begin, or indeed to end, a list of acknowledgements for a project which depended on so much goodwill, enthusiasm and effort by so many individuals and organisations. The biggest and most heartfelt thank-you must surely go to the many hundreds of volunteers, students, helpers and other community participants in the shared research and training effort. The decision has been taken not to try to name every individual participant: however we are sure that everyone concerned will recognise that this particular acknowledgement applies to them! Those project members who have contributed to the final publication and to the material on the ORA web resource are named as such. Thank you also to those who wrote a team biography, featured below (Chapter 7).

David Griffiths would like to thank the project team, Olaf Bayer, Joanne Robinson, Paula Levick and above all, Jane Harrison, for their exceptional commitment, hard work, and creativity. In addition, the assistance of William Wintle with geophysical survey was much appreciated. We created and shared a vision, and it worked!

Archeox would never have happened without the generous backing and support of Oxford University Department for Continuing Education (OUDCE), which housed and administered the project throughout. Its Director, Professor Jonathan Michie, former Deputy Director Philip Healy, and Operations Manager Sean Faughnan stand out as senior allies. Finance officer Janet Hufton, web designer Dave Balch, I.T. manager Jon Burt, librarians Sue Pemberton, Corinne Richards and Amy Wolstenholme, personnel officer Jo Nickless, marketing manager Gail Anderson, and programme manager Janet Leatherby all helped in myriad ways.

Chief among the funding acknowledgements must rank the Heritage Lottery Fund, and we are grateful to the wonderful, insightful Bridget Keegan who was our manager throughout the HLF grant. Exacting but kind in her advice, we benefitted enormously from her experience. We are also very grateful to Oxford University's John Fell Fund for providing the required ten percent match-funding to make the financial package (in total over half a million pounds) viable.

Within Oxford University we are also grateful to the Ashmolean Museum, in particular to Alison Roberts and Senta German who worked extensively with the project, and to the Pitt Rivers Museum. The School of Archaeology was supportive, and we are particularly grateful to Professor Chris Gosden for his personal enthusiasm, and to Professor Mark Pollard and Dr Peter Ditchfield for contributing their isotope research on the Bartlemas skeletons. The Vice-Chancellor between 2008 and 2016, Professor Andrew Hamilton, was a friend of the project and made profile-raising visits to our excavations and other events. The central public affairs directorate, and in particular the impact team, were always anxious to help and get involved.

In the city, we thank in particular David Radford, the city council's archaeological officer, for his steadfast support and advice. Chris Bell, supervisor of the City Parks Service (a former archaeologist) was also most helpful. East Oxford councillors Nuala Young and Graham Jones were keen advocates for our cause. The city council was generous in extending access to land at South Park, Brasenose Wood, and Minchery Paddock for fieldwork. Other permissions were provided by the Diocese of Oxford and Oriel College (Bartlemas), Fairacres Convent, Christ Church College, and by Rose Hill, Northfield, Cheney and St Gregory the Great schools, together with many private property-owners and householders.

Oriel College is thanked for our use of its sports pavilion at Bartlemas and we are grateful for the support of its former provost Sir Derek, and Lady Sue Morris, and the Bursar, Wilf Stephenson. The former vicar of Cowley, Revd. Adam Romanis, is also warmly thanked for his support. The enthusiasm and commitment of Christopher and Sarah Franks, residents of Bartlemas Farmhouse and custodians of Bartlemas Chapel, was a wonder to behold.

Within the East Oxford community, no greater thanks could be accorded than to the Ark-T Centre in Cowley, the project's local home and meeting-place for five years, and in particular to its then spiritual leader, Revd. James Grote. Other organisations which helped, hosted or otherwise played a role include Restore, Julian Housing, the Clock House Centre, The Links and Elder Stubbs Allotments, and the Iffley, Cowley and Littlemore historical societies.

Oxford Archaeology has helped in numerous ways. We are grateful to its Chief Executive Officer, Dr Gill Hey, and staff-members Anne Dodd, Ken Welsh, Paul Booth, Rebecca Nicholson, Julian Munby and John Cotter for all their help.

The research and production of this publication was dependent on the assistance of Anne Dodd (reviewer), Ian Cartwright (finds photography) and Alison Wilkins (illustration). We would also like to thank the following for their assistance and advice: Judith Curthoys (Christ Church archivist), Susan Lisk (Oxfordshire HER Officer), Neil Stevenson (Museum of Oxford), the archivists of Oriel College and Magdalen College, Jane Anderson (Oxford Brookes University), Mike Athanson (Bodleian Library Map Room), Jane Baldwin (Oxford Preservation Trust), Anni Byard (Oxfordshire Finds Liaison Officer for the Portable Antiquities Scheme), Dr Ann Cole (place-name scholar), Britta Wyatt (Oxentia), Andrew Smith MP, Professor Richard Bradley, Professor Roberta Gilchrist, Maureen Mellor, Dr John Naylor (Heberden Coin Room, Ashmolean Museum), Dr Abi Tompkins, and David Moon (Oxfordshire County Museums Service), Adam Stanford (Aerial-Cam), and the staff of Oxfordshire History Centre.

Chapter 1

Introducing East Oxford

David Griffiths

What and where is East Oxford?

Oxford is world-famous as a historic university city. Its centre is located on a gravel rise (or terrace) a short distance north of the confluence of the rivers Thames and Cherwell. Observed from its central concourse at Carfax, Oxford seems small and compact, a beautiful academic city dominated by higher education, tourism, and allied businesses such as publishing, bookselling, hotels, entertainment and retail. Less obvious from this vantage-point is Oxford's role as an important manufacturing centre, and its unusual and asymmetric geography. East of the Cherwell, separated from the historic city centre by a wide, green corridor of river-meadows, is a surprisingly large, diverse, and distinctively different part of the city.

Oxford-east-of the-Cherwell – 'East Oxford' – is viewed by many of its residents as much more than merely a peripheral area of the city of Oxford. It is a 'place apart' with its own identity. Composed of parishes and localities including St Clements, Cowley, Iffley, Headington, Blackbird Leys and Littlemore, its area stretches from Magdalen Bridge eastwards to the city boundaries, and southwards to the banks of the Thames. East Oxford's distinctiveness comes from its working-class traditions and its history of trades, making things, and immigration. Politically more radical, ethnically more mixed, less affluent, and socially less-dominated by the trappings of academe than other areas of Oxford, there is in East Oxford a distinctive sense of place, which is celebrated in fact and fiction.[1] External perceptions are, however, often of a mundane and unexciting nature: that Oxford's sprawling eastern districts are 'ordinary', or 'industrial', and are eclipsed to the point of disregard by the majestic architecture of the city's academic core. Guidebooks to Oxford, mostly unwilling or unable to see beyond the college cloisters, rarely mention the city's eastern districts. Yet any visitor who leaves the city-centre tourist trail behind and crosses Magdalen Bridge will discover an eclectic and vibrant area with a deep and fascinating history.

Two centuries ago, apart from a cluster of buildings around Old St Clement's Church at the eastern end of Magdalen Bridge, the landscape of East Oxford was predominantly rural and agricultural. Historic villages, which today are subsumed into the suburban townscape, such Iffley, Church Cowley, Temple Cowley and Littlemore, were then still small, rural parish communities separated from each other by open fields, marshes, meadows and commons. The spread of housing and industry across Oxford's eastern districts took place rapidly between the mid-nineteenth and mid-twentieth centuries, almost completely altering the character of the area. A glimpse of an agricultural landscape on the cusp of change is conveyed in the first edition one-inch Ordnance Survey Map of 1830 (Fig. 1.1) with the equivalent area and places depicted from the air today (Fig. 1.2).

'Inner' East Oxford, centred on the 'triangle' formed of St Clements, Cowley Road and Iffley Road, is today dominated by streets of Victorian brick-built terraced housing. Further out, towards the eastern periphery of the city council area, are several large areas of more modern housing, interspersed with parks and playing fields. The inter-war planned suburbs of Florence Park in Cowley, and Rose Hill near Iffley, were added to in the 1950s and 1960s with extensive estates of council housing at Blackbird Leys, Littlemore, Barton, and Wood Farm. These were built partly to re-house the inhabitants of densely-populated inner-city districts such as St Ebbe's (which occupies the south-west quadrant of Medieval Oxford), which were then described as slum areas, and subject to clearance and redevelopment. Oxford's eastern districts only gradually and incrementally came under the city's governance, having previously been rural (county) parishes. St Clements, at the eastern end of Magdalen Bridge was added to the city area in 1835, with Headington, Cowley and Iffley following in 1929, and more recently Greater Leys and Blackbird Leys in 1957,[2] and Littlemore in 1991.

In contrast to its largely agricultural character two centuries ago, with the exception of allotments and grazing paddocks, almost no active farmland survives within East Oxford, but still noticeable are a surviving number of open green spaces and allotments along the rivers, and upon rising ground towards the edge of the city. Remnants of the agricultural landscape of former times survive here, such as the field boundaries and ridge and furrow earthworks – the remains of long-disused cultivation strips in open fields, a fine group of which are preserved under grass in South Park (one of the last large stretches of open farmland near the city, it was incorporated as a public park in 1932).

Topography and landscape

The key to understanding the landscape of Oxfordshire is the geography of its principal rivers and floodplains, with areas of higher ground between them. The Thames (sometimes referred to in its Oxfordshire stretch as the 'Isis') flows from north-west to south-east through the county. As a topographic feature, the Thames Valley has evolved into its current form over the last two million years, and the position of the river itself within its floodplain has altered many times. The modern courses of the Upper and Middle Thames are mostly a relatively recent result of canalisation, stabilisation, re-cutting and flow management through the imposition of locks and reservoirs. In its pre-tamed state, the Thames was a wide, shallow braided stream which proliferated new and re-formed channels naturally as a result of the seasonal energy of its outflow. Some of these remain as side-channels, but many others have silted up to become palaeochannels, former river-

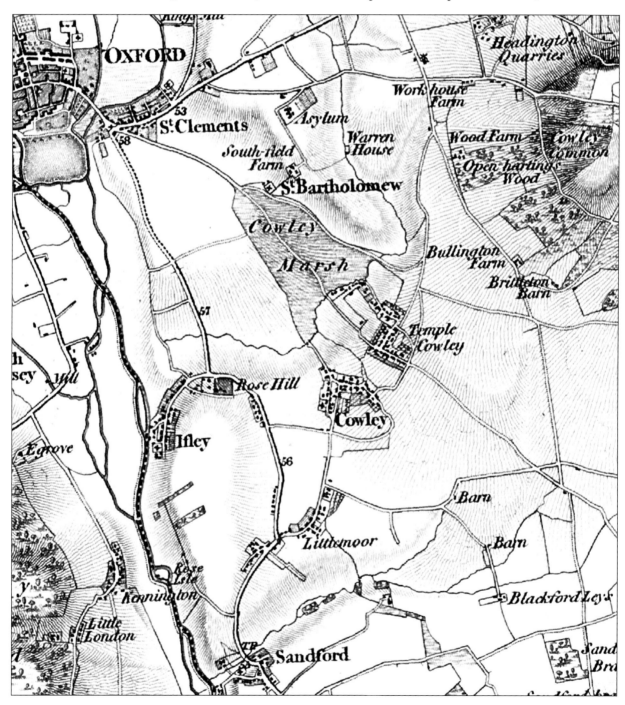

Fig. 1.1. Early Ordnance Survey Map, One inch to mile, 1830, source: Bodleian Libraries.

beds which remain visible in aerial photographs but carry no flow except in times of flood.

The early post-glacial Thames was the conduit and transport of millions of tonnes of alluvium: sand and gravel, which today form its flood-plains with low, flattish gravel terraces rising from the valley corridor. At junctions with tributaries, which bring their own alluvial loads downstream, the pattern of deposition is at its most pronounced. Oxford arose at just such a junction, where the gravel terraces forming a point of land between the Thames and Cherwell became a usefully-protected and resource-rich location for humans from the Palaeolithic period onwards. At

Oxford, the Thames runs through a wide gap between areas of higher ground to the west and east of the city. These are the Corallian Hills, formed out of oolitic limestones, mudstones, and sandstones, which were laid down in the Jurassic Period (c. 201-145 million years BP) when the region was covered with a warm, shallow sea. Wytham Woods, to the north-west of Oxford, with its neighbour to the south, Boar's Hill, form prominent ridges of limestone and greensand overlooking the city from the west. East of Oxford, the Corallian formations cause the topography to rise (Fig. 1.3). From the banks of the Cherwell in St Clements, the land rises steeply through the parish of Headington

Fig. 1.2. The same area as Fig. 1.1 viewed from above today, © GetMapping plc.

(and slightly less steeply through Cowley), before flattening briefly and rising upwards again to the crest of Shotover Forest. At 165m OD, this is the highest point in the Oxford landscape. A smaller but nonetheless prominent geological dome, Rose Hill, directly overlooks the village of Iffley and the Thames. Corallian limestone or 'Coral Rag' provided a ready source of building materials to Oxford, and the Headington quarries are the source of the honey-coloured stone famously characteristic of Oxford's colleges.

The solid geology of the East Oxford landscape is covered by a series of drift deposits. The flanks of the hills are overlaid with sands and clays, the limits of which coincide with spring lines where impermeable clays are overlain with sandier permeable soils. In the river valley bottoms of the Thames and Cherwell are extensive gravel formations and peats, the latter occurring where water has been slow-moving or stagnant in the distant past. Such an area is formed by Cowley Marsh. This is today taken to refer to a small stretch of open ground used as a public playing field, but was once much more extensive. Flat, low-lying and waterlogged, it occupied a broad shallow embayment between the edge of the Corallian rise towards Headington, and a slim gravel ridge aligned northwest to south-east, the line of which is traced by Iffley Road. Cowley Marsh was seasonally wet but provided good meadow grazing land. The higher ground around it is drained by small watercourses such as Boundary Brook, which traverses the East Oxford landscape from Headington through the Lye Valley into Cowley Marsh, and Northfield and Littlemore Brooks to the south-east of the city.

In Oxfordshire, as in the rest of southern England, the 'natural' landscape has long ago succumbed to the human-made changes, wrought initially by woodland clearance and early agriculture, and subsequently (and more profoundly) by land division and enclosure, roads, industry and modern suburban development. The growth of the city has brought both threats and opportunities to its urban archaeological heritage. From a rural perspective, there has also been serious concern since at least the 1940s at the rate of attrition of archaeological sites and deposits, particularly on the Thames gravels.[3] These urban and rural processes converge in East Oxford.

History of archaeological research covering East Oxford

Before the creation in the 1960s and 1970s of a professional role for archaeologists, most information on the archaeology of Oxford was gathered by individual antiquarian scholars and collectors working for their own interest. Early among these was Anthony Wood (1632-95), later styling himself à Wood, a member of Merton College, who was in contact with other antiquarian luminaries of his era such as Elias Ashmole, the founder of the Ashmolean Museum, John Aubrey, who drew Stonehenge, and the great English midland antiquary William Dugdale. During the difficult conditions of the English Civil War and its aftermath, Wood compiled material from college archives and local churches to form his *History and Antiquities of the University of Oxford*, a complex manuscript now held in the Bodleian Library. It was initially published in Latin in 1674, but with many errors, even according to its author. A more accessible edition in its original language of English was eventually printed in three volumes, edited by Andrew Clark, between 1889 and 1899.[4] Clark also produced a voluminous edition of Wood's life based on the antiquary's own writings.[5] Wood left some important notes on the history of St Bartholomew's (Bartlemas) Chapel. The first edition of Wood's *History and Antiquities* shared some of its illustrations with the splendid *Oxonia Illustra* (1675), a map of the city by the engraver and artist David Loggan. Wood's work remained a basis for various further writings and musings on the antiquities of Oxford in the eighteenth and nineteenth centuries, little of which strayed beyond the colleges and their memorials. A Society for Promoting the Study of Gothic Architecture was founded in Oxford in 1839, becoming in 1860 the Oxfordshire Architectural and Historical Society, and extending its remit to archaeology and antiquities (its journal, reconstituted as *Oxoniensia* in 1936, remains the principal annual periodical on Oxfordshire's archaeology).

At the end of the nineteenth century, a new group of Oxford antiquarian collectors emerged, with an interest in early Prehistory as well as the Roman, Medieval, and more recent periods, and whose activities touched upon East Oxford. Prominent amongst these was Percy Manning (1870-1917), a failed Classical undergraduate who undauntedly went on to collect and study and collect a wide range of archaeology, history and folklore from across Oxfordshire. The subject of a recent in-depth study,[6] Manning worked with Edward Thurlow Leeds (1877-1955), Assistant Keeper at the Ashmolean Museum and a pioneer of Anglo-Saxon archaeology,[7] Henry Balfour (1863-1939), Curator of the Pitt Rivers Museum, and he was joined in in his Prehistoric collecting interests by Alexander James Montgomerie Bell (1845-1920) (see page 18). All of these gentlemen (archaeology in those Edwardian days was more-or-less exclusively a male pursuit) left some notes with their collections to be curated at the two University museums. Some of these are highly precise, but in other cases they are rather rough and partial, and making sense of them in the modern age has been a challenge.

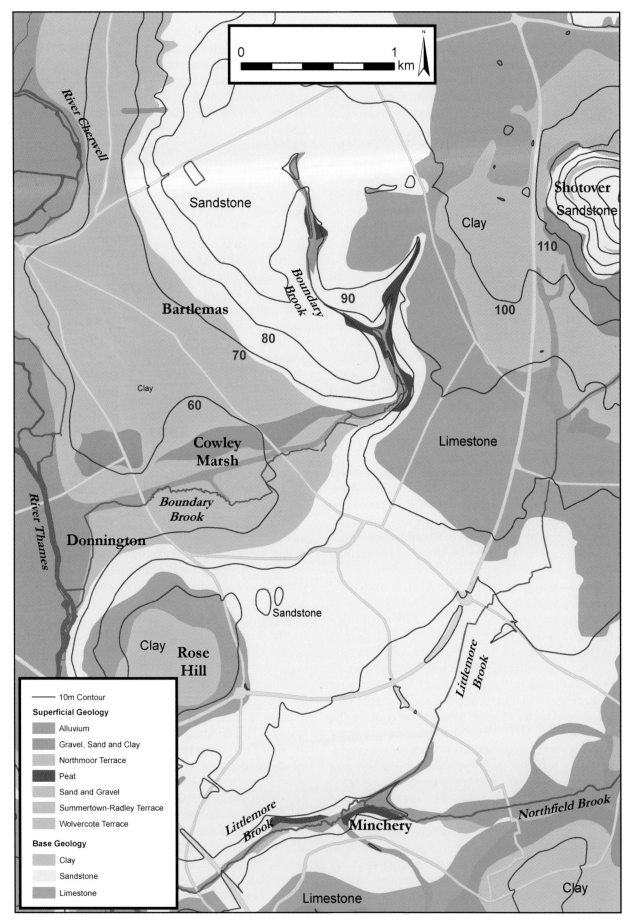

Fig. 1.3. Geology and topography of East Oxford.

The mid-twentieth century saw interest in Oxford's archaeology continue in hands of the next generation of practically-minded historical scholars connected to the university, such as W. A. 'Billy' Pantin (1902-73) and E.M. Jope (1915-96). Pantin, Jope and others, together with student members of the Oxford University Archaeological Society (founded in 1919), worked as best they could to record the vanishing Medieval heritage of Oxford before and after the Second World War, but the lack of any proper infrastructure meant that efforts were partial, and publication lagged behind. By the 1960s the pace of change brought about the creation of professional archaeological services. Beginning in 1965, Oxfordshire Museums Service developed a Sites and Monuments Record (SMR), containing information and grid references for every known or suspected archaeological site in the county. The SMR was maintained and enhanced by a series of active and knowledgeable field officers based at the County Museum in Woodstock, including Don Benson, Mick Aston and James Bond. They and their successors also liaised with local societies and individual experts through a series of advisory groups and committees. The SMR service was later transferred to Oxfordshire County Council and, in 2007, was renamed the Historic Environment Record (HER), encompassing standing buildings and below-ground archaeology. In the 1960s and early 1970s, as major urban redevelopment prompted a rising need for archaeological investigations, new field organisations or 'units' were formed in many English counties and cities to cope with the increased demand for information and excavation. In 1973, the Oxford Archaeological Unit (OAU) was formed (subsequently known as Oxford Archaeology or OA), to undertake 'rescue' excavations ahead of development, and its founding director Tom Hassall, with Trevor Rowley of OUDCE who became Staff Tutor in Archaeology in 1969, pioneered in-service training for the growing archaeological profession. Within the city, the Oxford Archaeological Unit provided advice on archaeological matters until the appointment of a professional archaeological planning advisor by the City Council in 2002. These changes allowed greater emphasis on the characterisation of the city's historic landscape, resulting in the publication of a series of resource assessments, and more recently, a research framework and an archaeological action plan for the city published in 2013.[8]

Since the introduction of professional archaeology in Oxfordshire, in built-up areas, particularly within the centre of Oxford, the timing and extent of excavations have been dictated by windows of opportunity presented by demolition and construction. As legislation gradually improved from the 1970s onwards, a series of rescue excavations took place on major redevelopment sites within the city. In 1990, the Government brought in a 'developer pays' system in England through Planning Policy Guidance Note 16 ('PPG16', a famous acronym to archaeologists). This had the effect of introducing competitive tendering for archaeological work within the planning process, and led to new organisations, and existing ones not based in Oxford, competing for contracts across the city. Evidence from excavations in central Oxford prior to 2003 has been summarised and synthesised in an important monograph published in that year, *Oxford Before the University*,[9] and major developer-funded excavations have continued, such as at Oxford Castle (1999-2005) and on the site of the Westgate shopping centre redevelopment (2014-16).[10]

In East Oxford, rescue and developer-funded archaeology has been considerably less intensive than in the city centre. The parishes to the east of the Cherwell have seen more modest levels of archaeological activity over the years, sufficient to discharge planning requirements, but there had been almost no research-led fieldwork. Urban redevelopment in East Oxford closest to the city centre was held up for many years as the result of a 1950s scheme to create an inner ring-road crossing Christ Church Meadow and the Cherwell, and cutting a swath through the streets of Cowley and St Clements. The inner relief road proposal attracted much local opposition, which contributed to its protracted delay and eventual downfall as a result of public expenditure cuts. Its threat was finally lifted in 1978, by which time extensive and often brutal urban redevelopment projects, involving widespread demolition and mass-displacements of working-class communities (such as had previously happened in the St Ebbe's district of central Oxford), were rapidly going out of fashion.

Further towards the eastern edge of the city, some major post-war planning developments did take place. In the early 1960s, the construction of the Cowley Centre (now Templars' Square) shopping precinct, high-rise flats and multi-storey car-park at Church Cowley, saw the virtual obliteration of the picturesque (if by then somewhat run-down) Medieval hamlet of Hockmore Street between Church Cowley and Temple Cowley. The building of the A4142 outer ring-road through Cowley and Headington in the later 1950s mostly crossed rural land and did receive some limited archaeological attention, but the construction of peripheral housing estates at this time passed through with little archaeological observation. This situation had improved somewhat by the 1990s, when a large area of new housing at Blackbird and Greater Leys, an extension to the car plant (at that stage owned by Rover) and the development of Magdalen College's Oxford Science Park between Littlemore and Sandford, all saw significant areas of excavation and subsequent publication.[11]

The sum of archaeological knowledge from Oxford, like that from most other historic towns, is therefore considerable in quantity, but unequal and patchy in coverage, with particularly large gaps occurring away from the city centre (Fig 1.4). For a wider geographic scale, the many past archaeological projects in the Thames Valley (covering its transit through all counties west of London) have recently been brought together in a series of synthetic monographs, co-ordinated by Oxford Archaeology

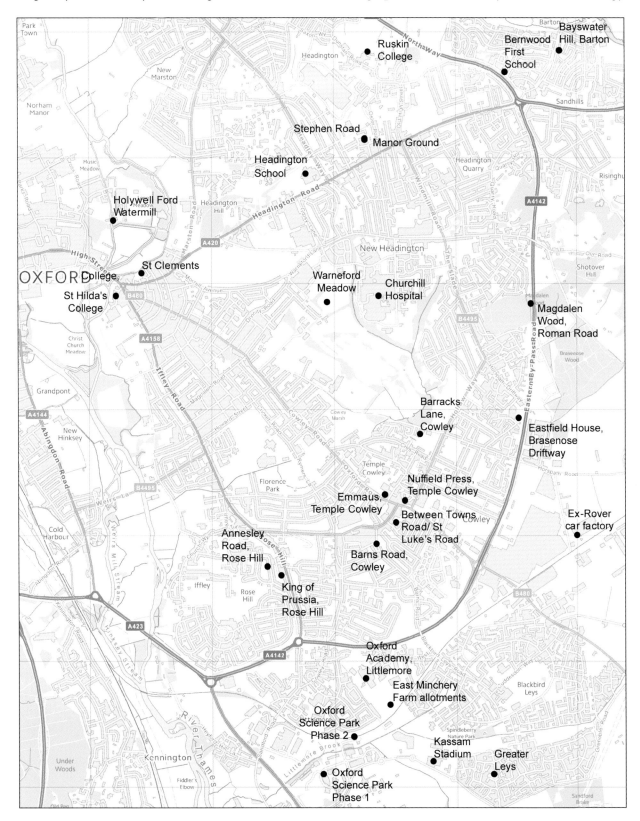

Fig. 1.4. Excavations in East Oxford under modern conditions by other organisations (Contains Ordnance Survey data © Crown copyright and database right 2019).

and funded by the Aggregates Levy Sustainability Fund (ALSF), known as *Thames through Time*.[12] These volumes provide an important, accessible and up-to-date regional benchmark for detailed archaeological studies within the Thames Valley. Together with the Oxfordshire Historic Environment Record (HER) and its city equivalent, archived documentary sources, and museum collections, these contributions form the background to present and future archaeological work within the county.

The Prehistory of East Oxford (from around 0.25 million years ago)

In Britain, footprints of early humans from around 0.25 million or 850,000 years ago have recently been detected at Happisburgh in Norfolk, and the earliest human remains, discovered in 1994 in a quarry at Boxgrove in Sussex, date to around 500,000 years ago. These are tiny, enormously fortunate glimpses of a time about which we know very little in human terms. The earliest Prehistoric traces of human activity in East Oxford, as detected in finds of Palaeolithic hand-axes, are considered to date very broadly to around 250,000 to 200,000 years ago (see page 18), although a continuous human presence (unbroken to the present day) may only be traced from the much later Mesolithic period (c.9600-4000 BC). Britain's last Ice Age separates these two distant eras, forming a vast timescale of over 100 millennia, during which we can assume that the area's earliest inhabitants had either died out, or migrated much further south to escape the cold. Evidence from the Lower Palaeolithic period (pre-dating the most recent glaciations) in Britain is extremely rare, but two sites in the Oxford area have produced concentrations of material of this exceptional age. Both were discovered by A.M. Bell (see page 18). In the 1890s, at Wolvercote Brick Pit, near the Oxford Canal on the north-west fringes of the city, Bell found a series of 322 worked flints, including Acheulian hand-axes, which are still perhaps the most impressive Palaeolithic objects from the county, and (unusually for this early date) indicate an *in-situ* tool manufacturing site. Another collection of 760 flint tools was amassed by Bell in East Oxford, much of it coming from Cornish's Gravel Pit, near Iffley (Location: see page 19). Until recently, the precise location of the gravel pit was uncertain, having not been recorded in detail at the time. However, recent scholarly detective work by Matt Nicholas of the Pitt Rivers Museum Characterization Project has been successful in finding the position of the pit, which has been determined from the first edition 1:2500 Ordnance Survey of 1875-78 as being at SP 5272 0450, under the present line of Arnold Road, where it joins Donnington Bridge Road (formerly known as New Iffley Lane). Here, Bell and Henry Balfour obtained

the Palaeolithic material including 28 Acheulian hand-axes, over several years of visiting. Pleistocene faunal remains including woolly rhino, mammoth and horse were also found in the pit, near the base of gravel on top of the underlying Oxford clay (mammoth teeth have also been found elsewhere in Oxford, notably under the New Bodleian Library in the late 1930s and the Ashmolean Museum forecourt in 1994). Unlike the Wolvercote finds, the Cornish's Pit lithic material had been rolled and transported in the gravel, and was therefore probably at least partially displaced from its original point of deposition. Bell also collected many other objects of slightly more recent periods from other gravel workings and field surfaces in the Iffley area, ranging from Mesolithic to Bronze Age in date. Bell's finds, despite requiring further study and cataloguing, draw our attention to the gravel ridge bordering the Thames at Iffley Fields as perhaps the most important identifiable location for Prehistoric finds of several periods from Oxford.

The landscape of Oxfordshire at the end of the last Ice Age has been described as a sparsely-wooded tundra.[13] The history of environmental change and vegetation cover across the Thames Valley has been studied through pollen records and molluscan evidence.[14] As the climate slowly warmed, the landscape saw a spread of deciduous woodland, the result that towards the end of the Mesolithic Period in c. 7000 BP (5000 BC) the region was largely forested. A major change in human settlement and lifestyle in Britain occurred between c. 4000–3500 BC, with the beginnings of the domestication of animals and plants and eventually the establishment of permanent settlements. Woodland clearance and early agriculture altered the landscape and hydrology, and the archaeology of ritual and burial became more visible and monumental (burials are barely detectable in Britain prior to this point). Defined by archaeologists as the Neolithic (New Stone Age), this series of changes and innovations was highly complex in its spread and progress across Europe and beyond, and almost every aspect of its origins remains the subject of scholarly contention. These developments continued, with the admixture of new technologies and burial practices, into the Bronze Age (c. 2500-800 BC). In Oxford, the gravel plateau (part of the Summertown-Radley gravel terrace) between the floodplains of the Thames and Cherwell which underlies the city centre and its northern fringes, appears to have been partially cleared by the middle Neolithic period. The excavated features, supplemented by aerial photographs of the University Parks which show yet more extensive and unexcavated ring-ditches and enclosures, show that the flat landscapes of central/North Oxford and Port Meadow were dominated by groups of ritual and funerary monuments by the early to middle Bronze Age (c. 2500 – 1600 BC). These are part of a pattern of several extensive linear barrow-cemeteries clustered on the upper and middle Thames gravels.

Peat deposits preserve pollen, an indicator of long-term landscape history, in their layers. The work of Adrian Parker and others shows that much of the dense post-glacial woodland of the Mesolithic period (c. 9600-4000 BC) was cleared, possibly using fire, to create a more open landscape during the Neolithic period (c. 4000-2300 BC) and Bronze Age (c. 2500-800 BC).[15] At the Kassam Stadium, Oxford Science Park and in Trench 1 at Minchery Paddock (Chapter 5), all of which fall within the Northfield and Littlemore Brook catchments, peat has been subjected to palaeoenvironmental coring and sampling, producing evidence of vegetational change over time. Relatively little is known about the people of the area in the Mesolithic era, with the worked flints from Bell's collection being one of the few glimpses of human activity. In contrast to later periods characterised by permanent settlements and agriculture, the semi-mobile hunting and gathering lifestyle of the tiny Mesolithic population has left only tangential traces in the landscape. At the Kassam Stadium and Oxford Science Park, developer excavations also revealed Mesolithic artefacts, contributing to a view that the locations of hunting and fishing camps favoured the sandy locations in the vicinity of rivers and streams. There are only limited hints of any Mesolithic presence on higher ground, such as a small collection of Mesolithic flints found during the redevelopment of the former Manor football ground, Headington. The impression gained is of a tiny population relative to modern terms, living in woodland clearings near to rivers, and moving with the seasons.

During the Neolithic period and the Bronze Age (c.4000-800 BC), people in the Thames Valley became settled in more permanent communities and some of the land was turned towards early farming. The combination of Neolithic and Bronze Age lithics in Bell's collection from Iffley Fields suggests long-term activity on the gravel ridge here (see Chapter 3), and a Neolithic axe was found prior to 1893 during building work at Chester Street/ off Iffley Road. At Blackbird Leys, excavators working ahead of a new housing development in 1995-6 found a series of pits producing 38 sherds of middle to late Bronze Age pottery, burnt stone and a decorated clay loomweight, the latter tantalising evidence for early settlement activity in the vicinity. At the nearby Oxford Science Park excavations in 1999, fragments of seven beakers and 48 other Neolithic and Bronze Age potsherds including pieces of Deverel-Rimbury ware were found. Other isolated finds of Bronze Age pottery include a Bronze Age collared urn from Donnington Bridge Road (close to the location of many of Bell's finds, and near an excavation conducted in 2013; see Chapter 3). The hoard of Bronze Age palstaves from

Leopold Street found in 1881 (see page 22) is the most prominent, but not the only, find of Bronze Age metalwork from east of the Cherwell, with single examples of socketed Bronze palstaves known from Iffley and Old Marston, and a spearhead from Littlemore.

The Blackbird Leys excavation of 1995-6 provided some evidence of settlement continuity from the Bronze Age into the Iron Age (800 BC AD 50), which was characterised by a penannular enclosure and ditches producing early to middle Iron Age pottery.[16] Plant remains from the Oxford Science Park excavation suggests that from the later Bronze Age into the Iron Age, the landscape was becoming wetter, with fen formation along the Northfield and Littlemore brooks. During the excavation of a ditch feature at the Rover (now BMW) Plant, Cowley, Bronze Age to middle Iron Age pottery was found.[17] Sites producing Iron Age deposits and finds include Eastfield House on Brasenose Driftway, the Manor Ground and Ruskin College in Headington, and Bernwood First School, Barton, where an enclosed settlement began in the early Iron Age and continued into the early Roman period, the latter marked by an early Roman pit burial. The enclosure ditches recorded at Bernwood First School were up to 3 metres wide and a gate structure, marked by post-holes, stood across an entrance causeway. Inside were further post-holes and a pit alignment. In two of the pits were three other crouched burials of probable Late Iron Age date.[18] At the site of the former 'King of Prussia' public house on the northern flank of Rose Hill, beside the A4158 road, evaluation trenches and a watching brief prior to redevelopment in 2011 found a series of re-cut ditches dated by pottery to the early to middle Iron Age, one of which was filled with probable redeposited bank material. The purpose of the features was interpreted as defensive.[19] This restricted glimpse of Iron Age bank-and-ditch defences on the steep flanks of Rose Hill raises an important question. Elsewhere in the Thames Valley, such as at Castle Hill, Wittenham Clumps, prominent hills in strategic positions overlooking the river are the locations of Iron Age hillforts (in the case of Castle Hill, succeeding and surrounding an earlier hilltop enclosure dating to the Bronze Age). Could Rose Hill have once been the site of a hillfort? This is an attractive hypothesis, but to prove it, yet more conclusive evidence would be needed.

The Roman Period in East Oxford (*circa* 43-450 AD)

The Oxford region came under Roman rule after Claudian invasion of Britain in AD 43. It is important to note that Oxford was never the site of a formal Roman town or fortress, unlike many other historic cities in England. The nearest Roman centres were Alchester, near Bicester, and Dorchester-on-Thames, which were linked by a north-south road which passes through Oxford's eastern districts along the flank of Shotover Forest, the line of which is partly followed by the A4142 eastern ring-road between Barton and Blackbird Leys. The Oxfordshire area was marginal to the Iron Age tribal territories of the Dobunni (to the west), the Catuvellauni (to the east) and the Atrebates (to the south). As these groups developed into the *civitates* or subject-peoples of Roman Britain, the influence of the rapidly-developing Roman economy grew. Far less dependent on localised and subsistence production than their Iron-Age predecessors, or indeed their successors in the early Anglo-Saxon period, the wealthier sections of society in Roman Britain embraced the advantages of large-scale regionalised production of consumer goods. These were distributed through extensive road and river-based trading networks, which were built, improved and secured by the Roman military presence, and financed by the Roman coin-using economy.

The main feature of the Roman period in the Oxford region is the development of an extensive pottery industry, producing tablewares and mortaria (see page 86), much of which was located on the eastern fringes of Oxford. To date, 30 kilns have been identified within the eastern boundaries of Oxford City, spread over 23 sites. The iron-free clays and extensive woodland resources of Shotover Forest, and the flowing water available from the Boundary Brook and Lye Valley, provided an advantageous location for the beginnings of the industry. Excavations at the Churchill Hospital, Headington, show that coarse wares were being produced as early as the first century AD, probably on a local scale at this time. In the second century, at a time of widespread change in rural settlement observed across Oxfordshire, pottery production shifted upwards in scale and towards fine table-wares, and the number of kilns expanded across the edges of the Corallian Ridge into Horspath, Cowley, Blackbird Leys and Rose Hill, near Littlemore Priory (Minchery Farm), and onwards towards Sandford, Nuneham Courtenay and Boar's Hill. By the later third century AD the Oxford kilns had become one of the largest pottery industry concentrations in Roman Britain, rivalling those of Hampshire and the Nene Valley. The Oxford mortaria, white slip 'parchment' wares and cream, red and brown colour-coated finewares, many of the latter imitative of the continental Roman Samian Ware tradition, spread out across the provinces of Britannia and beyond.

The Roman pottery kilns have been documented through excavation, but where did their workers live? and how were these settlements provided with food and resources? Identification of Roman settlement areas has been slower to come to light. A significant (if unquantifiable) proportion of the pottery workers were probably itinerant and lived in the area on a seasonal basis, returning to homes elsewhere at times of the year (e.g. harvest) when their labour was needed and pottery production possibly stepped down for some months. These workers would almost certainly have dwelt in very close proximity to the kilns, as their presence was needed through day and night, to stoke and watch over the pottery in its making and firing. Some excavations of kilns, at the Churchill Hospital and Annesley Road, Rose Hill, have indicated the presence of ancillary buildings which may have been workshops or housing. Several clusters of Roman finds and structures observed in excavations across the area imply the possible presence of rural villages or farmsteads. Evidence of what may be a Roman villa was found at Wick Farm, which lies north of Barton, when it was excavated by the antiquarian Llewellyn Jewitt in 1849,[20] together with a large quantity of coins and pottery of the third and fourth centuries AD. A 1940s excavation at nearby Bayswater Hill in Barton, located close to the line of the Roman road from Alchester to Dorchester, has been interpreted as a possible roadside settlement.[21] Sites at Headington School, Headley Way, Marston, and Eastfield House, Brasenose Driftway, Cowley, have all revealed traces of local settlement in the Roman period in the form of pits, ditches, and pottery finds, although in none of these cases did the evidence appear to amount to more than relatively low-density rural occupation. A number of probable Roman burials have been found across East Oxford, including several from the probable road-side settlement at Bayswater Hill in Barton, fifteen from Rose Hill, six from the Pressed Steel Works which was formerly part of the Morris motor factory complex, and several others from the military college in Cowley.

The locations of trade and communication routes remain important questions for the Roman period in East Oxford. The Alchester-Dorchester Roman road was observed as a truncated metalled surface during the construction of the ring-road through Magdalen Wood in the late 1950s.[22] A partially-preserved section of a hollow way, which may be its continuation to the south of the line of the ring-road, lies at the edge of Horspath Athletics ground, bordering the perimeter fence of the Pony Road Industrial Estate. Our attempt using geophysical survey to detect its position north of this position on open grassland in Brasenose Wood, close to its convergence with the line of the ring-road in 2012 did not meet with obvious success (see page 95), and we may have been working a little east of its true line. A further question concerns the river crossings. A possible Roman road leads eastwards from a ford on the Thames near Iffley, just south of the location of (modern) Donnington Bridge,[23] through Cowley towards the kilns at

Headington and Horspath. However to date no confirmed archaeological trace of its precise route has yet been established.

East Oxford in the Anglo-Saxon Period (*circa* 450-1050 AD)

The Oxfordshire Roman pottery industry came to a sudden end around AD 400 for reasons which must be related to the wider fragmentation and collapse of large-scale economic activity across Britain at this time. As imperial authority waned, people and activities which depended most on the integrated economy, coinage and transport networks under the Roman administration, suffered most. Villas, long-distance trade systems and major towns experienced a precipitous decline from the start of the fifth century. However, many other aspects of local Romano-British rural society were less drastically affected, and the picture of upheaval varies in intensity throughout the country. Traditionally, the fifth century is seen as the start of the 'Germanic' or Anglo-Saxon invasions, bringing people, new forms of burial, housing and pottery, and of course a new language which developed into English. Incoming settlers from northwestern Europe were probably already in the Thames Valley before the end of Roman rule (as indicated by late Roman burials with 'Germanic' style grave-goods from the Dyke Hills, near Dorchester on Thames).[24] The ways in which these settlers interacted with the existing inhabitants of later and post-Roman Britain was in all likelihood very complex, varied, and far from universally dominated by conflict and conquest.

In the Oxford region, we see hints of the gradual evolution of late Roman rural settlement forms into early Anglo-Saxon ones. There is in this area remarkably little evidence for large-scale migration, social fracture, warfare, upheaval, or discontinuity of settlement at this time. The onset of the Anglo-Saxon period seems rather to have seen an incremental adoption by the local population of new forms of burial, pottery, buildings and metalwork, perhaps aided by the influence of some incoming groups, but in a relatively muted form. Dorchester-on-Thames, and Barton Court Farm Villa, Abingdon, show evidence of new styles of sunken-floored buildings with early Anglo-Saxon pottery, and, in some cases loom-weights, constructed upon Roman sites in the fifth and sixth centuries. The principal discovery so far of the sixth and early seventh centuries in the East Oxford area comes from the 1999 excavation at Oxford Science Park, Littlemore, where over ten sunken-featured buildings, a total of 953 sherds of early Anglo-Saxon pottery (together with re-used Roman vessels) and one contemporary inhumation. A sunken-featured building was found during excavations at the nearby Peer's School (Oxford Academy) in 2009,[25] and further

isolated discoveries of sunken-featured buildings have occurred on the Headington/ Barton border under the northern ring-road.

Only occasional isolated burials of the early Anglo-Saxon period are known from East Oxford, a single inhumation was found in a pit dated by Anglo-Saxon pottery in excavations at Oxford Science Park, and a burial with an amber necklace and iron knife was found at Stephen Road, Headington.[26] An S form bronze Anglo-Saxon brooch with garnet decoration from the flanks of Rose Hill, above Iffley (see page 73), has been taken to be the sign of a possible burial, or even a cemetery, but further exploration has proved negative and it may be simply a stray find.[27] A fine Anglo-Saxon shield boss found in the bed of the River Cherwell under Magdalen Bridge in 1884 is detailed in a separate study (see page 26). A spearhead was also found nearby, but it is unclear whether this is from the same deposit.

The Oxford area does not seem to have had any particular political importance in early Anglo-Saxon England, although the wider Upper Thames region saw the development of the tribal group known as the Gewissae, which arguably gave rise to the later kingdom of Wessex. The nearby former Roman town at Dorchester-on-Thames was initially a more influential place in the Anglo-Saxon period, and became the site of an early bishopric. Oxford's location astride the confluence of two important rivers, and its role as a fording point across both of them, was however key to its foundation and rise to prominence in the middle and later Anglo-Saxon periods (c.650-1100 AD). The 'Oxen Ford' where traffic crossed the braided expanse of the Thames south of the city developed as a major strategic routeway from the middle Saxon period onwards.[28] St. Frideswide's Minster, the precursor of the present cathedral, was founded nearby, on the site later occupied by Christ Church College, probably in the later seventh or early eighth century. Its strategic presence on the gravel rise above the Thames crossing may have been the reason why, in the late ninth or early tenth century, a 'burh' (borough or fortified place) was founded beside it, by royal authority, on land held by the estate at Headington. The early extent of the burh was probably a square-shaped banked and ditched enclosure centred on Carfax, where its four main axial streets met. Later in the pre-Conquest period the burh area was extended, encompassing the site of Oxford Castle to the west, and stretching eastwards towards the edge of the Cherwell floodplain. The evolution of the burh's defences, street plan, churches, and its four principal gates, has been documented in a number of excavations around the city, and a recent discussion of these can be found in *Oxford before the University*.[29]

By 1000 AD, Oxford had become a prosperous and rapidly-expanding shire town. Like other growing urban centres at this time, it attracted traders and workers from far and wide. Danes (or Scandinavians in general) formed a distinctive part of Oxford's citizenry around 1000. A number of them may have been integrated and distributed throughout the town's population, but others may have been concentrated in St Clements, to the east of the city, grouping together rather as Jews later did in the ghettos of European and middle-eastern cities. Despite rising prosperity in towns, however, this was a most unstable and uneasy period in English history. The kingdom, under Æthelred II ('The Unready'), came under severe pressure from hostile military incursions sent by the Danish king, Svein Forkbeard, who had his eye on the English crown. In 1002, there occurred perhaps the most infamous act of Æethelred's reign, his decree ordering 'the slaying of all Danish men who were in England – this was done on St Brice's Day (13 November)'. Far from being an empty threat, this led to an atrocity in Oxford known as the St Brice's Day Massacre. It is described in Æethelred's renewal of privileges to St Frideswide's Monastery in 1004 (see page 214), occasioned by the minster church having been burnt down by the townspeople, with the Danish population of the city having sought sanctuary inside. The Danes, the renewal charter says, 'had sprung up in this land, sprouting like a cockle amongst the wheat.'[30] In the garden of Queen Elizabeth House, beside St John's College, north of the city centre, part of the ditch of a large Prehistoric henge monument was excavated in 2008, the upper fill of which contained the mutilated bodies of 37 male individuals dating from the later Anglo-Saxon or Viking period. These have been radiocarbon dated to around AD 1000 and, through isotopic analysis, it has been suggested that they were not local and may have been from northern Europe or Scandinavia.[31] If these individuals were Danes connected to the St Brice's Day massacre, their deaths must have been a sideshow to the main event in the minster church. After the massacre of 1002, it is not known whether, or in what numbers, any Danes remained in Oxford, or may have returned in more peaceful times following the accession of Svein Forkbeard's son Canute to the English throne in 1016.

The dedication to St Clement is associated with Danish settlements throughout Europe, as exemplified by the church of St Clement Dane in London.[32] It is likely that many of the Danish population of Oxford dwelt in this area. The old church of St Clement in Oxford, which stood until 1827 at the eastern end of Magdalen Bridge, was first documented as a royal chapel granted to St Frideswide's Monastery in 1122, but probably has earlier origins going back to the tenth or eleventh century. The few Viking-style finds found in the city, such as a twisted gold ring from St Aldate's, are reasonably well-distributed across its central area, but the discovery of two Viking stirrups on the Cherwell margins near Magdalen Bridge in 1884 emphasises the importance of this eastern city district, which John Blair conjectured may have been a base for Danish troops (see page 28). St Clements was known as 'brycg-gesett' (Bridge Settlement)[33] and may possibly have been a fortified outlier of the Anglo-Saxon burh. The semi-concentric shape of its street plan, as far to the east as Stockmore Street, is suggestive of a possible defensive enclosure, although no direct archaeological evidence of one has ever been found. (An alternative suggestion, that these streets echo the shape of strips in the open fields which once covered this area, seems equally hard to substantiate).

Medieval East Oxford (*circa* 1050 – 1550)

Away from the bridgehead settlement cluster at St Clements, East Oxford's history between the Norman Conquest and the mid-nineteenth century continued largely to be a rural and agricultural one. At the time of the Domesday Book in 1086, in Oxford 'within and without the wall' were 243 houses which paid tax, 500 other houses (22 of which were derelict), five fisheries, and two mills on the Cherwell. Cowley was held at Domesday by three landowners, Odo of Bayeux, Miles Crispin and Count Eustace, and there was a mill at Milham Ford, just downstream from Magdalen Bridge on the Cherwell. Iffley was held by Earl Aubrey, and its ornate late Norman parish church was built following a new foundation by Robert de St Remy around 1170 (see page 217). As the city of Oxford expanded, with extensive college and church construction, the limestone quarries of Headington became an increasingly important source of building stone.

Still evident within the now built-up and busy suburban townscape east of the Cherwell are the cores of the Medieval villages and hamlets that, until the mid-nineteenth century, stood largely independent and separated from each other by woods, lanes, fields and marshes (see Fig. 1.1). Headington, Iffley, Temple Cowley and Church Cowley are all located on ridges or slopes overlooking lower and wetter ground nearby. In the case of Iffley and the two Cowleys, they are perched on a steep edge as it drops to meet the Thames and Cowley Marsh. These clusters of Medieval and post-Medieval stone cottages and historic churches form the key surviving components of the area's former rural villages.

The semi-nucleated pattern of Medieval settlement in East Oxford is a fascinating one, its origins and development demand further archaeological and historical attention (see Chapter 3). The relationship of Medieval settlement patterns to earlier ones, in the Anglo-Saxon, Roman and even Prehistoric periods, offers us a significant research challenge. Elsewhere in

England, researchers have concentrated on this question, approaching settlement patterns through place-name and field-name research, geophysical survey and test-pitting. An earlier generation of settlement researchers concentrated on the earthwork remains of deserted Medieval villages ('DMV's), but these are now recognised as only one, perhaps quite distinctive, dimension of a broader picture. Currently-occupied settlements, where field researchers are obliged to negotiate the challenges of working within a living community, have more recently become a focus of research activity. These projects have inspired much that follows here.

The roads that radiated eastwards from Magdalen Bridge were, then as now, the key to East Oxford's developing role serving the approaches to the city, and contributed to its development as a suburb. Iffley Road follows the gravel ridge between Cowley Marsh and the Thames, which has been so productive of Prehistoric finds. One of the main roads eastwards towards London once headed from St Clements up the hollow way called Cheney Lane (now a minor no-through road), before joining the current line of Old Road, and then crossing over the highest point of Shotover Forest. Cowley Road once formed another major road in and out of the city to the East. Slightly north of its current line, one of the former eastern stretches of Cowley Road once skirted the fringes of the wet low-lying Cowley Marsh, along the line of the bridleway known in more recent times as Barracks Lane. At a strategic, if then somewhat isolated position along this road, well outside the Medieval city, at the point where modern Cowley Road and the line of Barracks Lane now diverge, a leper hospital dedicated to St Bartholomew was founded by Henry I in around 1126. The leper hospital was transferred to Oriel College in the early fourteenth century, when the chapel was rebuilt, and the site became an almshouse. Known locally as Bartlemas Chapel, it remains a hidden gem of surviving Medieval architecture in the heart of East Oxford (Chapter 4).

Another Medieval hospital once existed at St Clements, but apart from one reference to it in 1345, we know nothing more of its status or location.[34] Only a few archaeological glimpses of Medieval activity have so far been found in St Clements, pits and ditches with twelfth and thirteenth-century pottery have been found in York Place and Magdalen College School. In Jeune Street, a ditch containing thirteenth-century pottery was found in 2011, possibly indicating a tenement boundary. The circular roundabout 'island' in the centre of the busy Plain road junction at the eastern end of Magdalen Bridge preserves a reduced part of the old churchyard of St Clement. When the road tarmac on the eastern side of the roundabout was removed for reconstruction in 2007, several inhumations were found close to the surface.

Fig. 1.5. Stone relief shield with *cross pattée* above the main door at Temple Farm, Sandford.

Cowley Road runs eastwards from the Plain to Temple Cowley, which derives its name from an estate granted to the Order of the Knights Templar by Queen Matilda in 1139, where they established a preceptory (a manor or residence for members of the order, headed by a preceptor). The estate was transferred to the Knights Hospitallers in 1308 when the Templars were suppressed. However by this point, it is likely that no Templars remained in residence, as the preceptory had already been transferred to Sandford-on-Thames, to the south of Oxford, around 1240. Some Medieval fabric remains within historic manor buildings at Sandford, which are now part of a hotel complex, including a coat of arms possibly attributable to the Templars or to the Hospitallers who succeeded them as landlords after 1308 (Fig. 1.5). The locations of the Templars' site or sites at Cowley have proved hard to detect, with no substantive building or earthwork remains surviving above ground. An excavation in 1999 at the site of Temple Cowley Manor House (demolished in the 1950s), a structure which dated to the seventeenth century, revealed earlier foundations and pits. A wall slot, with a possible post-hole and entrance had been truncated by the later house. These were dated by pottery to the thirteenth century. These were built over a group of pits and ditches containing eleventh to thirteenth century pottery, suggesting the site was occupied well before 1136. The preceptory, if it was located on a different site, may have been partly uncovered during a watching brief at 169 Oxford Road in 2008.[35] Ditches and pits containing eleventh-century pottery were found underneath a series of walls including the corner of a building built with angular limestone blocks, which was later abandoned with the site becoming pasture. The Templars also possessed Littlemore Priory, known locally as the Minchery, between 1240 and their suppression in the early fourteenth century (Chapter 5), having been granted it by the Lord of Sandford. The priory, which was founded in the reign of Stephen in the mid-twelfth century continued, with varied fortunes, until it fell foul of diocesan inspections in 1445 and 1517. It was closed by a papal bull of 1524, its assets being sequestered by Cardinal Wolsey for the benefit of his newly-founded 'Cardinal College' in Oxford, now known as Christ Church.

The post-Medieval period and the growth of the modern city (circa 1500-1900)

Littlemore Priory had already closed by the time of the Protestant Reformation initiated by Henry VIII, and its buildings were plundered for building stone, with the nuns' dormitory on the east range surviving as farmhouse (latterly, in the 1960s, it became part of a now-demolished country club on the site, and most recently it was a public house). East Oxford suffered relatively little apparent disruption during the reigns of the Tudors, but was inevitably drawn into the major political and social fracture during the time of their successors, the Stuarts: the English Civil War. Between 1643 and 1646 Oxford acted as the principal centre of the Royalist government, London being in the hands of Parliament. Charles I initially repaired to Oxford after the inconclusive Battle of Edgehill, just north of the Oxfordshire-Warwickshire county boundary, in October 1642. The king pressed on south-eastwards intending to break Parliament's grip on London, but his failure there led to an increased Royalist presence in Oxford, and the Queen's household arrived in 1643. A Royalist arsenal was set up at St Mary's College (Frewin Hall) near Carfax, melting lead from roofs to produce musket balls, and defensive siege-works were thrown up around the city centre, including a ring of bastions surrounding the eastern end of Magdalen Bridge in St Clements. A defensive earthwork was constructed south-east of Magdalen Bridge (see page 102); it was still detectable as a surface feature under allotments in the early 1900s but has now disappeared from view under more modern buildings and landscaping.

Summer 1643 saw overcrowding in the city and a major typhoid epidemic broke out. The king summoned a royalist parliament to Oxford in January 1644. The modest heights overlooking the city from the east enabled the Parliamentarian army to keep watch over the king's headquarters inside the walls. The first of three sieges of Oxford took place in May 1644, ending when the king and other senior followers had left, and the thrust of the war passed elsewhere. The Parliamentarian troops encamped at Headington skirmished unsuccessfully in front of the Royalist defensive works surrounding the bridgehead at St Clements, allegedly watched by the king from Magdalen College tower. The second siege, in May 1645, saw a successful royalist sally against the Parliamentarian camp on Headington Hill where 50 roundhead soldiers were killed and 96 taken prisoner. In April 1646, at the start of the third siege, Parliamentarian troops mustered on Bullingdon Green to the east of the city (a formerly large open area, now occupied by parts of the Oxford Golf Club golf course and housing).[36] Their general, Sir Thomas Fairfax, oversaw the construction of new strong-points and siege works across the brow of Headington Hill, with a line down to St Clements to control the road heading east out of the city (see page 102). Fairfax's 'Great Fort' at Headington (its name is possibly something of an exaggeration for a scratch earth-and-timber defensive line) lobbed occasional cannon fire into the city, but did not seek to mount a full attack. The Royalist side was in disarray by this time, and the siege ended along with the 'first' Civil War, when a treaty was concluded at Marston in June 1646 and the keys of the city were presented to the representatives of Parliament.

We know a good deal about Oxford in the mid-seventeenth century from the writings of Anthony Wood, who recorded the colleges and churches of Oxford in the Civil War and its post-war period.[37] Wood described the rebuilding of the chapel and almshouse at Bartlemas in 1649–51, following their near-destruction and the robbing of their roof-lead by the Parliamentarians. The date 1651 is commemo-rated on the carved wooden rood screen. During the devastating cholera outbreak of 1832, the chapel was used as a convalescent ward for sufferers, presumably due to its separate water supply and relative isolation. By the time it was photographed by Henry Taunt at end of the nineteenth century (see Fig. 4.8) it was being used as a farm building, surrounded by lowly pigsties and farm implements, but was eventually to return to religious use in the twentieth century.

The story of East Oxford after the Civil War is one of gradual rural change, until the rapidly accelerated pace of development brought about by the spread of suburban housing and industry from the mid-nineteenth century. The coming of turnpike roads brought greater access for traffic, and the old coach road towards London via Cheney Lane and up over the heights of Shotover Forest was replaced by the new, wider London Road up Headington Hill in 1789. Vehicular passage at the east end of Magdalen Bridge was improved by the widening of the traffic junction known as the Plain, enabled by the demolition of old St Clement's Church in 1827 (Fig 1.6); the present parish church was built beside Marston Road in 1828. Other innovations around this time included the construction in 1824, by the Morrells brewing family, of Headington Hill Hall, an ornate Italianate mansion on the slope of Headington Hill, and the opening of a new open-air bathing pool complex next to the Cherwell in Bath Street, in 1827 (see page 222).[38] The enclosure of fields, which happened piecemeal across the area (with parts of Cowley enclosed as late as 1853) saw the end of the former open field system, the physical traces of which are still represented in the ridge and furrow earthworks in South Park (see page 98), in Headington Hill Park, and in the undulating surface of the allotments beside Bartlemas Chapel.

By parcelling up agricultural land into an easily saleable commodity, enclosure was a key enabler to process of urbanisation, when individual plots of land were bought freehold and developed for housing. The main thoroughfares: St Clement's Street, Cowley Road and Iffley Road, became joined together by a network of new streets upon which terraced houses were built by piecemeal private development. The social and architectural history of Victorian and modern East Oxford is a fascinating and rich topic, which this book and project address obliquely but not directly. For accounts of the modern local history of the area, the published works of authors such as Graeme Salmon, Annie Skinner and Liz Woolley, along with the Victoria County History, continue to enrich our understanding. The evocative glass-plate photographs of people and places in East Oxford by Henry Taunt (1842-1922) convey our richest series of glimpses of the vanishing rural character of the area on the cusp of industrialisation (see page 224). Taunt's lifetime covered almost perfectly the period of transition in East Oxford from timeless countryside to a modern, suburban townscape. It is from the vantage point of the busy, traffic-choked present that we must look back, though the eye of Taunt's box camera and beyond, if we are to find the history and archaeological answers we seek.

Research questions for a community investigation

Although many individual excavations have been conducted over the years, and the area mentioned here and there as part of broader studies of the city, East Oxford as a place distinctive in itself has never before been subjected to a dedicated archaeological investigation or synthesis on its own right. This would be a challenge enough in any terms, but to involve the community directly in researching its own past promised to add yet more complexity, impetus and potential (Chapter 2). A set of investigative themes were needed which served not just the narrow concerns of academic studies or council planning priorities, but brought together people and their heritage in a shared, accessible and inspiring endeavour. Rather than concentrating on separate, contained objectives period by period, an over-arching theme was required for this purpose. This is found most readily in the story of the landscape itself, from early traces of human activity towards the present.

Fig. 1.6. Old St Clement's Church from south, prior to 1816, after Mallet (1924).

However we could not hope to cover each and every period in equal intensity, so a series of linked research questions, derived from existing knowledge, were established. All of these were based on chronological developments, but were designed to serve the purpose of furthering the story of the landscape, and linking sites, past communities and livelihoods across time.

Investigative methods are described in more detail in Chapter 3, and have included:

- Studying archaeological and historical material in collections and archives

- Field surveys using geophysics and earthwork recording

- Test-pit excavations, usually 1x1 metre or 1 x 2 metres in size

- Targeted excavations

These went on concurrently, and their results were influential in shaping our next steps. The implications of new findings (and sometimes no findings!) and changing ideas were discussed at the regular project steering group meetings, and ways forward for the investigations were debated and agreed.

Prehistoric settlement on gravel ridges and river terraces is marked by clusters of worked flints, and a hoard of Bronze Age axes found during the construction of stables for horse-trams at Leopold Street in 1881 (see page 22). The area around Iffley fields and Donnington Bridge is of particular importance, due to the collecting work of A.M. Bell and Percy Manning over a century ago. The questions which arise from this are:

- Can studying finds in museum collections cast further light on the types and locations of settlement activity which existed in this period?

- Can we connect Prehistoric finds to their landscape context by doing surveys, targeted excavations and test-pits, particularly in and around the Iffley Fields gravel ridge?

- Would more work on sampling peat deposits help us to understand environmental change over long time periods?

For the Roman period, we already had good evidence for pottery production in the form of the spread of kilns. The East Oxford Roman pottery industry in its later Roman heyday must have provided a living for many people, considerably more than would have dwelt within the area previously. The presence of rural communities, farmsteads and roads is less well-understood in comparison to sites dedicated to pottery production.

- What can the analysis of test-pit finds contribute to our existing knowledge of Roman rural settlement and its relationship to roads and industry?

- Can we detect in geophysical surveys any hints of the lay-out of the Roman landscape?

For the post-Roman period a number of gaps and uncertainties exist. We have some glimpses of early Anglo-Saxon settlement from development sites such as Oxford Science Park, but as yet no overall pattern has emerged. Similarly to the Roman period, we asked:

- What can the analysis of test-pit finds contribute to our existing knowledge of post-Roman to middle Anglo-Saxon rural settlement?

- Can the study of place-names and documents such as charters help us to understand the origins and extents of early to middle Anglo-Saxon communities?

As described above, there is a somewhat greater stock of existing knowledge for the later Anglo-Saxon and Medieval periods. Research questions were posed as follows:

- What can the analysis of test-pit finds contribute to our existing knowledge of developing villages and parish centres during the later Anglo-Saxon period? Is the influence of the early town or burh of Oxford visible in the archaeology of its eastern rural hinterland?

- How did material culture and settlement change in the Medieval period? Can the study of finds in museum collections, along with those from test-pits, help with understanding this?

- How can studies of historic maps, alongside place-names, and Medieval histories of churches, colleges and organisations such as the Knights Templar give us new insights into the ways in which Medieval villages, manors, farms and field systems developed over time?

The Medieval religious houses of East Oxford are key to understanding many aspects of the landscape of the area. St Bartholomew's (Bartlemas) Chapel and Littlemore Priory are tantalising sites for which there are many unanswered questions:

- What was the detailed lay-out and burial ground of the Bartlemas leper hospital, its chapel and precinct? Using surveys, test-pits and excavations, can we make progress towards reconstructing these? How did it utilise the advantages of its landscape position?

- If (as suspected) burials exist at Bartlemas, what can these tell us about death, diet and disease in the leper hospital or later chapel communities?

- How representative was Bartlemas of Medieval leper hospitals in general?

- What was the extent and lay-out of the Littlemore Priory settlement? Where were its kitchens, middens, workshops and outbuildings?

- What more can the archaeological and historical study of Littlemore Priory contribute to the history of monasticism in Oxford, particularly of nunneries and the role of women in monastic communities?

- Can documentary study of these sites show us how they changed over time, and can later finds cast light on their subsequent uses?

For the post-Medieval period, arising from studies of open field systems and interest in the English Civil War (in part prompted by mid-seventeenth century activity at Bartlemas), we decided to pursue the following question:

- Can large scale surface survey of earthworks, coupled to studying aerial photographs and Lidar, help us to understand open field systems and also hopefully detect traces of Civil war defences and siegeworks?

We sought to bring these themes together in a common quest for understanding the development of East Oxford's landscape and communities over time. A focus on change and innovation was balanced with studying the effects of continuity from one period to the next. Industrialisation and immigration characterised the twentieth century, but they had also done so in much earlier times, such as in the third and fourth centuries AD. Long periods of apparent peace and quiet have been interrupted by interludes of upheaval, which was in some cases violent, but which inevitably died away again as passions cooled and events moved on. Modernity is no refuge from these pressures and turbulence, and the story continues into the present. Our philosophy is to see ourselves not as detached observers of East Oxford's history and community, but as part of them.

Since the *Archeox* project started, Oxford City Council has published a series of 'resource assessments' by period coupled with research agendas (2012), as a basis for a city archaeological action plan published in 2013.[39] These fascinating and useful overviews cover the whole city area, and are intended to provide a working framework for ongoing commercial archaeology and heritage. Much of their focus is inevitably on the city centre, but East Oxford is included. *Archeox's* research priorities contributed to some of their recommendations, and helped to develop a strong community archaeology theme in the action plan.

Notes

1   Attlee 2009.
2   VCH Oxon 4, 262.
3   Benson and Miles 1974.
4   Clark 1889-99 (3 volumes).
5   Clark 1891-1900 (5 volumes).
6   Heaney 2017.
7   Manning and Leeds 1921.
8   Oxford City Council 2012–2013. Available online at: https://www.oxford.gov.uk/downloads/20200/archaeology
9   Dodd 2003.
10   Poore *et al.* 2009; Munby et al. 2019.
11   Booth and Edgeley-Long 2003; Keevill and Durden 1997; Moore 2001.
12   Booth *et al.* 2007, Lambrick and Robinson 2009; Hey *et al.* 2011.
13   Parker and Anderson 1996.
14   Robinson 2011.
15   Parker and Goudie 2007.
16   Booth and Edgeley-Long 2003.
17   Keevill and Durden 1997.
18   MHS 2002.
19   JMHS 2011.
20   VCH Oxon 1, 318.
21   Atkinson and McKenzie 1946-7, 163.
22   Linington 1959.
23   Durham 1984.
24   Booth *et al.* 2007, 164-71.
25   Mudd *et al.* 2013.
25   Boston 2004.
27   Oxon HER.
28   Durham 1984, Dodd 2003, 13-17.
29   Dodd 2003.
30   Whitelock 1979, EHD, 127, 590-91.
31   Pollard *et al* 2012.
32   Crawford 2008.
33   Blair 1994, 161.
34   VCH Oxon 2, 158.
35   JMHS 2008.
36   Lattey *et al.* 1936.
37   Clark 1889.
38   Salmon 2010, 17-21.
39   All available online at: https://www.oxford.gov.uk/downloads/20200/archaeology

Alexander Montgomerie Bell (1845–1920)

Matt Nicholas

Alexander Montgomerie Bell was a classical scholar and teacher, as well as an enthusiastic amateur archaeologist, natural historian and anthropologist (Fig. 1). He spent his life collecting objects, many of which are now in the Pitt Rivers Museum. One of his major collections of Prehistoric artefacts is from East Oxford.[1]

Bell was born in Edinburgh in 1845. His father was a professor at the University of Edinburgh, and he followed him into teaching and academia. After graduating from Balliol College, Oxford, in 1869, he held various positions at the University as well as at schools and colleges across England and Scotland. Bell was primarily a scholar of classical Greek, but archaeology was his consuming hobby. What sparked this interest is uncertain, but it appears that his collecting began whilst teaching at Limpsfield School in Surrey in the 1880s, where he started to acquire Palaeolithic tools from nearby gravel pits.

In 1890-91 Bell moved to 7 Rawlinson Road, North Oxford, and his archaeological activities expanded. 1891 marks the beginning of his connection with the Pitt Rivers Museum when he donated his first three objects. In the following years Bell's attention turned to the Oxford area, firstly Palaeolithic finds from Wolvercote (on which he published several articles), and then Palaeolithic and later Prehistoric finds near Iffley, some of which came from a gravel pit known as 'Cornish's Pit'.

Little is known about exactly how Bell acquired the objects in his collection. It is likely they were amassed through a mixture of personal collection, purchases from workmen and acquisitions from fellow enthusiasts. Bell does not appear to have excavated any sites himself. His Neolithic tools from Iffley Fields were all surface finds, and his Palaeolithic tools were collected from gravel quarries and brick pits. However Bell recorded a detailed knowledge of the deposits from which artefacts came and, at least at Wolvercote, drew sections and took photographs.

Bell was an important figure in local archaeological organisations, giving exhibitions and lectures, and leading field visits. In 1894 he joined the Ashmolean

1. A.M. Bell whilst studying at Balliol College, Oxford, in the late 1860s. Reproduced by kind permission of Master and Fellows of Balliol College BellAJM-26-5.

Natural History Society of Oxfordshire, becoming one of the society's most active members and its President between 1898 and 1900. Bell was also involved in the foundation of the Oxford University Anthropology Society in 1909. Bell's Oxford collecting ended in 1911 when he moved to South Newington, near Banbury. He died in 1920, aged 74. During his lifetime Bell donated 260 objects to the Pitt Rivers Museum, but at the time of his death thousands remained in his possession. Shortly after Bell died, his son Archibald sold his father's collection to the Pitt Rivers Museum. Letters between Archibald Bell and the museum refer to an unfinished book that Bell had been working on prior to his death. The manuscript was never deposited with the museum and its current whereabouts are unknown, if it indeed still exists. As a result, much of the detail of the original location and context of the artefacts from Bell's collection is missing.

The Bell Collection of stone tools

Olaf Bayer

Bell amassed two significant collections of stone tools from the Iffley Fields area of East Oxford around the turn of the nineteenth to twentieth centuries. Both are now part of the Pitt Rivers Museum's collections. Much of his local collection of Palaeolithic stone tools came

from Cornish's Pit, a Victorian gravel quarry 250 metres north of Donnington Recreation Ground close to the junction of present day Donnington Bridge Road and Arnold Road (Fig. 2).[2] Dating from approximately 250,000 to 200,000 BC, this assemblage comprises around 185 pieces of worked stone, including a number of handaxes, and has been the focus of previous research. Much of the material has rounded water-worn edges so moved some distance in the river before being deposited in the Thames gravels at Iffley Fields.

Bell's other Iffley Fields collection consists of 529 lithic artefacts of Mesolithic, Neolithic and Early Bronze Age date. No records exist for the Bell Collection, so it is unclear exactly where all the objects came from. However, Percy Manning (another early-twentieth century Oxford archaeologist) made the following notes about discovery of the collection during a lecture given by Bell in 1907:

'Behind Fairacres House, towards Donnington House over about 10 acres. Gravel overlaid by humus about 2' 6", many flints found on the surface. In places shallow linear shaped hollows sunk down to gravel c.15' diam. Factory of flint numerous cores + flakes, cores mostly small, some larger. Mostly quite black = transparent, 3 or 4 fabricators (small fragment of entirely polished celt. [handaxe] surface)' (Percy Manning Archive).[3]

Based on this description, the collection was probably found between Fairacres Convent and Donnington Lodge. This places it on slightly raised ground overlooking the confluence of Boundary

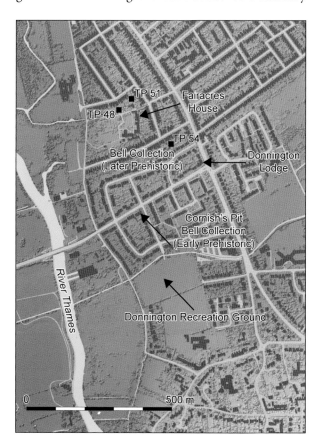

2. Location of the Bell collections and prehistoric finds from the Iffley Fields area. (Base mapping © Crown copyright/database right 2012. An Ordnance Survey/EDINA supplied service. Topography derived from a 1m resolution Lidar DTM © Environment Agency/Geomatics Group.)

Brook with the Thames, approximately 500m north of Donnington Recreation Ground. In the early years of the twentieth century this area would have been open fields. During 2012 and 2013 a number of test pits were excavated by *Archeox* in the grounds of Fairacres Convent and in gardens in the surrounding streets (see Fig. 3.4).[4] Although only a small number of lithics was recovered immediately to the north of the Convent, with a single find to the south-west, in the context of the Bell collection these confirmed a later Prehistoric presence in the area.

Building on two previous pieces of work researching the collection, *Archeox* volunteers studied and analysed the later Prehistoric element of the Bell collection in 2013.[5] The Bell Collection contains numerous datable artefacts including Mesolithic cores, microliths and microburins; Neolithic arrowheads and fragments of polished stone axe; and Early Bronze Age arrowheads and scrapers (Fig 3). The assemblage comprises both tools and debitage (the waste material created in making stone tools). The relatively high ratio of diagnostic tools to waste suggests that Bell, as with many other collectors at the time, collected easily identifiable tools at the expense of debitage. In all periods represented, the composition of the assemblage reflects the later stages in the stone tool manufacturing process, their use and eventual discard or loss. The types of tools present were used for hunting (microliths and arrowheads), cutting, scraping and piercing softer materials (scrapers, retouched and utilised blades and flakes, and awls), as well as heavier tools for felling and digging (axes and picks).

Analysis of the collection suggests the Iffley Fields area was a frequent focus of Prehistoric activity between the Mesolithic (c. 9600-4000 BC) and the end of the Early Bronze Age (c. 1500 BC). The lack of records detailing the exact location and circumstances of discovery make it difficult to say much more about the activities that created this assemblage. For example it is unclear whether all the material originates from one relatively tight area between Fairacres Convent and Donnington Lodge, or represents one of several foci of Prehistoric activity in the wider Iffley area.

Current thinking suggests that inhabitation during the British Mesolithic, Neolithic and Early Bronze Age was characterised by varying degrees of mobility rather than permanent settlement. The later Prehistoric element of the Bell collection assemblage is likely therefore to have been created over millennia of repeated episodes of inhabitation each lasting weeks, months or years, by at least partially mobile hunter-gatherer and early farming communities. Certainly the assemblage's raw materials indicate that the communities were part of patterns of movement, contact and exchange that reached beyond the immediate Oxford area.

3. Mesolithic, Neolithic and Early Bronze Age stone tools from the Bell collection, all © Copyright Pitt Rivers Museum, University of Oxford. 1. Mesolithic blade core, accession number 1921.91.405.1; 2. Mesolithic microlith 1921.91.405.9; 3. Mesolithic microlith 1921.91.405.11; 4. Mesolithic microlith 1921.91.405.10; 5. Fragment of Neolithic polished flint axe1921.91.405.211; 6. Base of Early Neolithic leaf-shaped arrowhead (tip missing) 1921.91.405.350; 7. Late Neolithic oblique arrowhead 1921.91.405.358; 8. Early Bronze Age barbed and tanged arrowhead 1921.91.405.359.

An interesting question raised by the collection is why this particular area was revisited over millennia? One school of thought on such 'persistent places' emphasises economic and environmental factors.[6] Thus groups of peoples' repeated return to the gravel terraces of Iffley Fields was driven by the continued availability of animal and plant resources in this slightly elevated location, overlooking the Thames and Boundary Brook confluence and Cowley Marsh. Another, and not necessarily mutually exclusive, explanation stresses the role of social factors in the persistence of places.[7] This suggests that over time, and through repeated episodes of inhabitation, locations developed resonance and history. Each repeated return

to this locale may have had as much to do with the area's associated memories, myths, stories, and traditions, as with its potential for hunting and gathering.

Notes

1   Extracted from a longer, fully reference article available online at http://england.prm.ox.ac.uk/ englishness-Bell-collection.html (viewed 06/03/2015).

2   Nicholas and Hicks 2013, 290-292 summarise previous work on Bell's Palaeolithic collection from Iffley Fields.

3   This extract of Percy Manning's archive is quoted in Nicholas and Hicks 2013, 292

4   For test pit reports on TPs 51, 54-58 and 71 excavated in this area see ORA data archive; Lithic artefacts from Archeox test pits are reported on by Olaf Bayer in the same archive.

5   Humphrey Case's article on Mesolithic finds from the Oxford area discusses five microliths from the Bell Collection (1953, 3-11). Robin Holgate's thesis on

Neolithic settlement in the Thames Basin summarises both the Mesolithic material (1988, 211 and 221) and the Neolithic material (1988, 253).

6   See Barton et al. 1995 for ecological explanations for the reuse of places in Prehistory.

7   See Pollard 1999 for social explanations for the reuse of places in Prehistory.

A Neolithic Axe from Chester Street, East Oxford

Valeria Cambule

Discovery

A Neolithic flint axe has been in the collection of the Ashmolean Museum (AN1893.177) since 1893. The entry in the accessions register records that Mr Roe, dealer in antiquities, St. Aldates, Oxford, purchased the object for £2 in Cardigan Street, Jericho. According to the entry, the axe was found by a workman about 4 feet (c. 1.30 metres) down during an excavation to build Chester Street, which is in Iffley Fields on the west-facing slope of the gravel ridge marked by Iffley Road.[1] There have been numerous other finds of Prehistoric lithic artefacts in this general area of East Oxford, including by A.M. Bell and other collectors. Although 17 July 1893 is the first record of the axe, it must be a few years after the date of its discovery. The note does not mention when building work on Chester Street began or how long the workman may have kept it. Chester Street does not appear on the Ordnance Survey map of 1886 but does feature on that of 1900. Therefore the axe must have been found after 1886 but before 1893. The find-spot is under the road at the junction of Chester Street and Warwick Street (SP 5279 0510).

Description

The axe is an impressive item, shaped using knapping techniques associated with the Neolithic Period (circa 3300-2350BC). It is a fine flint axe, ellipsoid in plan, from brown to greenish-grey in colour. The original flint nodule must have been large and shaped using bifacial flaking technology. The implement was well-flaked all round its periphery with no attempt at polishing. A semi-circular cutting edge, 7.1 cm wide, gradually decreases to 4.7 cm at the proximal end, over a length of 18.1 cm. The maximum thickness of the axe is 36 mm; it weighs 545 g.

The axe shows some distinctive characteristics:

- A small patch of residual cortex (33 mm by 21mm) with distinctive grey staining. The knapper was unable to remove it, because such an action could damage the form of the axe and compromise its intended function.

- A random distribution of chert patches.
- White sediments adhering to hinge fracture terminals all around the implement, especially around the edges.

1. Neolithic Axe from Chester Street. Ashmolean Museum Object no AN1893.177. Photograph by Ian Cartwright.

Topography and geology

Chester Street is a side street off the western part of Iffley Road. It drops from 63mOD at the north-east end to 56mOD at the south-west end, over a distance of 200 metres. The building of the street exposed Oxford Clay overlain by Summertown/Radley gravel.[2] As the residual cortex shows grey coloration, the Neolithic axe was probably found in the Oxford Clay deposit. However, the alternative might be a grey river silt deposit. A palaeochannel may have existed at the lower end of the street incised into the gravel. This channel would have filled with grey silts derived from Oxford Clay. The axe was therefore found in the lower zone below the middle of the street, which was probably subject to flooding.

Flint sources

The remaining cortex is thick and suggests the raw material for the axe was quarried from a deposit below the surface. According to the British Geology Survey there are no chalk deposits around Oxford. Possible supply points are elsewhere in southern England, from Neolithic flint mines such as Cissbury, Harrow Hill and Long Down in Sussex, or clay-with-flint on the Berkshire Downs and Chilterns. Peppard Common, in the Chilterns near Henley, is one of several good quality flint sources in the latter areas.[3] Comparing some flint examples from the pits of Site 2 of Peppard Common with the axe from Chester Street suggests this source of flint may be compatible.[4]

Hypothetical evidence of trade

Some trading or exchange may have existed between Peppard Common and the Upper Thames Valley zone. Individuals may have brought flint rough-outs from Peppard Common and then worked completed artefacts locally. The Ashmolean Museum collection produced comparable artefacts to the Chester Street axe: a polished axe from the Thames at Nuneham[5] and a partly-ground axe found around Headington.[6] These two axes show a flint source consistent with the Chester Street axe. Without any scientific analysis this

remains a hypothesis, but might support the idea that trade links existed, and consequently skilled knappers worked in the area. Indeed, all the implements illustrate a high standard of manufacturing: from the partly-ground axe from Headington, to the flaked Chester Street axe and a fully ground polished axe found at Nuneham.

Function and meaning of the axe

Axes are functional implements used in woodworking or as weapons. One detached flake on the Chester Street axe suggests it may have been used briefly for tree felling. But understanding the various uses of the axe is complex, as it has status and cultural meanings too. Its composition and good condition suggest the artefact was an important object, perhaps deliberately buried rather than casually lost. The axe may possibly have been a ritual deposition in or near to a 'watery environment',[7] given the proximity of Chester Street to the confluence of the rivers Thames and Cherwell, and to Cowley Marsh. This is only a hypothesis, but in Prehistory many artefacts of daily life were also part of ritual and belief. Perhaps the concentration of flint artefacts in the Iffley Fields area was evidence for a ritual deposition tradition in this area? This cannot easily be proven, but future discoveries in better-understood contexts could help to explain the distribution of artefacts discovered on the gravel terraces along the eastern banks of the Thames and improve our understanding of the Chester Street axe.

Notes

1. Ashmolean Museum accession records 17th July 1893, object no. AN177.1893, p. 678.
2. British Geological Survey Online Maps: http://www.bgs.ac.uk/discoveringGeology/geologyOfBritain/viewer.html (accessed 18/5/14).
3. Peake 1913, 39-40.
4. Russell 2000, 54.
5. Object no. AN1889.46.
6. Object no. NC-PREHIST.217.1865.
7. Bradley and Edmonds 1993, 204.

The Leopold Street and Burgess's Meadow Bronze Age Hoards

Jeffrey Wallis

Introduction

A hoard of Bronze-Age metal objects was discovered in Leopold Street, East Oxford, in 1881, and is held in the Ashmolean Museum. It closely resembles another metalwork hoard, also in the Ashmolean, which had been found in 1830 on Burgess's Meadow, on the eastern side of Port Meadow, a short distance north-

west of Oxford City. Both hoards also come from environments that could be described as 'watery': low-lying ground in the Thames drainage basin, at or near spring lines. Due to their strong affinities, the two hoards have been catalogued, studied and published together. The two hoards were re-examined and drawn under the aegis of *Archeox* by Jeff Wallis.

The Ashmolean Museum's archive includes extensive handwritten curatorial notes on the hoards. They are described together in a report by E.T. Leeds, dated 23rd March 1916, in the *Proceedings of the Society of*

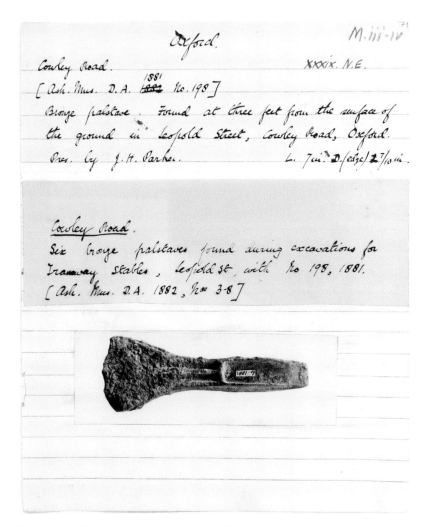

1. Archive notes on the Leopold Street Hoard © Ashmolean Museum.

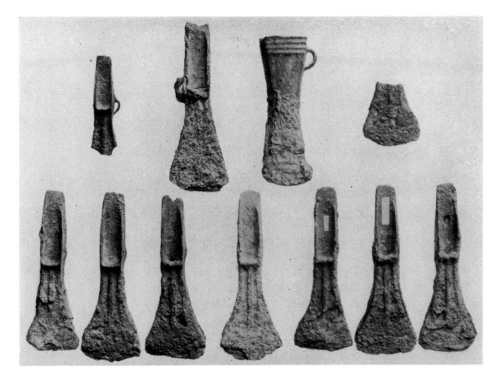

2. Reproduction of the photograph of the Leopold Street Hoard in Leeds's report (1916).

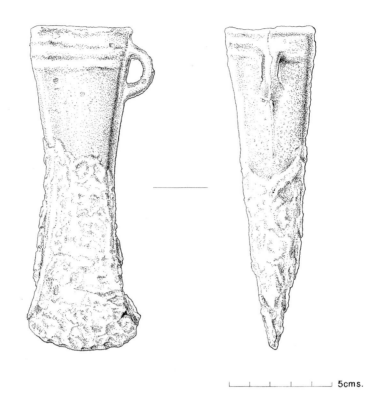

5cms.

3. Socketed, looped 'celt' from the Leopold Street Hoard, drawn by J. Wallis.

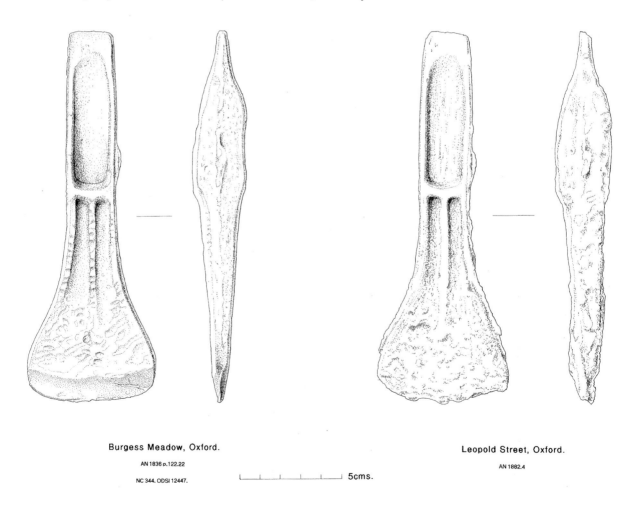

Burgess Meadow, Oxford.

AN 1836 p.122.22

NC 344. ODSI 12447.

5cms.

Leopold Street, Oxford.

AN 1882.4

4. Palstaves from Burgess's Meadow (left) and Leopold Street (right), drawn by J. Wallis.

Antiquaries of London.[1] Both were recovered without the exacting recording conditions required of field archaeology nowadays. The hoards consist of palstaves (hafted axes), socketed axes, spearheads, ingots, a chisel and a bronze smith's hammer from Burgess's Meadow.

What connects the hoards?

The palstaves from both hoards share the same mould, with the characteristic hallmark of the missing securing loops. (A further example cast from the same mould, found at Chislet, Kent, was identified by E.T. Leeds in the British Museum, and is described in his 1916 report). When observed laid side-by side the contrasting condition of the two Oxford hoards is startling. The smaller group from Burgess's Meadow is patinated (a thin greenish layer of corrosion). The hues were mid- dark green with some mint-green corrosion products. However, the underlying surfaces are well-preserved and can be easily inspected with the unaided eye. Sharply and softly delineated palimpsets of hammer work could be detected.

The poorer condition of all the elements of the Leopold Street Hoard is obvious. Corrosion products on most of the surfaces of the implements prevent any comment on their production technology. However, differences in states of corrosion products may allow some useful observations to be made. Looking at the Leopold Street objects as a group, one becomes aware of consistently severe and less severe states of preservation between the proximal and distal ends of individual artefacts. Their surface breakdown may be linked to wet/dry water-table fluctuations in the hoard's watery depositional environment: this is discussed further below. Examples of palstaves from the two hoards were illustrated alongside each other. The palstaves from these hoards share the same casting mould and have the common feature of missing hafting loops. Placing the two palstaves side-by-side on the page, confirms this – if overlaid they fit perfectly – and their weights are also very similar.

Of the two examples illustrated, the Burgess's Meadow palstave is in much the better state of surface preservation. A study of the photographs and drawing the surfaces brought the surface sculpture into sharper focus. The phases of hammer work were confined to the flanges and blade, probably with the intention of dressing and smoothing casting flashes from a bivalve mould-pour, and to aid hardening of relatively soft opencast grain structure. The primary hammer strikes left shallow and ovoid negative imprints. Could they have been carried out using the hammer in the hoard? To answer this question micro-signature marks on the palstave would have to be identified. A second overlaying course of hammering implied the use of a heavier, ball-shape hammer, as the five identified negative marks appeared much deeper. Did the bronze smith have at least two hammers at his disposal and by implication a rather large anvil? The texture of the cast surfaces in recessed areas between the flanges and curved fillets was very smooth and not granular as one would expect of a bivalve stone mould, suggesting these palstaves were cast directly into copper alloy moulds.

This leaves the problem of the missing loops. Looking at both hoards, where corrosion does not impair observation a slight protuberance is present on the flange of the palstaves where a loop could be positioned. The mould may have had a loop incorporated, which was blocked, possibly by smearing clay into the void to prevent casting this feature. One can sense the thumb of the smith smoothing the clay firmly into the holes slightly below the level of the surrounding surface resulting on casting in a slight bump in a relatively flat flange. But why do this? The blade has not been worked or even attempted to be sharpened for use. Usually a hone of sandstone or schist would have been used to produce a serviceable sharp edge and one could detect the vertical striae from grinding. However, there is no evidence of sharpening on this example. This, together with the broken scrap, suggests the hoards were bronze smiths' collections of new, tradable pieces and metal for recasting and perhaps not a deliberate placement. A future investigation could profitably look at the metallurgical assay of the alloys.

Geology and find contexts

Neither of the hoard locations was well-recorded. The Leopold Street hoard was an accidental discovery by construction workers digging footings for pony stables at the new Oxford Horse Tramway Depot. The Burgess's Meadow Hoard was discovered during ploughing. Burgess's Meadow borders Port Meadow, part of the Thames floodplain which has a rich archaeological palimpsest of crop marks and barrows. The subsoil is floodplain gravel with areas of alluvium and silted-up palaeochannels. Port Meadow still regularly floods today, and at the time of the hoard's deposition it would probably have been an even more extensive watery environment, with a complex system of channels and small islands, or eyots, of gravel.

E.T. Leeds's report on the Leopold Street Hoard states that it was found 'on a bed of clay with a bed of shells above it, 3ft below the surface'.[2] The presence of the shells (type not identified) is interesting and could imply a watery connection. The find-spot is also at the western edge of a once-extensive wetland area, later known as Cowley Marsh. A thin cover of Summertown-Radley gravels are recorded in this area, over the solid geology of Oxford Clay. Small streams and larger palaeochannels drain south-west from the high ground and flow into Cowley Marsh, and a spring or watery area probably spread across ground now occupied by St Mary and St John Church on Cowley

Road.[3] Bronze Age hoards have been linked to deposition in watery places or at springs, in many cases away from settlements.[4] The implements may have been contained in an organic container, and/or inserted vertically and partly into soft, fine-grain sediment as a deliberately-placed, ritual deposition.

Notes

1   Leeds 1916.
2   Leeds 1916, 149.
3   Allen *et al* 1970.
4   Yates and Bradley 2010.

Early Medieval weapons from the River Cherwell at Magdalen Bridge

1. An Anglo-Saxon shield boss and its reconstruction by Mark Viggers and Jenni Laird

In May 1884, dredging in the Cherwell uncovered an Anglo-Saxon shield boss along with a spearhead. The finds were discovered under an arch of Magdalen Bridge, the furthest one from Magdalen College, going east. Both the shield boss and the spearhead are now held by the Ashmolean Museum.

Shield Boss: Ashmolean accession number: AN1884.513

The accession records it as 'A well preserved iron umbo or boss of an Anglo-Saxon shield wanting only one of the flat circular headed rivets in the rim. The iron scarcely at all oxidised. The diameter 6 7/10" (16.7 cm); diameter of the central, or raised portion, only 4 2/10" (10.5 cm); projection of the boss from the shield: 4" (10.2 cm)'. The apex ends in a flat round projection or button. The sides of the raised portion are slightly hollow and have a ridge at the angle with the sloping top. The boss appears to have received a blow from a spear or arrow.[1]

Type and date

The shield boss was a stray find from the river bed, so lacks a context with datable grave goods. It may have been a ritual deposit in water, like we suggest the Viking stirrups found nearby were. However, because of its distinctive style, we can attempt to tell its story using other bosses of the same type. Initially we identified the Magdalen Bridge boss as a Group 4 type (based on Dickinson and Härke's typology) but reassessed this when we realised that the wider flange of the boss placed it into the Group 5 category. Boss Groups 4 and 5 are also unique in usually having only four boss rivets, and a spike or rod apex. In some cases a disc is brazed onto the end of the rod, but not on the Magdalen Boss. Group 5 bosses differ only in the greater flange dimension (25-31mm), and, where fitted, disc apexes are broader.[2]

Group 4 bosses are a small group, with 14 bosses in the Upper Thames area. Group 5 is even smaller with three bosses in the Upper Thames area and only one other from Bidford-on-Avon, Warwickshire. Group 5 bosses only differ from Group 4 in that the flange and disc apex are wider. These differences were so minor that we decided to look at Groups 4 and 5 together as they share a stylistic heritage and the finds group in an unusually concentrated area. The style of the boss can

17cm

1. The original shield boss in the Ashmolean Museum (Ian Cartwright).

2. The reconstructed shield boss.

be traced back to the early Roman Iron Age in the area to the east of the River Elbe, eastern Germany.[3] This Germanic boss style seems to disappear from cemeteries east of the Elbe in the later third and fourth centuries AD, but then reappears in cemeteries between the Elbe and west to the Loire in France in the later fourth and fifth centuries AD.

These bosses are more distinctive in appearance than other groups: this later style was developed for a completely different style of combat. Battles were being fought in a more massed formation using a shield wall, so later shields were physically bigger and wielded in a more protective manner. Early Migration period shields were smaller and used more offensively, in a period when fighting style was more individualistic, emphasising the warrior's skill, strength and bravery. The bosses are also higher and narrower than other groups.

Shield boss construction

A sheet of iron would have been heated and beaten creating a cylinder shape to form the wall. The bottom edge of this cylinder would then have been flared out to create the flange (to mount to the shield face with rivets). Another piece of iron would then have been heated and beaten to form the upper cone shape. The two pieces were joined by forge-welding around the circumference. This is where both parts were heated to a high temperature, joined and then beaten so the surfaces bonded to form one piece of metal. The spike, or rod apex, is brazed into place inside the cone.

We decided to recreate the Magdalen Bridge shield boss, working with an accomplished blacksmith friend, Jason Green of Wieland Forge. We worked with the original dimensions, along with numerous photographs and line drawings of the artefact.

Although Jason has vast experience of making similar bosses, he remarked on how technically difficult this particular style of boss was to manufacture. In his opinion, only a specialist blacksmith could have produced it. Bearing in mind the close proximity of other Group 4 and 5 finds, could it be that there was a specialist blacksmith in our area? Or did warriors from a specific area of the continent bring their shields and bosses with them when they settled?

Mark Viggers took on the challenge of fashioning an authentic Anglo-Saxon wooden shield to display this recreated boss, suggesting how it might have looked in the fifth or sixth centuries AD.

3. The finished shield, diameter 65 cm.

Damage to the shield boss

On the cone of the boss is an area that has suffered damage. Although we can only speculate from our experience of re-enacted battles, we would argue it was probably damage from a spear point. Most impact damage on a shield boss tends to be on the top (or upper) part, as in this case, because blows were delivered with a downward motion. On the flange there are two holes of roughly the same diameter and shape in close proximity. One of the holes would have been for the now missing rivet, but there also some damage to the hole. It is possible that the second hole was made to secure the boss after the initial hole was damaged or had deteriorated. Taking into account the boss's value and the high regard in which it would have been held, the first explanation is more likely.

In *Germania*, Tacitus mentions that the Germanic warrior's worst disgrace was to lose his shield in battle, and experience suggests that for many men a hard-fought battle would have left them with little or no shield-board, and all that would remain would be the more valuable metal boss. Re-fitting a new board to the remaining boss would not be difficult and it may therefore be that the boss itself held the symbolic significance.[4] Its deposition in the river could have been deliberate, as a ritual deposit, or an accidental loss as the result of an unrecorded local skirmish.

The Cherwell Crossing in Early Anglo-Saxon times

Although slightly less famous that the 'Oxen Ford' traditionally located to the south of the city, crossing the Thames (known after the Norman period as Grandpont), the Cherwell crossing at Magdalen Bridge has also been important throughout human history (its earliest historical mention is in the Headington Charter of AD 1004).[5] The bridge (today a much modified and widened late eighteenth-century stone structure) replaced older timber bridges and there was probably originally a ford here.

Might the discovery of this shield boss suggest the presence, perhaps transitory, of "foederati" or mercenary troops in the employ of local post-Roman administration centres, such as Dorchester-on-Thames? Dorchester is thought to have survived as a centre of Romano-British administration into the sixth century AD, and may have benefitted from the protection of the foederati. The Dorchester belt – an official insignia – has been presented as evidence that there were foederati there in the fifth century.[6] The Magdalen Bridge shield boss adds to the view that Germanic soldiers or mercenaries were probably present in the Oxford area, either in the very late Roman period or the early post-Roman period.[7] Although we do not know who owned or made this shield boss, we have used style typology and previous finds to propose a date. As is the case with many object

biographies, we have found ourselves asking more questions than finding answers, but the recreated object gives a vivid picture of how an early Anglo-Saxon shield would have looked.

2. A pair of Viking stirrups by Jenni Laird and Mark Viggers

Introduction

'Metal objects and bones found near Magdalen Bridge in 1884 are re-interpreted here as the likely remains of a Viking warrior and his horse, buried on an island in the Cherwell around the year 1000. This date, which has seemed improbably late for a "pagan" grave, makes more sense in the light of evidence from Scandinavia that furnished equestrian burial continued up to c. 1000. The man probably belonged to one of the armies that raided the region from the 990's, or even to Svein Forkbeard's army which attacked Oxford in 1009 and 1013. It is significant that the burial was so close to St Clement's, the possible site of a Cnut-period Danish "garrison".'[8]

So wrote John Blair and Barbara Crawford in 1997. We have reconsidered their interpretation, in the light of recent reports on similar sites, to ask whether the Magdalen Bridge site was a Viking burial, or something else.

The find and its location

In the late nineteenth century the Ashmolean Museum purchased a collection that included two fine, decorated stirrups. The stirrups are Anglo-Scandinavian (late Viking, probably of the early eleventh century), made of iron with decorations of

4. The stirrups © Ashmolean Museum.

inlaid brass wire (Fig. 4). They are not a matching pair, but were found together near Magdalen Bridge in Oxford. There were several other items found with them, which included a smaller stirrup, a spur, iron shears and a horseshoe, but it is not clear whether these were all from the same deposit. All were recovered from above the waterline on the southern edge of an eyot or river-island which underlies the bridge between the banks of the River Cherwell. The Register of the museum also records that 'horses' skulls and other bones' were found at the same spot. The bones were reportedly sold to a dealer in St Clements by workmen. Male thigh bones were also apparently found, and sold on to the University Museum of Natural History, but these can no longer be traced.

Oxford in the late tenth to early eleventh centuries

Oxford in this period had a Danish Viking population: many were massacred after taking refuge in St Frideswide's church on St Brice's Day (13 November) in 1002. The focus of Anglo-Scandinavian settlement may have been in St Clements, just over Magdalen Bridge from the city: Blair and Crawford suggested that it was significant that the putative burial was in the immediate vicinity of St Clements and the possible eleventh-century Danish garrison. The dedication to St Clement is found in Danish settlement areas across Europe, including the famous St Clement Dane's church in London. The local geography supports the possibility that St Clements was a garrison area. The eyot upon which the stirrups were found may have formed part of this. The Vikings preferred to use the sea, a river or marsh as protection on one side of their forts and garrisons. Viking camps such as Repton (Derbyshire), Torksey (Lincolnshire), and Reading (Berkshire), all made use of D-shaped enclosures or eyots within river courses.

The consensus that the original 'Oxen Ford' is on the north-south line of St Aldates, near Christ Church at the southern entry to the city, should not exclude the possibility of an important ford and bridge on the east side of the town, across the River Cherwell, near and probably just to the south of Magdalen Bridge. The Royal estate of Headington (east of the river) had lands on both sides at that point, and the crossing may have had been important enough for a bridge to be built there, even before it was first mentioned in the Headington Charter of 1004 (see page 214).[9]

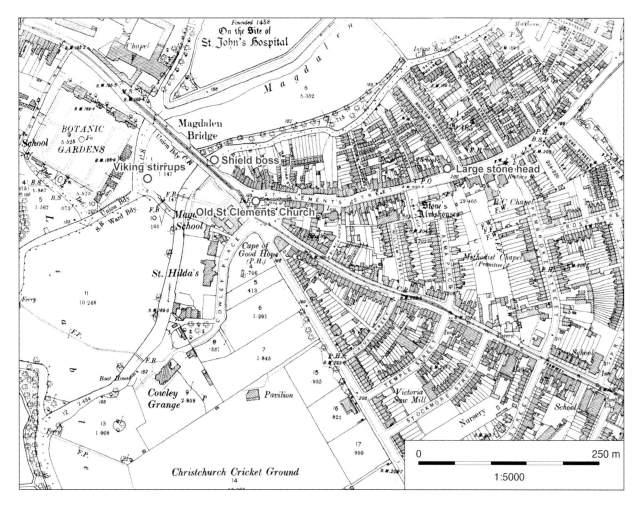

5. Map of St Clements showing find-spots. Base Map 1900 Ordnance Survey 6 inch to the mile (© Crown Copyright and Landmark Information Group Limited 2014).

Offerings in rivers

Christianity was widespread by Æthelred II's reign (978-1016), but some pagan practices recurred under Viking influence. This was perhaps demonstrated by an increase in river offerings or ritual deposits, marked by weapons and other items found in later times through dredging and other activities. Common to both Britain and Scandinavia,[10] these offerings were thought to have been a votive practice, giving thanks to the gods for success in battle or to ensure good luck in future battles. Deposits in the River Witham in Lincolnshire, which include a similar stirrup, and the Thames in London are particularly common. At Skerne (East Yorkshire), a number of animal skeletons and Viking metalwork were found closely associated with the oak piles of a bridge abutment or jetty. Four knives, a spoon bit, an adze and a Viking sword were also found. None of the animal bones showed signs of butchery for consumption.[11] These findings are similar to several in Scandinavia. A distribution of votive offerings seems to follow the movements of the Danish armies of 993-1016 along the Thames and Lower Severn valleys into East Anglia and Lincolnshire. Viking war bands were known to be mounted and mobile, and probably used stirrups. Whilst many Danish graves contained stirrups and other high-status horse equipment, the finds of stirrups in the Danelaw also attested to the presence of Danish cavalry in eleventh-century 'armies.'[12]

High-status burials?

Blair and Crawford suggested that the finds were the furnished burial of a Viking warrior and his horse. Review of the evidence has raised a number of doubts about this interpretation. An equestrian warrior's grave would probably have contained a shield, helmet, sword, spear and personal dress accessories, as well as horse trappings. Furthermore, the only human skeletal remains found were thigh bones, and no horse skull is recorded amidst the bones sold on. The horseshoe and smaller stirrup have also been dated as much later than the unmatched stirrups. It is hard to be sure given the standard of reporting in 1884, but it is therefore probable that the items were not all buried together at the same time, but could reflect a local tradition of deposit in this location.

Was there a garrison in the St Clements area? Would the Danish Vikings have buried a warrior and a horse so close to their garrison? There is now much more awareness and interpretation of votive offerings in the early medieval period, and these finds seem to fit this pattern better. Recent reports show offerings can include stirrups and can be found close to a bridge abutment or jetty. We would argue that, rather than a pagan grave, these finds mark a significant ritual location where Vikings (or indeed their enemies) made offerings to the river.

Notes

1   AN1884.513: by Prof. H. N. Moseley, Linacre Professor of Physiology.
2   Dickinson and Härke 1992.
3   Jahn 1916, 173.
4   Pollington 1996.
5   See study of the AD 1004 Charter in Chapter 6.
6   Kirk and Leeds 1952-53, 75.
7   The original artefacts are on display in the 'England 400-1600' gallery in the Ashmolean Museum.
8   Blair and Crawford 1997, 135.
9   VCH Oxon 4, 1-73, see study in Chapter 6.
10 Lund 2010.
11 Richards 1991, 116.
12 Graham-Campbell 1991.

Two stone heads

Nina Curtis

In 1912 the Ashmolean acquired Medieval stone sculptures of two heads (Accession no. AN 1912.2.c).

The small stone head

Small stone head: ? Headington limestone; face mutilated; hair curling round face; traces of red and green paint. Height 87 mm, Width 100 mm.

Dr Jim Harris, Teaching Curator in Western Art at the Ashmolean, and a scholar of Renaissance polychrome sculpture, has dated the piece to the thirteenth century. He believes it is the head of an angel, at some point separated from the rest of the body. There are remnants of the original polychrome colouring in several places, and it is likely that the head was painted twice: first with an undercoat of red, and then covered with green paint.

The small stone head was found in East Oxford during drainage works on Hurst Street, close to the corner of Leopold Street. It is difficult to know where the angel head would have originally been sited, but it almost certainly came from a church. It might have been part of an elaborate tomb decoration, part of a corbel or a column carving. .

The large stone head

Large stone head: ?Headington limestone, face mutilated; in cowl or wimple;
Height 332mm, Width 175mm; Depth 158mm; part of architectural detail. Source: probably Old St Clement's Oxford. Purchased. From site of old Almshouses, demolished (in 1912, on the site of Mission Hall, 56 St Clement's).

1. Small stone head from Hurst Street. Photograph by Ian Cartwright.

Dr Jim Harris felt it was definitely the likeness of a male individual, probably thirteenth century and probably carved from Headington stone. Marcus Cooper, professional stone mason and archaeologist, agreed that it seemed to represent a male. He observed that the carving was not sophisticated and thought it might have been part of a corbel table, sited high up in a church where fine details would not have been necessary.[1] A corbel supported stone arches springing up from the top of its head to the roof of a religious building. It also would have been painted. The head is both weathered and mutilated, making it difficult to envisage what it would have looked like. The lower right-hand side of the face/chin has been cut off, and finer details of the eyes, nose, hair and mouth have blurred with time, but we can still discern the main features.

While it is not crude, compared to some of the masterpieces in religious and academic buildings in Oxford, it seems likely that it was not carved by a master mason, but by a mason of lesser stature. In any case, our nominal date of the thirteenth century excludes many of the Oxford colleges which were built later. But not far from where the head was discovered, once stood the Medieval parish church of St. Clement, This was demolished in 1827, and is probably the origin of the large head, and may also be the source of the smaller head.

Background

We are not used to seeing sculpted stone figures painted in bright colours today, but in the Middle Ages, the interiors of churches, including the religious sculptures in stone or wood, would have been brightly coloured, to enhance their power to transport worshippers from often difficult daily lives into the glory of God's kingdom. Entering even a modest rural church would have been an inspiring and awesome experience, and the Medieval church was one of the most powerful influences in the community. Entering a church one's senses would have been assaulted: by works of art – paintings, carvings in wood and stone, stained glass, and walls, all painted in vivid colours – and the heavy scent of incense.

The raw material

The stone used probably came from a quarry in or near Oxford: Headington Quarry is the most obvious candidate, producing Corallian Limestone.[2] This was used extensively in Oxford's colleges and other buildings.[3] The stone would probably have been dislodged from the quarry by means of a puggle, a flat spear-headed piece of steel on a long pole.[4] This means of extraction resulted in the internal rock stresses being released in a gentle way, producing fewer cracks

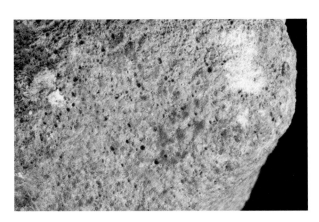

2. Paint traces on the small stone head. Photograph by Ian Cartwright.

3. Large Stone Head from St Clements. Photograph by Ian Cartwright.

compared to the modern 'fast' methods. When the stone arrived on site, a local mason would probably have carved the sculpture; he would have trained for many years as an apprentice to a master mason before becoming a maker of carved images.

The Reformation

In the sixteenth century the Protestant Reformation split Christianity into warring factions of Roman Catholics and Protestants. To the Medieval mind the head of a person not only housed the intellect, it was the home of the soul. Faces gave identity to depictions of human beings, and the expression was a key to the personality and character of the subject being depicted. Cutting the head off a statue was a gesture that destroyed the purpose of the sculpture and deprived it of meaning. Many beautiful works of art that graced the churches of England were destroyed, and those that weren't often had their colours hidden under a layer of whitewash: one of the reasons very few polychrome figures have survived. Further attacks on statuary occurred during the Cromwellian period. Sculpted heads had their noses smashed and were defaced, and it is possible that the angel's head was separated from its body at that time. Most of the nose and part of the mouth are missing, and although it is interesting and tempting to attribute it to Protestant or Puritan wrath, there is no conclusive evidence.

It is difficult for the modern viewer to imagine the power that art and objects displayed in the church had for the Medieval worshipper. The door of the church represented the border between earthly trials and deprivations of the here and now on the outside, and the sanctity and promise of salvation within. Once inside, the parishioner would explore with awe and wonder the extensive decoration which covered the interior of the church. Scenes from the Bible, lives of Saints, and real as well as metaphorical battles of the body and spirit were depicted. The extensive religious imagery carved into and emerging from the physical fabric of the church was designed to inspire and educate commoners and nobility alike, and as part of this potent iconography these stone heads would have played their part in enriching the lives of those who encountered them.

Notes

1   Marcus Cooper, stonemason, interviewed by the author, at the Ashmolean Museum, 24 April, 2014.

2   Arkell 1947.

3   Gee 1953.

4   A flat spear-headed piece of steel on a long pole, which was the only method of quarrying used in Oxford until the late-nineteenth century. Stephanie Jenkins, 'The Stone Quarries', on Headington Community website: 'History: Miscellaneous', viewed on 2 April, 2014 http://www.headington. org.uk/history/misc/quarries.htm

Chapter 2

Archeox: the emergence of a community

David Griffiths and Jane Harrison

Background: East Oxford and its population

As outlined in Chapter 1, East Oxford has a fascinating archaeological past, connected in every way to wider questions of early human habitation in the Thames Valley, and in later times to the development of the city. The formerly rural landscape has not completely disappeared, but has been in great part overwritten with housing, roads and industry. In the extensive network of green spaces which remain amongst the built-up areas, there has been a nearly complete change of use since the mid-nineteenth century. Land once in use as open fields for arable cultivation, hillsides used for foraging, quarrying and hunting, and commons with ancient grazing rights, have gradually lost their former purposes and been turned over to become parks, sports pitches, nature reserves, allotments, hospital grounds and a golf course. Woodland has been contained, tamed, managed and reduced, and wetlands have been drained. Much of what was once farmland is now divided into hundreds of small domestic gardens, and water-courses have been altered, bridged, channeled and culverted. The re-working of the landscape has served one purpose above all: accommodating a vastly increased population, which is now non-agricultural in its culture and economy. A few old families remain in Iffley, Cowley and Littlemore who can trace their lineage back to pre-industrial times, but folk-memories of a rural past in the area have faded beyond reach. An East Oxford childhood in the 1920s did mean a greater connection to country ways and smallholding life than is possible today,[1] but even then, the area was fast-changing. William Morris, later Lord Nuffield, had begun producing cars at Cowley in 1913, initially on the premises of the former military college, a private school founded in 1876 for boys from army families, which closed in 1896. Morris Motors became a huge manufacturing complex with several sub-factories, the easternmost part of which remains in business producing the BMW Mini. An increased influx of new inhabitants in the mid-twentieth century came through successive waves of immigration, in the 1930s from other less-prosperous areas of England and South Wales to work for Morris, and since the 1960s, increasingly from all over the world. Minarets now rise gracefully skywards from a townscape where only spires did previously. Of course, the area is no stranger to immigration. The Roman pottery industries must surely have attracted a multifarious workforce, and the spread of its products indicate the presence of long-distance traders and journeymen in their midst. Danes, who were victims of officially-sanctioned, ethnically-driven violence on St Brice's Day in 1002, Jews, Medieval pilgrims, civil war soldiers and fugitives, and students and workers at the growing university, all ensured that the population and cultural character of Oxford's eastern suburbs was never static, even well before the modern growth of the city.

East Oxford today, therefore, is a vibrant social mix. Its distinctiveness within Oxford is celebrated by its inhabitants, most spectacularly in the annual Cowley Road Carnival. Past planning struggles,[2] the development of an 'alternative' culture around Cowley Road from the 1970s onwards with its cluster of (often quirky) local shops and businesses, and its reputation as a 'working class' area have all served to distinguish East Oxford from some other parts of the city which are perceived as traditional, academic, affluent and less cosmopolitan in character. The area's most common self-image is one of diversity and informality, coupled with a concern for the environment. Cycling, and indeed recycling are popular! Life in East Oxford can be idyllic: widespread greenery and the beautiful downhill westward vista of South Park towards the 'dreaming spires' of Oxford, a community cinema and theatre, verdantly productive allotments, and characterful streets of pleasant terraced housing, are all amongst its attractions. The area is not without its problems, however. The Blackbird Leys Estate became briefly infamous in 1991 after an outbreak of youth 'joy-riding' in stolen cars, a problem which was solved by diligent community social work and policing, coupled with a redesigned road system. The 2013 conviction of a ring of seven men for extremely serious sexual offences conducted mainly in the area around Cowley Road over several years is a grim and worrying reminder that there is a less salubrious side to life in East Oxford. Homelessness, alcohol and drug-dependency support, family crisis and food bank charities are relentlessly busy. The fact that the quality of life for the majority of the population is not

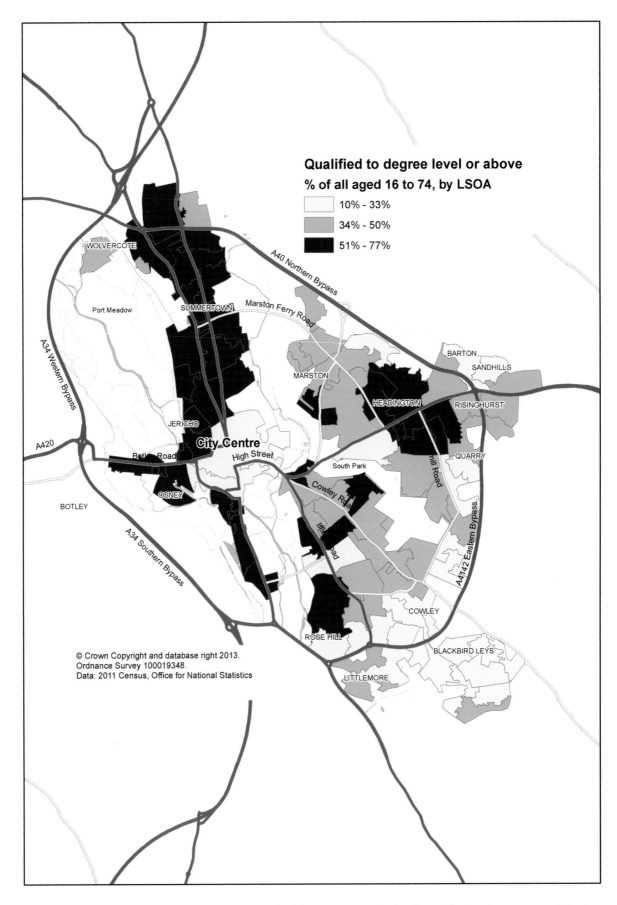

Fig. 2.1. Qualifications to degree level by area in Oxford ('LSOA', a statistical unit used by local government). Darker colours = higher, based on 2011 data © Oxford City Council.

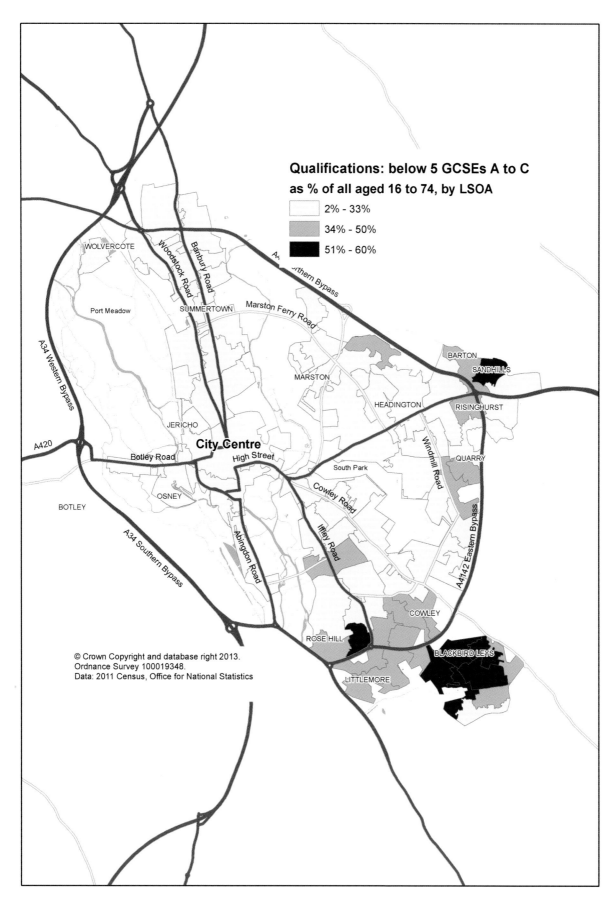

Fig. 2.2. Numbers of people by area with less than five GCSE's or equivalent in Oxford. Darker colours = higher, based on 2011 data © Oxford City Council.

seriously afflicted by these issues is a tribute to the tireless work of tackling, resolving and containing the area's problems on the part of local police, social care agencies, charities, the NHS, churches, and community support groups.

As a suburban part of a city dominated by two major universities, academia affects Oxford's eastern districts in influential ways. An area of the city which fifty or more years ago was dominated by the households of factory and shop workers, is now host to thousands of young people in higher education, many living away from their parents for the first time. Oxford 'dons' once tended to live in large, well-appointed houses in affluent North Oxford, and college servants inhabited humbler properties in the city centre and East Oxford. Today the high cost of housing means that most university academics can barely afford to live even in the most modest housing available within the city boundaries. The influence of the two universities on the economy and make-up of the local population has been strongest in areas of greatest proximity to their campuses in central Oxford and Headington. In the nineteenth century, playing fields established on Cowley Marsh and along Iffley Road caused students to venture in greater numbers to the east of Magdalen Bridge, but few undergraduates lived outside their colleges. Students and university employees now reside across most of the city, but remain a less dominant presence on its eastern periphery, particularly on the major housing estates. Pockets of relatively severe social deprivation in these areas give rise to an intense local patchwork of educational advantage and disadvantage which may be amongst the most pronounced anywhere in the country. These disparities are in some cases remarkably steep: for example, the affluent historic village of Iffley, populated with academics and professionals, sits cheek-by-jowl beside the sometimes-troubled social housing area of Rose Hill. In educational terms (Figs 2.1, 2.2), people with few or no qualifications, and those who have university degrees, cluster in contrasting areas, with the local authority housing estates of Rose Hill, Donnington, Wood Farm, Blackbird Leys and Barton forming concentrations of noticeably lower educational attainment. Any initiative which could seek to try to bridge these divides, and bring people of differing backgrounds together to further a common cause or interest, must surely be a good thing for the area.

Community archaeology: a fresh way forward for academic research

It is now a mainstream facet of academic research in Britain that it should wherever possible seek to engage communities beyond academia in the gathering and interpretation of scientific, historical or environmental research data. Indeed, by reaching out to existing social groups, such as to students or, local residents, new communities can be created around participation in a research campaign. Many public funders require 'impact' to be evaluated and reported upon, so no longer are university researchers able to hide in relative obscurity behind the closed doors of the library or laboratory. Some university teachers were initially sceptical of this development – daunted perhaps – but amongst forward-thinking academics, a positive sense has taken hold that engaging the public can potentially be a great asset to realising the potential of research. This is not merely to 'tick a box' for funders, but to appreciate that widening the appeal and resource base of university research beyond the walls of academe can actually strengthen its purpose and relevance. Approaches to community involvement can take the form of a professionally-organised project structure designed to reach out in terms of information or activity to members of the public, a 'crowd-sourcing' approach for 'Citizen Science' where self-selecting contributors voluntarily contribute information or resources to a central gathering-point for processing and interpretation, or a 'bottom-up' democratic structure where the collective participants in a research endeavour are also the organisers, thinkers and reporters. Each of these approaches has its merits, but no single one, by itself, is entirely applicable to an intensive community-based archaeological and historical research project.

An idea for a community-based archaeological research project in, and about East Oxford was dreamt up in the summer of 2008 by David Griffiths and Jane Harrison, both of whom are Oxford University archaeologists and also longstanding East Oxford residents. In conversation, after the long return journey from a six-week excavation in Orkney, in northern Scotland, the idea arose of starting a field project on our own doorsteps, with an all-year-round programme of investigations and studies, rather than just a few concentrated weeks in the summer season. Some of the key archaeological sites of East Oxford were already known about, even if there were as yet many unanswered questions about them: the Medieval leper hospital at Bartlemas, the spread of Roman pottery kilns, and the under-appreciated and little-investigated remains of Littlemore Priory. However, the links between these focal points in time and space, plus the plethora of smaller, piecemeal records of archaeological and historical interest, were then much less well-understood. A key context for the project idea from the start has been *Landscape Archaeology* – an approach which recognises that in order to understand any one site, feature, find or monument, it must be approached through the bigger picture of inter-linked land-use, settlement patterns and environmental change over time. Landscape Archaeology is a strong theme in the academic direction of the Archaeology programme at Oxford University Department for Continuing Education, where the project was based. Initially it was seen partly as an opportunity for students on part-time courses in Archaeology to gain some experience of working on field studies within Oxford. However from the beginning, a significant element of community involvement was sought, by appealing to participation by local residents. It was felt that, by attracting volunteers, we could expand the potential scope of the project to encompass many more areas, places and themes than would be possible with a small group of students alone. Moreover, it would give the project more meaning and relevance: archaeological research has all-too-often been done by the few, for the few. Evidence is taken from the ground, worked upon behind closed doors, and published in esoteric journals. More recently, there has been a drive to produce popular publications and online information, together with having open days, to 'show and tell' the public what the experts are doing. These approaches seemed underwhelming to us as a basis for the type of project we sought to create. Individuals may own land and buildings, but knowledge, and the right to carry it forward, belongs to everyone. Our starting point was to design and promote a research campaign where all of its participants felt a sense of co-ownership of the research endeavour and its results. A means of financial and institutional support was needed for a viable, robust research campaign, which could reach out and energise interest in archaeology and history within East Oxford and beyond, with a thorough programme of education and training, so that the volunteer recruits could receive guidance and experience in research methods and field practices. There was to be no slippage in standards, even if participants were sought from all educational backgrounds and none. The project would be externally funded, providing dedicated posts giving professional support, training, equipment and expenses for volunteers, and participation was to be free to all.

The educational context

Beginning in 1878, Oxford University began to offer 'extension classes' to the general public, where university academics could teach their subjects at centres across England, in the evenings, and on week-long summer schools.[3] The provision of education for the 'working population' in subjects such as politics, philosophy and history was a key tenet of later Victorian liberalism, in an age of gradually-widening voter franchise. Women were well-represented among the early extension students, although they did not gain the vote even on a restricted basis until 1918. The administrative needs of this endeavour gave rise to a 'Delegacy for External Studies', later known as the

Department for Continuing Education. By the 1970s, branching out into newer subject areas, the department had appointed full-time archaeology and local studies tutors (Trevor Rowley and Mick Aston), and as a result was offering an increasingly varied selection of courses, conferences and training programmes in archaeology. It was involved in the creation of the modern profession of archaeology and heritage, through its role in organising an archaeological response to the construction of the M40 motorway, and the founding of the Oxford Archaeological Unit (now Oxford Archaeology) in 1973. In more recent years, there has been a growing community involvement in its Oxfordshire training excavations, notably at Marcham-Frilford near Abingdon, and at Dorchester-on-Thames. Thousands of people from all walks of life have taken advantage of the department's courses to acquire a short encounter, a broader education, or even a research degree, in archaeology and/or local history. The courses mostly carry a fee, which with the gradual withdrawal (now complete) of government funding for Adult and Continuing Education, is unavoidable for the department to make ends meet, but this necessarily, and unfortunately, excludes some people who might otherwise be interested in learning and participating. The department's role is to extend learning beyond the traditional structures of the university, and to help to serve all aspects of the University's core aims and objectives, including that expressed in its Strategic Plan as follows: 'To contribute effectively to the cultural, social, and economic life of the city of Oxford and the Oxfordshire region'.

As the idea for a community-focused East Oxford Archaeology and History project progressed from the drawing-board, initial meetings with potential collaborators began in summer 2008. A pump-priming grant was obtained from Oxford University's John Fell Fund. This enabled David and Jane to organise a series of scoping meetings, to speak to local councillors and residents at area committees, in order to build a local profile for the project idea, and to explore other funding sources in more detail. Continuing Education was to be the host department within Oxford University for the planned project, but could not cover all eventualities by itself. The university's School of Archaeology, which teaches full-time students, runs excavations across the world, and operates a world-famous scientific research laboratory, was first amongst other departments to express an interest and to begin to point students towards the project to add to their experience. The two Oxford University museums housing archaeological material: the Ashmolean, and the Pitt Rivers, were also seen as necessary stakeholders because of their exceptional collections (both of which include locally-derived artefacts) but also because of their expertise in outreach, education and making their collections

Fig. 2.3. Jane Harrison leads a guided walk in the early stages of the project.

accessible. Oxford Brookes University's School of Architecture and Design came on board as a collaborator, offering its students opportunities to get involved in the creative side of the project (such as producing a highly successful exhibition event centred on the project at the Pitt Rivers Museum in October 2013, see page 48).

Beyond the two universities, the Oxford City Council Archaeological Officer, initially Brian Durham until retirement in 2008 and then his successor David Radford, offered support and guidance. The Oxfordshire Historic Environment Record, based at Oxfordshire County Council, indicated it was prepared to collaborate with the project. The leading professional archaeological organisation in the city, Oxford Archaeology, became the source of much good advice, encouragement and, as the project developed, became an essential partner in the post-excavation processing work. Members of the Oxfordshire Architectural and Historical Society (OAHS), which in Oxfordshire acts as the main 'county' archaeological society, showed considerable interest.

The project takes shape

By mid-2009 a head of steam was gathering around the idea for a community archaeological project in East Oxford. A working seminar of community-based archaeologists from around the UK was convened at the Asian Cultural Centre in Manzil Way, East Oxford in May 2009, from which we gathered commentary, advice and learned from the experience of others from up and down the country in promoting archaeological involvement for the public. Site visits took place to Bartlemas Chapel and (using the public bus service) to Blackbird Leys (it has been a maxim of the project throughout that we should aim wherever possible to use walking, cycling or public transport in preference to private or hired vehicles). Scoping meetings also took place with the Heritage Lottery Fund's offices in London, and with potential stakeholders in the community and charitable sectors around East Oxford, including the staff of the Ark-T Community Centre in Cowley, which was to become a key

supporter, meeting venue, and equipment base for the project. Features appeared in the *Oxford Mail* about digging up history in peoples' back gardens; guided walks (Fig. 2.3) and site visits took place, with up to 50 people participating. One-day practicals were arranged for older schoolchildren from Cheney School, who undertook geophysics on their playing field and measurement of the ridge and furrow earthworks in South Park (Fig. 2.4). South Park was also the location of the annual Cowley Carnival community fair, at which we had a project stall for several years (Fig. 2.5). Local environmental groups interested in archaeology received support and encouragement, with wonderful results when the Boundary Brook

Fig. 2.4. Jane Harrison teaches a student from Cheney School how to use survey equipment in South Park.

Fig. 2.5. David Griffiths and Nick Hedges with members of the public at *Archeox*'s stall at the 2012 Cowley Carnival.

Nature Park group (who manage a nature reserve on a former allotment site), were assisted in digging out a new pond, revealing a cache of Victorian and Edwardian bottles and jars, evidently the discarded contents of a chemists' shop which had been buried in the early years of the twentieth century (see page 57).

Such experiences and finds enhanced the reach of the project as word got around and more local people became interested. A website was created to promote the project and to provide contact information. It also had a 'sign-up' button where prospective volunteers could easily register their contact details and join in the growing project community. We were asked to think of a simple name or abbreviation for the website. An idea arose of abbreviating **ARCH**aeology of **E**ast **OX**ford as 'Archeox'. The new name quickly became accepted as a metonym for the whole project and the website became www.archeox.net from then onwards, keeping its title when it was later re-designed and expanded to become a data resource and event management tool.

The impetus given by the initial John Fell Fund grant led to the preparation, principally undertaken by Jane Harrison, of a Round 1 application to the Heritage Lottery Fund (HLF),[4] which sets out the aims and objectives of a proposal and, if successful, opens the way to the yet more complex, detailed and intensively-costed final Round 2. A favourable decision on Round 1 was received in September 2009, and development funding towards Round 2 was offered. This enabled the continued employment of Jane, who drafted the Round 2 bid. This involved the production of an extensive action plan, detailing all the activities which the project proposed to undertake, together with project designs, costings, risk assessments and methods of communication and dissemination. These were supported by guarantees of support from the university, and letters of recommendation from numerous people and organisations who had expressed an interest in volunteering or collaborating with the project, should it be successful in obtaining funding. Before the decision was taken, in February

2010, a site visit and interview took place by Lottery Fund assessors. This occurred at Restore's 'Bee Hive', a mental health charity centre, and included a short excursion to Bartlemas Chapel. The project team presented their ideas and costings for scrutiny and questioning. Volunteers and organisational representatives were invited to come and support the bid, with testimony and commentary on how the project could benefit them or their service-users.

After another anxious wait, in March 2010, the Heritage Lottery Fund's final decision was communicated. They had approved the full bid – forming a funding package of just over half a million pounds for a five-year project, to begin in September 2010. This total included a 65% financial contribution by HLF, backed up by 10% match funding which the John Fell Fund generously provided, with the rest accounted for as in-kind contributions in recorded volunteer activity hours. The project structure approved by HLF would have a Project Director or Principal Investigator (David Griffiths) whose time was covered by the university as part of its contribution; and two Project Officers who were employed to carry forward the activity plan on the ground: Jane Harrison (2008-15), and Paula Levick (2010-12), who left the project and was succeeded by Olaf Bayer (2012-14). The team was supplemented by the welcome addition of Joanne Robinson in 2012-13. A recent graduate with a flair for working with the public, Joanne's time on the project was funded by a Community Archaeology Training Placement Bursary, provided by the Council for British Archaeology. This scheme, also funded by HLF, enabled a series of one-year early-career placements to take place in archaeological projects and organisations around the UK. There were 100 applicants for the single advertised placement with *Archeox* – an indication of the profile which the project was rapidly building in UK archaeological circles.

In addition to assembling the HLF-funded core team, a project steering group was established, consisting of leading (or 'key') volunteers, representatives of stakeholder organisations including the City Archaeologist and the County HER Officer, and the project team. This met twice or thrice-yearly to review and comment on the range of activities undertaken and issues encountered by the project, and to contribute to forward planning. Continuing Education provided office space and the Ark T Centre offered part of its garden so a project activity and equipment shed could be constructed. Ark T was one of a number of church hall and community centre venues across East Oxford where numerous evening talks and weekend events were held, raising the profile of *Archeox*. An integrated google mail and contact list was established to handle the increasing numbers of volunteer recruits and to manage news and sign-ups to events (which increasingly became over-subscribed), a Facebook group, and Twitter and Flickr accounts were also set up. By the end of 2010, a vibrant community of budding archaeologists and historians, from all areas of East Oxford and beyond, was quickly taking shape.

Method and approach in 'Suburban Archaeology'

Having secured funding and created a management structure, and raised expectations with people all over East Oxford, the project team needed to begin implementing a practical, feasible and accessible programme of field and archive research, training and awareness-raising. The core theme of Landscape Archaeology has been referred to above. Seeing East Oxford as a segment of the wider Thames Valley landscape (Chapter 1) was an appropriate starting point and framework for the research design. The main research issues which have been explored in the Thames Valley over the years are as applicable within East Oxford as anywhere else on the Middle to Upper Thames floodplains, gravel terraces and surrounding Corallian limestone slopes and hills. However, the chief distinguishing characteristic of the project target area was its relatively built-up nature. This was to be a study in Suburban Landscape Archaeology. Suburbs have historically been relatively overlooked and under-sung places in which to conduct archaeological research. Archaeologists instinctively gravitate towards the open countryside, which bears the vivid imprint of thousands of years of human activity. From Dartmoor, to Salisbury Plain, to the North Yorkshire Moors, the sweeping narratives of Prehistory and early history have been played out in empty, wild, remote and beguiling places, not at all like the humdrum residential areas in which most archaeologists themselves have grown up. Another influential sub-set of archaeologists specialises in researching the centres of historic towns and cities, the busy and ever-changing hearts of our modern urban economy. From the 1950s onwards, urban archaeology has developed as a distinctive specialism and professional pathway. Unravelling deeply-stratified and often extremely rich and complex deposits, coupled with the challenge of working within a rapidly evolving world of redevelopment, has exerted a powerful pull on the practice of archaeology. Many of the most significant advances in excavation technique, stratigraphic analysis and in post-excavation management have occurred in urban archaeology. In many historic city centres, excavations over the years have been witnessed by thousands of members of the public from viewing gantries and through windows in hoardings, taking place in deep sheet-piled holes squeezed between towering department stores, office blocks, and multi-storey car parks.

By contrast, suburbs have been little regarded and less investigated. Some built-up areas on the peripheries of conurbations, such as Hendon in Greater London, or Stockport in Greater Manchester, have longstanding local archaeological societies or trusts which are committed to active field research. However most residential areas away from city centres lack such a focal group, and the profile of archaeological activity in English suburbia is generally low. Suburbs nevertheless come under the same planning laws as everywhere else, and planning conditions on (generally larger-scale) developments have produced a scatter of excavations, records and observations across built-up residential districts around the country. Largely unrelated to each other and mostly without an overriding research design, the outputs of such work tend to languish merely as routine entries in HERs and annual regional round-ups, or as 'grey literature'- the somewhat downbeat term for archaeological reports which are written up to a basic standard of completeness to fulfil a planning or contractual obligation, but do not make it past the ring-bound, photocopied stage to become proper publications. Rarely have they been brought together and interpreted within a landscape research synthesis.

Since the late 1990s, the rise in community-focused archaeology, and in many cases lottery funding, has favoured field research in residential areas in ways not seen previously. Instead of taking people to where the archaeology is perceived to be, the emphasis has moved onto investigations where people already live, work and play. Involving local residents has become key to unlocking popular history. Residents of the various village communities within East Oxford have been encouraged to get involved in geophysics, field-walking, artefactual and historical studies, and in digging test pits in gardens, grass verges and parks, peppering the area with small interventions which collectively have changed our understanding of village formation over the centuries. The late 'Time Team' archaeologist Mick Aston, who was a strong advocate of public engagement in archaeology, led a long-running community-based research project on the historic village of Shapwick, near his home in Somerset, which has been an inspiration to us.[5] In East Oxford, we have also benefited from the example of research projects such as the Whittlewood Medieval Settlement campaign,[6] on the borders of Northamptonshire and Buckinghamshire in the early 2000s, and CORS (Currently Occupied Rural Settlements), a Cambridge-based project whose volunteers have completed well over a thousand test pits across over fifty parishes, villages and small towns in East Anglia.[7]

Test pits (see Chapter 3) are relatively quick, simple and safe to carry out; they can be used to teach the basics of excavation, and are sociable and popular with adults and children alike. They are dug and recorded in accordance with a step-by-step guide, and a standard basic, low-value kit of equipment. The finds are saved for examination and synthesis later. Test pits rarely contribute major discoveries individu-

ally, but the more that are dug in one area, the better the return on the information they produce. Pottery, flints and other finds give an impression of the impact of past human activity. These are mapped and analysed digitally.

Medieval settlement researchers have been in the forefront of integrated community-based investigations within populated areas, but other models embracing all periods have also succeeded, notably the 'Thames Discovery Programme' which engaged volunteers in excavation and monitoring of the tidal river foreshore throughout Greater London.

Archeox: approaches, methods and highlights

When it was launched with a reception at 'Restore' in early October 2010 (with speeches by the Vice-Chancellor of Oxford University, Professor Andrew Hamilton, and the MP for Oxford East, Rt. Hon Andrew Smith, see page xvii), the *Archeox* project was already the beneficiary of a range of existing experience and methodologies drawn from elsewhere. These approaches, however, needed adapting to the particular circumstances of East Oxford. In a built-up and busy environment such as this, it was not possible to cover all avenues of inquiry with equal intensity. Direction, focus, and key research questions were needed to avoid an *ad-hoc* or scattergun approach. In many ways the varied character of East Oxford's districts shaped the project's direction, and the views of the Steering Group were key to evolving a series of questions and choices where to target our resources.

Where a strong demand emerged, in conjunction to the desire of residents' groups or local historical societies to see more investigation (such as happened in Iffley and Littlemore), we responded. *Archeox* chose to target its test-pit campaign on the cores of the Medieval villages, notably Church Cowley and Temple Cowley, Iffley and Littlemore, so as better to understand their spatial changes and chronological developments over the centuries. Another group of test-pits was conducted in gardens in Donnington and Iffley Fields, the area where Alexander Montgomerie Bell collected many Prehistoric stone tools in the late nineteenth century. Some of these areas were test-pitted in ones and twos, in others we held weekends of multiple test-pitting involving large numbers of participants over five or more test pits. In areas such as Littlemore and Blackbird Leys, the attendant energy and publicity surrounding such weekends brought more new people into contact with the project. Closely allied to the test pit campaign was a drive to reach out to the many allotment gardeners whose sites and plots are found in green spaces across East Oxford. These are the nearest thing left in the area to agricultural cultivation, and like farming, they involve repeated tilling of the topsoil, often turning up pottery, clay pipe

Fig. 2.6. Test pit 23 at Restore's Elder Stubbs gardens in Cowley.

Fig. 2.7. Test pit 29 at East Minchery Farm allotments.

fragments and other interesting finds. Allotment users who had kept such material in their sheds were often willing to allow it to be loaned and recorded by the *Archeox* team. In some allotment sites, this prompted the digging of more test pits, as in the Links site beside Bartlemas Chapel, the Rose Hill/Iffley allotment site and the Elder Stubbs gardens in Cowley, where the mental health charity Restore operates a vegetable garden (Fig 2.6, Fig. 2.7).

Test pits were far from the only practical research approach used by this project, indeed we could have managed many more of them if they had been. A range of other techniques were regarded as equally important, and volunteers were trained in their use and interpretation. Geophysical Survey is in many ways a typically successful way of characterising buried archaeology without, or before, excavation. Two mainstream field survey techniques, gradiometry (also known as magnetometry), and earth resistance (or resistivity) (Fig. 2.8) are used widely across Britain. These are very good at revealing buried traces of archaeology, particularly walls, ditches and pits – in the right conditions, but are affected by serious limitations as well.[8] They operate not as single point measurements but over a large gridded survey area, and it is only possible to make use of them in areas which have at least a 20 by 20 square metre space of uninterrupted ground surface (which excludes most domestic gardens). Magnetic techniques of survey suffer from the impediment that any ferrous material in the soil which has been introduced, through recent dumping or surface treatment, can obliterate with its very high magnetism any subtler signals coming from underlying archaeological features. It also cannot be done too close to fences or buildings, which have iron or steel in them which interferes with archaeological signals. This does not mean necessarily that the ancient features are not there, but for these reasons we often just cannot see them. Likewise, earth resistance survey, which relies on measuring patterns of moisture contrast in the ground, can be rendered futile by the interference of modern construction, drains, concrete and hard-core, and is also useless in soil saturated by a high water-table. All of these problems are much more pronounced in a busy, built-up environment than in the uncluttered realm of the open countryside, where the most impressive geophysical results are normally obtained by archaeologists.

We were keen to put geophysical survey to the test in as many open areas as possible in East Oxford, and to bring the experience and discipline of field survey and the digital processing of its results to as many volunteers as feasible. However, given the likely problems of using geophysics in a suburban environment, we proceeded with modest expectations of the results. Some apparently tempting open, green areas were written off after initial assessment due to high levels of metallic contamination, including several fields along the Thames margins near Iffley which had been used for landfill in previous decades. For use in more promising places, the project purchased two new arrays of UK standard 'workhorse' equipment in both magnetic and resistance survey: a Bartington Grad 601 dual array gradiometer, and a Geoscan RM15 electrical resistance meter. These enable fast, accurate survey and are not particularly difficult to

Fig. 2.8. Earth resistance survey training.

Fig. 2.9. Swii Yii Lim operates the project's Leica GPS Smartrover.

learn how to use, although operation requires some physical dexterity and fitness. Such equipment is also inadequate for landscape studies without proper survey control, meaning its results can be located and fixed on maps. The chief facility in this regard operated by the project was a Leica GNSS (or GPS) 'Smartrover'[9] a global positioning system which operates as a single independent unit receiving spatial correctional data to satellite links over a mobile telephone connection, and is accurate to within five centimetres on the National OS grid (Fig. 2.9). The Smartrover is also capable of recording three-dimensional data when measuring buildings and earthworks, and supplemented more traditional methods in this regard, such as plane-tables and elevation measurement using tapes, plumb-bobs and strings.

Surprisingly, some fragments of the pre-industrial landscape survive very clearly in East Oxford. This is perhaps most vividly represented in the Lidar plot which we obtained from the Environment Agency. 'Lidar' (Light Detection and Ranging) is an aerial remote sensing technique where a light-based signal is sent down to the ground surface from an aircraft and the differences between its millions of contact points are used to construct a detailed digital model of the

surface. It is well-known amongst archaeologists for its ability to 'see through' tree cover, where readings which have made genuine contact with the ground surface are interpolated to remove the 'false' reflections from vegetation. Earthwork survey, involving measurement and interpretation of the 'humps and bumps' visible on the ground, was an important adjunct to geophysics, test-pitting and Lidar, such as recording the faint traces of ridge and furrow earthworks which can still be seen amidst the vegetable plots in the Links Allotments next to Bartlemas Chapel. The most extensive combination of Lidar and geophysics which *Archeox* undertook was in its survey of South Park in winter 2012-13 (see page 98). This swath of open, sloping land, with its famous view of the Oxford skyline, was incorporated as a public park in 1932 from agricultural fields, the boundaries of which are still visible in some of its lines of trees and bushes. The surface of the park preserves a rich and relatively undamaged area of ridge and furrow – surviving because it has been left under grass for eight decades and not ploughed with modern machinery. Concealed amongst these agricultural earthworks are faint traces of other banks and ditches which occupy the crest of the hill, some of which are possibly remnants of siegeworks from the Parliamentarian occupation of the heights surrounding Oxford during the Civil War. In the case of South Park, due to its heavy public usage and our other priorities elsewhere, *Archeox* did not seek permission to excavate; the survey results were regarded as enough of an achievement in themselves. Sometimes the bigger picture counts for more than the relatively tiny areas which excavation is normally capable of tackling.

Excavation is also disproportionately heavy in its call upon resources in comparison to other field techniques. However there are research questions which cannot be answered in any other way. Geophysics and survey can give a reasonable impression of what lies in or under the ground. But testing those results, and unravelling the date and three-dimensional puzzle of buried features, is more properly the business of excavation. We wanted to make the point as clearly as possible to everyone involved that excavation is not the be-all and end-all of archaeology, and there are plenty of other possibilities for participation. Many people cannot dig and some do not want to, but are drawn to other aspects of the archaeological process, such as working with finds (Fig. 2.10), maps, images or making creative contributions. Others cannot afford the time to spend day after day getting muddy on site, but are able to participate in other, more flexible ways. It was, however, also clear from the beginning of *Archeox* that there was a substantial number of prospective volunteers who were strongly motivated by the chance to dig on interesting sites, to learn how to do it properly and develop

Fig. 2.10. Finds-sorting group at St Clement's Community Centre.

their own expertise, to guide and encourage others, and participate in the uniquely enjoyable social mix which occurs on excavations. Mindful of the need to engage and train volunteers in writing-up the excavations afterwards, and to process the usually-vast amount of site records, plans and artefacts which result, the project team and steering group opted to manage expectations and workloads carefully and to stage one significant excavation, of no more than five or six weeks' duration, for the years in the middle of our funded period (2011, 2012 and 2013). To have excavated in any later year could have left a burden of post-excavation work too close to the point when the project grant was due to expire.

As it turned out, only one of the three excavations undertaken by *Archeox* resulted directly from its campaign of geophysical survey – this was the last of the three, and the smallest – at Donnington Recreation Ground in September 2013. The other two came about by targeting known sites, to some extent aided by happy chance. The six-week excavation at Bartlemas Chapel (Chapter 4), which took place over the early autumn of 2011, was occasioned by the offer by *Archeox* to undertake the opening and archaeological monitoring of a relatively small new drainage circuit being dug to prevent the build-up of damp in the chapel. The chapel is maintained only by a small income from visitors' donations; the parish authorities gladly accepted *Archeox*'s offer of help, and a 'faculty' (permission, with conditions, to excavate) was obtained from the Oxford

Diocese. Oriel College gave permission to work on its own segment of the site, and also offered the comforts and facilities of its nearby sports pavilion for the team's use. The timing was perfect, producing a stimulating, productive and enjoyable first project dig which trained many volunteers, forged many new friendships, gained invaluable publicity, and generated a haul of fascinating finds, structural data and new information on the likely lay-out of the Medieval leper hospital.

Bartlemas also provided the project's principal encounter with the archaeology of human remains. Until 2011, the presence of a burial ground within the chapel enclosure was suspected but not confirmed. The trenches excavated by *Archeox* exposed a series of inhumations, together with charnel pits containing the mixed-up bones of people and animals, which had been reburied after disturbance in the past. Representing surely only a small proportion of what may lie buried there, 11 skeletons were exposed, cleaned and recorded to the standards and current ethical observances required in British Archaeology. The Diocesan Faculty forbade the removal of articulated human remains, so these were recorded *in-situ* before being re-covered at the end of the excavation. Removal of the charnel, however, was permitted, and this became the subject of a fascinating study and analysis, which contributed exciting new information on the illnesses and lifestyles of the people who had been buried there. Re-interment of any human remains was required by the Faculty within two years, and accordingly in

November 2013, a solemn divine service of re-committal back to the ground of these persons, or parts of persons unknown, was held, led by the parish priest of Cowley. A new trench, the size of a normal 1 x 1 metre test pit (TP 72), had to be dug east of the chapel to accommodate the reburial, and in the process yet another well-preserved skeleton was revealed and recorded, but not removed. Accompanied by a choir, a wicker casket containing the bones was lowered into place by *Archeox* volunteers who had participated in the 2011 excavation.

The second major *Archeox* excavation, undertaken in the early autumn of 2012, maintained the theme, established at Bartlemas, of investigating the archaeology of Medieval religious communities. On the south-eastern fringes of Oxford, on the boundary between Littlemore and Sandford, and overshadowed by modern buildings near to Oxford United's football stadium, stands a well-preserved, but rather neglected later Medieval building of Coral Rag limestone, with its ogival gothic windows and door-apertures reminiscent of some of Oxford's colleges. Originally a monastic dormitory, it is the only surviving upstanding remnant of Littlemore Priory, locally known as the 'Minchery', a Benedictine nunnery founded in the mid-twelfth century and dissolved in the 1520s (Chapter 5). Much of the priory site was subsequently demolished, but the dormitory building (one of the later and probably better-preserved structures built for the priory) was used as a farmhouse from the sixteenth to the twentieth centuries. It later became part of a 1960s leisure venue or 'country club' (the rest of which, consisting of modern buildings, was demolished after a fire in the 1990s), subsequent to which the Medieval building continued in use as a pub (Fig. 2.11), with the enigmatic

name of the *'Priory ...and ?'* until this closed in 2013. Thereafter the building has been empty and boarded up, with its future uncertain.

An important religious establishment, connected to Oxford, and with considerable rarity value as a Medieval nunnery, Littlemore Priory represents an extensive archaeological site. W.A. Pantin had written a historically-sound but archaeologically largely-speculative article about it which was published in 1970.[10] In more recent years there have been limited archaeological interventions for pipe-laying east of the pub, which revealed part of the burial ground. The overgrown and rubbish-strewn piece of land immediately west of the surviving building, owned by Oxford City Council, and known as Minchery Paddock, had been subject to a partial site evaluation by JMHS in 2006 in advance of expected housing development, which did not subsequently happen. The 2006 evaluation revealed clear potential for more of the priory site, confirming that walls, hearths and a well existed in the paddock area. *Archeox* applied to Oxford City Council for access permission to excavate three trenches in the Paddock, expanding upon the results of the 2006 evaluation and examining the wetland environs of the brook which lies at the northern limit of the site. In autumn 2012, if not in quite as perfect weather as that of the previous year at Bartlemas, six weeks of rewarding excavation ensued, producing a wealth of Medieval evidence, dating from the lifetime of the priory, with some important palaeoenvironmental data covering a much deeper timescale from Trench 1 beside the brook (see Chapter 5).

Our excavations at Minchery Paddock and Bartlemas were investigations at sites with both buried and standing remains, which form an interconnected

Fig. 2.11. The 'Minchery', the surviving building of Littlemore Priory (from north), shortly after the closure of the pub in 2013. Minchery Paddock (Chapter 5) lies to right of the path. The ground to the left, the site of the priory church, has since been excavated (see page 186) and built upon.

picture. The emphasis in the project's excavation work was on the sub-surface archaeology, but the work at Bartlemas in particular (where excavations were immediately adjacent to the chapel) illuminated key aspects of the chapel's architectural development. Elsewhere across East Oxford, a wealth of possibility exists for investigations of the built heritage. Churches, historic houses, pubs, and factory buildings interested many of the volunteers, and the Steering Group was receptive to suggestions that individual examples should be investigated. Perhaps the most in-depth study of a standing historic building undertaken by the project was that of St George's House, Littlemore (see page 195).

Maps, plans and old photographs contribute essential information, and building volunteers' experience in researching these became a key aspect of *Archeox*. Unusual and important buildings which have now disappeared have also been researched, such as old St Clement's Church, and the ornate, neo-classical bathing complex in Bath Street on the banks of the Cherwell, in St Clements (see page 222). The Oxfordshire History Centre in Cowley houses many important local documents, but many more were located in the Bodleian Library, in individual college archives notably at Oriel and Christ Church, in the national collections housed by Historic England, and online. With the freely-given support of a number of college librarians and professional archivists, groups were formed amongst volunteers which undertook specialist investigations. In several cases led by experienced local historians, these formed their own programmes of research into historic maps, place-names, and into the detailed histories of Bartlemas and Littlemore Priory. Links with local historical societies in Littlemore and Iffley ensured these areas were covered – indeed the Littlemore Historical Society, which had been struggling prior to *Archeox*, received a major boost in membership and activity as a result of its contact with the project.

Research into museum collections under the aegis of the project paralleled archival research. Volunteers who expressed a wish to work with the Ashmolean or Pitt Rivers museums to identify, catalogue and record material from East Oxford were encouraged to form interconnected groups, each one investigating a different type or class of artefact. The museums were only able to accommodate relatively small numbers in their work rooms, but larger workshops and handling sessions were also held, notably the occasion when Professor Richard Bradley, a leading prehistorian based at Reading University who resides in East Oxford, held a workshop for volunteers on the Leopold Street Hoard of Bronze-Age axes at the Ashmolean Museum in February 2012. The ongoing results of the excavation, archival and collections-based work were made available to the wider body of

volunteers and the general public in several ways. The archeox.net website carried photographs, reports updates and a series of quarterly project newsletters. Evening meetings at Ark-T and other venues heard updates from volunteers and specialists about their work. More immediate dissemination was provided by the *Archeox* Facebook page and Twitter feed and through 'Leigh's Blog', a frequently updated online account of the research campaign written by two volunteers, Leigh and Gill Mellor, who participated in almost every aspect of the project.

A further aspect of *Archeox* was the encouragement of creativity. Experiencing encounters with the past, through visiting sites or handling artefacts, is a stimulus to imagination. Writing formal archaeological reports and producing technically-accurate drawings is by no means all which can result from such encounters. Volunteers were encouraged to develop as broad an approach as possible to recording and symbolising their experiences. A group of archaeological re-enactors *Wulfheodenas*, led by volunteer Jenni Laird, supported the project in full Anglo-Saxon or Viking costume on numerous public occasions, especially on National Archaeology days and at the Cowley Road Carnival. Their skills in reconstructing ancient technology led to the creation of a number of highly accurate replicas of artefacts from East Oxford, most notably a decorated round shield based on the iron Anglo-Saxon shield boss from Magdalen Bridge which is in the Ashmolean Museum (see page 27). Joanne Robinson, the project's community archaeology bursary holder, led a series of workshops under the title *Artscape* for Julian Housing and dementia groups in East Oxford (see page 239). For those unable to participate in re-enactment or excavation, making replica Medieval floor tiles, based on actual archaeological examples, brought interest and fulfilment. Several talented artists contributed imaginary or semi-imaginary views and reconstructions of the sites which the project was working on, notably local painter Helen Ganly (Figs 4.7, 5.30). A group of first-year architecture and design students from Oxford Brookes University produced an ingenious series of sculpturally-mounted displays, inspired by, and physically including some of the more eye-catching finds from Bartlemas and Minchery Paddock excavations. This culminated in a highly popular short exhibition at the Pitt Rivers Museum in October 2013 (Figs 2.13, 2.14). Perhaps the most consciously artistic element of *Archeox*'s creative journey was an interactive installation, drawing on the Minchery Paddock excavation and interviews with volunteers, and staged in the grounds of Bartlemas Farmhouse in 2013. *Matrix* combined sound, music and visuals and was created by Tara Franks in collaboration with fellow musician Filipe Sousa and visual artist Lucy Steggals. Inspired by the 'Harris Matrix', a graphic form of the

Fig. 2.12. Mark Viggers (left) allows children at the Cowley Carnival to play with a reconstructed Anglo-Saxon shield.

Fig. 2.13. Gallery exhibition at Pitt Rivers Museum of Oxford Brookes students' art installations based on the project's finds.

Fig. 2.14. One of the Oxford Brookes art installations, featuring a piece of Medieval leaded stained glass (see Fig. 5.27) from the Minchery Paddock excavation.

Fig. 2.15. Listening to the 'Matrix' sound art installation, conveying recorded sounds from the project's excavations.

Fig. 2.16. Louise Bailey, an NVQ student, works on archaeobotanical material.

representation of archaeological stratigraphy, they explored how an archaeological dig is excavated, discussed and recorded. They captured visually and through sound the unique momentum and rhythmic qualities of archaeological activity, using live music, interactive sculpture and sounds heard through headphones (Fig. 2.15).[11]

Volunteering and training

A founding principle of the *Archeox* project has been that nobody who expressed interest in participating should be turned away. Individuals, couples, and families were encouraged to volunteer, whether or not they lived in the area. There was also an open invitation to local charities and schools to become involved, through tailored group-work sessions, work placements and practicals. An *espirit de corps* was generated on the understanding that it had to be open and non-judgemental, and welcoming to newcomers. Just as no individual could claim ownership of the area's heritage, no person or group could reasonably claim the project as their own: it was a collective effort. There was no typical volunteer (people from all ages and backgrounds signed up) nor any typical volunteer experience. Some people participated so regularly that they contributed significantly to everything which the project achieved. Others focused on whatever interested them – places, activities or techniques (see The shared thrill of discovery, below). Some were content to make occasional forays into the field, or to attend talks, exhibitions and evening events. No volunteer was made to feel less valued by comparison to any other, whatever the scale and intensity of their involvement. In order to maintain proper academic standards of fieldwork and research, a vigorous culture of training and education needed to be created at the heart of the project. The two project officer posts were appointed to take the lead on devel-

oping and delivering volunteer training, and these were supplemented by the CBA training placement. The core team set the tone and constructed a series of key pathways towards training and education, through organising talks, practical encounters with archaeological techniques, and writing guides to good practice which were posted on the archeox.net website and available to all.

A significant training initiative on the project was the provision of four funded places for volunteers to train for the National Vocational Qualification (NVQ) in Archaeological Practice, a UK-wide certified process which is co-ordinated by the Chartered Institute for Archaeologists (CIfA). Jane Harrison became an NVQ assessor, so *Archeox* had its own resident NVQ specialist. The first to qualify was an Oxford University archaeology student who wanted to increase her field experience but to do so while passing on her knowledge to others. The NVQ is achieved by logging and recording training and work through all possible methods of examination and was ideally suited to *Archeox*'s practical and training-led approach (Fig. 2.16)

From 2010 to 2015 the core project team was relentlessly busy in creating and equipping a programme of survey, excavation and post-excavation training. Activities from geophysical survey, to site and building recording, finds washing, soil sample sieving, botanical and zoological identifications, artefact drawing and archival research, required support, information and guidance so the results met all appropriate archaeological standards. For many volunteers it was the opportunity to receive training and education in archaeology and local history which was a major draw to the project, at least as much for some as participating in the thrill of discovery. There was a limit to what three or four professionals could achieve in terms of formal training for a growing community of several hundred eager and motivated volunteers firing on all cylinders. For *Archeox*, the answer was as simple in principle as it was complex in reality: the trainees became the trainers. Those who had already learned the basics or more were encouraged to pass this knowledge on to others, with the support and guidance of the project team. Experienced and inexperienced volunteers were deliberately situated next to each other on excavations and in workshops. The free-flow of wisdom, comment and reflection was encouraged. In this we were assisted by the diversity of the volunteer base, which reflects the character of East Oxford itself. All skills and educational backgrounds were welcomed.

Some of the volunteers were professional archaeologists or archaeology graduates. Students of archaeology and history, either in Continuing Education or full-time undergraduates and postgraduates, shared their own learning journeys with other volunteers. University academics in other subjects, schoolteachers and home-educators shared their knowledge of teaching and how to motivate others in a productive, organised and rewarding way. Librarians, IT specialists, illustrators, artists and writers turned aspects of their own specialisms towards the needs of the project. Builders, stone masons, gardeners, engineers and plumbers had a greater knowledge of how to deal with practical challenges, and charity administrators, health care professionals, fire fighters, bus drivers and police officers knew about disability, safety and security issues. Whilst relevant expertise was welcomed, it was certainly not compulsory or even assessed on entry. Driving, tea-making, and equipment-cleaning were all vital to the success of the project. Older people contributed their time, and in some cases their memories of the area in times past, and the young brought vitality and inquisitiveness. Volunteers worked together without concern as to their widely differing ages and backgrounds. Most importantly, they participated in every aspect of the archaeological research process, not just in excavations. From initial decisions and project planning, to a long-running series of post-excavation workshops, the volunteers did the work, ably trained and assisted by professionals. As the finds and records which the project had produced came closer to archiving and final deposit, the volunteers' enthusiasm and capacity for hard work remained essential. Abi Tompkins, an Oxford postgraduate student and a part-time curatorial assistant at Oxfordshire County Museum Service, led a group preparing for archive deposition, resulting in the *Archeox* finds from Bartlemas, Minchery Paddock and Donnington Recreation Ground becoming part of the permanent holdings at Oxfordshire Museums Store at Standlake (test pit finds were returned to owners, where requested).

The multi-authored nature of this publication is a reflection of the ways in which *Archeox* sought to involve its participants throughout the research process. Many of the contributors to this volume are achieving a print contribution to academic knowledge for the first time. Volunteers were encouraged to take ownership of their work through writing it up for archive, dissemination online and publication. This was not done 'by professionals' after 'the event', but was very much seen as an embedded part of the process. Test pit reports were written by those who had undertaken the work, to a relatively standard formula, although not one which was aimed at excluding original ideas or self-expression. Individual volunteers contributed 'object biographies' based on their own studies of artefacts, or accounts of their own experiences. Other reports, such as for geophysical surveys, excavation reports, or historical studies, tended to be co-authored by partnerships or groups. The project team guided, edited, ensured consistency and accuracy, and in some cases helped to reduce the word-count of these contributions to manageable proportions. 135 reports in pdf format, covering the entirety of the project's outputs, were put online for open access, many well before the end of the activity phase, on the project website. These have now found a permanent online and openly-accessible home within Oxford Research Archive (ORA) housed by Oxford's Bodleian Library. Indeed, we are grateful to ORA for seeing the potential in this project for public engagement, and making us a pilot study for inclusion.

Participation and evaluation

Archeox recorded the participation of its various members and contributors. Timesheets were signed by all participants as a condition of HLF funding until the initial estimated target had been so far exceeded, that in August 2012, HLF gave permission for the formal practice of timesheet recording to cease. Thereafter it was maintained on a more informal basis resulting in an overall estimate (see below). A 'Volunteer Day' was defined as a full day of activity (six hours or more) and half-days were also accounted for. By no means everything was recorded as in this manner, with many informal meetings, evening talks, school and group visits, and guided walks taking place with none or only nominal sign-ins. We never let such paperwork become a hindrance to the project's openness or to participation.

As the project went on, the decision was taken to capture and record many of the personal, social and

Table 2.1: summary figures for individual participation

Volunteer self-registrations on website (total)	642
Volunteer days signed for, Sept 2010 to Aug 2012	2056
Estimated total volunteer days (total) to Aug 2015*	6000
Open day visitors to three main excavations	1700

*this estimate includes two of the excavations, 2012 and 2013

educational impacts which our work was having. Our time was already overly busy with planning and preparing core archaeological and training activities, and we felt that unless a parallel effort was made to evaluate the outcomes and benefits of the project in research, social and educational terms, we would in some sense have failed to make the most of the experience. Our HLF grant conditions meant that we already had amassed a raft of information on volunteer sign-in numbers and activity hours, levels of participation in different activities, and had on record much individual feedback from volunteers and groups. We had conducted a volunteer survey in 2012 using the online software tool *Survey Monkey* which had produced some useful data on participation. The feedback obtained by this method was very largely positive. However the feeling remained with us that we might be missing out on certain aspects of how the project engaged and impressed itself on the public. As *Archeox* matured towards its final funded year, what we decided we needed was an objective, impersonal or anonymised review and assessment of the project against its stated aims, which could help us to make our final, in-depth report to the Heritage Lottery Fund on the use of their funds. After getting on for four years of intensive immersion in the project, we felt too close to the pattern of decision-making, and indeed too close to the people involved, for this reasonably or fairly to be conducted by ourselves. Therefore, having discussed it with the HLF first, we turned to the knowledge and technology transfer company Isis Innovation. This organisation (now renamed Oxentia) was founded by Oxford University to help provide consultancy and enterprise to its academic research endeavours. Two consultants, Britta Wyatt and Elena Andonova, undertook the evaluative work, and in close consultation with the project team, developed a series of interrogative approaches including interviewing people who had participated or those in organisations who had helped to facilitate the project ('stakeholders'), analysing participation data, and researching the project's impacts upon educational attainment, social cohesion, local planning and service delivery.

The Isis Innovation team had a busy few months of interviewing and data-crunching, resulting in a 140-page report completed in mid-2015.[12] Their constructive attitude, coupled with a sense of objective detachment from the project proper, led to a full and open-minded response form the people they interviewed. Personal stories were recorded for posterity and analysed, metrics established and suitably quantified, and external and media perceptions probed. An online survey was sent out to 642 volunteer email addresses, resulting in just over 100 responses, which at 17% is somewhat better than the consultants' initial expectation, based on common practice, of 10%. Amongst their findings were that 75% of volunteers who responded were local residents in East Oxford, 91% felt they had learned new skills, and 100% had enjoyed their experience and would volunteer again on a similar project. On the heritage of the area, 97% felt the project had positively changed their views of the archaeology and history of East Oxford, 89% agreed their own enthusiasm for learning had increased, and 83% felt they personally had made a positive contribution to the history of the area. A range of quotations were obtained:

'More people will have learnt something about and will have acquired a stake in the historic landscape of their area'

'They will have acquired new skills and experiences in the field, and thought in new ways about their physical surroundings. Blackbird Leys is a community living on the site of an extraordinary Roman pottery industry, not a modern housing estate without history'.

Individuals recorded their perceptions of how it had changed them:

'The main difference was actually for my son who undertook work experience with *Archeox* and ended up enjoying it so much he contributed to two further projects. It cemented his interest in history and archaeology which he went on to study at university'.

'The experience I had enabled me to put together a much better personal statement for UCAS than I would otherwise have been able to do'.

'As an archaeology student I was able to put my theoretical knowledge into practice'.

'It has sparked an interest where I have completed two adult learning courses'.

'The training and in-depth knowledge provided during the project has given me the confidence and understanding to participate in other Archaeology projects'.

'It has given me a lot more confidence. I have been able to do more than I expected and meeting people enabled me to get a job as I had been unemployed for some time'.

'I had a break in my career due to anxiety and depression, and this project came just at a point where I was well enough and looking for ways to do things outside of my home. I was finding it difficult to relate to people because of my anxiety. The people leading the project were allowing and understanding enough to deal with me, and let me get involved. It got me doing something practical and I was meeting people who I wouldn't have met any other way'.

Table 2.2: Summary table of activities

Date	Locations of evening events and talks	Research and fieldwork	Training workshops
Sept-Dec 2010	Blackbird Leys, Cowley and Iffley; Cheney School. Ashmolean Museum	Geophysics at Iffley, test pits at Bartlemas	Stone tools, Pottery, Excavation, Geophysics
Jan-April 2011	Jeune Street Methodist Church, St Clements Family Centre. Pitt Rivers Museum.	Test pits at Elder Stubbs and Bartlemas allotments; Littlemore and Blackbird Ley	Finds washing, Historic maps, Place-names
May-June 2011	Ark-T centre, Cowley	Test pit weekend at Iffley	Test-pit reporting
Sept-Nov 2011		Excavation at Bartlemas Chapel	Finds recording, Osteology
Dec 2011-March 2012	Littlemore, Iffley and Ark-T centre; Cheney School	Test pits in Church and Temple Cowley; survey and geophysics in South Park, Warneford Meadow, Rose Hill, Horspath	Historic maps, place-names; Leopold Street Hoard, Place-names
June 2012		Test pit weekend in Littlemore	Finds recording, Building studies
Sept-Dec 2012	Ark-T centre, Blackbird Leys	Excavation at Minchery Paddock, Littlemore Priory	Drawing, photography
Jan-May 2013	Ark-T Centre	Test pits in Iffley Fields	Finds workshops
June 2013	Ark-T Centre, St James's Church, Cowley	Test pit weekend in Temple Cowley	Environmental sample processing, Oxford Archaeology
Sept – Oct 2013	Ark-T Centre	Excavation at Donnington Recreation Ground	Collections research, Ashmolean
Nov 2013-May 2014	Rewley House	Processing data and writing up	Archaeobotany, Archaeozoology
May 2014-August 2019	Public conferences, Rewley House	Archiving, working on publication	Archiving

'I have been so impressed with how welcoming the team have been and so generous with their knowledge and expertise. I have had some amazing opportunities and have learnt so much'.

'I have found the project quite addictive and will be sorry to see it come to an end'.

Ultimately it is impossible in large part to quantify or seek a single explanation as to why it worked. Formal evaluation tends to focus on recording and analysing individual experience, but attempting to capture a group experience in objective terms is more difficult. Somehow, united by interest in a shared place and past, and helped on its way by the informality, generosity and friendliness of all of its participants, *Archeox's* own self-generated community flourished.

Notes

1   Surman 2009.
2   Skinner 2005.
3   Goldman 1995.
4   Now re-named as the National Lottery Heritage Fund.
5   Aston and Gerrard 2013.
6   Jones and Page 2006.
7   Lewis 2007, 2019.
8   Gaffney and Gater 2003.
9   GNSS is Global Navigation Satellite System; GPS is Global Positioning System.
10 Pantin 1970
11 http://www.tarafranks.co.uk/matrix last accessed September 2019
12 Andonova and Wyatt 2015.

1. A group talk on place-names in a pub garden in Iffley.

The shared thrill of discovery

David Griffiths, with Paul Booth and Mandy Bellamy

Working together in groups proved to be at the heart of the learning experience of most participants in the *Archeox* project. At public events such as Cowley Carnival days and national archaeology days, guided walks, site visits and exhibitions, potential new recruits could feel at ease as they encountered a project community which was welcoming, relaxed and great fun, whilst being passionate about our shared interest in the area's heritage and committed to what we were doing. Those who were new to the project expected as volunteers to be involved in digging, but were often surprised at the extent and depth of the other activities which formed part of the shared research effort. The digs were sociable and supportive environments for all. Digging was always the strongest motivation for some, but research, training and talks took place outdoors and indoors, all year round, including many full, tiring but absorbing days spent working together in community centres or in the teaching rooms at Rewley House, Oxford's Department for Continuing Education.

The archaeological material which was retrieved and bagged at test pit sites or excavations had only just begun its journey with us. Pottery and animal bone was initially cleaned and sorted by groups in community centres, and subsequently leading specialists such as Paul Blinkhorn (pottery) and Julie Hamilton (animal bone) led workshops where the material was identified, recorded and analysed. Unusual or special equipment was needed for some research activities, such as processing soil samples through wet sieving. In this we were fortunate to have the support of Oxford Archaeology (OA), one of the largest professional practices in UK Archaeology, and based in the city.

2. Sorting and recording animal bone from the excavations.

3. A pottery workshop in Rewley House led by Paul Blinkhorn (seated).

Under the supervision of its environmental archaeology staff, volunteers used the equipment in the wet processing area at OA to float and wet-sieve soil samples from the project's excavations and test-pits, and led by Dr Rebecca Nicholson, a series of sorting and identification workshops took place at Rewley House. Archival research, studying historic maps, and place-names were the subject of talks and many workshops, and research sub-groups became regular visitors to college archives, particularly at Oriel and Christ Church, as well as the Oxfordshire History Centre. Archaeology is now heavily dependent upon computing technology, so to assist with mapping and spatial analysis, a series of training sessions in GIS (Geographic Information Systems) were offered in the Computer Teaching Room at Rewley House and these proved to be extremely popular. Drawing training sessions were organised, overseen by expert finds illustrator Jeff Wallis.

A further series of group-work activities took place behind the scenes in the Ashmolean and Pitt Rivers museums. Under the supervision of curators, volunteers studied and recorded material from East Oxford, including the objects found many years ago by collectors such as A. M. Bell (see page 18). With Prehistory curator Alison Roberts, the Ashmolean group created

4. Rob McLean wet-sieving soil samples at Oxford Archaeology.

6. A drawing workshop.

5. A GIS training session at Rewley House.

7. Tea break at the Minchery Paddock excavation.

8. A visit to the Minchery Paddock excavaton by Oxford University Vice-Chancellor Andrew Hamilton (right), talking to Will Hemmings (left) and David Griffiths (centre).

9. Lucy Fletcher, discoverer of a Roman coin in Test Pit 12, Iffley Village.

a series of individual object web entries which were put online as part of the museum's British Archaeology collections. It is impossible easily to capture or record the extent to which people at these events networked, helped each other, and learnt together. Suffice to say they were abuzz with concentration and excitement, and almost all were over-subscribed. We were delighted when the project's activities received welcome recognition in the form of visits from the 'high-ups' of the University and City, and on these occasions it was important that the distinguished visitors met and spoke to the full range of volunteers and locals, not just to the project supervisors.

Example of a test pit find: a Roman coin from Test Pit 12, 26 Abberbury Road, Iffley

Paul Booth

One of the more striking finds from the test pit campaign was a third-century Roman coin (Fig. 10). This is a characteristic 'radiate' of Emperor Postumus (AD 260-269), minted in Gaul. The obverse shows the bust of the emperor with the prominent radiate crown which gives the type its name (we do not know for certain what name the Romans used to identify this type of coin, and the commonly-found term 'antoninianus' is not now favoured by specialists). The legend, IMP C POSTVMVS P F AVG, which can be translated as 'Emperor Caesar Postumus, pious, fortunate Augustus', follows very widely-used conventions. The reverse carries the legend PROVIDENTIA AVG – 'the forethought of the emperor'. It shows the figure of Providentia facing left with a long sceptre and a globe held in her right hand. This is again a common type favoured by a number of emperors in the later third century, but it appears only to have been used by Postumus only in the middle part of his reign, so the coin can

10. Roman coin of Postumus, diam. 16mm (Nick Hedges).

probably be dated *c* AD 263-265. In this period most of Postumus' coins seem to have been struck at a single Gallic mint, which was probably based at Trier in Germany.

Postumus was the first of the so-called 'Gallic' emperors. A series of crises on both northern and eastern frontiers of the empire had put the military organisation under enormous strain. Postumus, left by the legitimate emperor Gallienus to defend the Rhine frontier, was proclaimed emperor by his troops late in AD 260. Britain and Spain followed the German and northern Gallic provinces in supporting Postumus, and parts of the resulting political unit survived until AD 274 when it was reincorporated by Aurelian. Meanwhile the 'Gallic Empire' had undergone its own interior upheavals and Postumus had been murdered by his own men at Mainz in 269, following which the provinces of Spain switched their allegiance back to the central empire. As part of the Gallic Empire from 260-274, Britain received large quantities of the coinage issued by its rulers, and issues of Postumus, Victorinus and the Tetrici, and irregular copies of these issues, are therefore common finds on British sites. This is a good example of the standard low-denomination coin of this period.

Example of an East Oxford object in the Ashmolean Museum: a historic key
Mandy Bellamy

For over fifty years when I have been out and about I have carried my front door key with me and in all that time I have not given it a second thought. At the Ashmolean Museum among artefacts in the Percy Manning collection I spotted this key (Fig. 11).

Museum Number AN1921.288: Iron (pin-) key; oval bow; plain shank; rather elaborate wards. Length 16.2 cm, Width (bow) 6.1 cm, labelled 'From the Manor House, Temple Cowley Oxon'. Percy Manning collection. The key resembles early post-Medieval keys, and is possibly from the early seventeenth century. These keys were hand-made, often quite large, crudely forged and had a large loop handle. The wide bow and bits at the working end of the key show that elaborate, possibly quite stiff works were used. Such locks were fitted to higher-status buildings such as Temple Cowley Manor House. Iron locks were expensive hand-made items, and usually only needed or affordable for the houses of wealthier people.

It wasn't only the key itself that interested me, but also that it was from Temple Cowley Manor House. In 1139 Queen Matilda gave land in Cowley to the Order of the Knights Templar, hence the name Temple Cowley. I know Temple Cowley well: my mother was born there. When I was a child she would often take my brothers, sisters and me to Temple Cowley Library and point out the old cottage that was once her home as a child. When I was four years old I started school in Cowley at Our Lady's Convent School, next door to The Original Swan public house. On the opposite side of Oxford Road on the corner of Hollow Way stood Temple Cowley Manor House. There is no direct evidence to show that the Temple Cowley Manor House I knew existed before the seventeenth century. It was demolished in 1957.

11. Key from Temple Cowley Manor House (Ian Cartwright).

Archeox at Boundary Brook Urban Nature Park

Janet Keene

Boundary Brook Nature Park, just north of Florence Park, was created by Oxford Urban Wildlife Group in 1990. At that time allotments were not in great demand and many were abandoned. The site had become very overgrown and urban wildlife had made it a home. The allotment holder suggested we should establish a nature park on the site, and the City Council agreed to lease us some of the land. After the initial success of the conversion, the site was extended. Then, while digging a pond in the eastern extension to the Nature Park in 2008, some fascinating Victorian and Edwardian glass and pottery bottles and jars were discovered, together with other small items such as a china medicine spoon. Many of them would have once been in a chemist's shop a century or more ago, so we believe that in the days before modern rubbish collections, possibly around the time of the First World War, someone had buried discarded pharmacy stock at the end of an allotment, perhaps when the shop moved or closed down. Many of the jars were undamaged or slightly-damaged stoneware items bearing the names of local Oxford businesses, others were glass bottles for cod liver oil, mineral waters, and other medicinal drinks. One unusually small, narrow cylindrical clear glass bottle was embossed [Mrs Winslow's] 'Soothing Syrup'. We discovered that this syrup was an American-made opiate remedy once given to teething babies to stop them crying. It was first marketed in 1845, and was well-known and used

1. Some of the collection, Mrs Winslow's Soothing Syrup bottle on left.

widely in the USA and Britain in the later nineteenth and early twentieth centuries, with its name even figuring in the title of one of Edward Elgar's compositions. However, it was a dangerously powerful drug, and after dozens of babies died from overdoses, it was eventually banned in 1930.

The first *Archeox* practical training session was held at Boundary Brook Nature Park in November 2009, when volunteers learnt high- and low-tech methods of surveying a site. An excellent drawn survey of the topography – lumps and bumps – of open ground in the park was produced. In July 2011

2. A Victorian advertisement for Mrs Winslow's Soothing Syrup.

Archeox continued their training at Boundary Brook, when volunteers gathered to dig two test pits (TPs 2 and 3), learning excavation techniques and how to record all the work. A good range of Medieval pottery was discovered in the Boundary Brook pits, as well as a fragment of Roman tile. Unfortunately there is no more conclusive sign of a Roman settlement here as yet! Volunteers also plotted the old outlines of allotments and paths in the grass of an orchard area. The experience raised awareness among volunteers that caring for archaeological and natural heritage goes hand-in-hand.

3. Test pit excavation at Boundary Brook Urban Nature Park.

Chapter 3

Investigating a suburban landscape

Jane Harrison, Olaf Bayer and Leigh Mellor

Part one: The test-pitting campaign

Jane Harrison, with Leslie Wilkinson and Leigh Mellor

A key aim of the *Archeox* project was to understand more about the changing ways in which the landscape was shaped through the development of the villages and other settlements over time. Some information could be brought together at the outset from previous archaeological finds and investigations, but the project's campaigns of test pit excavation and geophysical survey were seen as ideal ways in which to investigate the landscape whilst working in a wide range of different locations across the project area – from back gardens to playing fields – and, importantly for a community project like this, to draw as many people as possible into the programme of research.

What can be learnt from test pits?

As mentioned above in Chapter 2, test pits were an essential technique in our campaign of discovery. They are one or two metre-squared sized small excavation trenches, which can be dug with simple hand-tools, recorded, and backfilled in one or two days, and the ground surface restored with minimum lasting impact. Often taking place in domestic gardens and allotments, these mini-investigations allow archaeological research to go into inhabited areas.[1] Many other projects have used test pits in and around rural villages, such as the Whittlewood, Shapwick and CORS ('Currently Occupied Rural Settlements') projects mentioned in Chapter 2, or in historic towns such as Wallingford. *Archeox* showed that digging test pits in urban suburbs could also help to 'reconstruct the development of occupation sites, villages and landscapes'.[2] The total number of test-pits reported upon here (72) is enough for a meaningful coverage, given the relatively localised scale of our study area, and compares, for example, with the 59 completed at the time of publication of the recent Wallingford Research Project.[3] It must also be kept in mind that this was only one research technique amongst many which we devoted ourselves to pursuing.

Archeox volunteers dug seventy-two test pits across the project area between 2009 and 2013 (Fig 3.1). Most were one metre square, and a few were enlarged to two by one metres because we encountered walls or pits, or they needed to be dug deeper. All were excavated down to the natural geology, or as deep as it was safe to go (usually about one metre depth). Contexts were recorded using plans, sections and photographs. All the soil was sieved, unless it was very clay-rich in which case it was carefully hand-sorted; all the finds, the pottery, bone and flint as well as the glass, clay pipes, metal, shell and tile were cleaned, photographed, weighed, counted and identified. Where an undisturbed context was identified, occasionally soil samples were taken for floatation, which yielded important evidence such as the charred cereal grain from Test Pit 1 which gave us a radiocarbon date of the Anglo-Saxon period. The finds were sorted, washed and recorded by work groups which included many people who for various reasons were unable to dig. Photographing the cleaned finds together in groups by layer or context proved very useful: specialists and report-writers could see at a glance what had come out of each context (Fig 3.2). The individual test pit reports were written up by the people who had done the work on site and indoors thereafter.

How did we decide where to dig the pits? Once the project became known in the community, many residents offered their gardens. We focused particularly on the areas within and around the cores of the historic villages, and one cluster was excavated in and around Fairacres Road in Iffley Fields, an area on a low gravel ridge above the Thames which is known to have produced numerous finds of Prehistoric flint in the past. We were offered far more sites than we could take on, so we were also able to select and target certain locations of enhanced research interest, for example in the gardens of some of the oldest buildings in the historic village centres. To balance this, and to introduce an element of randomness, some test pits were dug in areas with no known focal point of archaeological discovery in the past. This generated a healthy mix of randomness and targeted sites.

Finds discovered in test pits are indicators of past activity in the landscape. The challenge is to extract as

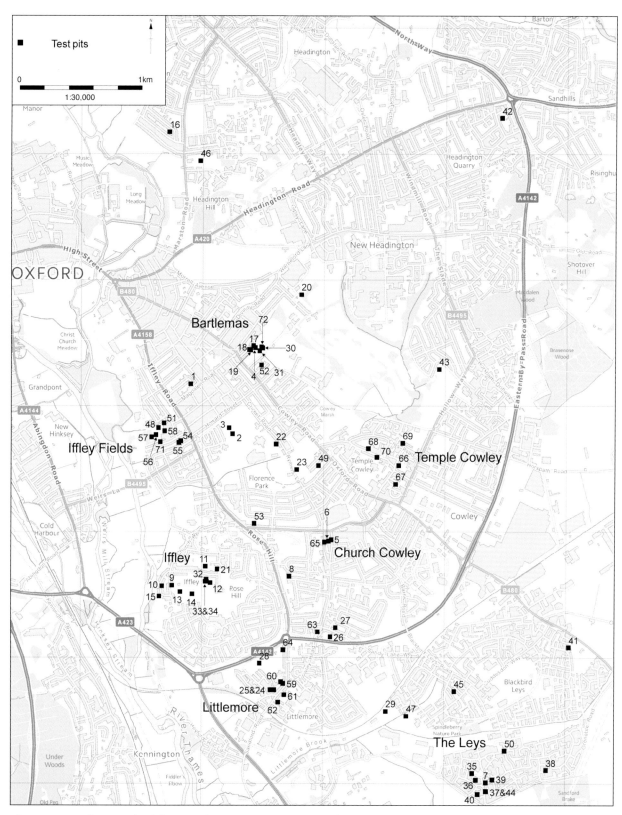

Fig. 3.1. Map of East Oxford showing the numbered locations of all 72 test pits (Contains Ordnance Survey data © Crown copyright and database right 2019).

much information as possible from small pieces of worked flint and (mostly) broken and worn pieces of pottery, about the nature, extent and distribution of that activity, its date and how it changed over time.[4] Theorising about what people were doing from the

type, quantity, condition and vertical and horizontal distribution of test pit finds is far from an exact science, and depends on inferences made about the objects discovered. We had to come to some decisions about what a few artefacts retrieved from about a

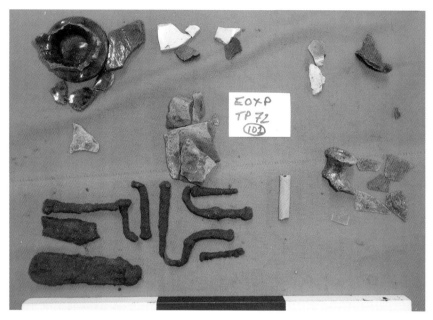

Fig. 3.2. All the finds from one context (102) in Test Pit 72, after washing and sorting.

cubic metre of soil might represent. Did it help if we thought about the means by which they got into the soil, how they survived there and how they might have been moved about in it?

Flint and other forms of worked stone artefacts are very durable, but also very portable and can easily be redeposited. Pottery of some periods is hard-fired and survives well, whereas from other periods it survives rarely or poorly. Prehistoric pottery is mostly hand-made, not hard-fired, and generally survives less well than Roman, Medieval and later wheel-made fabrics. Hand-made early Anglo-Saxon pottery is also much rarer because of its fragility. Carenza Lewis, a pioneer of test pit excavation in Medieval landscape studies, wrote that just two crumbly Anglo-Saxon sherds 'may reasonably be interpreted (if with caution) to indicate occupation of that date in the vicinity'.[5] Even just one sherd of earlier Anglo-Saxon pottery in a one metre-square test pit might indicate people actually living close-by – rather than just working the land. The pre-AD 850 collection of Anglo-Saxon pottery from the Whittlewood Project test pits, for example, was small in relation to other periods.[6]

For more durable Roman and later Medieval pottery types, more sherds would be needed to draw the same conclusions. Broadly, for the period from c.850 to c.1500 (Ceramic Phases 4-6; Table 3.1) we proposed that a total of three or fewer sherds per metre deep test pit (so 1m³ of soil) was likely to result from agricultural activity away from the actual settlement. Such a small assemblage might also be the result of manuring: spreading organic waste from a dung heap, including kitchen debris, being brought out to fertilise the fields.[7] These 'manuring scatters' can be identified more confidently if the pieces of pot are especially small and worn, generally indicating ploughed and

fertilised fields, and, in the Whittlewood Project were 'differentiated from settlement sites by their density *and* levels of abrasion'.[8] So by comparing the distribution and locations of these collections of pottery over time, we might gain some idea of which areas of the landscape were under the plough. We proposed that 4-9 sherds were evidence of people living or working near or close-by (particularly if the sherds were of a reasonable size and condition). More than ten sherds (perhaps more than twenty for the Roman period) from a single test pit were taken to be a probable indication of settlement or industrial activity.

The soil contexts from which pottery was collected were also important. The most informative layers were those which had remained undisturbed since the pottery entered the soil. If, for example, finds of Medieval pottery came from layers with no later material, this could mean the layers have probably been undisturbed since the Medieval period. Such 'undisturbed' contexts are relatively rare in test pits dug in occupied places, but they enable more secure interpretations to be made. For example, if pottery came from highly organic layers, this rich soil often resulted from domestic activity nearby, especially if animal bone or other finds such as building stone were also part of the mix. On the other hand, field soils ploughed regularly in the past can be identified by their homogeneity and the worn state of the finds.

We viewed the size and condition of the sherds as important information. Potsherds weighing over 5g are more indicative of better-preserved archaeology than those less than 3g; fewer larger sherds in good condition are more suggestive of settlement than more, small and abraded sherds (in particular for the Medieval period). Sherds are also more significant if they come from a restricted number of layers, or

Fig. 3.3. Test Pit 6 in the Ark-T Centre garden being recorded.

contexts. Even a lack of pottery can be informative to some extent. Test pits with little or no pottery from any or all periods were clearly on land which was either alluviated, or not cultivated or settled, such as meadow, pasture and woodland, or wood pasture (we would always have to discount the possibility that later disturbance, for example levelling of ground had not simply removed all the archaeology).[9] Gaps or fall-offs in the sequence of pottery types might indicate a former settlement being abandoned, or when ploughed fields had been laid down to pasture.

Local circumstances are all important in making an interpretation: as more clusters of test pits were completed, we were better able to make judgments about what their findings might represent. Where possible, we also compared the test pit assemblages to those recorded from larger excavations in the same areas, and looked for clues in place-names historic maps and documents (Chapter 6). We therefore tried to use all the available evidence to suggest ways in which settlement and other activity in the landscape had changed over time. Inevitably we could have dug more test pits if time, funding and other pressures had allowed, so our suggestions stand as something for future researchers to amplify, improve or challenge.

Analysing the test pit evidence

This chapter now goes on to discuss the evidence from the 72 test pits. All individual test-pit reports and specialist reports are deposited online with the Oxford Research Archive (see table of contents for DOI). What follows here is a synthesis of the evidence, written in relation to the project's research questions (see page 15). Although many other types of finds and material evidence were encountered, the emphasis throughout our research was on collecting and analysing worked flint (mostly for the Prehistoric period) and pottery (for all periods).

Pottery finds were the key to our chronological analysis of the test pit data. Table 3.1 shows the Ceramic Phases (CPs) into which the pottery from the test pits was divided. This was not a straightforward process to determine, as deciding the period over which any one pottery fabric was used in any particular area can be complex: some fabrics were very long-lived; some went out of fashion in one area while they were still being produced or used elsewhere; others were slow to be taken on and/or in use beyond their production dates. The fabrics found in East Oxford were assigned to Ceramic Phases based on existing knowledge of their local use and distribution.[10] Inevitably there is overlap in the date ranges: Medieval pottery fabrics OXAM (Brill/Boarstall Ware, c. 1200-1500) and to an extent OXBX (Late Medieval Brill/Boarstall Ware, c. 1400–c. 1600), as some of the most common fabrics in the area, and in production for hundreds of years, were divided between the relevant Ceramic Phases (5-6 and 6-7). This made little difference with the later fabric OXBX in Ceramic Phase 7 as there were only 27 OXBX sherds in total from all the test pits and no one test pit had more than five, whereas there were just over 200 sherds of fabric OXAM and allocating these between Phases 5 and 6 had a significant impact. However, in instances where there was very little or no pottery of either an earlier or later phase, the OXAM Brill/ Boarstall sherds were assigned to the phase with more pottery (see also discussion of the Donnington Recreation Ground pottery, below). The number of test pits and the pottery recovered and the challenges of phasing the pottery mean the results should be regarded above all as indicating relative trends within and between phases.

Table 3.1: Ceramic phases

Periods: approximate date range	Fabric code *Total from all test pits*	Wares: approximate date range
CP1: Prehistoric: c. 800BC–AD43	Iron Age (IA) *3 sherds*	c. 800BC–AD43
CP2: Romano-British: c. 43–400	Romano-British (RB) *173 sherds*	c. 43–400
CP3: Early-Middle Anglo-Saxon: c. 400–850	E/MAS Anglo Saxon hand-built *2 sherds*	c. 400–850
CP4: Late Anglo-Saxon: c. 850–1050	OXB Late Saxon Oxford Shelly Ware OXR St. Neots Ware OXZ Stamford Ware *73 sherds*	c. 790–1025 c. 850–1200 c. 900–1250
CP5: Medieval: c. 1050–1400	OXAC Cotswold-type Ware OXBF East Wiltshire Ware OXY Medieval Oxford Ware OXBK Medieval Shelly Coarseware OXAG Abingdon Ware OXAW Early Brill Coarseware OXAM Brill/Boarstall Ware, *c. 380 sherds, dominated by OXAM*	c. 1050–1350 c. 1050–1400 c. 1070–1350 c. 1100–1350 c. 1075–1400 c. 1180–1250 c. 1200–c.1500
CP6: Later Medieval: c. 1400–1550	OXAM Brill/Boarstall Ware, OXBG Surrey White Ware OXBX Late Med Brill/Boarstall Ware *c. 70 sherds*	c. 1200–c. 1500 c. 1250–c.1450 c. 1400–c. 1600
CP7: Post-Medieval 1: c. 1500–1700	OXBX Late Med Brill/Boarstall Ware OXCL Cistercian Ware OXST Rhenish Stoneware OXFH Border ware OXEAH Midland Blackware OXDR Red Earthenwares *c. 220 sherds, dominated by OXDR*	c. 1400–c. 1600 c. 1475–1700 c. 1480–1700 c. 1550–1700 c. 1580–1700 c. 1550+
CP8: Post-Medieval 2: c. 1650–1800	OXCE Tin-glazed Earthenware OXBESWL Staffordshire Slip-trailed Earthenware OXEST English Stone ware OXRESWL Polychrome Slipware OXFM Staffordshire White-glazed English Stoneware OXBEW Staffordshire Manganese Glazed ware OXFI Chinese Porcelain *35 sherds*	c. 1600–1800 c. 1650–1800 c. 1688 + c. 1600–1700 c. 1720–1800 c. 1700–1800 c. 1750 +
CP9: Modern/Victorian: c.1800 onwards	WHEW Mass-produced white earthenware *c. 2,800 sherds*	c. 1800 +

The Landscape in Prehistory: worked flint and pottery from test pits (Ceramic Phase 1) Fig. 3.4

Fig 3.4 shows the distribution of worked flint and Prehistoric pottery collected from the test pits. A total of 71 pieces of worked flint were recovered from 31 of the 72 test pits. Most of the flint artefacts are likely to be residual – moved from the place they were first dropped and worked into later layers, either by natural processes or subsequent human actions. However, few of these finds were likely to have moved more than a few metres from the point where they were originally lost or discarded. As a result their find-spots can be taken to indicate the general locations of areas of Prehistoric activity.[12]

The majority of the test pit flint finds consisted of unmodified and relatively undiagnostic debitage (waste created during the manufacture of stone tools), which dominates larger lithic assemblages, in for example TPs 5, 10 and 70, and accounts for most of the smaller collections in other test pits. These undiag-

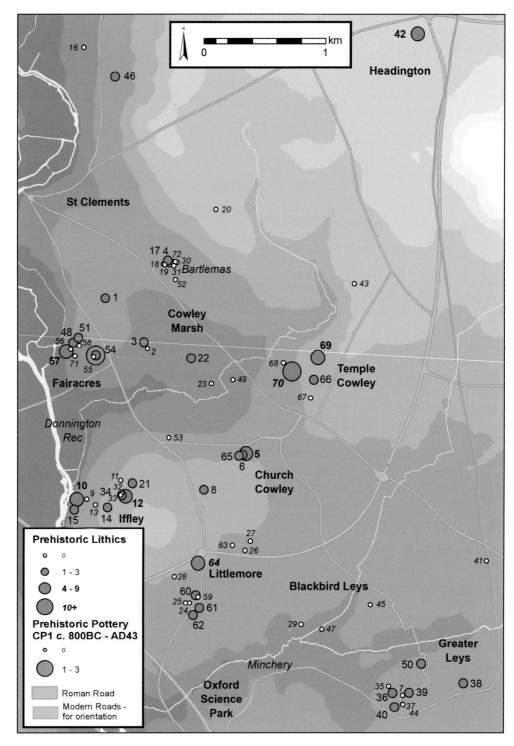

Fig. 3.4. Test pit distributions of Prehistoric lithics and pottery (Ceramic Phase 1).

nostic fragments are not identifiable as a particular tool. However, analysis of the technological traits of the fragments indicated they resulted, broadly, from either the later Mesolithic or Early Neolithic period (c.7000-3300 BC) or from Neolithic to Bronze Age (c. 3300-800 BC). Their distribution also suggests that Neolithic and Bronze Age activity had been dispersed quite widely across the East Oxford area, with occasional hints of earlier activity from the Mesolithic and/or the Early Neolithic periods. The majority of the test pit

flint finds came from test pits on slopes and spurs overlooking lower, damper ground and streams, for example the Fairacres area, Iffley, Church Cowley and Temple Cowley; such topographical locations were clearly attractive to East Oxford's prehistoric hunter-gatherers and early farmers (see Fig. 1.3).

Three small sherds of undiagnostic Iron Age pottery (Ceramic Phase 1) were found in Test Pit 54 in the Fairacres Road area. These were very worn, with a shelly fabric and were not elements of either rims or bases. Four test pits in that area including TP54 (and TPs 48, 51 and 57) also produced earlier Prehistoric worked flint, suggesting this locale continued to be a focus of human activity throughout Prehistory. However, the sherds of Iron Age pottery in TP54 were the only Prehistoric pottery found in any of the test pit excavations, although 13 equally small and abraded fragments of shelly Iron Age pottery were found worked into the later plough-soils in the Donnington Recreation excavation (below), around 300m to the south of Fairacres Road and just across the course of Boundary Brook. Both these areas overlook the Thames and Cowley Marsh, a clustering which is supported by the results of earlier investigations as described in Chapter 1.

In terms of individual artefacts, lithic finds from the test pits included the oldest and youngest stone tools discovered by the project (Fig. 3.5). The oldest was a Late Mesolithic microlith from TP22 on Cricket Road. This dates from between 7500-4000 BC and would have formed part of an arrowhead or barb, possibly lost by someone hunting in Cowley Marsh. The most recent was an eighteenth or nineteenth century gunflint from TP17, close to Bartlemas Chapel. This formed part of the firing mechanism of a flintlock gun, creating a spark to light the gunpowder.

Other interesting Prehistoric finds came from Test Pits 5, 70 and 10. TP5 in Church Cowley contained six flints altogether, including a possible Neolithic-Early Bronze Age flake found in a test pit layer undisturbed since the sixteenth century, and a redeposited Mesolithic-Early Neolithic blade from the lowest layer, dated by the pottery to AD 780-1050. TP70 in Temple Cowley produced seven unmodified flakes of flint suggesting some tool manufacture or modification may have occurred there, as might the similar number of flakes and chunks found in Test Pit 10 in Mill Lane in Iffley. These were in the upper layers, but with a mixed assemblage of pottery of all periods from Roman onwards. As with Fairacres and Church Cowley, test pit

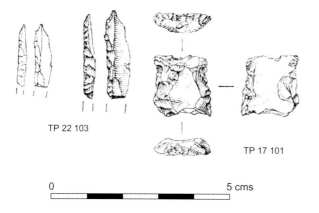

TP 22 103

TP 17 101

0   5 cms

Fig. 3.5. Fragment of a Late Mesolithic flint arrowhead or barb: between 7500–4000 BC (L), and a flint from the mechanism of a flintlock gun, 17th–18th century (R).

flints from Temple Cowley and Iffley along with the finds from the Donnington Recreation excavation provide slight but noteworthy hints of earlier Prehistoric activity in very plausible locations: overlooking water-ways and on a sandy or gravelly slopes and ridges in places that continued to be popular for settlement.

The majority of the Prehistoric worked flint finds were made from raw material from within, or close to, geological chalk deposits. The closest such geology is on the Chilterns and the Berkshire Downs at least 15km south of Oxford. Only one artefact among the finds was made from water-worn flint, which could have come from a wider range of gravel/pebble flint sources, potentially much closer to Oxford. This range of raw materials shows that Prehistoric communities were either moving around and/or had contacts and exchange networks with groups beyond the immediate area. The find of Iron Age pottery in Test Pit 54 is a tantalising if limited glimpse of further evidence for later Prehistoric settlement in the Fairacres Road area, which is close to the Donnington Recreation ground excavation described below.

Landscape and settlement in the Romano-British Period: 43–400 AD (Ceramic Phase 2)
Fig 3.6

Earlier chapters depicted Romano-British East Oxford as a busy landscape of industry and scattered rural settlement: people were making the most of natural resources and it is likely very little unmanaged or unexploited land remained. Christopher Young's summary (see page 86) shows how the numerous kiln sites of the pottery industry were distributed on the higher ground of Headington, Rose Hill and Church Cowley, north of Littlemore and across Blackbird Leys. Until now, it has not proved easy to identify the Romano-British rural settlement areas whose population and agricultural output must have supported the pottery industry. The test pit campaign did not identify any new kiln sites, but has been able to suggest some probable locations for those rural settlements, as well as of the ploughed fields worked by their inhabitants.

The most unexpected settlement evidence came from test pits in the extensive grounds of Fairacres Convent (in the Fairacres area), and the Project's 'field walking' exercise on its extensive cultivated vegetable patch. 40 sherds of Roman pottery were collected from the three test pits dug in the grounds (TPs 56, 57 and 58) and 20 from the vegetable beds, with the vast majority of them (51 sherds) coming from the vegetable patch and just two contexts in TP56, the test pit sited closest to the vegetable beds. Those two layers in TP56 otherwise only yielded four very small abraded sherds of Medieval Brill/Boarstall ware, which were almost certainly intrusive – that is moved down

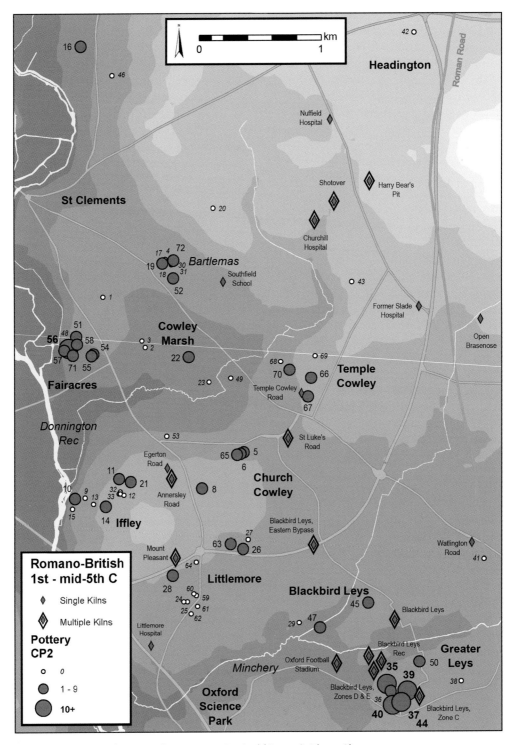

Fig. 3.6. Test pit distributions of pottery from Roman Period (Ceramic Phase 2).

after they had been deposited by rooting or worm action. The pottery cut-off between the layers and those above was also sharp, with the upper contexts almost totally dominated by pottery later than c. 1200. The Romano-British layers were relatively undisturbed, and as the pottery sherds were also large and crisp-edged this suggested people were living there or very close by in that period. The pottery assemblage was domestic in content rather than characteristically kiln-related, but included mortaria of the types

produced in the Oxfordshire industries, so the Roman settlement in Fairacres was likely to have been a farm connected in some way to the potteries.

Test pits only 50m south and east of the Fairacres Convent grounds (TPs 54, 55 and 71) produced only two or three smaller sherds of Roman pottery; two test pits about the same distance north (TPs 48 and 51) produced no and little Roman pottery respectively. These results provide possible limits for the Roman settlement-related activity and suggest there was a small farmstead located in close proximity to TP56, centred within the current convent grounds and overlooking and bounded to the west by the then braded courses of the Thames. The Fairacres Road locality is also well-known for Prehistoric flint finds as discussed above, and close to the only Iron Age pottery found in a test pit (TP54). So this area – with light sandy soil, set on a low gravel spur looking out over the nearby river and with springs running close by – had attracted people to live and/or farm there for thousands of years. The Roman inhabitation does however seem to have been followed by a break in actual occupation in the immediate area of the convent until perhaps the thirteenth century, with the few small, worn earlier Medieval sherds found in the test pits and vegetable beds more likely to have resulted from the manuring of fields with domestic and farmyard waste.

Just over half a kilometre to the south-south-east, near to the tail-end of the same gravel and sand terrace, the Donnington Recreation Ground excavation (see below) also produced Roman pottery in quantities that suggested a domestic/farm building very close-by. Unfortunately no evidence of buildings or yards or ditch boundaries had survived the thorough ploughing or gardening of the later Medieval and Victorian periods.[13] But the assemblage of 75 sherds of Roman pottery derived from the small excavation trench suggested that the later agricultural activity had probably destroyed Roman features, perhaps related to another farm mirroring the one on the Fairacres gravel ridge to the north; the thirteen Iron Age sherds from the excavation may be an indication that the ploughed-out settlement had earlier roots. There may therefore have been two or more Roman farms on the ridge (running along Iffley Road) east of the Thames, providing an element of the infrastructure necessary to the pottery-making industry.

There was little evidence for Roman settlement in the area around Iffley church. Despite one test pit (TP12) yielding a late Roman coin (of Emperor Postumus: reigned c. 260–269; see page 55), only scatters of small and worn Roman pottery sherds were discovered (in TPs 10, 11, 14 and 21), implying this area was ploughed or perhaps travelled across rather than lived on. However, just to the east, on the eastern flanks of Rose Hill at Annesley Road, excavations conducted in the 1930s had discovered possible settlement directly associated with pottery industry kilns (see above, Chapter 1); some of the people living there may have worked those fields, or perhaps the fields were linked to a Roman farm at Donnington Recreation Ground, or another as yet undiscovered agricultural settlement in Iffley.[14] It is also possible that the scatter of Roman pottery and finds between the Rose Hill kilns and the Thames reveal the route of a track joining a river-crossing to the kilns around

Annesley Road and then on to the group of kilns located in Church Cowley.[15]

Several of the test pits dug in Greater Leys, already known from previous excavations to be a concentration of the Roman pottery industry, produced more than ten sherds of Romano-British pottery (TPs 35, 37, 39 and 40). The obscuring effect of the modern housing estate's landscaping meant we could deduce little from this pottery as the layers were so disturbed, and none of these test pits produced more than 20 sherds of pottery. Interestingly, none of the pottery assemblages produced finds indicative of the immediate environs of a kiln, rather they closely resembled the fabric range discovered at Fairacres Road, and so may be related to domestic areas and perhaps the potters' houses and middens. This group of test pits were located on slightly higher ground overlooking a number of known kiln sites (Fig 3.6): other test pits in the Blackbird Leys area on lower ground closer to the local watercourses produced fewer and more abraded sherds (TPs 45, 47 and 50; four or fewer sherds) and so were apparently dug in agricultural or more peripheral areas. The small number of worn sherds found in pits along the northern edge of Littlemore also suggest the manuring of agricultural fields rather than settlement (TPs 26, 28 and 63; fewer than 10 sherds), as did those recorded for Temple Cowley (TPs 66, 67 and 70), and around Bartlemas (TPs 19, 52 and 72; and including the 22 very worn sherds from the Bartlemas excavation itself). These results suggest that other Roman farms, from which those fields were worked, may remain to be discovered: near Temple Cowley, Bartlemas, Church Cowley and Littlemore/Iffley. To the likely cultivated areas suggested by these discoveries we can add agricultural activity detected in previous archaeological investigations.[16]

Two test pits revealed undisturbed Roman features of probable agricultural origin. One of the Project's Church Cowley (Ark-T Centre) test pits uncovered an undisturbed ditch with Roman pottery in its fill (TP6). Both of the other test pits in the grounds of Ark-T, and the watching brief on Centre's playground clearance, produced small amounts of pottery (TPs 5, 65 and Watching Brief), so this area was probably on the edge of the kiln site discovered in previous non-Project excavations just to the east (St Luke's Road area).[17] (A local resident from Crowell Road, about two hundred metres south of Ark-T, mentioned at a Project talk in 2010 that her husband, unfortunately by then deceased, had over years of gardening collected many tesserae in their garden). While this could not be confirmed, it raises the intriguing possibility of a small villa having possibly been located to the south-west of the Church Cowley kiln site, overlooking agricultural land to the south, with links to the kiln sites, river crossing and farming land to the west). Finally TP22 revealed a possible Romano-British outdoor yard surface, associated with two sherds of contemporary pottery, indicating that land in Cowley Marsh was being used for a variety of purposes in that period, including arable and possibly settlement.

Those test pits without Roman pottery might indicate a distribution of pasture and woodland or wood pasture: perhaps pasture around Cowley Marsh, Bartlemas and Temple Cowley (TPs 1, 2, 3, 4, 17, 18, 23, 30, 31, 49, 68 and 69) and the eastern reaches of Blackbird Leys (TPs 38 and 41); and wood pasture or managed woodland around Iffley (TPs 9, 12, 13, 15, 32, 33 and 34), and the higher slopes above Bartlemas and Temple Cowley (TPs 20 and 43). The complete blank in the centre of Littlemore may reflect pasture or rougher ground (the *mōr* 'moor'; TPs 24, 25, 59, 60, 61 and 62) deriving from the limestone geology of that area. Pollen analysis from Minchery Farm, Littlemore, also indicated an open grassy landscape with patches of woodland during this period.[18]

Considering the extent of the Roman pottery industry across the East Oxford area, and the very close proximity of some of the Archeox test pits to known kiln sites, such as those in Church Cowley, it is perhaps surprising that we did not find more focused evidence for Roman industry. Instead, the majority of finds of Roman pottery from the test pits and from the three larger project excavations, seem to favour field scatters and rural settlement. These discoveries nevertheless help to answer an important gap in our knowledge about the broader landscape in this period, and their implications are further considered by Christopher Young in his contribution on the pottery industry (see page 86).

Landscape and settlement in the Early to Middle Anglo-Saxon period, c. 400–850 AD (Ceramic Phase 3) Fig. 3.7

Settlement and farming in the East Oxford area must have been affected by the rapid decline of the pottery industry around 400 AD, but there is little apparent evidence that this included widespread abandonment of farmland. For Ceramic Phase 3, only one test pit at the Ark-T Centre (Church Cowley) produced pottery, but this meagre record primarily illustrates the point discussed above: fragile, lower-temperature fired early Anglo-Saxon pottery generally survives very poorly in disturbed soils. Although there is thus relatively little that can be gleaned from the test pit record, pottery from the Donnington Recreation Ground excavation added to the picture (see below).

Two of the key questions about this early Anglo-Saxon period are the extent to which settlements continued in the same locations as in the Roman period and whether there was a contraction in agricultural land use. In the Project area, at least three

farms may have continued in the same place from the Roman into the early Anglo-Saxon period: two suggested by *Archeox*'s results – on the Ark-T (Church Cowley) plot and the area of the Donnington Recreation Ground excavation – to add to a possible example from a previous excavation at Oxford Science Park. Conversely, the Roman settlement detected in the Fairacres area did not survive into the post-Roman period: no material of this CP3 was discovered in any of these test pits (48, 51, 54-58 and 71). However, in the Donnington Recreation Ground excavation (below), 76 sherds of Early-Middle Anglo-Saxon pottery were recovered from the investigation's small trench; and although the much larger area at the Oxford Science Park excavation produced nearly a thousand sherds, the Donnington collection of this rarely-surviving pottery is significant.[19]

At Donnington Recreation Ground, later ploughing through at least the eleventh to fourteenth centuries and in the Victorian period had completely destroyed any Anglo-Saxon features that would have helped to contextualise the pottery, but a surviving assemblage of that size must almost certainly be derived from a settlement. The Donnington pottery was contemporary with and similar in fabric types to the sixth to seventh century assemblage from the structures recorded in the Oxford Science Park excavation, and we suggest there were probably buildings at Donnington analogous to those found at Oxford Science Park. There, between ten and twelve sunken featured buildings (SFBs) of the sixth and earlier seventh centuries were discovered spread across the gentle southern slope of Littlemore Brook.[20] The un-straightened brook was then wide and slow-flowing; the buildings were located on the sand above the damp low-lying ground and below the limestone-topped crest of the slope. The excavators concluded that only three or four of the SFBs were standing at any one time, and that the farm's cluster of buildings moved along the slope with time. The northern slopes of the brook were used for arable in the Roman, Medieval and post-Medieval periods: their use in the early Anglo-Saxon period is less certain, although environmental evidence from the Oxford Academy excavation just to the north argues that the area was probably also farmed in that period.[21] The more limited investigations at the Academy also uncovered a sunken featured building, which was possibly contemporary with those found at Oxford Science Park.

At Donnington Recreation Ground site there was very likely a break in occupation after the early-middle Anglo-Saxon period until the later eleventh century; there may have been a similar hiatus at Oxford Science Park but it was not possible to be certain. However, for the Church Cowley area there was ample ceramic evidence that the site was used for occupation throughout the Medieval period. Thus, although the evidence is limited is does suggest more continuity in

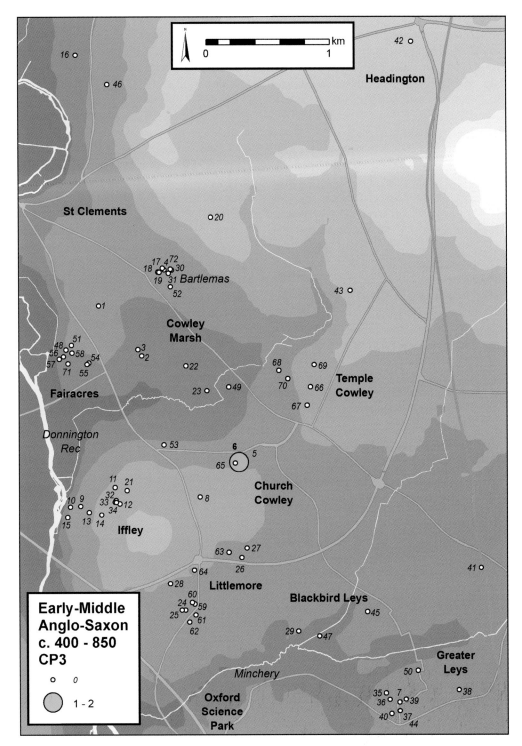

Fig. 3.7. Test pit distributions of pottery from the Early/Middle Anglo-Saxon Period (Ceramic Phase 3).

settlement location across the East Oxford area from the Romano-British into earlier Anglo-Saxon periods, with the possibility that there was some alteration in the pattern into the later Anglo-Saxon period.

Environmental evidence from the excavations at Oxford Science Park demonstrated that a great deal of the land there had been cleared well before the Anglo-Saxon period, and that there was no obvious loss of this open land in the Early Medieval landscape, which continued as a patchwork of relatively small fields,

managed woodland and scrub.[22] Pollen samples taken near Shotover in the 1990s also indicated there was no diminution in the amount of open land used for agriculture – whether grazing, hay or arable – from the late Roman to later Anglo-Saxon periods.[23] Nothing in this Project's research contradicts or materially adds to this picture. However, TP43 (Fairview allotments) east of the upper reaches Boundary Brook and in the foothills of Shotover, contained sherds of Late Anglo-Saxon pottery (especially OXB: Late Saxon Oxford

Shelly Ware) suggesting the area was ploughed from later in the Anglo-Saxon period, thus supporting the pollen evidence from further upslope.

At the Ark-T Centre, TP6 (Church Cowley), two sherds of fifth to ninth century early hand-made Anglo-Saxon pottery – one of them quite large – indicate that this site, with evidence from Prehistory, continued to attract occupation, especially as there were also over 40 sherds of Later Anglo-Saxon St Neot's Ware from both TP6 and other test pits in the area (fabric OXR: c. 850-1200; TPS 5, 6, 65 and Watching Brief). At Oxford Science Park, at Yarnton north of Oxford, and in other areas in of southern England such as Mucking in Essex, excavations have demonstrated that earliest Anglo-Saxon settlement was dispersed, comprising small clusters of sunken featured buildings and post-built timber halls.[24] We might therefore suggest that in Church Cowley, and at Donnington Recreation Ground, as well as above the Littlemore Brook, settlement at this time comprised small dispersed groups of early-middle Anglo-Saxon sunken-featured buildings sited on light sandy or gravelly soils, probably clustered around a post-built hall and shifting regularly across the slopes or higher ground where there had also been Romano-British settlement very close by, if not in exactly the same location.

Landscape and settlement in the later Anglo-Saxon period, c. 850–1050 AD (Ceramic Phase 4) Fig 3.8

During the later Anglo-Saxon period the landscape probably began to take on some of the character which was still discernible on a map of the area from 1830 (see Fig. 1.1). Churches and manors provided a core of inhabitation in each parish, and the settlement pattern became more stable within estates owned by king, church and lords. But it is still very difficult to answer certain crucial questions: when were any new, larger, communally-farmed open fields laid out; when and exactly where were the elusive beginnings of settlements, later identifiable as established villages – settlements with church, manor house, and peasant dwellings sitting in small fields and gardens. Indeed did East Oxford follow the trajectory of 'nucleated' settlement development at all? The test pit evidence suggests the area may have remained more varied, supporting a range of settlements of various forms, many of which remained dispersed at this time and surrounded by more scattered farmhouses and hamlets, with woodland and smaller fields surviving around the open fields in the centres of the parishes.

The test pit pottery assemblages identified only two possible settlement locations for Ceramic Phase 4: one at the heart of the later village of Church Cowley and one on the edge of Cowley Marsh. The pottery

evidence from Church Cowley only allowed us to infer that this place had continued to be a favoured location for settlement prior to this period. Three test pits in the grounds of the Ark-T Centre produced 38 sherds of pottery of this phase (TPs 5, 6 and 65: fabrics OXB, OXR and OXZ). TPs 5 and 65 also included undisturbed layers from this period. However, some distance to the west, the first test pit dug by *Archeox*, TP1 (Stanley Road: beside Cowley Marsh), like TPs 5, 6 and 65 located on higher ground above Boundary Book, produced equally interesting results. While the overwhelming proportion of the pottery assemblage from TP1 was nineteenth-century in date (158 sherds out of 169), there were two sherds of later Anglo-Saxon pottery, one of which was reasonably large. A charred barley grain from the layer underneath the Anglo-Saxon pottery produced a radiocarbon date spanning the later eighth and ninth centuries AD (cal AD 767-895; SUERC-49315: at 88% probability). Although we cannot be certain, because of a degree of later disturbance, the date suggests there may have been a small Anglo-Saxon settlement on the edge of the gravel terrace, looking south-east across Cowley Marsh and to Church Cowley. TP1 also produced a great variety of species of animal bone, including domestic fowl, sheep, pig, cattle and pike, some of which came from its lower and less-disturbed layers.

What about the surrounding landscape? The evidence is so far fairly sparse. Collections of pottery indicating the manuring of arable fields came from TPs 3 and 22 in the Cowley Marsh area. The earliest sherds found in test pits in what was to be one of the Medieval centres of Littlemore come from this period, and were two single sherds of St Neots Ware in TPs 24 and 25 in the grounds of the Manor House and Village Hall respectively. As neither produced any pottery at all in the subsequent phase, these sherds may be sparse remnants of the manuring of the locally very thin soil. The single sherds of later Anglo Saxon pottery found in TP54 in Fairacres Road, in TP11 in Iffley, and in TP43 in the Fairview Allotments, could also result from the a similar process. However TP43 had no pottery later than c. 1400 and the land may have been laid to pasture later in the Medieval period.

A considerable number of test pits produced no pottery for this phase, suggesting large areas of both pasture and wood pasture on the slopes of the Headington ridge around Bartlemas and Temple Cowley, across Blackbird Leys, Greater Leys and Littlemore. The Fairacres Road area of Iffley Fields, inhabited in distant Prehistory, may conceivably have been laid to pasture, while much of Iffley Village seemed to continue as wood pasture. Woodland provided an important resource for timber, forage and grazing, charcoal and hunting; pigs in particular thrived on pannage. The forest of Shotover was, and remains today, the largest area of mixed woodland

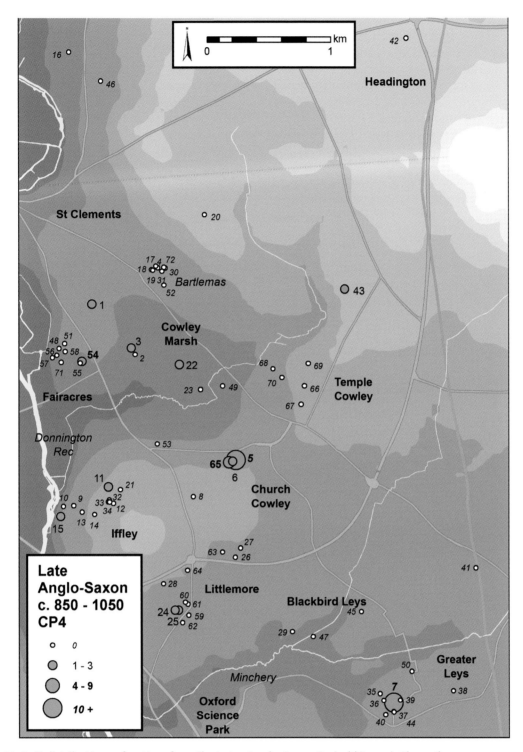

Fig. 3.8. Test pit distributions of pottery from the Later Anglo-Saxon Period (Ceramic Phase 4).

bordering the East Oxford area, and must have been in existence in the later Anglo-Saxon period since it is mentioned in Domesday Book of 1086.

Inevitably, more evidence and more test pits are needed to help strengthen any conclusions, but on the basis of the information we have gained so far, Church Cowley probably developed as a focused settlement in this phase, but there is as no conclusive sign of Iffley, Temple Cowley or Littlemore having as yet on taken their later form as clustered or nucleated villages; these

settlements may therefore have only have begun to take shape as such after the Norman Conquest (CP5). The Temple Cowley test pits produced no CP4 pottery, and Littlemore only a tiny assemblage likely to be the result of ploughing (TPs 24 and 25; see below). The small collection of sherds from Iffley Rectory, TP15 (three sherds) may however have resulted from activity around the periphery of a house rather than ploughing, as it was located on the crest of a relatively steep slope, immediately above the river. The vast majority of the test pits in Iffley however produced no CP4 pottery (TPs 9, 10, 12-14 and 32-34). Neither the Bartlemas nor Littlemore Priory excavations produced more than a thin scatter of pottery from Ceramic Phase 4 and Donnington Recreation Ground only one sherd. The combined results of the excavations and test pits point towards most of East Oxford's historic villages taking shape after 1050, with dispersed farms or hamlets continuing to dominate the settlement pattern prior to this date.

The villages and farms of East Oxford in the Medieval period c. 1050–1400 AD (Ceramic Phase 5) (Fig. 3.9)

For this Ceramic Phase, during which the historic villages of East Oxford began to take shape towards those we recognise today, the evidence will be discussed mainly by village area. A further cluster of test pits, around Bartlemas Chapel, is discussed in Chapter 4.

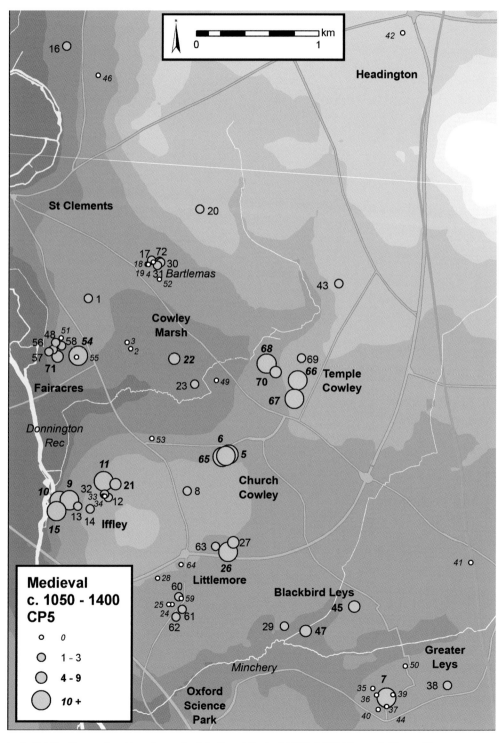

Fig. 3.9. Test pit distributions of pottery from the Medieval Period 1050-1400 (Ceramic Phase 5).

Iffley Village (Fig. 3.10)

The date of the origin of Iffley Village remains uncertain with only four sherds of earlier Ceramic Phase 4 pre-Conquest pottery (and no earlier post-Roman fabric) having been discovered in the ten test pits dug across its environs. Yet as well as having an Old English *leāh* ('wood pasture') place-name element (see Chapter 6), Iffley was referred to in the 1004 AD Headington Charter (see page 214), so a settlement must have existed here in CP4, sufficiently distinguished to be referred to in the description of the charter bounds (perhaps the location of at least part of that settlement was indicated by the CP4 pottery in TP15). In the nineteenth century a bronze, S-shaped brooch set with garnets, probably a sixth-century Frankish import, was discovered somewhere in the Abberbury Road area (that is around TPs 11-12, 21 and 32-34). It was donated to the British Museum in 1874 (accession no. 1874, 1105.1). How and exactly where it was found are unclear. It has been suggested the brooch came from a disturbed burial, but absolutely no evidence of this was found in any of the test pits in the vicinity.

The fine Romanesque parish church of St Mary the Virgin (see page 217) was constructed in the later twelfth century, so it is certain that Iffley Village was significant enough to require a church by this time. We cannot be certain if there had been an earlier church on its site, but this seems likely given that Iffley is mentioned in Domesday Book. The test pit pottery for CP5 confirms that, around the church site, the village was growing in CP5. Four test pits yielded ten or more sherds of pottery (TPs 9, 10, 11 and 15); one test pit with a considerable number, over 30, was on Mill Lane (TP10), the site of what was recorded later on, in the sixteenth century, as a substantial farmhouse. The Mill Lane test pit located north-west of the church, certainly seems to indicate that there was Medieval habitation on the sloping banks of the Thames. The pottery assemblage retrieved from the test pit dug in the garden of the sixteenth-century Rectory (TP15), less than 40 metres north-west of the church, was also sufficient to suggest a Medieval dwelling in the near vicinity. However many of its small, worn sherds of pottery were probably the result of backyard or garden-linked activity. The area may even have been part of an orchard behind the Rectory.

Test Pit 11, over 500 metres north-east of Iffley Church, may have been situated beyond the emerging village core, but taken together with the results from

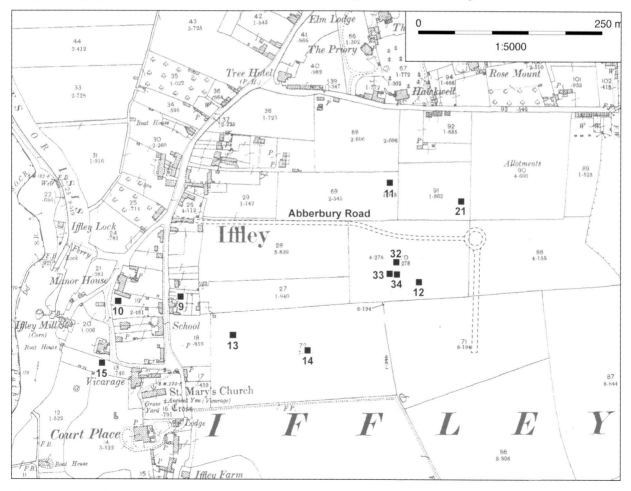

Fig. 3.10. Test pit locations in and near Iffley Village. Base Map 1900 Ordnance Survey 6 inch to the mile (© Crown Copyright and Landmark Information Group Limited 2014).

TP21, there is the possibility of another focus of settlement on the north-eastern slopes of the hill. Deep organic deposits were excavated in both pits, washed down from slightly further up slope, probably during the Medieval period. These contained sherds of this phase (21 in TP11 and eight in TP21); the pottery will have originated in settlements immediately above the test pits, brought downslope with the movement of soil resulting from the clearing of land for dwellings and from agriculture. Thus there are hints in this evidence that Iffley may have developed originally as a 'poly-focal' village with at least two small clusters of settlement, one around the church and one to the north-east strung out along the relatively gentle middle slopes of Rose Hill, at the spring line, and below the thin soils lying over the eroded limestone cap on its upper slopes and crest.

Five of the test pits, all in the same higher topographical situation, were dug through sandy clay to limestone bedrock and produced little or no pottery from this phase: TPs 12 and 14 close to the crest of the hill produced fewer than three small, scrappy sherds, while TPs 33 and 34 close together and just to the north-east produced none. These suggest limits to, and perhaps a break between, the church-linked settlement to the west and the possible dwellings to

the north-east. The land on the rounded summit of the hill above the dwellings may well have continued as wood pasture (hence the -ley *leāh* or 'wood clearing' name). Horticultural or agricultural activity just east of the church was suggested by a few sherds of Medieval Oxford Ware produced by TP13, on the edge of what was later the glebe field. The only other test pit dug in Iffley was located close to the church: TP9 on Church Way. This contained eight small, scrappy sherds of pottery from CP5 and this would suggest that this area, very close to TP13, was also either a kitchen garden or ploughed field rather than necessarily in the immediate ambit of a dwelling.

Iffley Fields and Donnington (Fig. 3.11)

Results for Ceramic Period 5 from the eleven test pits excavated around Fairacres Road and Donnington areas to the north of Iffley Village add interesting insights to the story of Medieval settlement along the Thames. Ploughed and manured fields were perhaps indicated by the few, small and abraded sherds found in TP 1 on the lower land to the east of Fairacres Road. Meanwhile Cricket Road (marked by the line of TPs 22 and 23) and Barracks Lane (just east of modern Cowley Road) were long-established routes running

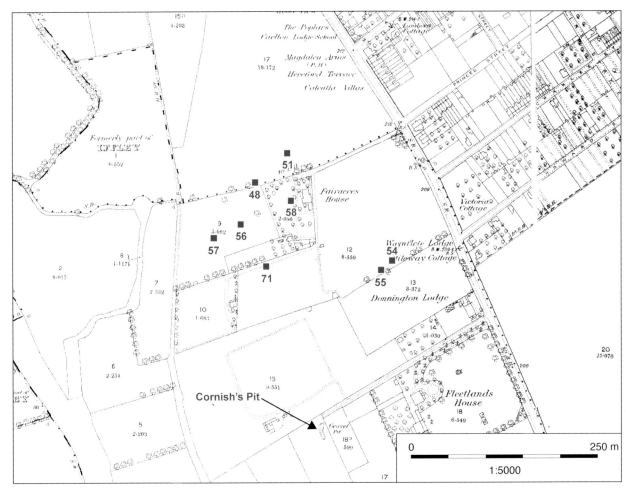

Fig. 3.11. Test pit locations in and near Iffley Fields/Donnington. Base Map 1900 Ordnance Survey 6 inch to the mile (© Crown Copyright and Landmark Information Group Limited 2014).

alongside the edges of the common pasture land of Cowley Marsh proper, and the pottery from this phase in TPs 22 and 23 may result from activity along the western of these routes. On the Iffley Fields gravel ridge, two of the test pits on the edges of the area yielded no pottery of this period (TPs 51 and 55) and may, as in Iffley Village, suggest areas of orchard and/or wood pasture. Manuring scatters of one or two sherds came from TPs 48, 56, 57, 58 and 71, a pattern arcing south around the heart of Fairacres Road, perhaps indicating gardens or peripheral activity around what turned out to be the most productive test pit in this area, TP54.

Test Pit 54 at 15 Fairacres Road produced 48 relatively large and unworn sherds of CP5 pottery (including at least 13 sherds of OXAM assigned to this phase), the majority of these came from contexts that had probably not been disturbed after about 1400. This pottery must have come from a Medieval farmstead close to TP54, with the ambit of the farm probably indicated quite tightly by the manuring scatters in test pits only metres to the north-west, west and south (TPs 48, 56, 57, 58 and 71). The area immediately to the north-west (TPs 56-58 in Fairacres Convent) had been the site of the Romano-British

farm which, like its Medieval successor revealed in TP54, had benefited from the river-side location, close to pasture and productive arable areas.

To add to this picture of the development of farms along the gravel terrace it appears that, after the break in settlement in the later Anglo-Saxon period, another Medieval farm grew up near to the Donnington Recreation Ground site. The 2013 excavation there, about 500m to the south of the Fairacres farm, produced nearly 300 sherds of CP5 pottery (see below). Although from a bigger volume of soil and generally quite small and worn, this assemblage from a relatively small excavation suggested disturbed features rather than just manuring of ploughed fields. So the rural settlement beyond Iffley village and along the river in the Medieval period very probably continued to be relatively dispersed, with at least two farms within a kilometre to the north of Iffley Village.

Littlemore (Fig. 3.12)

There is nothing in the test pit evidence to suggest that settlement in the Littlemore area continued to be anything more than scattered and relatively sparse before Ceramic Period 5: only the land around the village hall produced any pottery from the previous

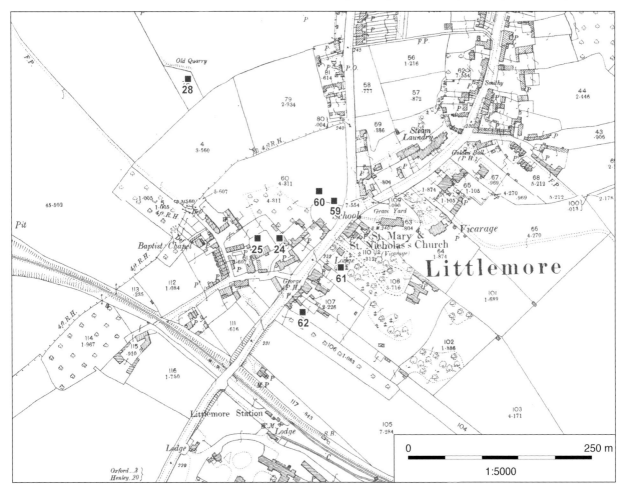

Fig. 3.12. Test pit locations in Littlemore. Base Map 1900 Ordnance Survey 6 inch to the mile (© Crown Copyright and Landmark Information Group Limited 2014).

period (CP4; TPs 24 and 25). However, these test pits provide some support for the argument that Littlemore began to grow as a village in the twelfth century, perhaps stimulated by the foundation of Littlemore Priory to its south-east (Chapter 5). Like Iffley, Littlemore appears to have developed as a poly-focal or perhaps more accurately a straggling, amorphous village. The test pit evidence from here is not yet conclusive, but might indicate settlement both along the line of the long-established route running between Sandford to the south and Church Cowley (modern Sandford and Cowley Roads) and also to the north-east around TPs 26 and 27.

Seven test pits were excavated in Littlemore. TPs 24 and 25, dug where some of the older buildings in this part of Littlemore cluster, despite having had a few bits of pottery in CP4, drew a blank in this phase. However, the ground immediately around both may well have been levelled in later periods and the lack of pottery may simply be the result of the removal of soil, especially as the only other pottery in these test pits was nineteenth and twentieth century. Those test pits, along with two in the grounds of St George's House (TPs 59 and 60) (see page 195), did however demonstrate that the older sixteenth and seventeenth-century buildings in the village were built directly onto the limestone bedrock with very shallow foundations. The higher ground in Littlemore is capped with rafts of limestone which sit very close to the surface. These provided builders with excellent grounding for their thick-walled, stone-built houses and ensured that buildings occupied the thin soils away from the better-quality land needed for arable, meadow and pasture. This was perhaps more critical in Littlemore than in some other areas, due to its variable soil quality, some thin and clayey, and considerable marshy areas associated with the brook and its tributaries, meant good agricultural land was at a premium. At least some of the small population of the locality were probably dependent on Littlemore Priory for their livelihoods.

Of the remaining test pits in Littlemore, several yielded CP5 pottery. TPs 61 and 62 across the road from TPs 24 and 25, having had no CP4 pottery pieces, did contain a very few sherds of this period, although one or two of the sherds were larger and in better condition. Again we suspected there had been a good deal of disturbance at the time the modern houses were built. At the northern 'end' of this part of the emerging village the test pit evidence was also quite difficult to interpret. St George's House, built on one of the limestone platforms, hosted two test pits (TPs 59 and 60). TP59 right next to the house recorded the levelling of shallow soil close to the building for its construction and contained no pre-seventeenth century pottery. TP60 behind the house showed the opposite: the building-up of organic soils

to create gardens and orchard land. Deep down at the limit of pit excavation in an undisturbed buried soil were two sherds of CP5, including one large (18g), unworn sherd of Medieval Oxford Ware, hinting at the possible presence of a dwelling on the site.

North of this test pit cluster, on the boundary with Church Cowley and just north of the gentle summit of the rise which Littlemore straddles, TPs 26, 27 and 63 all contained CP5 pottery. TPs 63 produced just two small sherds indicating an area on the edge of dwellings, or in ploughed fields. TP27 contained seven sherds but TP26 contained 13 and a few larger sherds and both may have been close to a house. TPs 28 and 64 to the west produced no sherds at all and were perhaps sited on pasture; this established a possible break between dwellings around TP26 and those near to TP60 to the south. Although the evidence is patchy there seems to have been at least some settlement developing along the road in Littlemore, with arable land and pasture on surrounding slopes. There may also have been ploughed land to the north-east, as environmental evidence from the non-project excavation on land belonging to the Academy school and just south of TP26 also suggested the area was farmed in this period.[26]

Blackbird/Greater Leys (Fig. 3.13)

Unfortunately the scope of the published report on the Oxford Science Park excavations renders it difficult to assess fully its Medieval assemblage, but it is evident that agricultural activity continued both immediately south and north of Littlemore Brook in the area west of Littlemore Priory and south of the developing village.[27] The Science Park excavators also suggested that a small farmstead may have been located on the limestone-capped higher ground above sand soils of the slopes, but any building remains had been completely quarried away. This suggests that as at Iffley, there were separate farms around the developing and also likely dispersed village of Littlemore.

The picture of Medieval settlement is less clear in the area of Blackbird Leys Farm (now extensively built over with housing) to the east of the Littlemore Priory site: of the nine test pits in Blackbird/Greater Leys (TPs 7, 35-40, 44 and 50) only two produced sherds of pottery from CP5 (TP7 with over 20 sherds and TP38 with two). The high number of CP5 sherds in TP 7 could suggest there had been a house or midden here. Nearer to Littlemore Brook, TPs 47 and 45 contained a few abraded sherds. TP 29 just north of the Brook on East Minchery Farm allotments produced a few sherds of Medieval pottery; these were in a context that was probably undisturbed since before 1550, and associated with an arrangement of post-holes, and so they may represent a building. A later, more extensive excavation by Thames Valley Archaeological Services ahead of development in this area discovered more

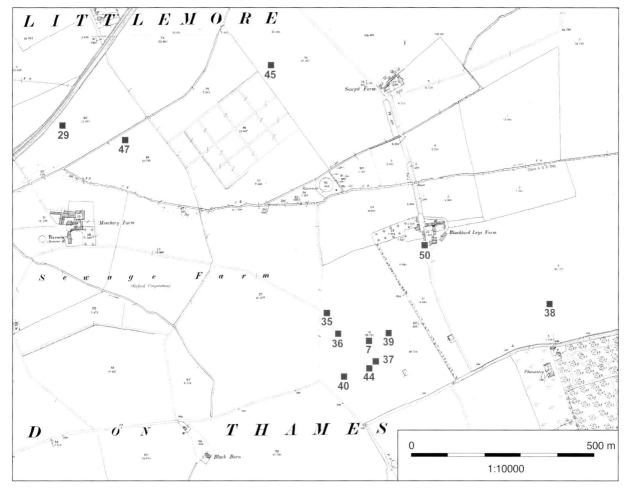

Fig. 3.13. Test pit locations in Blackbird and Greater Leys. Base Map 1900 Ordnance Survey 6 inch to the mile (© Crown Copyright and Landmark Information Group Limited 2014).

evidence of Anglo-Saxon and Medieval occupation.[28] TP41, much further east near the Roman road line contained no pottery of this period.

Church Cowley and Hockmore Street (Fig. 3.14)

During Ceramic Phase 5, the settlement at Church Cowley expanded, focusing around the church of St James and its adjacent manor house. Temple Cowley village evolved around its manor and, after 1139, the Knights Templar Preceptory, which probably took over and acted much like the preceding secular manor. Between them in the dip between the ridge of Church Cowley and the slopes of Temple Cowley, on a winding track, was the hamlet of Hockmore Street (an area now built over by the modern shopping centre).

The area around the Ark-T Centre (TPs 5, 6 and 65), immediately north-east of the church of St James in Church Cowley, has produced evidence of settlement since the Romano-British period, and, as TPs 5, 6 and 65 all produced worked flint, including possible Neolithic tools, the location probably supported human activity for thousands of years even before that time. The three test pits in the grounds of the Ark-T Centre (Church Cowley) produced considerable assemblages of pottery. The collection from TPs 5, 6

and especially TP65 with c. 50 sherds, including several large sherds from two deep layers undisturbed since about 1400, amounted to nearly 80 sherds. This collection is perhaps not surprising as the test pits were all within an 'eye' of land on Beckley sand created by Beauchamp Lane and Crowell Road. Both those routes are long-established, and probably fossilise an early configuration of tracks whose shapes may indicate the outline of a village green between them.

St James's Church dates from the twelfth century but may have earlier origins, having been established as the manor church before the Norman Conquest. And yet, surprisingly little archaeology for CP5 has been uncovered in previous excavations that have been conducted in the Church Cowley area over the years. No Medieval archaeology of note is recorded from the investigations of the Roman pottery kilns on St Luke's Road, the Telephone Exchange or Barn's Road.[29] TPs 53 and 49 to the north, and on lower ground, both contained no CP5 pottery. Other isolated test pits included TP49 within Cowley Marsh and TP53 near the border of Iffley and Cowley, and on clay soil. Church Cowley thus remains the most enduring settlement location identified by *Archeox*'s test pits.

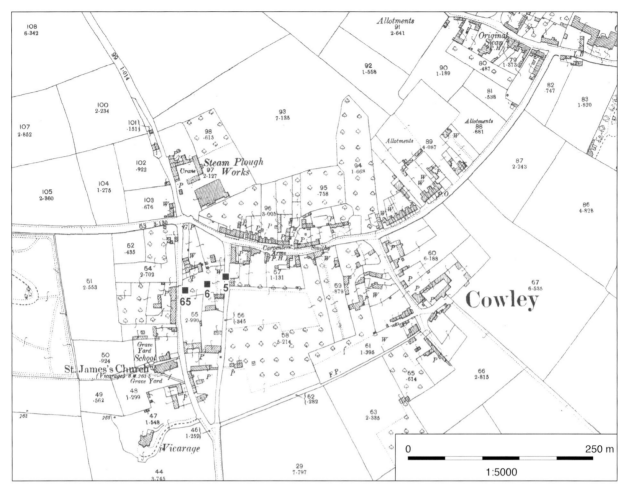

Fig. 3.14. Test pit locations in Church Cowley. Base Map 1900 Ordnance Survey 6 inch to the mile (© Crown Copyright and Landmark Information Group Limited 2014).

Temple Cowley (Fig. 3.15)

In Temple Cowley, both TP 68 and TP70 on Temple Road produced undisturbed Medieval layers and large, unworn sherds of CP5 pottery. The garden of TP70 had been very built up, but the lowest layer in a small sondage was undisturbed and contained one large sherd of pottery. TP68, further down the slope and north of Temple Road, but still on the Beckley sand, produced 19 sherds of CP5 pottery, including several large fragments, in the two lowest layers which in fact contained only pottery of this phase. A third test pit, TP66 on Junction Road just to the east, again on the slopes of the ridge and on sand, contained nearly 30 big sherds of CP5 pottery also deep down in layers undisturbed after around 1400. TP67 immediately to the south, was much more disturbed but still produced almost ten sherds of the relevant pottery; the natural geology could not be reached in this pit but the soil was much more clayey than in the three pits just discussed. The deep undisturbed layers in the three pits yielding post-Conquest and pre-1400 pottery must indicate settlement, possibly starting a bit before but certainly contemporary with the Templars' Preceptory. Some may relate to the earlier

manor that was given to the Templars. Whatever that occupation was in form, it left a footprint stretching from TP66 down Temple Road as far as the sandy soil reached. TP69, on a much more modern road to the north, provided a limit to the Medieval settlement in that direction: no pottery of CP5 was unearthed there. The village core at Temple Cowley seems to have started after the Norman Conquest, as none of the test pits produced CP4 pottery; indeed its growth was probably greatly accelerated by the arrival of the Knights Templar. As outlined above in Chapter 1, we still do not know the precise location, plan or extent of the Templars' Preceptory, although a fishpond was identified during archaeological work ahead of the building of the swimming pool and library complex just south of TP70. Ditches, pits and walls also emerged from excavations in the area of the seventeenth-century Temple Cowley Manor in the 1990s.[30] Large-scale archaeological evaluation in 2005, before new housing was built south of Temple Road, discovered no more convincing Medieval evidence.[31] It is probably significant that those new houses were located on clay geology rather than on better-drained sand just to the north and east, within which TPs 66, 68 and TP70 were excavated.

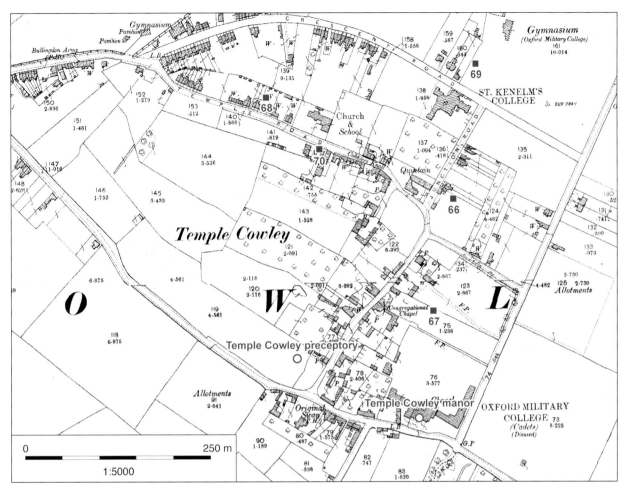

Fig. 3.15. Test pit locations in and near Temple Cowley. Base Map 1900 Ordnance Survey 6 inch to the mile (© Crown Copyright and Landmark Information Group Limited 2014).

Conclusion to Ceramic Phase 5

Into the fourteenth century the pattern of village settlement in the East Oxford area was well-established, with a mixture of clustered village settlement at Church Cowley and Temple Cowley, more linear and probably poly-focal villages in Iffley and Littlemore, with separate farms sited to exploit zones of better agricultural land. Nearer the city St Clement's was developing just outside the city walls. The landscape was also articulated by ecclesiastical buildings: the leper hospital at Bartlemas (Chapter 4); the Preceptory at Temple Cowley; the Priory including its church near Littlemore (Chapter 5); and churches at Iffley, Church Cowley and St. Clement's. These institutions and the walled town of Oxford with its expanding university were creating a demand for food, workers and services which must have provided opportunities for the inhabitants of the farms, hamlets and villages detected in our test pits.

Landscape and settlement in the later Medieval period c. 1400–c. 1550 (Ceramic Phase 6)
(Fig 3.16)

This relatively short Ceramic Phase, distinguished from CP5 only by the dominance of certain distinctive

later Medieval pottery types such as the later Brill/Boarstall wares, demonstrates that the broad settlement pattern established earlier in the Medieval period persisted and developed towards the end of the period. Around villages of varied forms, outlying, dispersed farms continued as a feature in the landscape. There is some evidence for settlement expansion, for example in Iffley and possibly in the Iffley Fields/ Fairacres Road area, and conversely, we can say with a little more certainty that settlements in Temple Cowley, perhaps Church Cowley and Littlemore, and at the Donnington Recreation Ground site, had contracted towards the end of the fourteenth century, likely reflecting the impact of the plagues and famines of the 1300s on the inhabitants of East Oxford's farms and villages.

Iffley Village

Iffley appears to have developed as a linear village, possibly with two foci. TP10 close to the church on Mill Lane produced over ten sherds of pottery in this shorter phase and, while the Rectory TP15 only gave six sherds these were large and unabraded. To the north-east, TP11 also contained over ten sherds thus continuing the pattern from the previous phase. TP9, between the

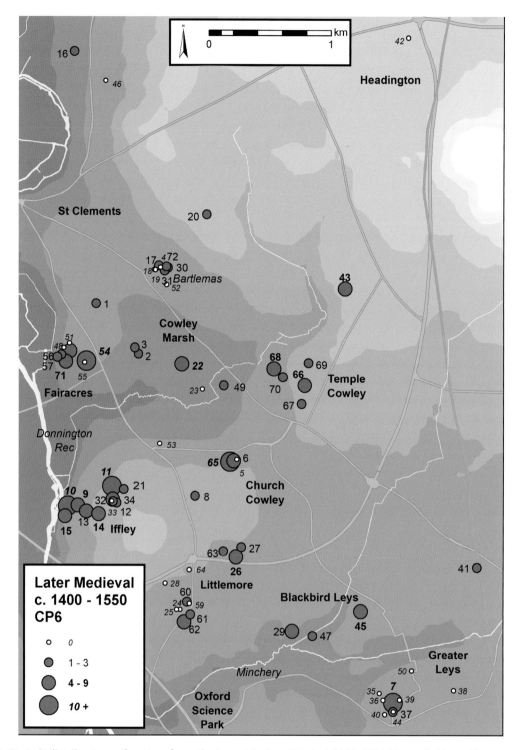

Fig. 3.16. Test pit distributions of pottery from the Later Medieval Period 1400-1550 (Ceramic Phase 6).

two apparent settlement foci, produced fewer than ten sherds and TP13, in the same vicinity, two large unabraded sherds. This suggests the church-focused settlement had at least not contracted. However, the increase in the number of test pits in Iffley giving evidence for the manuring of arable land or kitchen gardens hinted at an increase in agricultural and horticultural activity around the village: together TPs 12, 14, 21, 32 and 34 indicate cultivated areas or increased activity spreading up the middle slopes of the

hill above the village. Only TP33 produced no pottery, but as this pit had very thin soil with much lost to later landscaping it may reflect only that, rather than indicating a patch of surviving pasture or wood pasture.

Iffley Fields and Donnington

Several test pits in the Fairacres Road area of Iffley Fields yielded no pottery of CP6 (TPs 48, 51, 52, and 55) suggesting the gravel ridge was probably used for pasture, orchard or wood pasture; ploughed fields or perhaps kitchen gardens were indicated by the three or fewer worn sherds in TPs 56, 57 and 58. As in for CP4 and CP5, Test Pit 54, just to the south, produced the largest number of pottery sherds in the vicinity – nearly 20. The Donnington Recreation Ground excavation (see below) produced a large assemblage of 283 sherds of Brill/Boarstall ware, 190 of them from stratified contexts: evidence of a dwelling in the immediate vicinity during the Medieval period. However, Paul Blinkhorn has proposed that the tiny and worn collection of later pottery (14 sherds of fabrics from before the nineteenth and twentieth century) and most significantly the lack of late Medieval Brill/Boarstall fabrics confirmed the settlement was abandoned towards the end of the fourteenth century.[32] Later ploughing then disturbed the remains of Donnington's Medieval dwelling-place. The area close to TP22 along what was later Cricket Road may have continued to be the place of a barn or small habitation: the test pit contained seven sherds of pottery. The scatter of pottery in TPs 1, 2 and 3 implied the area of Cowley Marsh to the north-west was established as ploughed fields. Thus the settlements in Donnington, Fairacres and beside Cowley Marsh – hamlets, farms or other buildings – continued to be relatively contained, and dispersed amidst pasture and fields.

Church Cowley, Hockmore Street and Temple Cowley

Church Cowley and Temple Cowley were, by CP6, well-established settlement centres. However, the overall reduction in the amount of pottery found in Phase 6 might reflect the effects of the hard years of the fourteenth century on the rural population, although this may also be partly a consequence of a shorter phase. Although TP65 in Church Cowley produced nearly 20 relatively large sherds of Phase 6 pottery, TP6 contained only one or two and TP5 no sherds. As all these test pits had very few sherds for both CP7 and CP8 it may be that activity in this part of Church Cowley either declined or changed in character from the 1400s.

In Temple Cowley TPs 67, 69 and 70 yielded only four or fewer sherds, with only TPs 66 and 68 holding as many as seven. This may indicate a quite considerable contraction in the occupation of the village over the fourteenth to fifteenth centuries, hit by the loss of the Knights Templar Preceptory as well as the more generalised hardships of the period.

The scatter of pottery found to the north-west in the area around Bartlemas Chapel, which had by this period become an almshouse, must have been linked to small-scale horticulture or agriculture in the grounds of the institution (Chapter 4).

Littlemore and Blackbird/ Greater Leys

The test pit evidence for CP6 suggests the village of Littlemore continued to develop as a straggling or polyfocal settlement. The northern centre around TPs 26, 27 and 63 remained small – perhaps still a hamlet – as TP63 yielded only a single sherd of this phase. However, it is perhaps significant that the location of this possible settlement – on the sandy mid-slopes of the spur of higher ground running to Rose Hill – mirrors that of Church Cowley. These were sought after positions. The second centre of Littlemore Village, to the south-west, meanwhile may have contracted or been abandoned as a place to live, as only a scatter of pottery came from TPs 60, 61 and 62, suggesting the manuring of fields or gardens. It is possible this change in fortunes for that part of Littlemore was linked to the declining fortunes of Littlemore Priory and its eventual dissolution in the sixteenth century.

The farm or small settlement in Blackbird Leys close to TP45 may have continued into CP6 but as there are fewer sherds and it produces no pottery for CP7, it may have been abandoned in the 1400s. TPs 29, 47 and 41 to the west and north-east of TP45 may indicate ploughed fields. TP7 contains 27 sherds of OXAM fabric but has a similar profile to TP45, with a range of fabrics for the previous phase CP5 but almost none for the CP7. Thus it is possible that this farm was also abandoned for some time during CP6 and the surrounding area of Greater Leys mostly under pasture.

Conclusion to Ceramic Phase 6

The period from around 1400 into the 1500s seems to have been one of settlement contraction or re-organisation. Some of the individual farms or hamlets may have been abandoned, perhaps as their inhabitants were drawn into the villages, or attracted to the city of Oxford. A drive to greater agricultural efficiency may have also have led to the eradication of some farms. The villages are still clearly evident in the landscape but the possible decrease in activity, perhaps despite the movement into villages from outlying farms and hamlets, suggests that populations may have been reduced by the plagues and famines of the fourteenth century.

Landscape and settlement in the early post-Medieval period c. 1500–1700 (Ceramic Phase 7) (Fig 3.17)

Covering the beginning of the post-Medieval period, Ceramic Period 7 witnessed changes in the concentration and pattern of settlement, or perhaps alterations in what people were doing, that significantly affected the amounts of pottery entering the ground. The Donnington Recreation Ground excavation site had been abandoned and was by then used as agricultural land. Around Fairacres, the amount of pottery found for CP7 decreased: the same test pits produced pottery, but no pit more than 12 sherds. Thus, while settlement continued in the

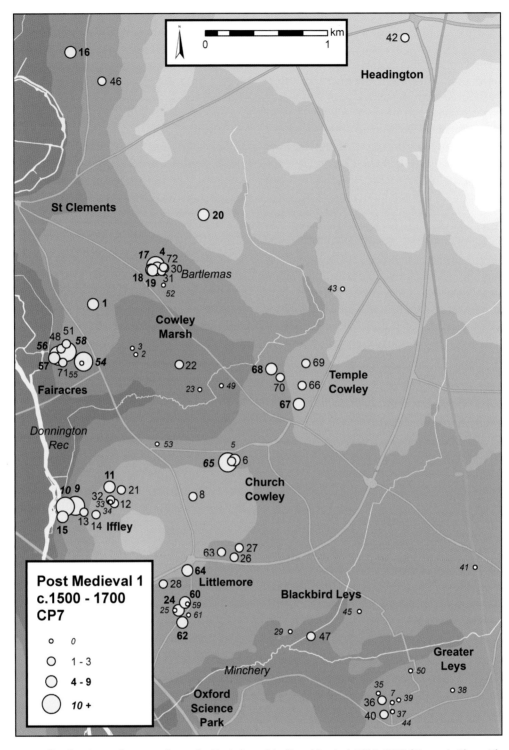

Fig. 3.17. Test pit distributions of pottery from the Early Post-Medieval Period 1500-1700 (Ceramic Phase 7).

same places, either the number of people or the level and type of activity had changed. The number of sherds in the surrounding test pits indicating manuring, of ploughed or worked land, also decreased (TPs 2 and 3 yielded no CP7 pottery), but this might reflect different ways of using agricultural or domestic waste for fertilising the land. Towards the end of this period, for example, across the country more fragmented bone begins to be found in fertiliser.[33]

The earlier inhabitation around TP45 in Blackbird Leys appears to have gone, although there is more evidence for land being worked to the south-west (TPs 29 and 47). Activity in the northern part of Littlemore had lessened, but more sherds of pottery were collected in the south-western area of the village around TPs 24, 60 and 62. Quantities however were still relatively small; on this basis the village does not seem to be flourishing at this time, perhaps affected by the closure of Littlemore Priory (Chapter 5). Similarly the dwelling or agricultural building alongside Cricket Road had probably been abandoned (TP22) and the village of Temple Cowley contracted further. In Iffley the village may have refocused on the area around the church: pottery amounts dropped-off in the test pits around TP11. The amount of pottery found in the Church Cowley test pits also reduced slightly.

This general pattern observed in the established centres of population strengthens the argument that changes in the inhabitants' lifestyles were influencing the amounts of pottery being thrown away or deposited close to houses. Perhaps fewer people were reliant on kitchen gardens, or household waste was being disposed of in different ways. The test pits around Bartlemas Chapel, however, produced more pottery for CP7. It is possible that this increase is associated with the occupation of the chapel and its grounds during the English Civil War (Chapter 4).

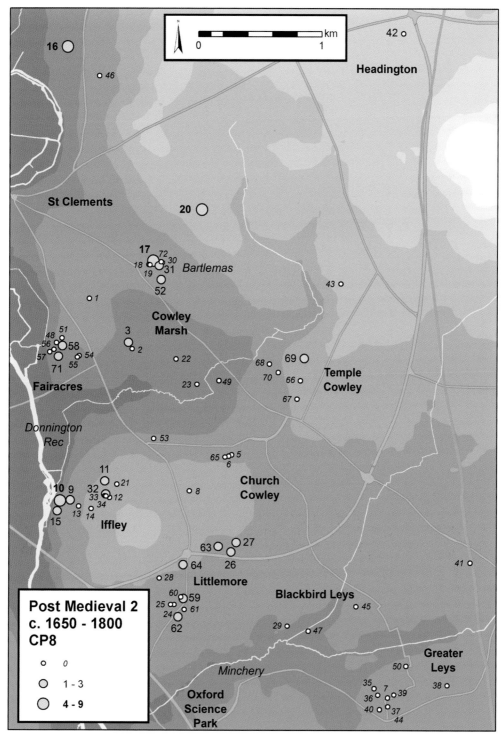

Fig. 3.18. Test pit distributions of pottery from the Later Post-Medieval Period 1650-1800 (Ceramic Phase 8).

Landscape settlement in the later post-Medieval period c. 1650-1800 (Ceramic Phase 8) (Fig. 3.18)

For this period, the last fully rural era in East Oxford, there is a general and dramatic drop in amounts of pottery collected. No test pit produced over 10 sherds and only five 4-9 sherds (TPs 10, 16, 17 and 20 and the much larger area of the Fairacres Convent vegetable patch). It is difficult to extract much more information from the CP8 ceramics except to note that areas interpreted as ploughed fields in previous phases were by then obviously fertilised differently or used in other ways as the spread of manuring scatter pottery had disappeared (from example around Blackbird Leys and the centre of the area). Over all, it seems that the later seventeenth and eighteenth centuries were one of the quieter periods in East Oxford's developmental history, seeing little expansion of economic activity or dramatic change in the extents of settlements and population.

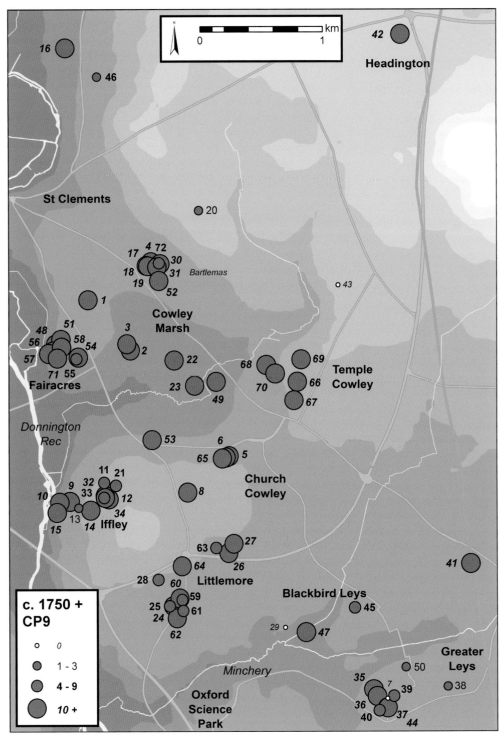

Fig. 3.19. Test pit distributions of pottery from after 1750 (Ceramic Phase 9).

Landscape and settlement after c. 1750 (Ceramic Phase 9) Fig 3.19

In contrast to the relatively meagre finds from the preceding period, the haul of evidence found in test pits from the end of the eighteenth century, and more particularly the nineteenth century, was much more dominant. The effects of industrialisation and mass-production here and elsewhere were evident. Broken plates, cups, bowls, pipes, glazed tablewares and jars were common finds, indicating the spread of new suburbs and consumer lifestyles across the area in Victorian times. Three quarters of the test pits produced upwards of 10 sherds of this period, and there are almost no nuances in the distribution. The majority of the pottery is mass-produced white earthenware (fabric WHEW), typical of the nineteenth to early twentieth centuries. This dominance under-lines the rapidity of the suburbanisation of East Oxford, and the increased availability and affordability of factory-made domestic items with the coming of the railways, mostly from around 1850 onwards.

Other finds from test pits

Although not our primary research target in terms of artefact retrieval and spatial analysis, plenty of non-lithic and non-ceramic finds, including quantities of archaeozoological material, came up in the test pits, and these were of great interest to many volunteers. There were plenty of pieces of assorted broken glass, which was mostly Victorian or later window glass. There were also numerous metal objects, but with only occasional exceptions such as a Roman coin of the Emperor Postumus from Test Pit 12 in Iffley (see page 55), these were mostly broken cutlery or rusty ironwork of relatively modern date, consisting of nails, wire offcuts and pieces of broken garden tools and household fittings. Much of it came from topsoil. The animal bone material was assessed by a faunal specialist and a report is included in the online database.[34] 356 fragments of bone were found in the test pits although only 139 of these could be identified to species. Most of the identifiable bone came from sheep/goats[35] with a smaller number from cattle and pigs. This range of animal bone is what we might expect to find in the general household waste from farms and small settlements over many centuries, reflecting what people were eating and which animals were being farmed locally. The nature of test pit layers – predominantly disturbed and archaeologically mixed – means without extensive (and expensive!) radiocarbon dating these bones cannot be fitted securely into our chronology, so they only give us some very limited insights. The relatively large collection of rabbit bone fragments from recent layers was probably the result of natural deaths of a wild population (or pet burials).

Bones from domestic fowl – probably mostly chickens – was concentrated in three test pits: TPs 1 (Cowley Marsh), 48 (Fairacres Road) and 68 (Temple Cowley) and may have been either pre-modern farm animals or more recent garden-kept birds.

A few of the bone assemblages could be associated with dateable layers and provide information on diet and the keeping of animals. Test Pit 1 (Stanley Road) produced one of the largest total assemblages and the greatest variety of species from fish (pike) to cattle, sheep, pig and fowl. TP48 in the Fairacres area to the south-west of TP1 also produced one of the larger collections of bone, including part of a sheep skeleton, as well as the fowl remains. A partial sheep skeleton was also found in TP54 very close by on Fairacres Road. The sheep remains in TP54 belonged to an undisturbed Medieval layer suggesting that sheep were begin eaten and/or penned or grazed in Fairacres at that time. A partial fowl skeleton in TP68 in Temple Cowley was discovered with Medieval pottery in a lower sequence of undisturbed layers dated to 1050-1400. This layer was probably a spread of Medieval kitchen midden (rubbish), and the fowl bones therefore perhaps the remains of someone's meal.

The remaining larger assemblages of identified bones were found in Church Cowley (TPs 5, 6 and 65) and Iffley (TPs 9, 10 and 15), which included cattle and pig as well as sheep, and around Bartlemas Farmhouse (TPs 17, 18 and 19), which lacked pig bone but produced one of the only two horse bone fragments. Thus all the more notable bone collections came from areas which, as discussed above and in Chapter 1, were the centres of long-lived agricultural settlement originating in the Roman to Medieval periods.

Notes

1. Lewis 2007, 133.
2. Lewis 2007, 2019; Gerrard and Aston 2007, Aston and Gerrard 2012; Jones and Page 2006; Christie *et al.* 2103.
3. Christie *et al.* 2013, 27.
4. Jones and Page 2006, and Gerrard and Aston 2007.
5. Lewis 2007, 139.
6. Jones and Page 2006, 88.
7. Jones 2005.
8. Jones and Page 2006, 93.
9. Jones and Page 2006, 108.
10. This was done in discussion with pottery specialist Paul Blinkhorn.
11. See report in online data by Olaf Bayer.
12. Beckley and Radford 2012.
13. Blinkhorn 2014.
14. Harden 1936.
15. Notes and Reviews in 1940 *Oxoniensia* 5: 163; Notes and Reviews in 1941 *Oxoniensia* 6: 9; Young 1973; Green 1983. A coin of Postumus (260-269) was found in TP12 (see page 55).

16 Booth and Edgeley-Long 2003.
17 See note 6.
18 Parker 1996: 136
18 Blinkhorn 2014.
20 Moore 2001.
21 Mudd and Brett 2013.
22 Moore 2001, 215-218.
23 Day 1991.
24 Sunken featured buildings were small, relatively low
    structures dug slightly into the ground and in this
    area built of timber, usually with a large roof-post at
    each short end.
25 Salzman 1939, 315.

26 See note 15.
27 Moore 2001.
28 McNicoll-Norbury 2014.
29 See note 6.
30 Muir *et al.* 1999; Fitzsimons 2008.
31 Ford 2005.
32 Blinkhorn, 2014, 4.
33 Gerrard and Aston 2006.
34 Information in assessment report by Chris Faine
    2014, in ORA online resource.
35 It is very difficult to distinguish between sheep and
    goat bones, although most of these are likely to be
    sheep.

The Oxfordshire Roman pottery industry

Christopher Young

From the mid-third to the end of the fourth century AD, Oxfordshire was home to one of the three or four major pottery industries of later Roman Britain, with a history of production back to the first century. Oxfordshire wares were traded across a broad band of southern and central Britain from the far south-west to Kent and East Anglia. Outlying finds reached northern Britain as far north as the Mull of Kintyre and even to the other side of the English Channel. These wares included mortaria (gritted mixing bowls which were essential to Roman cookery; Fig. 1), fine red table wares, and also white wares with red-painted decoration. The industry also made ordinary kitchen wares which were used locally. Several examples of local wares are on display in the Ashmolean Museum.

Pottery manufactories were located according to the availability of raw materials, communications and other land uses. Kilns producing these widely traded wares were spread along the Roman road from Alchester south to Dorchester, beginning to the north of Headington and extending south to the Thames at

Dorchester. There is a major concentration of potteries in the area of the East Oxford Archaeological Project, with groups of known sites in Headington, particularly at the Churchill Hospital; around Shotover; at Blackbird Leys and Greater Leys; Between Towns Road; Cowley; Rose Hill; and Littlemore. These discoveries show clearly how East Oxford's industrial history, with some gaps, goes back nearly 2,000 years.

The first sites were discovered over a century ago and discoveries have continued up to the present day. The industry was studied in depth some forty years

1. A Roman mortarium made in the Oxford potteries (C.J. Young).

2. An excavated kiln at the Churchill Hospital site (C.J. Young).

ago and from that study there is a reasonable understanding of the products, and their dates and distribution.[1] During that study, the major production site at the Churchill Hospital was excavated (Fig. 2). This investigation of around 5,000 square metres provided a clear picture of the organisation of production into small workshop units within pre-existing ditch systems, probably the boundaries of fields within which the workshops were placed

The work published in 1977 was essentially an analysis of what was already known and recovered. Apart from the opportunistic Churchill excavation, conducted ahead of development, it was not a project involving field work and was never planned to be so. As is always the case, this study left many questions unanswered. One of these was the social and spatial context of the industry. While we know quite a lot about the products and how they were produced, we have no idea of where the potters lived and little idea

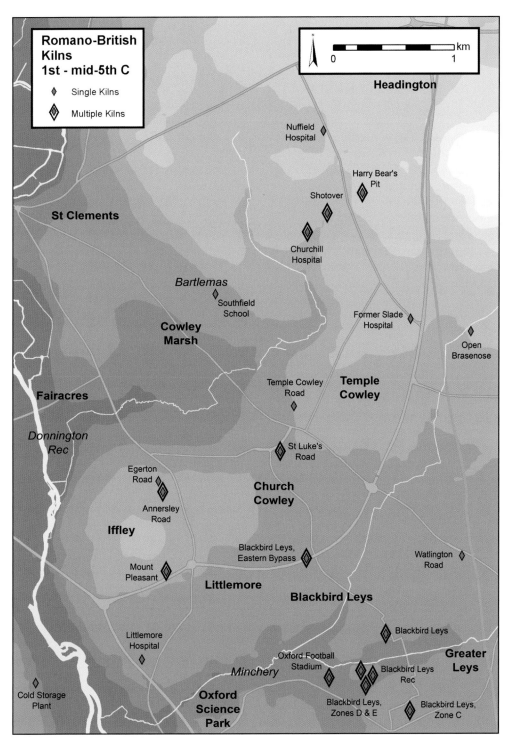

3. Map of Roman kiln sites.

of what other activities took place in this landscape through the Roman period. We also know little of sources of raw material (clay, sand, mortaria grits, fuel, water) beyond identifying potential areas based on the geology of the area, but suspect that some materials may have had to be moved at least five kilometres. Similarly, we know little definite about the ways in which the finished products were moved to their markets though it is likely that water transport was used as well as roads.

The *Archeox* project area covers much of the Roman pottery industry. Its 72 test pits and other pieces of work provide a sample of archaeological deposits across East Oxford. They therefore provide some insight into the context of the Roman pottery industry as well as into other periods of activities. The distribution of test pits was not planned specifically with the Roman pottery industry in mind but nonetheless provides a useful sample of Roman activity in the project's area. In Littlemore, Rose Hill, Temple Cowley and Blackbird Leys there were many test pits close to known production sites (Fig 3).

Of the 72 test pits, Roman pottery was found in 39. In eight of these, more than ten sherds were found, probably representing a significant Roman presence. There were concentrations of find spots in the area of Fairacres Road, close to a possible crossing point of the Thames, on Rose Hill, at Blackbird Leys, in Iffley Fields and in Temple Cowley. The excavations at Donnington Recreation ground and Littlemore Priory also produced quantities of non-kiln site Roman pottery, with a lesser amount from Bartlemas Chapel. There was a notable absence of Roman material from test pits in central Littlemore and between the Iffley and Cowley Roads.

None of these finds indicated new production sites, which are unmistakable because of the sheer quantity of finds and the presence of waste material. The absence of production material, given the closeness of some test pits to known production sites, suggests that they had firm boundaries and operated in specified

areas. This is perhaps indicative of a landscape which was divided up into a variety of uses. The finds represent occupation sites for the local population which would have included the potters and therefore indicate the potential location of settlements across the landscape.

These discoveries are a major step forward since for the first time we have evidence of potential settlement and can therefore begin to consider further the context of the pottery industry. It is clear that, with a few exceptions, there is the possibility of finding Roman material through much of the study area. There is the possibility at some point in the future to carry out more extensive investigation in, for example, the area of Fairacres Road and Donnington where there are open areas as opposed to gardens and streets. As well as looking for settlements, finding evidence of agriculture and other forms of land-use, in the form, for example, of field ditches or of environmental material, would be valuable.

Archeox has demonstrated the interest in their past of the residents of East Oxford and has shown that the area still has rich archaeological resources despite the extent of modern development over the last 150 years. It has also demonstrated the effective role that communities can play in improving knowledge of their own past through identifying and investigating known resources. On the basis of work to date, it would be possible to develop a future programme targeted at further improving understanding of Roman settlement in East Oxford and placing part of the Oxfordshire Roman pottery industry within its local context. The discoveries should also inform planning decisions on development proposals to allow appropriate investigation of potential archaeological sites.

Notes

1   Young 2000 (updated version based on a 1977
     British Archaeological Report).

Medieval pottery found in Oxford

Paul Blinkhorn

Pottery has been found in many excavations in Oxford and across the county, creating a recognisable series of wares characteristic of Medieval sites in the region.[1] (see Table 3.1, page 63).

Early and Middle Anglo-Saxon Pottery
(c. 450–850 AD)

Most excavations in Oxford's city centre have produced relatively small collections of Early/Middle Anglo-Saxon pottery, and by far the largest assemblage,

totalling nearly 1,000 sherds, came from excavations in advance of the construction of the Oxford Science Park, near Littlemore in 1999.[2] It is interesting then, although perhaps not entirely surprising, that the *Archeox* project also discovered relatively large quantities of such pottery during the excavations at Donnington Recreation Ground (see below).

Late Anglo-Saxon and Early Medieval Wares
(c. 850–1050 AD)

In the later Anglo-Saxon period, Oxford was, for the most part, supplied with two different types of pottery, St Neots Ware (fabric code OXR) and Oxford Shelly

1. St Neots Ware (Maureen Mellor).

2. Cotswold Ware (L) and Oxford Sandy Ware (R) (Maureen Mellor)

Ware (OXB). The former is from sources to the north, the latter from south of the Thames, or possibly London, although we do not know the exact place of manufacture for either. It is possible that the choice of pottery reflected the background of the inhabitants of the new town of Oxford, with St Neots Ware used chiefly by people originally from Mercia, and Shelly Ware more by those from south of the river, in Wessex. In the mid-eleventh century, both of these pottery types ceased to be used in the city, and pottery from the Cotswolds (OXAC) became the norm.

Medieval Pottery (c. 1050–1400 AD)

Shortly afterwards, two new wares, Oxford Sandy Ware (OXY) and East Wiltshire Ware (OXBF), appeared. We do not know where OXY was made, but the composition of the clay suggests somewhere to the north of the city was the most likely source. The pots were mainly unglazed jars used for a variety of everyday tasks, but also included the first glazed pottery in the form of tripod pitchers: jugs with three

small feet on the base. East Wiltshire Ware (OXBF), despite its name, was actually made near Newbury in West Berkshire. A kiln that had produced this pottery was found in the Savernake Forest during the construction of the Newbury by-pass. It is now generally known as Kennet Valley Ware. All these wares were found at the excavations at Bartlemas and Littlemore Priory (below, Chapters 4 and 5).

3. East Wiltshire Ware (Maureen Mellor).

4. Brill/Boarstall Ware (Maureen Mellor).

Later Medieval Wares (c. 1200–1550 AD)

Not long after the beginning of the thirteenth century, potteries producing very high quality glazed wares were established at Brill, near Boarstall in Buckinghamshire (OXAM), and these quickly came virtually to monopolise the pottery supply in Oxford for the rest of the medieval period. In the fifteenth and sixteenth centuries, small quantities of pottery from the London area ('Tudor Green Ware'), Northamptonshire ('Cistercian Ware') and the Rhineland ('German Stoneware') were imported, with the new pottery types being mainly cups and mugs.

Notes

1   Mellor 1994.
2   Moore 2001.

Part 2: Geophysical surveys in East Oxford

Olaf Bayer

The East Oxford suburban landscape is characterised by a relatively large amount of open space. In order to build the landscape theme in conjunction with other types of investigations, we made extensive use of geophysical survey techniques to investigate the parks, recreation grounds and playing fields. The locations of all the project's surveys are shown in Fig. 3.20. We could not hope to cover all of the available open spaces in full, so survey locations were selected on the basis of the presumed archaeological potential of particular sites based on past finds or landscape position, our ability to secure permitted access, and the openness and technical feasibility of the spaces to be surveyed. The minimum survey area which our equipment could attempt was one 20 by 20 metre grid square, so this meant that nearly all domestic gardens were too small for the equipment to function. Results were most productive on land which had been subjected to relatively minimal modern interference, which is rare in a busy suburban area. Those from school and university playing fields were generally disappointing due to the high levels of sub-surface drainage and surface levelling, often involving introduced materials, which had occurred. Parts of the Thames floodplain within the city boundaries have also been used for landfill and dumping in the nineteenth and early twentieth centuries, even though their appearance today is of tranquil grassed meadows and paddocks. This section summarises the techniques used by the Project and presents an illustrative range of survey results.[1] A selection of our surveys are covered here; those undertaken at and around Bartlemas Chapel are covered in Chapter 4. Several other surveys were conducted by the project, at Christ Church Meadow, Warneford Meadow, Scout Hut Field (Iffley), Northfield School (Blackbird Leys), Lark Rise and St. Gregory's schools (Florence Park) and St Michael's school (Marston). These located relatively little in the way of archaeological features, mostly due to modern land-use changes or the presence of historical landfill. This is not to say that there is no archaeological potential in these areas, merely that it did not show up using these techniques. All reports are available in the ORA online archive.

Gradiometer (or magnetometer) survey was the principal geophysical survey technique used by the project. Most surveys were conducted using a Bartington Instruments Grad 601(2) dual array gradiometer. This instrument is widely used as an archaeological prospection tool for locating sites in landscapes, and enables the relatively rapid collection of high-resolution data over large areas. It works by detecting small variations in the earth's magnetic field caused by buried features and objects. These variations can be produced by subtle traces of archaeological features such as pits, ditches, walls, surfaces, hearths and kilns.[2] The gradiometer also picks up the often stronger magnetic distortions caused by modern features, structures and iron-rich objects. This is usually less problematic in a rural setting, but presents a real challenge in a suburban landscape such as East Oxford where the magnetic signatures of services (pipes and cables), fences and made ground often obscure archaeological features.

In addition to gaining an understanding of the area's archaeology, the surveys were used to train project volunteers in geophysical survey techniques. As a result the methodology adopted by the project was designed to allow large numbers of volunteers, most with no previous experience of geophysical survey, to collect good quality data. Data was collected along traverse lines clearly marked at metre intervals, and the sample speed of the gradiometer varied to suit the pace of each individual (these lines are visible in Fig 3.21). Before starting to collect data each new surveyor walked a number of practise traverses to accustom them to carrying the instrument, and to the speed and rhythm of data collection. The instrument was re-calibrated between walkers, and each new person was scanned with the gradiometer to minimise interference from iron-rich objects attached to their clothing or footwear. Results were regularly checked in the field, and any areas affected by poor data collection were resurveyed.

The project also had a Geoscan RM15 dual probe earth resistance meter (see Fig. 2.8). Resistivity (otherwise known as earth resistance survey) was used to survey the precinct of Bartlemas Chapel (see page

120). This technique depends on subsoil moisture patterns revealing archaeological features. The probes are inserted into the ground, passing a weak electrical current through the soil, the resistance to which is measured and plotted across a systematic grid of readings. It is well-suited to finding subsurface building remains where walls stand out as high resistance (drier) features against moister surrounding deposits, and unlike a gradiometer it is not affected by metallic interference. Large mobile arrays with GPS

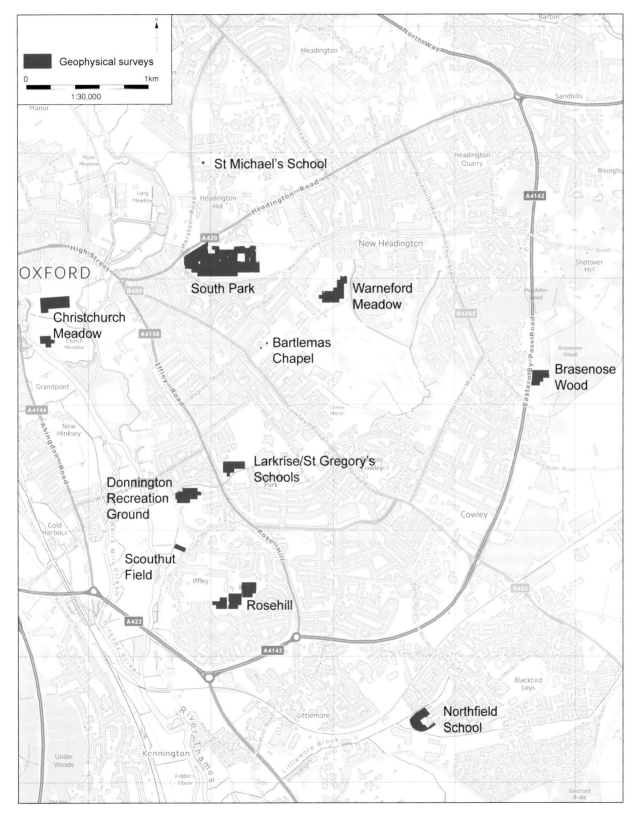

Fig. 3.20. Locations of *Archeox* geophysical surveys (Contains Ordnance Survey data © Crown copyright and database right 2019).

tracking can now be operated by tractor, but in its unmechanised form it is comparatively slow and cumbersome as a landscape prospection tool, and not well-suited to attempting large area coverage. Hence, here it remained used as a secondary technique, used in specific circumstances, but one which, when used more widely in addition to gradiometer survey, could add some useful complementary data to the picture.

Another increasingly mainstream geophysical technique available to archaeologists is Ground Penetrating Radar (GPR). This technique uses a mobile surface antenna to pass radar signals of varying strength into the ground and measures the patterns of response, often represented vertically as a 'time-slice'. It is particularly well-suited to detecting and visualising voids such as tombs, wells, or detecting barriers such as buried floors or other hard surfaces. The archaeological utility of GPR has made enormous progress since the *Archeox* project began in 2010, and it is now in use as a three-dimensional mapping and modelling technique, with impressive extensive landscape potential – an outstanding international example is the survey of the Roman city of Carnuntum on the Danube (Austria) by the specialist research and development organisation LBI ArchPro.[3] Our decisions to equip the *Archeox* project in the context of 2010 were driven by cost, accessibility, and ease of operation for trainees, hence instead we opted for the other techniques as described above. However this approach was never intended to be the last word in archaeological research in the area, and GPR could still be used to cast useful light, particularly on structures associated with Bartlemas Chapel for instance, or on the site of Littlemore Priory.

South Park

At 11.8 hectares in area the South Park Survey was the most extensive geophysical survey undertaken. The work was completed in a mixture of freezing fog, snow and sunshine in mid-winter 2012-13 (Fig 3.21).

The park was chosen for survey partly as one of the largest publically- accessible open spaces in East Oxford, but also because it encompasses the probable location of temporary siegeworks relating to the siege of Oxford (1643-1646) during the English Civil War (see page 102).[4] Any traces of Civil War features have not been readily apparent as distinctive features in the gradiometer data. The interpretation of the earthworks is discussed below, page 98 .

The results of the South Park survey (Fig 3.22) are in many ways typical of those seen in gradiometer results across East Oxford. Large magnetic anomalies caused by modern ferrous objects (for example cables, pipes and removed fencing) dominate the data. Smaller magnetic anomalies are likely to be caused by iron-rich objects lost or discarded during the modern

Fig. 3.21. Collecting data in the snow: South Park. The ground lines are visible either side of the surveyor, David Pinches.

usage of the area as a public park, and venue for fairs and concerts. These numerous minor anomalies make it extremely difficult to identify the smaller, focused archaeological features such as buried pits and post holes. The location of the annual Oxford City Council bonfire slightly to the east of the centre of the survey area demonstrates the magnetic enhancement of soils caused by extreme heating.

Rose Hill

The project carried out a large area of gradiometer survey on the summit of Rose Hill in the summer of 2012. Given its pronounced hilltop location and a number of late Prehistoric and Roman finds from its flanks, the survey area had some potential for further archaeological discoveries, possibly even an Iron Age hillfort.[5] However, as can be seen in the survey data, clear results were not forthcoming (Fig 3.23). Magnetic features caused by the survey area's proximity to suburban development since the 1930s (including areas of made ground and removed football posts) made it difficult to identify older features. However, as a known site of the Romano-British pottery industry lies very close on the eastern flank of Rose Hill, it is not impossible that some of the highly magnetic anomalies were caused by kilns and related spreads of highly-fired material, rather than modern ferrous material.[6] Clear archaeological features were limited to elements of the post-Medieval landscape and included grubbed-out field boundaries and a trackway. Several linear trends in the data suggest the presence of now levelled Medieval ridge and furrow cultivation. This was

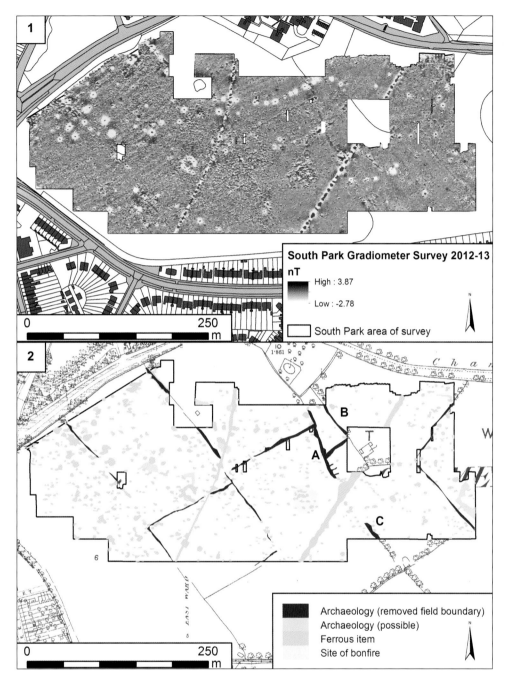

Fig. 3.22. South Park: geophysical survey results and interpretation (Historic mapping © Crown Copyright and Landmark Information Group Limited 2014).

further borne out by the presence of slight corresponding topographic features in lidar images of the survey area.

Brasenose Wood

Also in summer 2012 the project carried out a small area of gradiometer survey on land between the eastern by-pass and Brasenose Wood. This survey area was located to include the projected line of the Dorchester to Alchester Roman road.[7] The projected road line corresponded with a slight linear feature observed in the field and is shown on successive

phases of Ordnance Survey mapping. The survey aimed to discover the line of the road and any contemporary roadside settlement or other activity.

The survey shows a number of modern ferrous features generated by a buried cable/pipe, street lights on the nearby by-pass, and the presence of a largely demolished Second World War military camp (Fig 3.24). Also visible is a herringbone pattern of slight features caused by land drains. Perplexingly the data yielded no definite traces of the Roman road. Although there are very faint linear trends in the survey data in approximately the same location as the projected road line, the more substantial traces of the

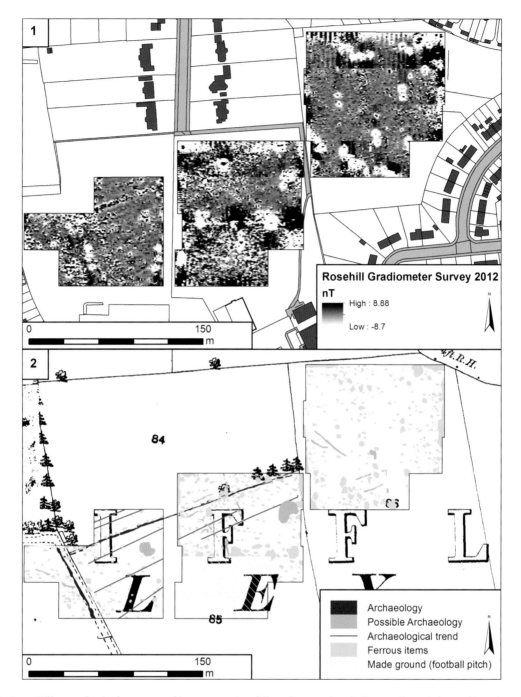

Fig. 3.23. Rose Hill: geophysical survey and interpretation (Historic mapping © Crown Copyright and Landmark Information Group Limited 2014).

road encountered in excavations and surveys at other sites nearby were not encountered.[8] There are a number of possible explanations for the apparent absence of the road. The road's construction materials may have been deliberately removed, or there may be insufficient magnetic contrast between the road and the surrounding geology, making it invisible to gradiometer survey. Equally the projected road line may be incorrect and might actually lie outside the survey area, probably just to its west under the ring road. No other clearly identifiable archaeological features were detected by the survey.

Donnington Recreation Ground

Donnington Recreation Ground is an unremarkable area of flat mown grass, which is well-used by dog walkers and weekend football players. At first glance it is an unlikely place to discover traces of some of the earliest settled communities in the Thames Valley. However, geophysical survey and excavation carried out here in 2012 and 2013 provided the project with a glimpse of East Oxford's Neolithic past.

The recreation ground is situated in one of the lowest lying areas of East Oxford, on the floor of the shallow

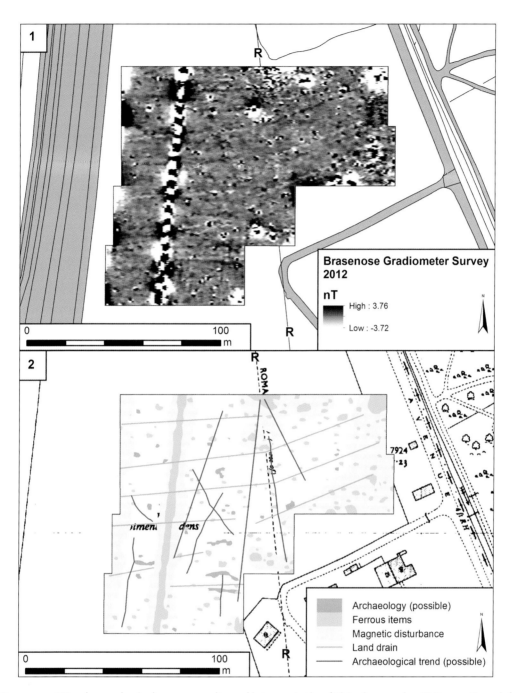

Fig. 3.24. Brasenose Wood: geophysical survey results and interpretation (Historic mapping © Crown Copyright and Landmark Information Group Limited 2014).

valley of the Boundary Brook, close to its confluence with the Thames (see page 19). It was this location near the river that first drew our attention to the area. A number of important sites of all periods have been found on the gravel terraces of the Upper Thames valley.[9] One of the aims of the *Archeox* project was to investigate areas of gravel terrace in the East Oxford area. Extensive areas of gravel terrace associated with the Thames and Cherwell exist within the area but a significant proportion have been disturbed by building, landscaping, quarrying, or, all too often, by early twentieth-century rubbish dumping. By studying a combination of historic maps, geological maps and

Lidar data, as well as making site visits, Donnington Recreation Ground was identified as a surviving pocket of potentially undisturbed gravel terrace surrounded by housing, an abandoned school football pitch, to the south-east, a now grassed-over rubbish dump.

This site was one of several to be investigated in a week of geophysical surveys in June 2012. Unlike many of the other sites discussed above, the recreation ground proved to be relatively free of magnetic contamination, and in some areas the gradiometer survey revealed subtle, but potentially interesting magnetic features. Fig 3.25 shows the results of the survey. Much of the survey area was masked by

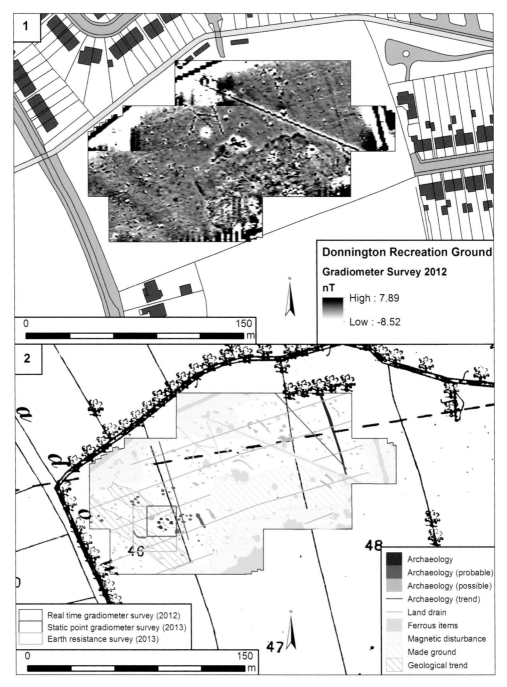

Fig. 3.25. Donnington Recreation Ground: geophysical survey results and interpretation (Historic mapping © Crown Copyright and Landmark Information Group Limited 2014).

'magnetic noise' caused by gas pipes, fencing and hard-core brought in to level out parts of the recreation ground area, but a swathe running across the centre of the site gave much clearer results. Although cut across by removed field boundaries, land drains and by patterning in the underlying natural gravels, a number of probable archaeological features indicating buried pits and ditches were detected. Particularly interesting was a small, roughly circular group of similar anomalies towards the western end of the survey area. Measuring approximately 10m in diameter, enclosing an internal area slightly over 5.5m wide, and with an

apparent gap in its south eastern side, this grouped feature consists of a ring of six or seven smaller magnetic anomalies, presumed to be buried pits, each approximately 2-2.5m in diameter. This feature is similar in shape to a number of ritual monuments called either pit circles, timber circles or segmented ring-ditches, which date to the mid to late Neolithic Period (3300-2350 BC). Although slightly larger in size, a local comparison is 'Site IV', 13km downstream of Oxford at Dorchester-on-Thames, excavated by Richard Atkinson in the late 1940s.[10] There a circle of pits, also with a gap in its south eastern side, once held

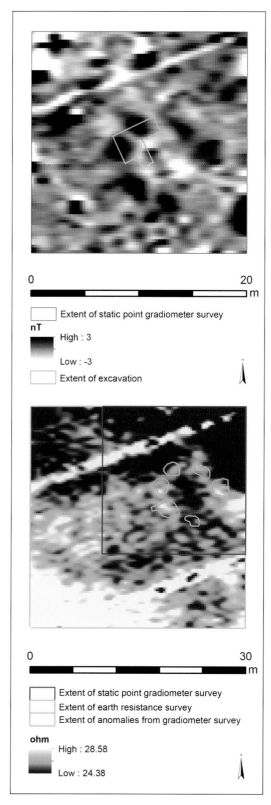

Extent of static point gradiometer survey

nT
■ High : 3

Low : -3

Extent of excavation

Extent of static point gradiometer survey

Extent of earth resistance survey

Extent of anomalies from gradiometer survey

ohm
High : 28.58

Low : 24.38

Fig. 3.26. Donnington Recreation Ground: static point gradiometer and earth resistance surveys.

Fig .3.27. Marking out features from the geophysical survey at Donnington Recreation Ground, prior to excavation.

surveys with the aim of adding more detail to the results. First was a more detailed 'static point' gradiometer survey (Fig. 3.26, upper). Instead of collecting streams of data along walked traverses, as described above, the surveyor stops still at 0.25m intervals along each survey traverse line, and while stationary, manually takes each reading. Although time-consuming, this removes the need for much of the post-survey data processing and produces much clearer, more detailed data. The second was an earth resistance survey (Fig 3.26, lower). The combined results of both surveys increased the definition of the feature, enabled the project team to plot its shape on the ground and to start thinking about where to position an excavation trench (Fig 3.27).

Conclusion

Archeox's use of geophysical survey was unusual in that it took a technique normally used in rural contexts, and applied it in a suburban landscape. The mixed results of many of the project's gradiometer surveys were to some extent predictable. At many sites magnetic survey has yielded much more information about very recent activity than it has about that from preceding periods. The close proximity of these sites to modern settlement has resulted in high levels of 'background noise' created by strongly magnetic modern objects which drown out the weaker traces of earlier activity. Working in areas with these consistently high levels of magnetic contamination makes interpreting survey results difficult. There is a tendency to identify linear features and features with an unusual or recognisable morphology/shape before detecting smaller, point-focused features such as individual pits.

However, even the most magnetically contaminated sites produced some glimpses of pre-twentieth century activity, such as traces of Medieval ridge and

substantial upright timber posts, which were later removed and cremated human remains inserted into the tops of the holes left by the posts.[11]

We returned to the recreation ground in summer 2013 to conduct two smaller targeted geophysical furrow or removed post-medieval field boundaries. At other sites the results are as frustrating as those encountered on any site, rural or urban, where the data is a challenge to interpret. At Brasenose Wood the apparent absence of a Roman road raises questions about the nature of the road's construction, the suitability of gradiometer survey to locate it, the possibility of its deliberate removal, and the possibility that historic mapping has placed it in the wrong location. At South Park, a Civil War siege line, rather than being a large earthwork, was probably a relatively slight feature emphasised by local topography, and reworked and incorporated into later phases of landscape use. Yet the results from Donnington Recreation Ground excavation, discussed below, show that a combination of background research and an element of good luck can successfully reveal areas of subtle archaeological features even in this 'noisy' suburban context. At that site it was the particular arrangement of a group of features that captured attention and led to further investigation.

Beyond the purely archaeological outcomes of the work, the practice of carrying out geophysical surveys with groups of volunteers from the local community was a great success. A large number of people, with no previous experience of geophysical survey, were taught the survey methodology, worked together

closely, and successfully collected good quality data. These surveys have provided valuable, if sometimes difficult to interpret, windows into East Oxford's past.

Notes

1   Results of all of the *Archeox* surveys, including those discussed in this section, are available in the digital archive at ORA.

2   For further information on gradiometer (magnetometer) survey see Gaffney and Gater 2003, 36-42 and 61-68.

3   https://archpro.lbg.ac.at/case-studies/case-studies

4   Lattey et al. 1936, 172.

5   Chapter 1, on Bronze Age, Iron Age and Roman East Oxford.

6   See Christopher Young's contribution on the Roman pottery industries.

7   For more information on the Dorchester-Alchester Roman road in the Oxford area see Beckley and Radford 2011d, 27.

8   Lewis 2009 and Linington 1959.

9   For more information on the archaeology of the Thames gravels see Thames through Time: Hey et al. 2011; Lambrick et al. 2009 and Booth et al. 2007.

10 See Atkinson et al. 1951 for information on the 1940s excavation at Dorchester-on-Thames.

11 See Gibson 1992, 87 for a revised interpretation of Dorchester site IV.

South Park: interpretation of earthworks

Olaf Bayer

South Park is a major public park stretching eastwards and uphill from St Clements, bounded by London Road, Cheney Lane and Morrell Avenue, with Warneford Lane at the top (eastern) end. It was created in 1932 when the trustees of the Morrell family estate sold sixty acres (24.3 hectares) of disused farmland to the Oxford Preserv-

ation Trust, which were later transferred to the city council on condition it was kept as a public park.[1] The purchase from the Morrell Estate was financed in part by a donation from David and Joanna Randall-MacIver,[2] an act of generosity commemorated on a stone obelisk on the western boundary of the park carved by Eric Gill. South Park is one of the largest publically-accessible open, green spaces in East Oxford. It preserves extensive surface traces of Medieval and post-Medieval cultivation ridges, and the remains of former field boundaries including surviving trees and

1. Ridge and furrow in South Park, visually accentuated in light snow (David Griffiths).

2. Lidar slope model of the lower end of South Park (© Environment Agency copyright and/or database right 2012). The inset shows the data collected by the tractor-mounted GPS.

bushes, effectively fossilising a fragment of nineteenth-century agricultural Oxfordshire (Fig. 1). As such, it is one of few places in the East Oxford area where a 'rural' landscape archaeology approach can be taken.

An account of the geophysical survey in South Park is given in above in Chapter 3 (see pages 92–3). A combination of desk-based and field survey techniques was used to investigate South Park's surface archaeology. Earthwork features were surveyed on the ground and mapped from lidar data. Lidar (Light Detection and Ranging) is an airborne laser scanning technique used to create detailed, three-dimensional models of landscapes.[3] The lidar data used by this Project was collected by the Environment Agency (EA) as part of a nationwide survey to predict areas at risk of flooding, but has the added bonus of clearly showing archaeological earthworks. Due to its proximity to the Thames and Cherwell, EA Lidar coverage was available for most of East Oxford[4] and proved to be a valuable research tool for the project. This image (Fig. 2) was created by projecting 16 separate light sources across a Digital Terrain Model (DTM) of the park to maximise the visibility of often subtle archaeological features. As an experiment in mechanised data-gathering, the project GPS smart station sensor was fixed to the front of an Oxford City Council grass-mowing tractor, recording close-interval data over the earthworks (Fig. 2, inset).

Lidar provided an overview of the park's micro-topography, from which the location and morphology of often very slight earthwork features could be mapped. Several types of archaeological field survey[5] were then used to understand and interpret these features. The simplest of these techniques was 'walkover survey'. The whole park was examined on foot (with printed extracts of historic or lidar mapping hand), and observations about the character and relative sequence of archaeological features were annotated on sketch maps.

Interpretation

The most prominent pre-park features that can be detected are the remains of field boundaries, some of which are marked by surviving trees, which once divided the area of the park into a series of smaller enclosed fields. Also prominent in the lower, western half of the park are the earthworks of a ridge and furrow cultivation system of probable later Medieval date. Those features survive as low 'corrugated' earthworks (Fig. 1) and are easily traced in the lidar image of the survey area (Figs. 2 and 3).

The pronounced break-of-slope which runs north-west to south-east across the centre of South Park (between points X and Y in Figure 3) attracted particular attention. In this location, multiple phases of

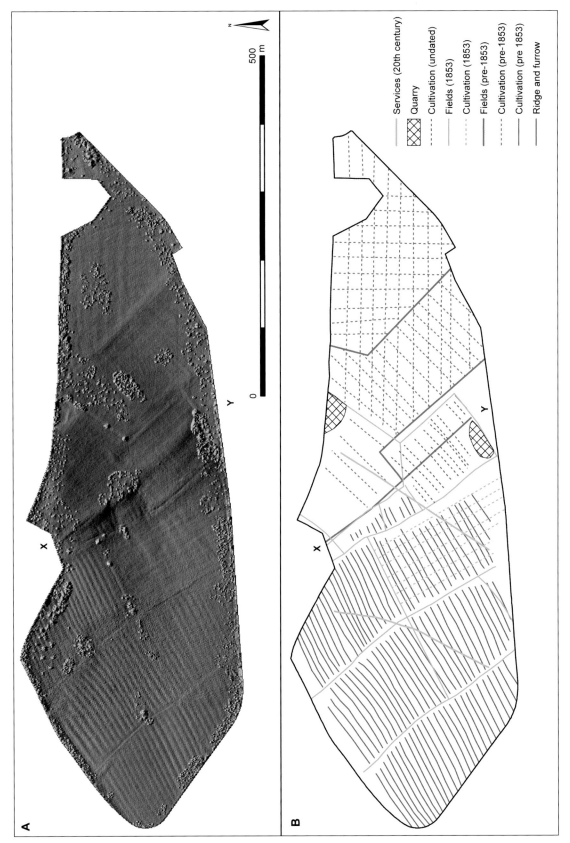

3A. A multidirectional hill-shade model of South Park derived from 1m resolution lidar Digital Terrain Model (© Environment Agency copyright and/or database right 2019. All rights reserved). 3B. Interpretation of lidar data.

field boundaries (and traces of associated cultivation) converge with a natural topographic feature, the sharp break of slope. Views of the city from this position are unrivalled. Here, more detailed analytical earthwork survey techniques were used to unpick this complex sequence of features. Both hand (analogue)[6] and computerised (digital)[7] survey methodologies were used to produce detailed plans, enabling a fuller understanding of this area. A north-south bank or lynchet appears to have emphasised the break of slope at this point (see below).

Figure 3B summarises the results of analysis of lidar data, walk-over survey and analytical earthwork survey, with information from historic mapping and the geophysical survey. At least three phases of fields and/or cultivation are evident in South Park. The first phase is evidenced by the slightly curving east to west corrugations which are clearly visible at the western end of the park (shown as solid and dashed red lines in Figure 3B). These are the remains of medieval 'ridge and furrow' cultivation probably originating in the twelfth or thirteenth century. Formed by oxen-drawn mould-board ploughing, the ridges would have increased the cultivable surface area, improved drainage, and divided the open fields of St Clements parish into a series of narrow, elongated strips. Evidence of ridge and furrow cultivation is widespread in central lowland England, but its surviving extent has been vastly diminished by modern deep-ploughing.

Whilst the preservation of ridge and furrow is clearest at the lower lying, western end of the park, it is likely to have been much more extensive in the past, and it may well underlie traces of later cultivation in the central and eastern areas of the park. Ridge and furrow cultivation is likely to have gone out of use in the later Medieval or early post-Medieval period, possibly as early as the enclosure of this area of St Clements parish in 1565.[8]

A second phase of fields and associated cultivation is visible at the eastern end of the park (shown as solid and dashed blue lines in Figure 3B). Fields are defined by a series of broad banks, or lynchets which are probably post-medieval in date. It is assumed that their origin is broadly contemporary with the fields shown in green below, differing only in that that had been removed by the time completion of the St Clements parish tithe map in 1853.[9] These fields have been cultivated in two directions probably representing the 'cross-ploughing' (at 90 degrees) of earlier ridge and furrow.

The final phase of fields is visible in the western and central areas of the park as a combination of slight earthworks and intermittent lines of trees (shown as solid green lines in Figure 3B), and appears on the 1853 St Clements tithe map. These broadly rectilinear fields are probably contemporary in origin with the second phase of fields, being only distinguished by their

survival into the early-twentieth century. Aerial photography of the park shows that these boundaries survived much more extensively in the mid-1940s.[10] The tithe map and apportionment show that only the eastern end of the area that later became South Park was under cultivation in 1853. It was probably this cultivation that slighted earlier boundaries in this area.

Two substantial depressions are visible in the lidar data (shown as cross hatched areas in Figure 3B). The first lies on the northern edge of the park close to one of its entrances is probably a small quarry. The second close to the southern edge of the park is harder to interpret. It lies in the corner of a post-medieval field and could be another quarry, a spring, or the remains of a hollow way cutting through the slope (it has a somewhat linear shape on the ground). Two slight linear features cutting diagonally across the park (shown as orange lines in Figure 3B) are caused by twentieth century pipe or cable trenches and are clearly visible in the geophysical survey results.

A particularly interesting conundrum is presented in the central area of Figure 3A between X and Y. Here the pronounced lynchet (bank or terrace) running along the top of the break of slope (shown in blue) appears to be overlain by a series of perpendicular cultivation furrows (shown as dashed purple lines). This relationship is significant, if these furrows are the remains of medieval ridge and furrow it indicates that the underlying, and therefore pre-existing, lynchet is early Medieval or earlier, possibly even Romano-British or Iron Age in date. The alternative explanation (and the one favoured here), is that these particular furrows are the result of nineteenth or early twentieth century cultivation taking place within one of the later fields (those shown in green), and that the underlying bank is more likely to date to the post-Medieval period, and hence could feasibly be feature from the English Civil War.

Figure 4 shows the eastern half of Bernard De Gomme's 1643 map of Oxford's Civil War fortifications. The defences of Royalist Oxford are visible, including at the eastern bridgehead of Magdalen Bridge, which is defended by a substantial redoubt entirely enclosing Old St Clement's Church. Some distance to the south-west across the Thames at approximately SP 517048 is a small star fort. Towards its eastern edge, the map also shows the lines of a substantial opposing Parliamentarian siegework complex lying immediately upslope of the break-of-slope on the flank of Headington Hill, across the line of Cheney Lane, which De Gomme labels as London Road. This feature appears to be in a different ink to the rest of the map and may have been added on later, possibly as late as 1646. The location of this depiction suggests that the west-facing line of the parliament-arian siege work straddles Cheney Lane in a north-south direction, and therefore its southern half should

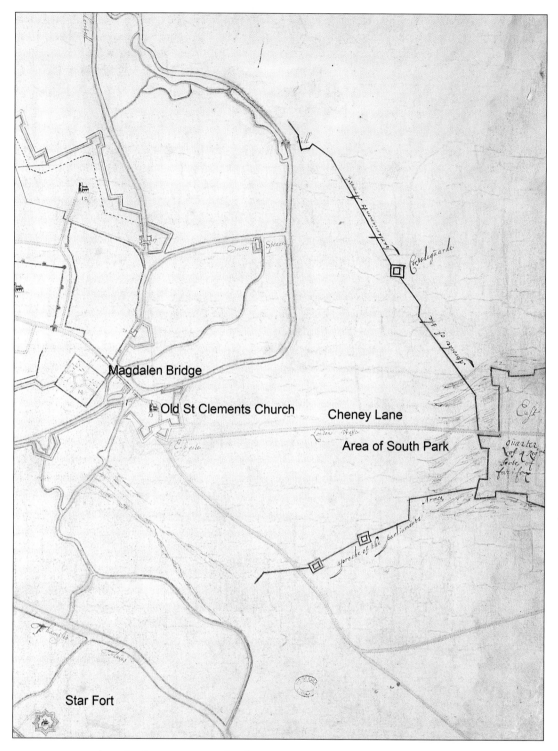

4. Eastern area excerpt from De Gomme's Map of Oxford's Civil War Defences, 1644/46 © Bodleian Library, University of Oxford, with our annotation.

lie within what is now South Park.[11] Given this apparent topographic position, with commanding views across St Clements and the eastern approaches to the city, the top of the break-of-slope crossing South Park is an obvious location for the siegework. We were excited to find that the bank on the break of slope appears to coincide with De Gomme's depiction of the line of siegeworks. We did not find, in either the geophysical or earthwork surveys, any clear traces of a

defensive structure or ditch in this location, in fact the evidence for any such features is slight. The siegework was short-lived in duration, so it is likely that elements of it were merely a temporary enhancement of the natural break of slope (perhaps using lightweight portable materials such as wooden palings and bundles of thorns), meaning that after over 350 years later, they have become more-or-less invisible to both archaeological survey techniques. If this is the case, then the combination of the post-Medieval lynchet and field boundaries running along the top of the break-of-slope may preserve, but also overwrite and partly obscure the line of the siegework. To find out more, a larger, more intensive survey on both sides of Cheney Lane, coupled with the possibility of targeted excavation, might consolidate the picture.

Notes

1 Salmon 2010, 29.
2 David Randall-MacIver (1873-1945), of Queens College, was a famous Oxford archaeologist and Egyptologist.
3 For more information on lidar see https://historic england.org.uk/images-books/publications/light-fantastic/
4 Lidar data for East Oxford can be accessed at http://environment.data.gov.uk/ds/survey/index. jsp#/survey?grid=SP50
5 For more information on analytical earthwork survey see https://historicengland.org.uk/images-books/publications/understanding-archaeology-of-landscapes/
6 For more information on analogue earthwork survey techniques see https://historicengland.org.uk/images-books/publications/with-alidade-and-tape/
7 For more information on digital earthwork survey using a Total Station Theodolite (TST) see https://historicengland.org.uk/images-books/publications/traversingthepast/ and using a Global Navigation Satellite System (GNSS) see https://historicengland.org.uk/images-books/publications/where-on-earth-gnss-archaeological-field-survey/
8 VCH Oxon 5, 258-266.
9 Copies of the 1853 St Clements tithe map and apportionment are available from the Oxfordshire History Centre. The fields also appear on the Cowley Enclosure Award, see Chapter 6.
10 See 1945 aerial photography on Google Earth.
11 Lattey *et al.* 1936.

Part 3:
Donnington Recreation Ground 2013: the excavation

Jane Harrison

At Donnington Recreation Ground, in September 2013, an excavation trench (Site code DR13) was laid out over the geophysical anomalies discussed in Part 2 above, to investigate the cluster of potential pit-like features revealed by the geophysical survey (see Figs 3.25 to 3.27). It was five metres (NW-SE) by three metres (NE-SW) with a 1.5 metre by 3.3 metre extension to the south-west (Fig. 3.28). The trench was positioned to enable excavation of half of each of two large pit anomalies, as well as a smaller pit, which appeared in the

geophysics as central to the possible pit-ring. Only one of the larger features (Pit 2028, in the western part of the trench) proved to be an archaeological feature; the other (Pit 2022) was less certainly of archaeological origin and interpreted as a tree-throw. The pottery and flint finds from all the features in the trench, and the Medieval and later plough-soils sealing them, when combined with results from the environmental samples and radiocarbon dating, revealed human activity in the Donnington area of the Thames gravels from the Mesolithic Period to the present.

Reports on the excavation by Jane Harrison, on pottery by Paul Blinkhorn, lithics by Olaf Bayer, archaeobotanical evidence by Diane Alldritt, radiocarbon dates by Seren Griffiths, and iron finds by Ian Scott, can all be found in the ORA online archive.

Fig. 3.28. Donnington Recreation Ground excavation: looking north.

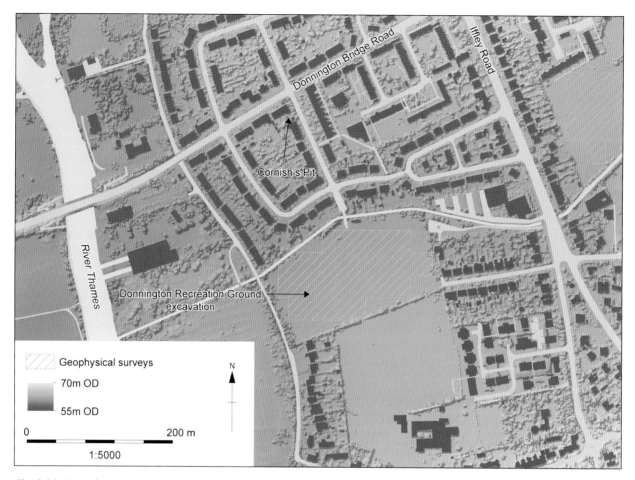

Fig. 3.29. Donnington Recreation Ground excavation: location map (Base mapping © Crown Copyright/database right 2012. An Ordnance Survey/EDINA supplied service. Topography © Environment Agency copyright and/or database right 2019. All rights reserved). For geophysical survey, see Fig. 3.25.

Summary

The excavation uncovered one large, deep pit nearly two metres in diameter [2028], the source of one of the geophysical anomalies. Finds of flint tools and two radiocarbon dates from hazel shells indicate this had been created during the early to middle Neolithic Period (c. 4000-3000 BC). A shallower and more uneven filled-in hole in the north [2022], which had generated another of the larger pit-shaped responses, lacked the coherence and depth of [2028] and was most probably a tree-throw. Tree-throws are created when a tree falls, pulling out its root-bole and leaving behind a characteristic, ragged hole. In the past these were sometimes re-used as places to dump waste material. The smaller geophysical anomaly, central to the pattern of pits, reflected an area of old animal burrows and filled-in large horizontal and vertical tree root holes. It was excavated in two small sondages (2030 and 2034). Roots had badly disturbed the south-eastern side of pit [2028], suggesting a large tree had rooted into the pit-fill to exploit the moister and more humic soils. The stratigraphic relationships between the contexts are shown in diagrammatic form as a 'Harris Matrix'[1] (Fig. 3.31).

Both the Neolithic pit and the tree-throw had been truncated (upper layers removed, so only their lower extents remained), and the highest of those surviving layers had been disturbed by Medieval and later ploughing. Ploughing had also eradicated any archaeological features from the Romano-British and Anglo-Saxon periods, leaving behind pottery worked into the plough-soils. Although there were no recognisable features in the trench other than the pits, tree-roots and animal disturbance, the amount of pottery found suggested that there had been settlements from both of those periods in the very near vicinity, and possible within the area of the trench. Paul Blinkhorn noted that the Early to Middle Anglo-Saxon (Ceramic Period 3) assemblage of 76 sherds of pottery was; 'one of the largest from the environs of the modern city of Oxford'. An Anglo-Saxon settlement of this period would probably have been characterised by sunken-featured buildings similar to those discovered in the Oxford Science Park excavations.[2] Some of the more diffuse 'blob-like' anomalies in the Donnington Recreation Ground geophysical survey (see Fig. 3.25) may even hint at the survival of such structures.

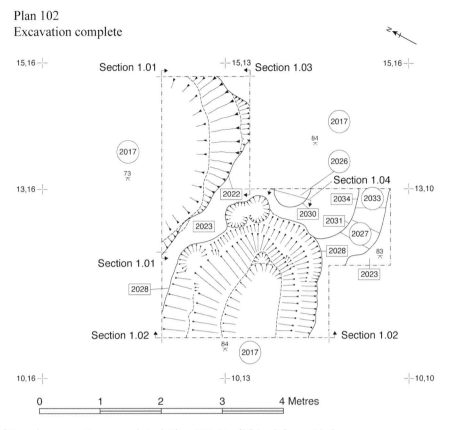

Fig. 3.30. Plan of Trench, excavation completed, Plan 102. Neolithic pit lowest in image.

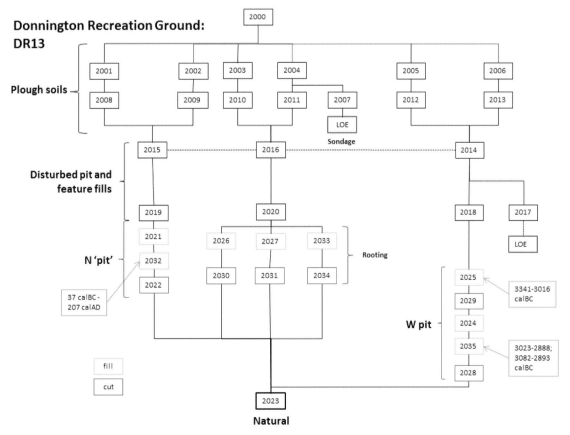

Fig. 3.31. Donnington Recreation Ground excavation: stratigraphic matrix, Neolithic pit sequence to right.

DR13

Section 1.02
Pit 2028

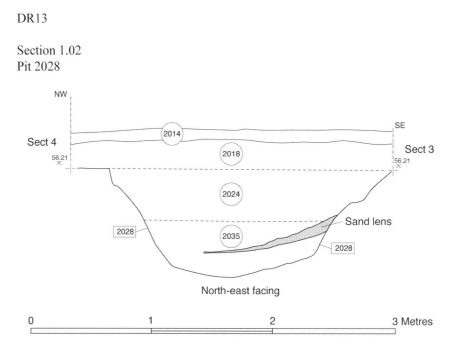

Fig. 3.32. Drawing of half-sectioned Neolithic pit [2028], section 1.02.

All of the Medieval pottery (c. 400 sherds) in the plough-soil was from the mid-eleventh to fourteenth centuries, and may indicate that a dwelling was situated nearby during that period. This was probably abandoned when the field was converted to pasture after the fourteenth century with only a tiny scattering of sherds of pottery (13 in total) discovered from later periods before the nineteenth century, when ploughing recommenced. Some of the more recent pottery probably resulted from the time when Donnington Recreation Ground area was incorporated into allotment gardens. Very little animal bone was found.

A total of 338 worked flint fragments were also found during the excavation. The majority were debitage – the waste created during the manufacture of stone tools. Most (238 in total) were also retrieved from the plough-soil layers, so had been disturbed from where they were finally dropped or thrown in Prehistory. However, 95 fragments were found in the Neolithic pit and five in the tree-throw. Of those flint finds, five had clear evidence of having been re-worked so they could be used as tools (see Fig. 3.35). The flint assemblage represented two episodes of human tool-making and use around the site: one late Mesolithic to early Neolithic and the other from the late Neolithic to early Bronze Age. The radiocarbon dates from Pit [2028] also indicated that broadly the same two phases of activity had been recorded in environmental remains – charcoal and hazel nutshells – from its fill.

The Neolithic Pit

The earliest feature discovered in the trench, cut into the natural gravel and sand, was the large sub-circular pit in the western area of the trench [2028], 1.86m maximum in diameter and nearly one metre deep, with a U-shaped base. The pit had been truncated by later ploughing, so had probably originally been quite a bit deeper. The south-eastern side had been badly damaged by large tree roots and animal burrows. This pit was half-sectioned, meaning that all the material filling one half of the pit was carefully removed to leave a vertical slice through its contents (Fig 3.32). The first and lowest fill of the pit (2035) was sandy, but contained concentrations of burnt clay, charcoal and silt and a large quantity of worked flint, mostly found in an area of more charcoal-rich material within the fill. Of the 64 worked flint fragments collected, two were identified as small serrated cutting blades, probably later Mesolithic (c. 8/7000-4000 BC), or possibly early Neolithic (c. 4000-3300 BC). The upper pit fills (2024 and 2025) were very similar and produced 31 worked flints of which three had been re-touched to form blades or flake tools.

The soil samples from the pit fills produced considerable amounts of charcoal, together with some very well-preserved hazelnut shell fragments. All of the charcoal was of either oak or hazel, with oak dominating. This suggests that people were gathering fuel and nuts from surrounding mixed deciduous woodland, which probably included some more open areas. The excellent condition of the nut shells and charcoal in the lowest layers suggested that, probably in the Neolithic, people were disposing of the remains from hearths that had been constructed close by, straight into the pit. Radiocarbon dating on burnt material from these deep layers produced an interesting result: two dates on hazelnut shell spanned the ranges 3030–2890 cal BC (SUERC-51280) and 3090–2890 cal BC (SUERC-51281), within the later Neolithic. However, the date on hazelnut charcoal from the charcoal-rich deposit found higher up (2025) was *earlier*: in the middle Neolithic 3350–3010 cal BC (SUERC-51283). This reversal of dates and the mixture of flint tools from two distinct periods probably arose because, after the pit was dug in the early-middle Neolithic period, the people collecting up and burying burnt hearth debris and other waste from that period also swept up worked flint fragments and charcoal from an earlier phase of human activity. People had been gathering food and fuel, making tools to cut and scrape food and raw materials, and lighting fires and cooking, close by the pit during at least two distinct periods.

The tree-throw

The tree-throw to the north of the trench [2022] was sub-circular and shallow, with very uneven, root-disturbed and undercut edges (Fig 3.33). The lowest sandy fill (2032), contained only three fragments of flint debitage, and was probably comprised of surrounding soil eroding and settling into the hole after the tree had fallen. Subsequently the tree-throw was filled in with slightly organic sand (2021) and this layer also contained a little pottery and worked flint. Two sherds of pottery – one early-middle Anglo-Saxon and one Medieval – were swept in from the surrounding ground with two fragments of flint debitage. The contents of the environmental samples were sparse, and the charcoal and burnt plant remains heavily degraded, suggesting the tree-throw was on the margins of activity in the dated periods or that material had been blown in from nearby burning. A single

barley grain from the lowest layer returned a radiocarbon date of cal AD 01–140 (SUERC-51282), so some of that activity took place in the Romano-British period. The layers within the tree-throw were so disturbed that is difficult to suggest when the tree toppled – although probably not much before the early Roman period indicated by the radiocarbon date – or when the hole was finally filled in, but the process may have happened quite quickly. The pottery found in the uppermost layer was most likely worked into the top of the fill of the tree-throw by Medieval ploughing.

The plough-soils

Plough-soils sealed the pit, tree-throw and tree-root channels. There were three broad layers: the sandy subsoil (2014-2020) below the grass of the recreation ground, and a lower and upper plough-soil (contexts 2008-2013 under 2001-2006). On excavation these soils had been divided up into four equal parts in the main trench and two in the extension to keep better control over the location of the finds. Most of the flint finds came from the disturbed upper fills of the two large cut features that had been ploughed up into the subsoil.

Together the two plough-soils clearly represented a remnant Medieval plough-soil; the ploughing had probably disturbed Romano-British and early-mid Anglo-Saxon archaeological remains, before being further reworked by nineteenth-century ploughing. 68 sherds of Romano-British pottery were fairly evenly distributed between the plough-soil layers. 76 sherds of rarer, hand-made, Anglo-Saxon pottery from the sixth to ninth-centuries were concentrated in the lower plough-soil, where they may have survived better. Finding so many sherds of this fragile

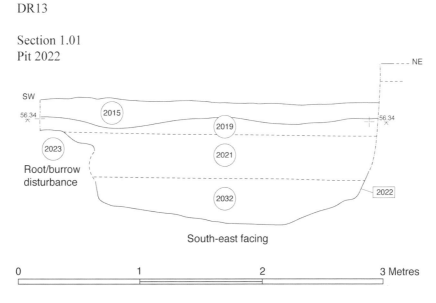

DR13

Section 1.01
Pit 2022

Fig. 3.33. Drawing of half-sectioned tree-throw [2022], section 1.01.

Fig. 3.34. Completed trench looking west, Neolithic pit at top of image.

pottery in such a small excavation (Fig. 3.34) suggested a settlement from that period had been, if not within the footprint of the trench, then very close at hand.

Summary of the finds

Olaf Bayer and David Griffiths

Reports with listings on lithics by Olaf Bayer, pottery by Paul Blinkhorn, and on iron finds by Ian R. Scott can be found in the ORA online archive for Chapter 3.

Of the 338 lithic artefacts were recovered during excavations at Donnington Recreation Ground, the majority (238) were unstratified, coming from the overlying plough-soil and top-soil. 95 lithic artefacts were recovered from the fills of western pit [2028] and a further five came from the fills of the northern pit or tree-throw [2022]. With the exception of a single piece of quartz from [2022], all lithic artefacts were struck from flint. Where present, cortical surfaces suggest that most of their raw material was derived from *in situ* chalk-flint or clay-with-flints deposits, and must therefore have been imported over distances of at least tens of kilometres. A much smaller portion of the raw material was derived from more locally available water-worn 'pebble' flint.

A combination of typological and technological analyses, and differences in artefact patination, indicate the presence of two distinct phases of stone working within the assemblage. The first phase probably dates to the late Mesolithic Period (c. 8/7000 –4000 BC), or less probably the early Neolithic (4000-c. 3300 BC). The second probably dates to the mid to late Neolithic (c. 3300 BC–2500 BC). It is likely that later material is contemporary with the three radiocarbon dates from the western pit [2028], which span 3350-3010 to 3090–2890 cal BC. We suggest that this later component of the assemblage is contemporary with the creation of pit [2028], and that the fill of this pit incorporated residual traces of *earlier* Mesolithic or early Neolithic activity, presumably derived from the surrounding land surface. The relative lack of lithic finds from northern pit or tree-throw [2022], particularly its lower fills, calls into question its date. Approximately 14% of the lithic assemblage shows signs of burning. This proportion of burning is consistent across both components of the assemblage and is considered likely to reflect accidental burning in a hearth.

The composition of the assemblage indicates that in addition to the manufacture, use and discard of stone tools, a range of cutting and scraping tasks were carried out in the immediate area of the site during both periods evidenced. Notable artefacts include:

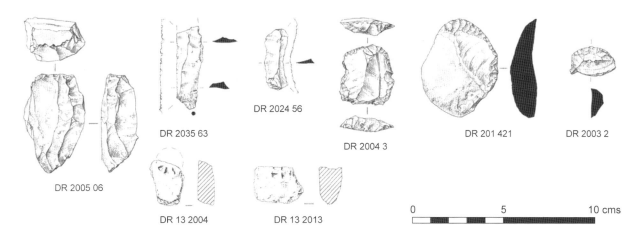

Fig. 3.35 Selection of the finds. Drawings by J. Wallis. **Upper row**: 2005 (6) Opposed-platform blade core of probable late Mesolithic date. 2035 (63) Serrated blade of possible late Mesolithic or early Neolithic date. 2024 (56) Serrated blade of possible late Mesolithic or early Neolithic date. 2004 (3) Double-ended and side scraper of probable Neolithic date. 2014 (21) Side and end scraper of probable Neolithic date. 2003 (2) Snapped scraper of probable Neolithic date. **Lower row**: 2004, Anglo-Saxon pottery fabric F2. Stamped sherd. Black fabric with a light brown inner surface. 2013, Anglo-Saxon pottery fabric F2. stamped sherd. Black fabric with a light brown inner surface.

- Context 2005 (SF 6), an opposed-platform blade core of probable late Mesolithic date from which long narrow flint blades were made.

- Contexts 2035 (SF 63) and 2024 (SF 56), serrated blades of possible late Mesolithic or early Neolithic date, possibly used for extracting plant fibres.

- Contexts 2004 (SF 3), 2014 (SF 21) and 2003 (SF 2), scrapers of probable Neolithic date used for cleaning hides or wood-working.

The pottery assemblage comprised 608 sherds with a total weight of 2,209g, the earliest among which are six Iron Age sherds, and 75 Roman sherds. The rest of the pottery assemblage is dominated by Anglo-Saxon and Medieval wares. 76 sherds of Early/Middle Anglo-Saxon hand-made wares are a significant find, and represent one of the largest excavated groups of pottery from this era within East Oxford. Two sherds from contexts 2004 and 2013 (Fig. 3.35) have stamp decoration associated with a sixth-century date. These are similar to pottery found at the Oxford Science Park excavation near Littlemore, which was associated with sunken-featured buildings.[3] The Anglo-Saxon sherds from Donnington are residual in plough-soils, but their presence and number implies the relatively near proximity of a settlement, possibly on the gravel terrace immediately to the north of the site.

The Medieval pottery assemblage is typical of the range of pottery types utilized in the Oxford region from the mid-eleventh to fourteenth centuries. It is all highly fragmented and apparently the product of secondary deposition, with the bulk redeposited in nineteenth-century plough-soils. The assemblage is dominated by Brill/Boarstall wares, mainly in the form of sherds from glazed jugs, although rim sherds from a bottle and a jar were also present. The lack of later Medieval Brill/Boarstall fabrics is paralleled by the absence of 'developed' late Medieval vessel types such as dripping dishes and bung-hole cisterns, which confirms that there was probably no activity at the site after the fourteenth century. The rest of the Medieval assemblage consists largely of fragments of unglazed jars in fabrics such as Cotswold-type wares, Medieval Oxford Ware and North-East Wiltshire Ware. A few fragments of glazed Medieval Oxford Ware tripod pitchers, a typical late eleventh to twelfth century vessel type, were also present. The post-Medieval assemblage comprises as small number of small sherds, and seems very likely to be the product of manuring, suggesting that the site has largely been used as agricultural land since its abandonment in the fourteenth century.

There were also 54 iron objects (58 fragments) which includes 37 nails, mainly from ploughsoil and topsoil contexts. Among these was a fourteenth-century barbed and socketed Medieval iron arrowhead, two horseshoe nails, two refitting fragments of thin strip or binding and an L-shaped staple or holdfast. The nails are mainly from plough-soil contexts (2002) and (2003). There are six miscellaneous pieces include a plain iron ring, strip, wire and sheet.

Conclusion

This small excavation confirmed some aspects of our interpretation of the geophysics, but also added new and unexpected information. This relatively flat area of Thames gravels, now used as a recreation ground, had been repeatedly visited and used in Prehistory, as was the area of Iffley Fields around Fairacres Convent, only 500m to the north, where many Mesolithic, Neolithic and Early Bronze Age flint tools have been discovered. The geophysical survey raised hopes that there was a curved line of pits, possibly all of Neolithic date. Whilst there is good evidence of human activity in the area in prehistory, on the present limited evidence we must stop short of interpreting this cluster of anomalies as being part of a Neolithic ritual monument, such as 'Site IV' at Dorchester-on-Thames.

The light and sandy soils close to the confluence of Boundary Brook with the Thames continued to attract farming and settlement from the Romano-British, through the Anglo-Saxon and Medieval periods. Pottery finds suggest that an Anglo-Saxon dwelling lay in the immediate vicinity. Just like the Fairacres gravel ridge to the north, this area beside the Thames was for millennia a good and productive place to live and work.

Notes

1   A representative form of depicting stratigraphic relationships, named after Edward Harris who invented the technique whilst digging in Winchester.
2   Blinkhorn in Moore 2001.
3   Moore 2001.

Chapter 4

St Bartholomew's (Bartlemas) Chapel, surveys and excavations

Jane Harrison, with Ruth Barber McLean, Pam England, Sarah Franks, Christopher Franks, Nathalie Garfunkle, David Griffiths, Graham Jones, Christopher Lewis, Rob McLean, Leigh Mellor, Gill Mellor, Steve Nicholson, Paul Rowland, William Wintle and Swii Yii Lim

St Bartholomew's Chapel, commonly known as Bartlemas, lies to the north of Cowley Road in the heart of East Oxford. The chapel is part of the Diocese of Oxford, and the parish of St Mary and St John, Cowley. It stands within a rood of church land (equal to 0.25 acre, or 0.10 hectare) surrounded by land owned by Oriel College, Oxford, with playing fields and gardens to its north and west, and allotments to its east and south (Fig 4.1). Surrounded by green space, trees, and isolated from the traffic and hubbub of Cowley Road, Bartlemas now feels like a sanctuary, but this calm belies a past marked at times by disease, conflict and neglect. The documented history of the site begins with the foundation of a leper hospital by Henry I in the mid-1120s.[1] One of the most historic places in East Oxford, Bartlemas and its landscape became a key research target for the *Archeox* project. We initially researched the site and its environs using documentary research, test pits, and geophysics. Following a request to assist with ground preparations for a drainage scheme (see below), we excavated three trenches, surrounding the chapel, and to its west and south, in October and November 2011 (Site code BC11, Trenches 1-3). Subsequently a further test pit (TP 72) was dug in 2013, to enable the re-interment of human remains found during the 2011 excavation.

Bartlemas and its landscape

The Bartlemas cluster of historic buildings, in their secluded and peaceful enclave, are today largely hidden from view, and many local residents are unaware of their existence or historical value.[2] Approaching the site up a narrow lane leading northeast from Cowley Road between gardens and allotments, Bartlemas Farmhouse appears on the left. The farmhouse (Fig. 4.2) is an appealing jumble of styles: the central range dated by dendrochronology (dating of structural wood) to the early sixteenth century, with later additions from the seventeenth,

eighteenth and nineteenth centuries.[3] The southern lower wing may be earlier, perhaps a surviving section of the hospital chaplain's house.

To the right of, and perpendicular to the lane is Bartlemas House (Fig 4.3), a double-fronted stone house of simpler and more symmetrical style than the farmhouse. This very probably stands on the site, and may echo the size and plan, of the Medieval leper hospital's infirmary; it was substantially rebuilt in 1649 after damage caused during the English Civil War, but has remained virtually unchanged since then. At the heart of this small group of buildings is St Bartholomew's or Bartlemas Chapel, built around 1336, to replace a previous chapel, which was by then in poor repair. It is small, single-chambered, rectangular and buttressed, built in pale yellow limestone, with a steep roof (reconstructed in 1649 and renovated in the 1920s) rising above the trees (Fig 4.4). A simple belfry aperture is located near its apex above the west door, and there are five windows of varied styles and sizes, including four with Medieval gothic stone tracery (Fig. 4.5).

Lawns surround the Chapel to the west, south and east, with thicker vegetation and trees encroaching to the south. Two large yew bushes stand to the left and right of the west door, and the landscaped garden of Bartlemas House lies to the north of the entrance path. A substantial limestone wall curves around the chapel site to the south and east. This wall is almost certainly Medieval in date, and it is evident on an 1840 estate map held in Oriel College's archives (Fig 4.6), it also appears on a sketch of the farm buildings of roughly the same date (Fig. 4.28) and is clearly visible in a photograph taken by Henry Taunt around 1900 (Fig. 4.29). Now covered in ivy and barely visible or accessible through the dense undergrowth, it includes some impressive masonry with stones of nearly a metre in length.

Bartlemas lies on a gentle south-west facing slope. As was all too apparent with project volunteers struggling to excavate hard-baked ground in a

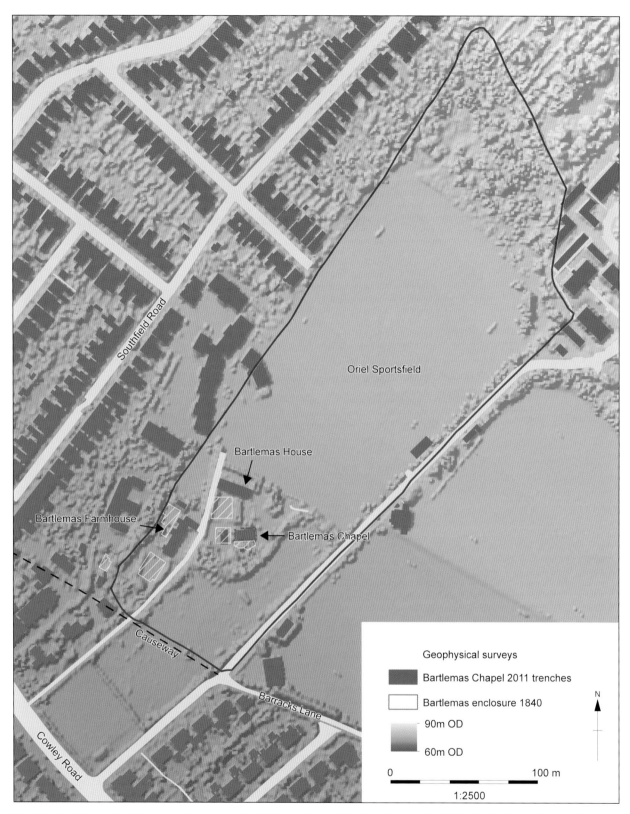

Fig. 4.1. Bartlemas location map (Base mapping © Crown Copyright/database right 2012. An Ordnance Survey/EDINA supplied service. Topography © Environment Agency copyright and/or database right 2019. All rights reserved).

wonderfully warm early autumn in 2011, the chapel sits on clayey ground, but this gives way to sandier soils about 300 metres upslope to the north-east. The junction of permeable and impermeable surface geology creates a natural spring-line within a plantation to the north-east, above Oriel College's playing fields. Many people believe that this spring line marks the site of the holy well which attracted the lepers. Water rising here feeds a ditch which leads downslope and its line marks the western margin of

Fig. 4.2. Bartlemas Farmhouse, east-facing frontage.

Fig. 4.3. Bartlemas House, south-facing frontage.

the Bartlemas enclosure. Visible on the 1840 map, this minor water-course was evidently one route by which fresh water was provided to the site, and perhaps effluent taken away. However, a curved water feature marked in blue on the 1840 map to the east of Bartlemas House indicates there was a second source of water nearer to the chapel, and this is the other obvious candidate for the probable site of the holy well. This water feature may once have been a Medieval fishpond, but has been altered in recent years, and in 1990 was recreated and sealed to form a walled ornamental garden pond. The persistence of the groundwater here has helped to cause the damp

problems in the north-east corner of the chapel which led to the 2011 investigations.

When the modern pond feature was created in the eastern grounds of Bartlemas House in 1990, there was an archaeological excavation conducted by Brian Durham of the Oxford Archaeological Unit. A possible later Medieval bank and ditch was discovered, following a similar alignment to the southern boundary wall of the chapel enclosure (also echoing the line of the original main road).[4] This ditch contained fifteenth-century pottery, and ran between Bartlemas House and the chapel, hence it may have been part of a late Medieval reconfiguration of the site. Perhaps it was

Fig. 4.4. Bartlemas (St. Bartholomew's) Chapel, from north-west.

Fig. 4.5. Chapel 3-D exterior scan, viewpoint from south-west, conducted by *Archeox* in conjunction with Mollenhauer Group, 2011.

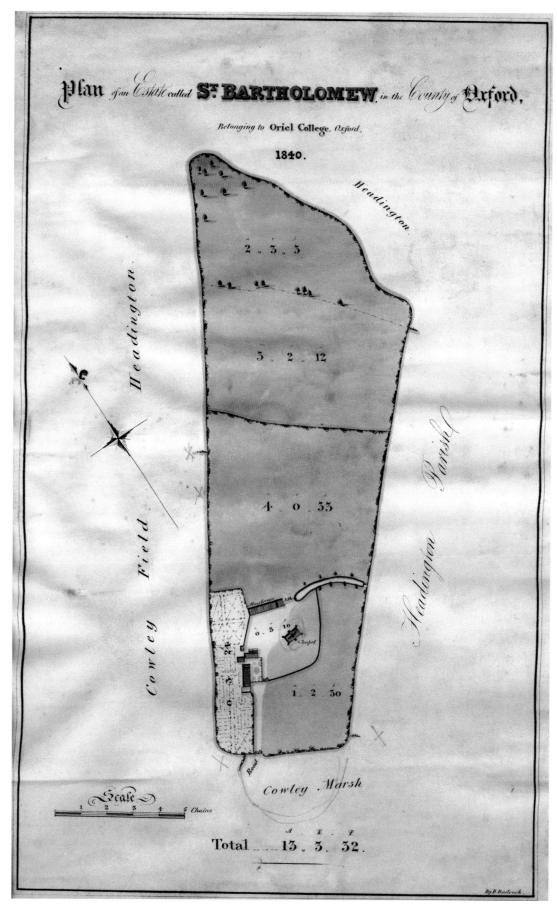

Fig. 4.6. 1840 Estate Map © Oriel College, Oxford, showing the chapel in its enclosure, the adjacent buildings and water feature.

created, once the change in purpose from hospital to almshouse had become established, more clearly to separate the two buildings.

The Medieval community at Bartlemas was established outside the city in a favoured place. The antiquarian Anthony Wood recorded the agreeableness of the breezy, rural location shaded by fine groves of trees; it was certainly in demand from the fourteenth century as a tranquil refuge for ailing Oriel dons from the bustle and dirt of Oxford. The land surrounding the hospital extended to six acres and the hospital brethren were responsible for cultivating it, growing cereals, including rye and barley. They kept doves and raised livestock, probably cattle, sheep and pigs. The ground surface around the chapel enclosure was altered and built-up over the centuries to improve drainage and develop fertile soils for the gardens. Until the nineteenth century, a road leading east from Magdalen Bridge towards Bullingdon Green ran past Bartlemas, on a route closer to the chapel than the modern line of Cowley Road. It is still visible in the neighbouring allotment site as a slight linear rise forming a causeway across the northern edge of Cowley Marsh (the southern boundary of the Bartlemas Estate on the 1840 plan (Fig. 4.6) follows its line), and it continues east along the bridleway known as Barracks Lane.

A brief history of Bartlemas

St Bartholomew's Hospital was founded in 1126 or 1127 by Henry I for twelve lepers and a chaplain. It was certainly in existence by 1129 when it is recorded in the Pipe Roll.[6] Henry gave the six acres of land on the south-western edge of his royal manor of Headington and, as Henry was also having Beaumont Palace built on the northern edge of the city, it is possible that surplus building stone from that enterprise was used at the hospital. Another original annual royal donation is recorded: two loads of hay from the king's meadows at Oseney,[7] so the hospital evidently possessed cattle, sheep or horses from its beginnings. Other donors gave land and financial bequests and, although Bartlemas was never rich, until the documented mismanagement of the later-thirteenth into fourteenth centuries, it was probably a reasonably secure foundation. Its location on the road leading east to and from Oxford allowed it to make an income from pilgrims, and it possessed a collection of saintly relics including a piece of the skin of St Bartholomew (see page 144). The hospital was assisted by papal edict from Gregory IX in 1238 when it was granted immunity from paying tithes (or tax-in-kind) on garden produce, copse wood and any increase in its herds of animals. Indirectly we can infer the

Fig. 4.7. Conjectured reconstruction of Bartlemas Chapel and it surroundings during the Leper Hospital period, from west. Artwork by Helen Ganly.

presence of gardens, of access to fire wood, probably from the nearby Forest of Shotover, as well as from its own groves.

By the early fourteenth century the hospital had entered a difficult phase. The number of brethren had been reduced to eight, two of whom had to be healthy enough to carry out work on the estate. Leprosy had by this time declined in prevalence and those afflicted with the disease were perhaps less likely to attract patronage. In 1330, its income was only seven pounds, excluding returns from the farm, and a succession of previous wardens had been accused of mismanagement and corruption. Adam de Weston was perhaps the worst offender, accused of neglecting the buildings, of retaining a concubine for his own comfort and of dismissing not only the servants who helped on the land, but, worse still, the chaplain, so depriving the brothers of spiritual solace. He had sold vital provisions – rye, malt, hay and straw – without consent. Again here was evidence for the farming context of the hospital: land to be worked and agricultural produce, either donated or harvested from its own acres, exploited in this instance for personal profit. Adam de Brome was appointed Warden in 1326, after more complaints by the brethren of maladministration. Two years later in 1328, Bartlemas was granted by Edward III to the new college which de Brome had founded in Oxford: the

College of the Blessed Virgin Mary, known as Oriel. The chapel was rebuilt in 1336, and the hospital's saintly relics were eventually moved to the college. The last mention of lepers residing at the hospital among the brethren is recorded in the will of John de Vintner dated 1342.[8]

From 1328 onwards there were tensions about the purpose of Bartlemas. The take-over by Oriel led to disagreements between the civic authorities in Oxford and the college about who should be making use of its facilities. In 1367 Oriel complained to the king that the hospital brethren were disobedient to them, and in response the king ruled that they were to live chastely, wear their habits outside, and not to admit any who were married or in debt.[9] Although there are records of considerable but unspecified repairs undertaken to the buildings in the fifteenth century, revenue from Bartlemas may well have been diverted to benefit Oriel. Increasingly used as an almshouse and less so as a hospital, the history of the site next faced serious upheaval in the seventeenth century, when it was reported by Anthony Wood as having suffered greatly during the English Civil War sieges of Oxford during 1644–1646. Royalists cut down a grove of elm trees north of the site and burnt down the almshouse, perhaps as part of their scorched earth approach to reducing the chance of Parliamentarian ambush and encampment. The Chapel was also reported as

Fig. 4.8. Henry Taunt's photograph of the Chapel, circa 1900: HT3004 © OHC.

damaged when, despite the Royalist efforts, Parliamentarians set up camp on site: probably during the third siege of 1646. Wood declared the Chapel was 'ruinated almost to the ground' with the lead stripped from its roof to make musket balls.[10] In 1645 the Warden's house (Bartlemas Farmhouse) had been let out as an alehouse, providing an additional attraction for the soldiers. After the sieges, the chapel was restored and re-roofed in 1651 (a date commemorated on the carved wooden roodscreen) and the almshouse rebuilt in its present form (Bartlemas House).

Disputes between college and town about the management of Bartlemas continued to grind on, and its role never seemed entirely settled or secure. After the chapel had been used as a cholera ward in 1832, during an epidemic that struck St Clements especially hard, the buildings were used as a farm (Fig. 4.8), although a few college individuals seem also to have continued in residence. It is clear that despite the conflict and disputes, the land had remained viable for agriculture. Towards the end of the nineteenth century, almsmen no longer lived on site and the obsolete foundation was dissolved. In 1913 the chapel with its rood of surrounding land was transferred to the care of the Church of England and the parish of SS Mary and John. By that time the city had expanded to surround the estate. The houses and their gardens are now privately owned, but Oriel College retains the remaining land, including the playing field and allotments.

Drainage work around the perimeter of St. Bartholomew's Chapel 2011

For some years prior to 2011 the chapel had suffered increasingly from damp penetration to the floor and walls, particularly to the north and east. In July 2005 pluvial flooding threatened to lap over the north door threshold when the single drainage gully east of the door was overwhelmed. This was due to changing climate and new building development and landscaping to the north of the site interfering with natural age-old underground watercourses in the area, exacerbated by root creep from the undergrowth. The church architect recommended that a pebbled filled trench should be dug around the perimeter of the chapel, with edging to keep the undergrowth back from the walls. He also recommended laying drainage pipes along the north and east side of the chapel running into a large soakaway positioned down slope to the southeast of the chapel. *Archeox* gained permission from the Diocese to hand-dig parts of the proposed drainage trenches surrounding the chapel to investigate for earlier foundation and possible burials, before the pipelaying and backfilling. This partnership of drainage works and community archaeology excavations proved extremely successful for both parties and produced

new and exciting insights into the long and varied history of this extraordinary and historic place.

Investigations before the excavation

We aimed to discover more about the landscape setting of the Chapel and to add to what was known about the history of the chapel and other buildings on the site. There were some specific questions: we know the chapel was rebuilt in 1336, so what type of structure existed before this? There must have been a graveyard, but where were the bodies? It was strongly suspected that the ground within the chapel precinct must have contained burials but there had as yet been no archaeological confirmation of this. In 1708, grave-diggers working immediately to the east of the present Chapel had discovered a stone vault containing three skulls and many other bones.[11] Thus a grave was being prepared for at least one person in the enclosure at the beginning of the eighteenth century, which disturbed earlier and presumably relatively important interments in a vault, but nothing more definite was known about burial around the chapel – it was not even known whether lepers had been buried at the site.

The western ditch and fields outside

Redevelopment of the site of a former nursery school immediately west of Bartlemas Farmhouse but outside the south-west to north-east running boundary ditch required some archaeological work (by Oxford Archaeology) in 2008 and 2010.[12] The stream's ditch-bound route for that stretch was likely the original one as discussed above. Very little was found in these investigations, but the evidence suggested the area of land immediately west of the leper hospital site had been a ploughed field for some considerable time, perhaps since the Roman period. Although a small investigation across the boundary ditch carried out during those works produced no pre-eighteenth century finds, the ditch had clearly been recut, and probably several times. A test pit on the eastern bank of the ditch (TP 18) produced both Medieval and Roman pottery and further evidence for re-cutting and maintenance of the ditch in the past.

Archaeological recording in the Links Allotments to the east and south

The neighbouring allotment site provided an opportunity to explore the landscape east of the chapel. Students from OUDCE recorded the ridge and furrow which is still faintly discernible when following the network of grassy paths dividing up the allotments south of the chapel. As mentioned above, an earlier causeway along the edge of Cowley Marsh carried a road out from Oxford south-east and ran closer to the chapel than the modern Cowley Road. The route of the causeway can still be traced crossing the allotments and running north-west to south-east about 60m south-west of the now-ruined and overgrown chapel enclosure wall. Its camber is still evident, and the buried stones of the road surface continue to pop up in the garden topsoil along its course.

Two test pits were dug in the allotments (TPs 30 and 31). Test pit 30 was located east of the chapel boundary wall as it runs north-east, and almost level with the east end of the chapel. Lots of fragmentary nineteenth- and twentieth-century pottery testified to the recent work of farmers and allotment holders, but there were also some large, crisp-edged sherds of Medieval pottery in the clayey soils, as well as pig and sheep bone. This supported the hypothesis that this northern area of the allotments had not been ploughed in the Medieval period and was perhaps an orchard, or area with outbuildings. Test pit 31 was dug just south of the chapel boundary wall and was probably on the margin of the ploughed field to the south. Finds were only discovered in one disturbed layer and the pottery, although mostly nineteenth- and twentieth-century, included some from the

preceding two centuries. In neither location was the land as built up as immediately around the chapel.

Surveys and test pits around Bartlemas Farmhouse

In 2009, OUDCE students carried out a geophysical survey in the farmhouse gardens. Immediately behind the house they picked up the paths of the formal garden visible on the 1840 estate map (Figs 4.6, 4.10). TP 17 was dug in the back garden of Bartlemas farmhouse and revealed deep, disturbed layers of clayey soils mixed with domestic rubbish. The layer immediately above the natural clay may have been a Medieval ground layer: it was much more homogenous and included some Medieval pottery.

Test pit 4, dug in the front lawn east of the farm-house, was one of the few test pits that uncovered *in-situ* building remains. A stoutly-built wall was uncovered on an alignment that would have joined the farmhouse barn to the north with the original course of the approach track to the chapel from the earlier causeway to the south. This established a different boundary from that on the 1840 estate plan and indeed the gravel of a nineteenth-century garden

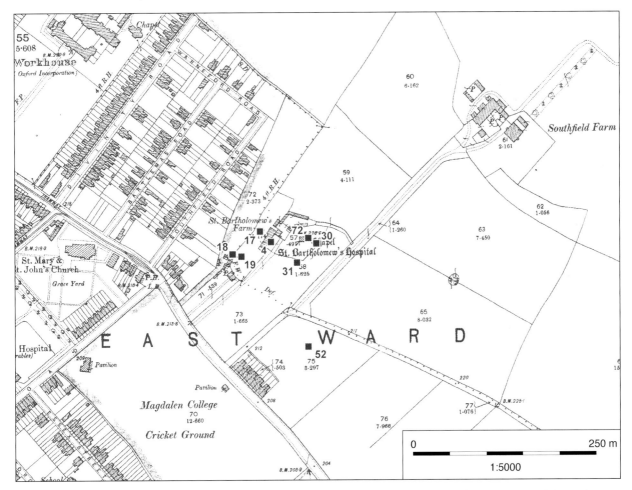

Fig. 4.9. Bartlemas test pit locations. Base Map 1900 Ordnance Survey 6 inch to the mile (© Crown Copyright and Landmark Information Group Limited 2014).

path covered the neatly dismantled wall. Most of the pottery was nineteenth and twentieth-century in date, with a small collection of post-1550 red earthenware sherds. The land in the front garden has been raised at some point, as the windows are below ground level, and the test pit itself produced yet more evidence for earth-moving and alterations on the site.

Two test pits, TP18 and TP19, were excavated in the gardens south-west of the farmhouse. TP18 was dug south of the point where, in the nineteenth century, the western stream ditch had been diverted west from its original Medieval course. The edge of the original backfilled ditch was discovered but, unfortunately, most of it was inaccessible under dense hedge-growth. A small ditch found feeding into the main north-east to south-west channel was similar to land drains discovered on the Nursery School site and may have marked the edge of a ploughed field to the north. The land into which the test pit was excavated was once near to a forge or smithy, and the soils and backfill of the land drain were packed with discarded iron fragments and slag. Unlike the test pits dug closer to the chapel, undisturbed clay was reached very quickly. Test pit 19 was dug just east of TP18 but within the hospital enclosure and, although there was also relatively modern smithing waste in the upper layers, the soils were deeper. In four of the five test pits eventually dug within the leper hospital's grounds (TPs 4, 17, 30 and 72) at least half a metre of built-up and redeposited ground was discovered before Medieval levels were reached. The land was probably being deliberately raised and altered for some time after the hospital was established.

Geophysical surveys within the hospital enclosure, close to the Chapel

For explanations of techniques, see Chapter 3, Part 2. Due to the confined exterior spaces around the buildings at Bartlemas, and the presence of many metal fences and other constraints, Gradiometry was of little use. The earth resistance survey done in 2009 however produced interesting results from west of the farmhouse (see above) and on the grassed area just west of the chapel (Fig 4.10). The higher, white coloured, patterns of response imply spreads of stone beneath the surface and intriguingly the shape of the response west of the chapel seemed to echo the outline of the west wall of the chapel and its buttresses. Either these are other structures beneath the lawn, or spreads of rubble resulting from

Fig. 4.10. Geophysical (earth resistance survey) results overview, by William Wintle. (Base mapping © Crown Copyright/database right 2012. An Ordnance Survey/EDINA supplied service).

demolition or reconstruction work. The results from the lawned area of the front garden of Bartlemas House, immediately to the north, also indicated possible walls and structures, which may well be the remains of nineteenth-century farm outbuildings which are just visible in Taunt photographs (see Fig. 4.29). Unfortunately, due to a difference in ownership and permission, no excavation work was carried out on the garden lawn.

Bartlemas: the 2011 excavation

The excavations followed in part the drainage scheme around the chapel detailed above, but also took in two further areas. Three trenches were excavated: Trench 1 ran around the chapel to one metre out from the walls; Trench 2 (Fig. 4.11) lay a few metres to the west of the chapel and was ten metres near north-south by maximum five metres, and Trench 3 (three metres by two metres) was positioned just over four metres south of the south-western stretch of the chapel wall. A long, narrow pipe trench extended south into the chapel yard (locations, Fig. 4.12).[13]

The excavations demonstrated how much destruction, rebuilding and change had happened over the centuries at Bartlemas: in all three trenches, but especially in Trench 1 around the chapel walls, the soils were packed with Medieval and later floor and roof tile fragments and building stone rubble – some

Fig. 4.11. Trench 2, working shot, from west.

of it with architectural detail. This substantiated the broad sequence already established: of neglect, rebuilding, ruination, rebuilding, decline and restoration. Most of the archaeological layers were very disturbed by later changes and the site had suffered from periodic water saturation. There was no evidence for major ground-raising work around the chapel before it was built, it may have been sited deliberately on a slight rise, but the area to the west had definitely been lowered sometime after its construction, perhaps when pigsties and other farm structures were cleared and the chapel reinstated for worship in the early twentieth century. All this activity meant that a great deal of the pottery was in poor condition, having been moved, crushed and worn, and that there was no material suitable for scientific radiocarbon dating preserved, apart from human bone. The archaeobotanical specialist summed up state of the small amount of charcoal surviving on the site as reflecting 'building activity, demolition and disturbance'.[14] Yet despite this, the excavations have added a great deal to the story of Bartlemas.

There were hints in the excavations of activity on the site before the hospital was founded. A small amount of Prehistoric worked flint and Roman pottery was recovered: there was probably settlement and some farming activity nearby, and there was also a Roman pottery kiln 500 metres to the south-east. Pottery found within the floor of a small, semi-sunken, timber building identified in Trench 2 west of the chapel (see below), included Cotswold-type ware (fabric OXAC, c.1050-1350), the earlier range of which could potentially indicate activity prior to the hospital foundation. This small building also lay on a different alignment to all subsequent structures, and so could possibly pre-date the hospital, even if it then carried on being used for a while after the arrival of the lepers. The building was levelled at some point before the later Medieval period, as burials from that time were cut into its infilled footprint.

1120s–1320s: St Bartholomew's Leper Hospital

Buildings

Trench 1, which surrounded the chapel, revealed limestone rubble wall-foundations and the bases of buttresses, which clearly pointed to the existence of an earlier, smaller stone-founded building, which we interpreted as an earlier chapel, indeed very probably

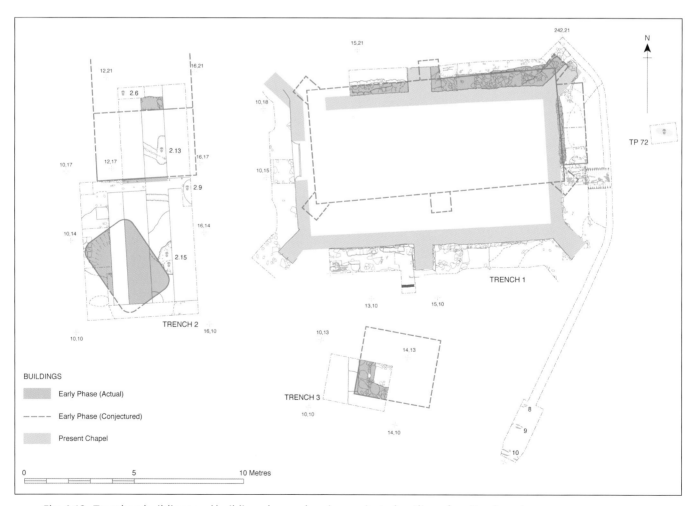

Fig. 4.12. Trenches, buildings and building phases, showing projected outline of earlier chapel.

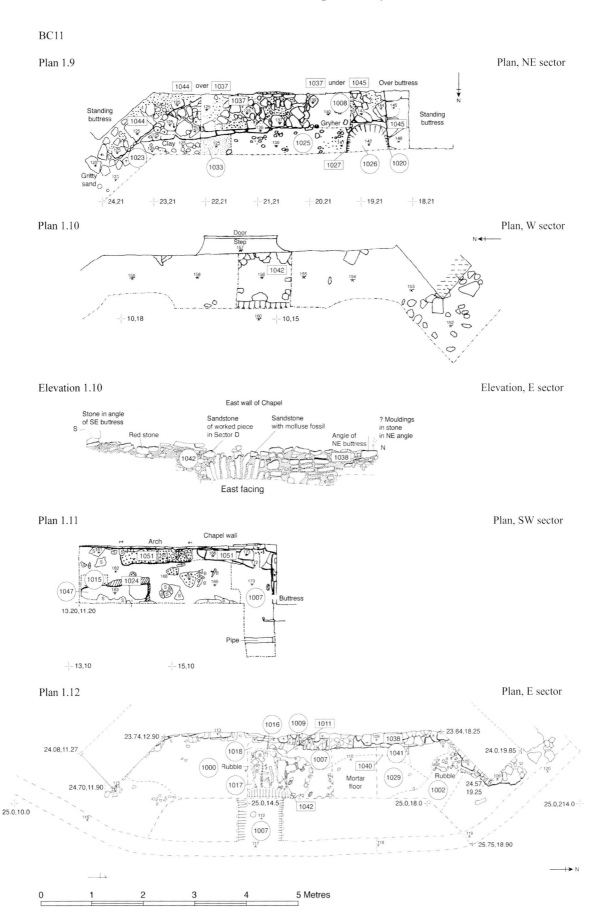

Fig. 4.13. Trench 1, surrounding the chapel, plans of early phase stone foundations.

the original chapel of the leper hospital. This structure was about four metres wide by no more than 11 metres long, and on a slightly different alignment to the current chapel. The earlier foundations project at most nearly a metre out from under the northern wall of the later chapel and appeared under and incorporated into its eastern wall and foundations (Figs. 4.13, 4.14). Although most of the building was clearly dismantled, five courses of secure foundation stonework were left to provide a base for the new, longer and wider building raised by Oriel College in 1336.

The possibility that the first hospital chapel could have been made of timber cannot be ruled out, but as this was a Royal foundation, it is more likely that the stone foundations encountered in Trench 1 do represent the initial twelfth-century chapel. At some point, an extension was erected against the eastern end. It was impossible to be sure of the size or shape of the addition but thirteenth-century pottery was associated with its fragmentary walls and surviving patches of floor. The stone foundations revealed on the north and east sides of the chapel also bore the scars of later disturbance. Post-holes had been sunk into the stonework, their spacing and location close to the standing chapel suggested these had held the bases of scaffolding poles, perhaps set up to aid construction of the fourteenth-century building, or possibly for the post-Civil War rebuilding.

The earlier chapel was not the only Medieval building to be identified by our excavations within the inner enclosure of the leper hospital. In the small Trench 3, to the south of the chapel, were discovered

Fig. 4.14. Foundations of the earlier phase chapel protruding from under the current N wall, from west.

Fig. 4.15. Wall foundations in Trench 3.

Fig. 4.16. Medieval Oxford Ware OXY, SF 46.

the remains of the corner of another masonry structure, which had probably been dismantled in the fourteenth century (Fig. 4.15). We could not be certain of the size of this building, but it may not have been much more than four to six metres square. The floor had been flagged with stone and very little was found within its floor layers to provide clues as to its purpose, except for a very few sherds of pottery (Fabric OXY; date range 1075-1300) and some fragments of human bone. This may have been a vault or ossuary, maybe even a small chapel, but a building discovered during excavations at the Hospital of St Mary Magdalen in Partney (Lincolnshire) founded by 1115, suggested an alternative.[15] There, a small detached stone building by the chapel was interpreted as a bell-tower. The Bartlemas brethren may have rung a bell for services, and to attract the attention of travellers on the road just to the south.

The remains of two smaller, less substantially-built buildings were found in Trench 2 west of the Chapel (see Fig. 4.12). One lay in the south of the trench and was presumably constructed from wood, or wattle and daub: this was the building mentioned above that may have been associated with a farm pre-dating the hospital. There were no stone foundations, but the small rectangular building (about four metres by two and a half metres) had been dug down slightly into the natural clay, with a roughly paved area outside to the north-west, probably by the door, and perhaps the start of a path. There may also have been a gravelled yard by the building, and the sunken footprint of the structure was partially lined with clay before at least one more floor was laid. The earliest surviving patches of undisturbed floor contained some of the earliest pottery on site including a large, crisp rim-sherd of OXY fabric pottery with the range c. 1075-1300,

which had probably escaped crushing, tucked into the corner of the building (Fig 4.16; SF 46).

With its north-west/south-east alignment, different to all the other buildings, this structure may just feasibly have existed before the establishment of the hospital. Alternatively, it might have served as one of the first leper cells. A fine pierced honestone or whetstone for sharpening tools or knives (SF 48, see page 135), as well as the scraps of everyday pottery cooking pots and jars indicate a practical and domestic space. Archaeobotanical samples from within and around the building contained abundant charcoal: perhaps from the remnants of domestic fires. The subsequent history of this building is very difficult to untangle as any subsequent and Medieval floors were either very disturbed or entirely removed by Civil War activity, and later yards and walls, so could not easily be dated. It is quite likely the small, wooden building was demolished by the later Medieval period, perhaps when the chapel was rebuilt by Oriel College in the early fourteenth century.

In the northern end of Trench 2, mortar-rich floors were discovered which dated from the leper hospital era, and are associated with the remains of stone-founded buildings. These seemed to follow a similar alignment to the first stone Chapel, either parallel to or at right-angles to the lie of the chapel. A short stretch of west-east aligned stone wall was found almost on a line extended west from the northern chapel wall and, lying parallel to that, another fragmentary, largely demolished wall about three metres to the south across an intervening floor. This building may have been an extension of another to the north, of which we only discovered a floor, or the southern part of a longer structure. The walls were relatively narrow so possibly supported a wooden or wattle and daub superstructure. Nothing in the pottery suggested these building were other than dwellings, perhaps the successors to the first leper 'cells', or the southern end of a longer range lying at right angles to the chapel. Again it is plausible that these buildings were radically altered or even demolished after Oriel College took over the hospital in 1328.

A relatively small collection of fragmentary animal bone can be related to this period.[16] The analysis of those bones revealed that meat was brought to site in large portions to be butchered further, then cooked and eaten. Only 36 of 275 fragments found in Trench 2 could actually be identified to species: these were cattle, sheep, pig and deer with in addition a few bird bones (mostly domestic fowl). Those living and working at the hospital were therefore eating beef, mutton and poultry. This diet, combined with the relatively utilitarian Medieval pottery implies, as might be expected, that the brethren were living relatively comfortably but far from extravagantly. More unexpected is the evidence for the consumption of pig and deer, indicating a more varied and perhaps higher-status diet. Does this reflect the food produced for the hospital's senior staff and patrons? The deer

may have been gifts or taken from the hunting forest of Shotover, which lies a short distance to the north-east. And indeed a barbed and socketed iron arrowhead of a type from as early as the thirteenth century and used in hunting was found in the Medieval layers at Bartlemas (SF 31, see page 135).[17] The pottery sherds came from ordinary domestic jars and cooking pots, sooty from use; the only more unusual vessels that may have been used during the lepers' time were slender Brill-Boarstall ware bottles for oil or vinegar. Were these perhaps vessels holding oils used in attempts at basic palliative care for the lepers? Other Medieval objects were found reworked by rebuilding into later layers and included quarter of a cut, voided long cross silver penny of Henry III, minted at Winchester and dating to 1248-50 (SF 37, see page 135).

Burials

Another of the research questions it was hoped the excavation could answer concerned the extent of Medieval burial at the site. Despite a reference to vault construction in the early eighteenth century, previously there was no conclusive evidence for graves in proximity to the chapel. However, our investigations

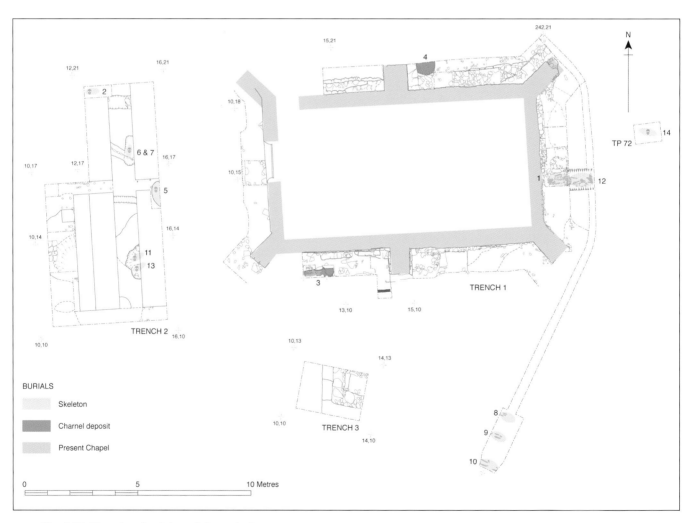

Fig. 4.17. Trenches, burials and charnel pits.

revealed that the walled chapel enclosure is almost certainly packed with burials, with some of the earliest having been disturbed by the construction of the current chapel in the fourteenth century (Fig. 4.17). Lepers had definitely been buried around the first stone chapel, perhaps mostly to the south of the building, but so over the centuries so were many other people, including children. The quantity of disarticulated human bone fragments found in the all the soils excavated in Trench 1 running around the chapel, and the discovery of inter-cutting graves, disturbed burials and two charnel pits – where loose bone was reburied – indicated the graveyard was well-used, but also perhaps at times not well-respected. The successive building works and non-religious use of the grounds – for example during the Civil War – had led to the digging up or turning over of many burials, parts of which were reinterred in the charnel pits.

The 'faculty' (permission) to excavate issued by Oxford Diocese stipulated that only disarticulated human remains could be removed from the ground, and that articulated remains (partial or complete skeletons) could be studied but were to be left *in situ*. Eleven articulated burials were uncovered, recorded and then reburied without disturbing the remains (Skeletons SK 1, 2, 5, 6-7, 8, 9, 10, 11,12, 13 and the

Fig. 4.18. Inhumation exposed in Test pit 72, east of the Chapel. North to right of image.

burial found in TP72). None of these were observed to be of lepers. But we know lepers were buried around the chapel, because bones bearing the marks of the disease were found in the back-fill of a later grave against the east wall of the chapel and in a charnel pit against the southern wall of the chapel. A leprous jaw-bone found in the fill of the burial east of the chapel was radiocarbon dated to 1013-1155 cal. AD (SUERC-49304), and must have come from someone who was buried at the hospital in its early years.[18] It is possible that the corner of a stone-lined grave found just on the edge of Trench 3 south of the chapel, and the original stone-lined grave [1024] into which the charnel pit against the southern wall was dug, were also from this earlier period.

One relatively undisturbed burial from the leper hospital period was discovered, in a test pit (TP72) dug after the excavations were complete (Fig 4.18). The faculty permission stated that any disarticulated human bone removed for study had to be reburied within two years. The reburial of the charnel human bone, in a wicker casket, took place on 9 November 2013 during an open-air service conducted by the parish vicar of Cowley St Mary and St John, with music selected to reflect the historical periods lived through by the people being re-interred. To bury the casket, another hole had to be dug east of the chapel, which became Test pit 72. Unsurprisingly, this came down on the central two-thirds of a west-east burial and a fragment of likely Medieval stone wall foundation (possibly relating to the eastern annexe of the chapel, or perhaps some form of vault).[19] There were no signs of leprosy on this skeleton, but it was radiocarbon dated to 1220-1298 cal. AD (SUERC-51233).[20] Not only did this test pit confirm that the cemetery was well-used but suggested that the officers of the hospital – chaplains and wardens – or patrons may have been buried to the east of the chapel. The rebuilding of the eastern end of the chapel after the Civil War probably disturbed other burials, as a considerable amount of disarticulated bone was recovered from the back-filled construction trench relating to that reconstruction work. Some of the skeletal elements collected from this wall-side location showed considerable amounts of compact bone on their surfaces, one of the characteristic indications of secondary infection from leprosy.

Bartlemas under Oriel College: c. 1328 to the English Civil War

This is the period of the site's history for which it was hardest to extract archaeological information: reworking of the layers by later building, landscaping and disturbance during the Civil War and Victorian periods had dispersed the evidence for these three

Fig. 4.19. Trench 2, working shot, from south-east.

hundred years. However, it is likely that Oriel College's take-over and subsequent rebuilding radically altered the layout of the chapel enclosure. The small buildings around the chapel were most probably levelled when the chapel was enlarged and rebuilt in 1336. There is no clear evidence for anything other than paths or possibly yard surfaces west of the chapel for this time. The ditch and bank found north of the chapel in 1990 and referred to above, may have been part of a new separation of the chapel and its immediate surroundings. The cemetery would then have resembled a more conventional graveyard, with fewer or no small buildings within its confines.

Buildings

In the rebuilding of the chapel in around 1336, the earlier chapel's foundations were re-used in the north and east by Oriel's masons, and thus survived. The incorporation of the east wall of the first chapel into the new building has been mentioned. This process also involved the construction of one of the three structural relieving arches discovered in the foundations of the fourteenth-century chapel: one in the reworked east wall and two in the new southern foundations (Fig 4.20, arch [1048] in the southern wall). These supporting masonry features helped to spread the weight of the walls over less stable areas and were perhaps built over patches of softer, wetter ground at

the site. The amount of building rubble recovered from Trench 1 around the chapel demonstrated the scale of the works undertaken over the site's history. Some of that rubble probably resulted from the fourteenth-century alterations as it included fragments of earlier Medieval roof tile. The cut for the new foundation trench of the 1336 chapel was visible to the south of the southern wall, and the back-fill of that trench (1004) contained many fresh sherds from a single and probably fourteenth-century Brill/Boarstall jug with 'metal copy'-style decoration.[21] The presence of this pottery and the structural integrity of the relieving arches suggested that, although there was some later disturbance to the uppermost level of the construction trench-fill, later post-Civil War reconstruction is most likely to have affected the upperworks, rather than the lower parts of the 1336 chapel.

Burials

There was more evidence for the use of the cemetery in this period, although some of the earlier burials of lepers may have been lost under the footprint of the larger chapel whilst others were disturbed by the alterations. The charnel pit just south of the chapel (the bones collectively SK3: Figs 4.17 and 4.21) was probably created to re-bury bones unearthed during the building of the 1336 chapel: they were dug in a coveted location under the eaves' drip and thus may

Fig. 4.20. Relieving arch [1048] in southern wall of chapel.

Fig. 4.21. Trench 1, Charnel pit 1015 (SK 3) to the south of the chapel.

have been seen as splashed by sanctified rainwater running from the chapel roof. This charnel pit re-used an earlier stone-lined grave and contained human bones with indications of leprosy, including a jaw-bone. Bones from at least five human skeletons had been re-interred together. There was some animal bone in the top layer. The upper back-fill of this charnel pit was disturbed again later, perhaps during the disruptive Civil War period, perhaps also during the subsequent reconstruction, and it is possible that the animal bone was added at that time.

Sometime after the current chapel was built, a robust young man with an extremely good set of teeth was buried lying west-east and supine (on his back) (SK 1), with his head very close to the east end of the chapel: so taking another coveted location for burial, this time in close proximity to the altar (Figs 4.17 and 4.22).[22] The grave was also partially stone-lined, making use of the remains of the stone foundations of the original eastern annex to create its northern side. The southern side of the grave was also partially stone-lined with rubbly limestone courses held together with rough lime-mortar. It is notable that both this burial and the thirteenth-century one found in Test pit 72 (see above) were stone-lined and re-used adjacent wall-lengths, suggesting an area of higher-status burial. SK1 was buried with his head up against the chapel and showed no signs of disease. Stable isotope analysis of a sample of his bone (see page 142) revealed that this man had eaten a more varied diet than some of the other people buried to the south and west the chapel. Whilst all of the nine skeletons whom we tested produced evidence of having eaten a typical terrestrial diet – cereal, plant and animals – SK1, interred at the east end of the chapel, and SK10, a skeleton encountered at south of the chapel at the far end of the drainage trench (see below), had probably also eaten fish and perhaps shellfish.[23] This, together with the site of his burial, led us to wonder if SK1 at least may have been either an official or a patron of the chapel. However, because the full length of his grave was not marked, or because pressure on space in the graveyard was so acute, another later burial had disturbed his resting place. Where this young man's knees and lower legs should have been was another grave cut with the skull of another skeleton (SK12, Fig 4.23) lying further to the east.

Brethren lacking the benefit of a prime position were buried a little further from the Chapel, and the evidence suggests they were in neat rows. When the soakaway for the new chapel drainage system was dug, extending to 11.6 metres south of the Chapel, the poorly preserved and fragmentary remains of three skeletons were discovered (Fig 4.17; Skeletons 8-10). These people had been laid to rest lying west-east and apparently in a closely packed row; Skeleton 9 was only c. 14-16 years at the time of death. Radiocarbon dates on two teeth from two adjacent skeletons gave dates of cal. 1388-1440 AD and cal. 1288-1399 AD.[24]

To the west of the chapel in the northern end of Trench 2, the legs of another skeleton, possibly buried during the same period, were uncovered lying just west of where the stone buildings had been in the previous period (SK 2). This person was also buried west-east and on their back and the grave had been dug from a similar ground surface to that of the three skeletons to the south. Two slightly different burials were also discovered in Trench 2 (Fig. 4.17, SK11 and 13). Their graves were dug into the edge of the south-eastern corner of the dismantled and filled-in semi-sunken building described above. Only the skull of the earliest burial in the north (SK13) was uncovered, but the position of the skull suggested that although the grave was aligned west-east the body had not been laid in it flat on its back. Parallel, slightly to the south and cutting into that grave was the resting place of Skeleton 11. This person had been buried with their hands tucked up by their turned head: the whole body may have been lying on its side, but we could not be certain as only the skull and upper arms were visible. Both graves may have been lined with charcoal and ash. The backfill of the later grave contained joining sherds of a thirteenth-to fourteenth-century jug, so these burials may have been from a broadly similar or perhaps slightly later period to the others, but following a different burial practice.

There were another two burials found in Trench 2 which indicated that burial practice became less

Fig. 4.22. Trench 1, SK 1, east of chapel, west at top of image.

Fig. 4.23. Trench 1, SK and SK 12, intercut east of chapel.

Fig. 4.24. Trench 2, Child burial SK 6-7.

orderly over time. Two child burials were discovered west of the chapel's western door (Fig. 4.17, SK 5 and 6–7). These were unexpected, as the official hospital brethren and college members should have been at least of teen age. Both interments were of very young individuals and both were buried aligned north-west to south-east rather than west-east; the burials were also relatively shallow compared to any others on site, except the charnel pits. The child in the northern of the burials (Fig. 4.24) was about five years old, and a line of upright stones erected to support an internal partition within a later building had cut across the grave and parted the skull (SK 7) from the rest of the body (SK 6). The second child skeleton (SK 5) was about six or seven, but part of the burial stretched outside the trench so that the upper body and skull were not seen. There was a tradition in Medieval England of burying unbaptised children secretly in consecrated ground: children who would otherwise be condemned to unchristian burial.[25] Were the Bartlemas children examples of this practice? If these were hurried, unsanctioned burials that would perhaps explain the unusual orientation and lack of depth. In the backfill of the older child's grave, touching the skeleton, were two large sherds of a delicate thin-walled Tudor Green Ware lobed cup, of fifteenth or early-sixteenth century date (Fig 4.25).[26] This fragile vessel would have been quite a luxurious item in its day and its presence suggested it was laid in the grave with the child. We do not know exactly when either child was buried, but a fifteenth- or sixteenth-century date would fit the sequence of the other archaeological evidence.

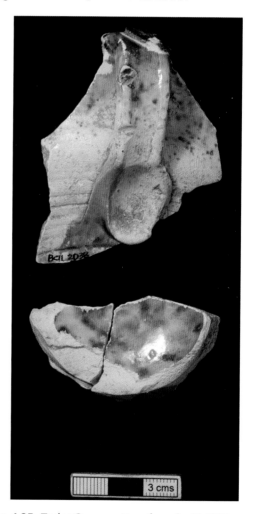

Fig. 4.25. Tudor Green pottery found with SK 5.

Bartlemas during and after the Civil War (1644–1651)

We know from Anthony Wood's accounts that Bartlemas was damaged and disrupted during the English Civil War, and unsurprisingly the archaeology shows activity and disruption immediately around the chapel during this period and in its aftermath. The evidence discovered also resonates more with an encampment of soldiers rather than those of a religious site: not only was the chapel damaged, but the graveyard was disturbed.

Some of the objects found around the chapel in archaeological layers of this period also accord well with a time of military occupation. Most of the animal bone evidence for cooking probably comes from this period and a concentration of worked bone found in Trench 3 might plausibly have been left by soldiers occupying their hands as they waited and smoked – clay pipes datable quite tightly to around the Civil War period were found in all the trenches. With smoking went drinking: the sherds of black-glazed drinking vessels or 'tygs' (fabric PMBL) mainly found in Trench 2 could have come from the alehouse established in the Farmhouse, or another such establishment nearby. This might also explain some of the German Frechen stoneware or 'Bellarmine' bottles or jugs which were also discovered on site. Wood reports that the lead roof of the chapel was stripped for making shot and several unfired lead musket balls were indeed discovered in the trenches (Fig. 4.26). The chapel was also reported to have been used as a stable, and part of an iron harness fitting was found in Trench 3; horseshoe nails were retrieved from Trenches 2 and 3, although these could relate to later periods. Also recovered from the disturbed upper backfill of the construction trench in Area D was a Nuremberg jetton: an inscribed coin-like token used in financial calculations (see page 135). It was unfortunately too worn to attribute it to a specific maker, but the style dated it to the sixteenth to mid-seventeenth centuries. Jettons were used to perform calculations in accounting, for example by traders, but plausibly also by army paymasters, or in gambling.

The fabric of the standing chapel bears witness to the damage inflicted by the Civil War. The upper foundations show evidence of patching and the non-matching window traceries may be the result of Oriel making repairs using stonework from the college's stock of worked stone elements salvaged from buildings elsewhere on its estates. However, it is impossible to be certain whether all of the walls were equally damaged and so of the exact extent of the post-Civil War rebuilding. And it does appear that more graves were disturbed, as the archaeological stratigraphy indicated that the charnel pit north of the chapel originated in the upheaval of the Civil War period and its aftermath (Fig. 4.27; bones collectively

Fig. 4.26. Three lead musket balls, probably manufactured on site.

SK4). Almost all of the long bones in the earlier charnel pit to the south of the chapel had shown characteristic signs of changes produced by secondary infection from leprosy; by contrast, there were very few signs at all of infection in the lower limb bones found in the earliest layer of northern pit. That lowest and original layer of bone in the pit, consisting mainly of long bones, was laid carefully and regularly, but a final and later layer was probably added when the pit was re-opened at a later date. The upper deposits had human bones jumbled in with cattle bones and a dog skull, but included two leg bones (femora) which show evidence of rickets, one of which was radiocarbon dated to cal.1635-1684 AD.[27] This bone along with three others have been drilled at their ends, presumably so a skeleton could be hung as part of an anatomical display (see page 141). The leg bones, which the radiocarbon date indicates are of a person who had died in the seventeenth century,

Fig. 4.27. Trench 1, working shot of charnel pit 1026 from east (bones collectively SK 4).

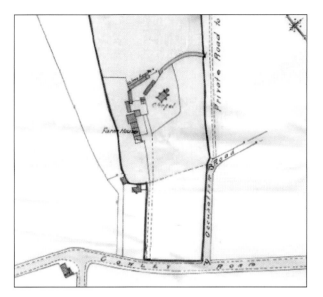

Fig. 4.28. Sketch of Bartlemas Farm, dated 1837, with smaller intermediate buildings since removed © Oriel College, Oxford.

could therefore have been used for display for some decades at least, and deposited long after their death. It should be noted in this regard that a surgeon named Samuel Glass is named in Oriel College's tenancy records as living in Bartlemas Farmhouse in 1771, although no connection with the interment of the bones can be proven.[28]

Bartlemas as a farm

The evidence for Bartlemas's more recent history concerns its period as a Victorian farm. Small, now vanished, buildings such as wooden sheds and pigsties

left slight traces in Trench 2, including stubs of walls and yard surfaces, while a lean-to building was erected against the east end of the chapel re-using some of the footprint of the Medieval extension in this position. This tiny annexe was marked on estate plans of the early nineteenth century (Fig. 4.28), and the roofs of small agricultural buildings and a caravan-type hut can also be seen in Henry Taunt's photograph of Bartlemas from around 1900 (Fig. 4.29). A wide, shallow wall footing from this later period was discovered running across the southern end of Trench 2, in a south-west to north-east orientation, temporarily dividing the space inside the chapel enclosure by joining the south-west corner of the chapel to the wall beside the lane. There was plenty of domestic pottery from the nineteenth century, and contexts from this period in Trench 2 produced a good deal of animal bone, which showed a considerable amount of mutton in particular was being eaten.

Summary of the finds

The objects found on the dig reflect the full history of Bartlemas,[29] with some interesting Medieval and post-Medieval objects including some probably related to the military occupation of the site during the English Civil War. There are also numerous objects from later periods with a spread of iron nails, broken crockery, clay pipe fragments and other discarded items, mainly from the chapel's time as part of a Victorian farm. As a Medieval ecclesiastical site which later saw lower-status agricultural use, there are similarities between the Bartlemas finds from 2011 and those from the following year's excavations at Minchery Paddock,

Fig. 4.29. Henry Taunt's photograph of Bartlemas (© Historic England), taken from south in adjacent field (now allotments) showing ridge and furrow (foreground) and sheds behind precinct wall.

part of Littlemore Priory (Chapter 5), although the latter excavation was more extensive and produced a more varied assemblage.

There is a small scatter of material from before the leper hospital, but nothing was retrieved from the 2011 excavation which points to significant occupation on this site before the twelfth century. Eight pieces of struck flint including one scraper of probably Neolithic or Early Bronze Age date imply some general activity in the Prehistoric landscape hereabouts, although no features from this long ago were detected in the trenches. The occurrence of 22 small and relatively worn sherds of Roman pottery is unsur-prising, given the local proximity of the East Oxford pottery industry: most excavations and test pits in East Oxford have produced at least some Roman pottery sherds. Among the finds from the excavations, there are some sherds of Late Anglo-Saxon or Saxo-Norman pottery (St Neots and Cotswold-type wares). These (Fig. 4.30) hint at possible occupation at the site before the hospital was founded, but are seen by John Cotter as typical of Oxford pottery assemblages of the time, and therefore could have been brought in as part of manuring scatters or with 'hard core' from elsewhere when the leper hospital was being built. The bulk of the Medieval pottery assemblage dates to the twelfth century or later, is mainly domestic in character, and is dominated by Oxford and Brill/Boarstall wares. There

are some items from further afield, perhaps reflecting the influence of longer-distance trade, travel or pilgrimage, including Tudor Green ware from Surrey or Hampshire, and two sherds of Raeren stoneware from Germany.

Highlights among the finds dating to the period of the leper hospital include a 'spearpoint' hunting iron arrowhead which could be from as early as the thirteenth century (Fig. 4.31) and a silver coin (a voided long cross penny) of Henry III, minted at Winchester, dating to 1248-50 (Fig. 4.32). The upper part of a pewter or lead-tin spoon handle (Fig. 4.31) with a decorative acorn knop is of a somewhat later Medieval date, probably from the fifteenth century.[30] Two hones or whetstones are also likely to be Medieval in date, one of which (SF 48) is a rather fine pierced example. A small but finely-turned bone object (Fig. 4.34) does not lend itself to easy identification but could be part of a musical instru-ment: dating it is difficult, but it could be from as early as the fifteenth century (a bone tuning peg, probably from a zither known as a psaltery, was found at Minchery Paddock, see Chapter 5).These Medieval finds come from Trench 2, where earlier layers were somewhat less disturbed than in the area immediately around the chapel (Trench 1).

Metal finds of the early post-Medieval period from Bartlemas include a Nuremberg jetton of the sixteenth

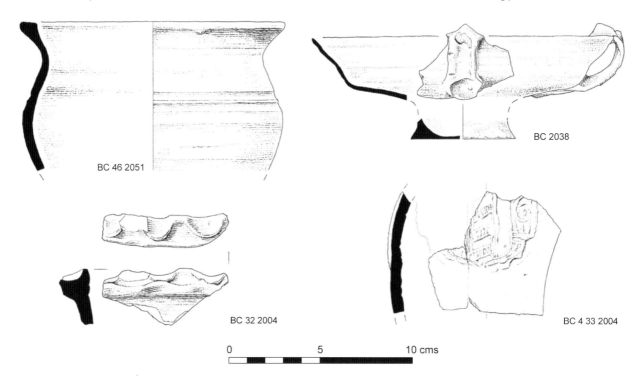

Fig. 4.30. **Top left:** Medieval Oxford ware pot, date c. 1075-1300, Context (2051), from layer associated with Medieval graves in the south of Trench. 2; **Bottom left:** Late Medieval Brill/Boarstall ware pot. dish/bowl rim with rare piecrust decoration, date 1575-1640, Trench 2, Context (2004); **Top right:** Tudor Green ware pot, splayed pedestal base, date c. 1380-1525, Trench 2, Context (2038) fill of grave containing skeleton SK5; **Bottom right;** Frechen stoneware pot: two joining body sherds from 'Bellarmine' jug with part of heraldic medallion (probably a German town or merchant), date c. 1600-1630, Trench 2, Context (2004). Drawings by J. Wallis.

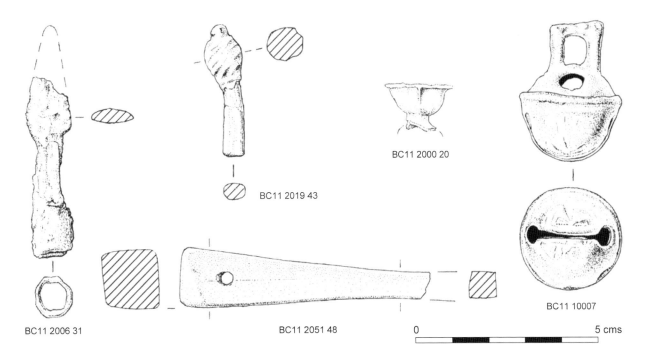

BC11 2000 20

BC11 2019 43

BC11 10007

BC11 2006 31   BC11 2051 48   0   5 cms

Fig. 4.31. **Left:** Barbed and socketed iron arrowhead, 'Spearpoint type', date: 1200-1400; Type 16 in *Museum of London Medieval Catalogue*.[33], Trench 2, Context (2006); **Centre, left:** Pewter or lead-tin spoon handle terminal with acorn knop, date: 1400-1600, Trench 2, Context (2019), surface exterior to buildings; **Centre, right:** Small lead or lead-tin bowl, with base broken off suggesting it was part of a larger object. Possibly a toy, or a lighting implement, or possibly a patten from a casting process, date, post-Medieval, Trench 2, Context (2000), topsoil; **Right:** Copper-alloy cast crotal bell with integral suspension loop, upper surfaces marked with bell-founder's hammer and initials WG (probably William Gwyn, 1770–1813). Trench 1, Context (1000 D), topsoil. **Bottom:** Pierced whetstone, tapered by wear from use, incomplete, Trench 2, Context (2051), layer over pit (2057). Drawings by J. Wallis.

Fig. 4.32. (obverse and reverse views) Cut quarter of a voided long cross silver penny of Henry III, minted at Winchester. Radius 0.9 cm, Weight 0.2g. Date: 1248-50. SF 37, Trench 2, Context (2017), a layer forming a rough external surface.

Fig. 4.33. (obverse and reverse views) Copper-alloy jetton, worn. Probably from Nuremberg. Rose and orb type, wording of inscriptions too worn to identify maker, date 1500-1650. SF 26, Trench 1, Context (1004 D), 17c disturbance to construction trench for 14c chapel.

Fig. 4.34. Turned bone cylinder with screw thread. Length 2cm, diam 0.9 cm. SF 22, Trench 2, Context (2004), surface immediately west of chapel.

Fig. 4.35. Four views of a copper-alloy cast crotal bell with integral suspension loop, upper surfaces marked with bell-founder's hammer and initials WG (probably William Gwyn, 1770-1813). Height 3.5 cm, diam 2.8 cm. SF 7, Trench 1, Context (1000 D), topsoil.

Fig. 4.36. Decorated glass button with metal suspension loop, date Victorian. SF 29, Trench 1 (Context 1000), topsoil.

to seventeenth century from Trench 1 (Fig. 4.33). Jettons are copper alloy counters or tokens produced in German city-states, which became relatively common at ecclesiastical sites in England in this period, and reflect the increasingly international trade patterns of the Tudor and early Stuart periods. They are often identifiable as minted by masters such as Hans Krauwinckel, but this example, whilst characteristic of the 'Rose and Orb' type, is unfortunately a little too worn to identify a clear maker attribution. Also from this period, or slightly later, is a tiny lead-tin bowl, from Trench 2, with a broken-off base, the exact purpose of which is unknown (Fig. 4.31). Geoff Egan lists miniature metal vessels from Southwark under the heading of toys, but none of the ones he illustrates is quite like this one.[31] An alternative explanation may be that this is part of a decorative lighting implement, possibly a candelabra. Small bowl-like objects were also used as patterns for casting bells and other objects.

Three lead musket balls from Trenches 1 and 2 (Fig. 4.26) are almost certainly evidence of military activity at Bartlemas during the Civil War occupation in the 1640s, indeed matching a description from Anthony Wood that the chapel roof was melted down for ordnance at this time.[32] Clay-pipe bowls, and a copper alloy buckle of the seventeenth century also date from, or just after, the Civil War period. A decorated salt-glazed Bartmann or 'Bellarmine' jug fragment dates to 1600-1650 (Fig. 4.30), so may also be associated with the Civil War; there are in total 31 sherds of German 'Frechen' stoneware from the Bartlemas trenches. Sherds of black-glazed 'tygs' or drinking vessels date to around the Civil War period and probably reflect the presence of the alehouse which is known to have existed here at this time. Post-Medieval red earthenwares are common local finds from the seventeenth and eighteenth centuries, and bowls, and pipkins and mugs are represented here. The Raeren and Frechen wares and Red Earthenwares were also found at Minchery Paddock (Chapter 5), implying they were not unusual in the Oxford area.

From the mid-eighteenth century onwards, English domestic pottery became more uniform with mass-production of transfer-printed porcelain wares, and we see the widespread emergence of Staffordshire china. Oxford colleges had their own monogrammed pottery, and a sherd of Exeter College tableware is represented here (perhaps surprisingly, as Oriel owned the site!). Also found was a small crotal bell (possibly from a bridle) of the eighteenth century (Fig. 4.35), inscribed with the initials WG, which may be the maker William Gwyn (1770-1813), of Aldbourne, Wiltshire, and a fine mid-Victorian glass button (Fig. 4.36), which was no doubt a grievous loss to its owner. A Victorian penny was also found. The three trenches were scattered with small iron objects, many of which came from mixed topsoil layers. Wire, nails, horseshoe fragments, chain fragments, an iron shoe-patten were found, mostly dating to the seventeenth to nineteenth centuries; part of an iron object known as a 'joiner's dog' indicates the presence of craft and repair at the site, particularly during the Victorian period.

Conclusion

The 2011 excavation at Bartlemas Chapel happened during an exceptionally balmy and bright autumn, and the beautiful surroundings and weather only enhanced the feeling of tranquillity. Yet the work revealed dark and dramatic episodes in the history of the site, including conflict, destruction, disease and tragically early death. Despite its sense of seclusion today, Bartlemas was clearly a significant local institution and an East Oxford landmark for many centuries, providing shelter for the needy, refuge for the sick, work for locals and spiritual support for pilgrims. Not only did our excavation assist the process of improving drainage at the chapel and thereby safeguarding its future, it also gave many residents of East Oxford and beyond valuable archaeological experience and a new sense of the historical significance of an important, if not widely appreciated, historic site in their area. Many local people had been unaware of the existence of the place: by the end of the excavation, hundreds had visited and been drawn into the exciting and engaging story of Bartlemas, and its lepers, pilgrims and soldiers.

Notes

1 Charters of William II and Henry I, Sharpe 2014 (H1-Oxford-STBart-2014-1, Creative Commons).
2 The relevant literature on leper hospitals and leprosy includes Clay 1909, Magilton *et al.* 2008, Palmer 1982, Rawcliffe 2006, Roffey 2012 and Satchell 1998.
3 Clark, D. 2009, *Oxfordshire Buildings Record Report: OBR.65 Bartlemas Farmhouse, Oxford OX4 2AJ.*
4 Durham 1990. Unfortunately there is insufficient detail recorded of this work to be able to glean anything certain about the purpose or extent of this boundary.
5 This was detected in both excavation and in the test

pits excavated around the chapel

6   VCH Oxon 2, 157-8.

7   See Graham Jones, below.

8   Satchell 1998.

9   VCH Oxon 2, 157-8.

10 Wood, 'Oxford', p. 517.

11 VCH Oxon 2, 158.

12 *Former Bartlemas Nursery School, Oxford: Revised Archaeological Evaluation Report*, February 2010, Oxford Archaeology Unpublished Report.

13 All the detailed excavation reports and specialists' reports noted below, including those animal and human bone, pottery, radiocarbon dating, environmental remains, and several related research papers can be found in the Project online archive in ORA for Chapter 4.

14 Alldritt, D. 2012 Archaeobotanical Report.

15 Atkins and Popescu 2003.

16 Hamilton, J. 2013 Archaeozoological Report.

17 Scott, I. 2014, Report on Iron Finds.

18 SUERC-49304: cal AD1013-1155 (95.4% probability).

19 Report on Test Pit 72, ORA data resource.

20 SUERC-51233: cal. 1220-1298AD (95.4% probability).

21 Cotter, J. 2012 Report on Pottery.

22 The burial must have taken place after the building of the fourteenth-century chapel as it was so close to the wall that any work would have disturbed it.

23 Ditchfield, P. 2015, Laboratory Report on Isotope samples.

24 SUERC-51231: cal. 1388-1440 AD and SUERC-51232: cal. 1288-1399AD (95.4% probability).

25 Levick, P. 2012, Human Bone assessment.

26 Cotter, J. 2012, Report on Pottery.

27 SUERC-49303 cal.1635-1684 AD (95.4% probability) see also Boylston, A. 2012 Palaeopathology Report.

28 Information from Oriel College archive.

29 Finds reports with listings on Small Finds by Anni Byard, Iron Finds by Ian Scott, on Pottery by John Cotter and on Lithics by Olaf Bayer can be found in the Project online archive for Chapter 4.

30 For examples see Egan 1998, 244-52.

31 Egan 2005, 126.

32 Clark 1890, 517.

33 Ward-Perkins 1940, 66.

Leper hospitals, lepers and leprosy

Jane Harrison and Swii Yii Lim

Leprosy was a relatively common disease in Medieval England but the contemporary attitude to sufferers was complex. They were not simply feared social outcasts for leper communities played a distinctive role within society, as shown by leading medical and social historian Carole Rawcliffe.[1] This in part reflected a contradiction in the Bible. The Old Testament Book of Leviticus stigmatises 'unclean' lepers, with their suffering visible punishment for spiritual sickness and sexual excess, but the New Testament describes Jesus spending time with and even curing leprous pariahs.[2] When leprosy asserted itself in England in the twelfth century, one response was inevitably to fear, avoid and segregate lepers, but over time their special status 'outside' society saw them increasingly targeted as suitable recipients of charitable provision from wealthy patrons. Establishing leper hospitals and endowing them with land, money and provisions became a way of demonstrating piety, enhancing local standing, as well as helping to smooth the patrons' path through purgatory. This approach was reinforced by the Pope: the Fourth Lateran Council of 1215 encouraged the giving of alms to leper hospitals.

Leper hospitals were usually founded outside towns but were prominently situated alongside main roads where, as they approached, people could appreciate the generosity of local benefactors before diverting to the chapel to offer alms and ask for intercessory prayers. Some of the hospitals' lepers might beg at the roadside,

while others took part in services and prayers; the less sick could perhaps be seen working on the hospitals' land. Proximity to water sources: wells or springs, was also an important and recurrent feature, with washing and purification a key part of their daily ritual. Leper hospitals and their inmates had a recognised place in the urban hinterland.[3] Of over 300 leper hospitals which are known to have been founded in England the majority were in service during the period c. 1050-1350. Only 17 chapels survive today and, because of their location just outside Medieval town centres, the sites of leper hospitals have generally been subsumed by more recent urban sprawl. The hospital buildings and other domestic structures surrounding the chapels rarely survive intact.

As a result, we know relatively little about the arrangement of buildings within hospital precincts or enclosures, but the publication of several recent excavations have begun to generate new information.[4] Excavations at Chichester, West Sussex, dealt mostly with the cemetery of the hospital, uncovering nearly 400 skeletons[5], while recent excavations at St Mary Magdalen, just outside Winchester, Hampshire, have provided rare information about the lepers' and wardens' accommodation and lifestyles.[6] Here, from its reconstruction in the mid-twelfth century, the lepers were accommodated in a long, aisled infirmary which was north of, and parallel to, the chapel. A tower-like structure existed in part of the site, and the burial ground was internally demarcated with lepers in their own special area. We know as yet little about the immediate contemporary landscape setting of the hospitals.

Although lepers often lived semi-monastic lives, following vows of obedience, chastity and humility, their routines entwined with the rhythm of church services, there is no evidence the hospitals were routinely laid out like monasteries. Early foundations, mostly in Kent and the south-west seem to have developed piecemeal, initially from basic timber buildings, and often with separate, small cell-like houses for the lepers.[7] Again the Pope had intervened. The Third Lateran Council of 1179 stipulated that all leper hospitals must have separate housing for the inmates and their own chapel and priest (ratified in England in1200, so too late to have constrained the original design at Bartlemas). But the overall layouts probably varied, especially as the foundations often underwent changes in use over their history: there are not enough excavated examples to be certain. The edge-of-town location of the hospitals had another advantage. It allowed them to attain a degree of self-sufficiency with the endowment of surrounding land for use as gardens, orchards, paddocks and fields. Much of the hospitals' grounds would have resembled secular farms with animal pens and shelters, outbuildings and workshops, arranged around kitchen gardens and yards. Sufficiently fit lepers might work in the fields or tend animals, but their efforts must have been supplemented by non-resident local workers or healthier hospital inmates.

Despite the general lack of excavated evidence, a range of buildings would be encountered at a twelfth to fourteenth-century leper hospital complex, amidst the infrastructure of a small farm: a chapel, usually with a cemetery; leper accommodation (either separate, scattered cells or stalls in a long hall built parallel to, or joining and at right-angles, the chapel); a warden and/or priest's house, and perhaps some housing for lay helpers. The core of the complex was likely to be delineated by a precinct enclosure, and a source of fresh water was vital for therapeutic washing as well as drinking and cooking. Bartlemas had all of these attributes. A long section of the substantial curved precinct wall survives, although overgrown and crumbling in places, and surrounds the Medieval cemetery. The nearby springs were a reliable source of fresh water, and at least one may have been known as a holy well.

The 2011 excavations demonstrated that the standing chapel was the direct successor of an earlier structure, which was almost certainly the leper hospital chapel. The current chapel was rebuilt a short time after the hospital became an Oriel College almshouse in the early fourteenth century. Despite being altered and rebuilt over the centuries, the two historic houses at Bartlemas may also preserve early architectural elements dating back to the period of the leper hospital. If the St Mary Magdalen, Winchester, excavations serve as an example, a long, narrow-aisled infirmary building may have existed to the north of, and parallel to, the chapel. This comparison would seem to point towards the shape and position of Bartlemas House quite strikingly (Bartlemas House was reconstructed in 1649, but the ground-plan, and parts of the foundations and masonry from its predecessor, may have been re-used). Bartlemas Farmhouse is probably also the successor of some of the hospital's domestic accommodation, possibly parts of the farm, or even the warden's house. The disturbed stone foundations of a north-south aligned building found in the 2011 excavations also showed that there were also smaller, less permanent buildings in the close vicinity of the chapel; these may have housed lepers, but we cannot be certain of this. During the twelfth and thirteenth centuries the leper hospital complex supported a special and in some cases needy community, and held a notable position in the East Oxford landscape, next to an important road, and symbolising royal generosity and charity.

Notes

1 Rawcliffe 2006.
2 Matthew 8: 1-4; Mark 1:40–45; Luke 5:12–16.
3 Roberta Gilchrist sees leper hospitals as 'liminal': marking a transition from the environs of the town to 'wilderness': again placing lepers in an ambiguous if acknowledged position (1995, 40).
4 Swii Yii Lim 2012 *The English Medieval Leper Hospital in Context* see ORA online data resource.
5 Magilton *et al.* 2008.
6 Roffey 2012.
7 Rawcliffe 2006 and Satchell 1998.

Leprosy at Bartlemas

Swii Yii Lim and Anthea Boylston

Lepers and leprosy have long exercised a particular fascination in the popular imagination. The stereotype of the medieval leper – an itinerant outcast suffering from terrible physical disfigurement – is a powerful image that still persists, yet the reality was far more complex. Major historical studies have been dedicated to lepers and leprosy, but work on leper hospitals remains scarce.[1] This is particularly true of the archaeology. Recent excavations such as those at Winchester and Chichester, however, have done much towards addressing this shortfall, complementing the recent work of historians.[2] What the archaeological evidence provides is an emerging picture of lepers not as outcasts, but as people integrated into the social fabric of Medieval society and treated with some measure of dignity and respect.

1. Stone corbel in Lincoln Cathedral showing facial changes of leprosy, published by permission of Jo Buckberry.

Leprosy in Britain

How and when leprosy first arrived in Britain is still uncertain. Skeletal evidence from Cirencester and Poundbury Camp, Dorset suggests that the disease was already present during the Roman period.[3] Now commonly known as Hansen's disease, leprosy is an infectious, air-borne disease that can be traced archaeologically by changes in the skeletal structure, most often in the facial area and the extremities.[4] It is caused by *Mycobacterium leprae*, a pathogen belonging to the same family as tuberculosis. Symptoms can range from very mild (tuberculoid) to extremely severe (lepromatous), with tell-tale deformity of the face (Fig.1) and extremities in individuals with low immune resistance.[5] As a disease, it does not appear to have been a significant problem in England until the eleventh century and was already on the decline by the fourteenth century.[6]

The social perception of lepers

During the Middle Ages 'leprosy' was a fluid term used to designate a whole host of skin – and even venereal – diseases. So long as it looked like lepra, it was effectively lepra. A strict medical definition would have been foreign to the medieval mind-set, which did not differentiate between physical and spiritual aspects of disease. To the medieval Christian, physical symptoms of leprosy were manifestations of an underlying spiritual malaise – the sign of a diseased soul and evidence of a sinful nature. The disease was also thought to make the afflicted lustful, sexually profligate, and beast-like.[7]

However, as the doctrine of purgatory developed in the Middle Ages, lepers also came to be regarded in another light: rather than being sinful penitents, lepers were an elect few enduring Christ-like suffering and purgatory on earth in exchange for surety in the afterlife.[8] This elevated status meant their intercessory prayers were thought to have special efficacy and were

particularly attractive to wealthy hospital benefactors seeking to build up spiritual credit while alive.

Leper hospitals

Medieval hospitals were complex places providing more than simply medical treatment or a cure. They saw themselves and were seen as houses of religion: hence the alternative name of *domus dei* or *maison dieu*, 'house of God'.[9] The purpose of hospitals often changed over time. In the twelfth century, hospital establishments could be hospice or hospital. In later times, they often served as almshouses as well, with many offering a combination of two or more of these services.[10] This was particularly true for leper hospitals which converted into almshouses or hospices after the devastation of the Black Death and as leprosy petered out in the fourteenth century.[11]

An awareness of the social perception of leprosy and lepers is thus vital to understanding how and why medieval leprosaria cannot simply be seen as isolation wards for social outcasts or the unwanted sick. They provided shelter, nursing care and, in the case of the seriously ill, medication and treatment. But above all, the quasi-monastic lifestyle expected of the inmates catered to their spiritual needs as well.

St Bartholomew's Hospital

Bartlemas or St Bartholomew's Hospital in Oxford was among the first leprosaria to be founded in England. These foundations were generally composed of a collection of cottages and a chapel surrounding a green, often with a well in the centre.[12] Sixteen leprosaria situated mainly in the south of England took the name of the apostle Bartholomew, owing to the saint's perceived medical powers. As the old hymn quoted by Sir Norman Moore states: 'lepers he cleanses, the sick he restores'.[13] Furthermore, St Bartholomew was martyred by being flayed alive.[14] There is an obvious association with skin diseases, which is reinforced by the fact that a piece of his skin was one of the relics preserved at the leprosarium and later acquired by Oriel College as a source of revenue (see page 145).

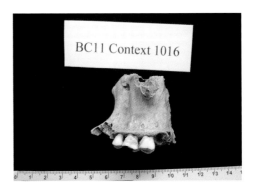

2. Leprosy seen in an upper jaw bone from context (1016).

Evidence of leprosy from the 2011 excavation

Bone changes of the disease are seen mainly in the nasal area and small bones of the hands and feet. There were two left upper jaws which exhibited the facial changes of leprosy within the cemetery soils. One was from Context 1016 in the grave fill of Skeleton 1 in Trench 1 (Fig. 2) and the other was from Context 3002 in Trench 3. The front teeth had been lost before death and the bone surrounding the nasal area had become rounded and smooth. Three foot bones from Charnel Pit 2 (SK3) also showed definite evidence of leprosy. They probably came from the same foot. The joints of the big toe showed septic arthritis and destruction. Two other toe bones were porous and misshapen, indicating inflammation (Fig. 3).

The shin bones are also affected in leprosy when infection spreads upwards from damaged feet. This is indicated by new bone formation on their surfaces. Both shin bones from Context 1015/5 showed evidence of inflammation. Other bones from Charnel Pit 2 with similar changes were a left tibia (Context 1007), a right fibula (1015/16) and fibula shaft fragments (1015/17) and a fibula from Trench 1 (1049). In summary, the excavations at Bartlemas provided convincing evidence of leprosy leaving traces on some of the earlier burials from the cemetery.

3. Foot bones affected by leprosy from context (1015/5).

Notes

1   Richards 1977; Rawcliffe 2006.
2   Rawcliffe 2006; Gilchrist and Sloane 2005.
3   Manchester and Roberts 1989, 266; Reader 1974.
4   Ortner 2008.
5   Manchester 1984, 167.
6   Magilton 2008, 9.
7   Orme and Webster 1995, 26.
8   Magilton 2008, 12; Rawcliffe 2006, 60-61.
9   Orme and Webster 1995, 35.
10   Knowles and Hadcock 1953, 40.
11   Knowles and Hadcock 1953, 310-11.
12   Clay 1909.
13   Clay 1909, 252-3.
14   Rawcliffe 2006.

Rickets at Bartlemas and anatomical dissection at Oxford

Anthea Boylston

The leg bones from the skeleton of a woman who had had rickets in childhood were found in context 1026 from Charnel Pit 1 to the immediate north of the Chapel, which has been dated to the middle part of the seventeenth century, during the English Civil War. This skeleton is extremely interesting because the bones had been drilled at both ends and in other places in order to turn them into an anatomical specimen (Figs. 1 and 2).[1] They thus possibly form part of the very early history of anatomy at Oxford University. Rickets was first named as such in England early in the seventeenth century by a Dutchman, Daniel Whistler.[2] A detailed description of its clinical signs in infants was published by Francis Glisson in 1650, approximately contemporaneous with the burial of this skeleton.[3] This volume represented a comprehensive study by a committee of the Royal College of Physicians into this mysterious affliction. In fact, it has been described as 'the outstanding disease of the seventeenth century'.[4] At the time, a lot of blame was laid at the door of wet nurses, because the group who appeared to be affected most were the

children of the nobility. Nurses were also blamed for trying to stand young children on their feet too early, thus causing the bones of their lower limbs and shoulders to become bowed.[5]

Rickets usually occurs between the age of nine and eighteen months when infants start to walk and is due to inadequate mineralisation of bone; most children recover by the age of two to three years. However, the curvature in their leg bones remains and for this reason healed rickets is a common finding in adults. Vitamin D can be acquired from the diet or from sunlight and the disease became more frequent as industrialisation proceeded and many people migrated from the countryside to the towns.

Anatomical dissection

Dissections were first performed at Oxford University in 1549[7] during the reign of Edward VI, when his Visitation of the University began. It was laid down by statute that medical students had to attend two 'anatomies' during their six-year training period and doctors studying for their MD, two to three. In 1624, the first public anatomical dissection took place. During the seventeenth century these events were almost theatrical and drew members of the public in a way that seems strange at the present time.[8] In the same year, the Tomlins Readership in Anatomy was

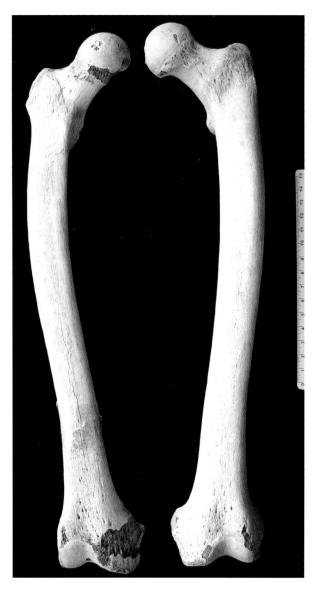

1. Rickets in both femora (thigh bones) of a female from context (1026) in charnel pit 1.

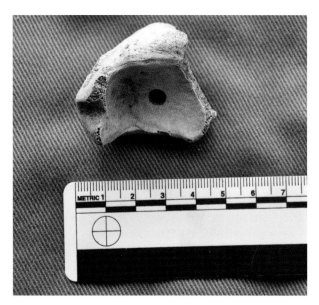

2. A drilled hole in bone from context (1026).

established. Indeed, Oxford was the first university in Britain to endow an academic post in the discipline. Richard Tomlins, a wealthy London merchant, paid the Reader £25 per year to demonstrate anatomy and he, in his turn, paid a surgeon £3 per year to perform the actual dissection and prepare the body.[9] A further forty shillings was allowed for collection and 'decent burial of the body and all necessaries thereunto'.[10] The main candidates for dissection were members of the criminal class who had been sentenced to death and hanged. 'A Sounde body of one of the Executed persons' was procured at the Lent Assizes.[11] In addition, the Great Charter of Charles I decreed that any person executed within 21 miles round Oxford should be made available for dissection.

These procedures happened within a day or two of death because there was no way of preserving the body; they certainly could not take place in summer in the early days.[12] Both men and women were hanged, the latter often for killing an illegitimate child. There were no assizes in the Michaelmas, or autumn, term but the Reader would give a lecture in Osteology then or at other times of year at the Anatomy School in the Bodleian Library.[13] One is recorded on 3 December 1632, and for this presumably a prepared and mounted skeleton would be necessary to demonstrate anatomical or pathological features. The Reader would discuss 'the skeleton or History of the bones with theire Situation Nature and Office'.[14] In 1634, Thomas Trapham is recorded as having prepared a skeleton at Oxford for use in anatomy teaching.[15] Furthermore, in 1654 the writer John Evelyn recorded seeing 'two skeletons which are finely cleansed and put together' in the library at St John's College.[16]

Interestingly, there is a link between Francis Glisson, who studied rickets so intensively, and George Joyliffe, the Oxford anatomist who discovered the lymphatic system. Joyliffe was trained in Oxford probably by Thomas Clayton, the first Tomlins Reader in Anatomy, and was known as 'that dexterous Dissector'.[17] Joyliffe later met Glisson at Cambridge and Glisson recalled learning about the lymphatic system from Joyliffe.[18] It naturally follows that the subject of rickets, which was the new disease of the seventeenth century, should have been of great interest to those who were teaching medical students in Oxford at the time. Taking into account the growing awareness of the skeletal manifestations of rickets, in conjunction with an increasing interest in anatomy, it is probably not surprising that the lower limbs of the woman from context 1026 ended up in the dissecting room and lecture theatre, only to find their way into the charnel pit at St Bartlemas' chapel once they were no longer required. Evidence for the use of prisoners in dissection was found during the excavations at Oxford Castle.[19] A total of 60-70 burials were recovered, dating to the sixteenth-eighteenth centuries. Several of these individual had undergone post-mortem processes such as sawing through the cranium. They had not received a Christian burial in consecrated ground but had been eventually consigned to the moat. Removal of the top of the cranium is seen in an illustration from the Corporis Humani Disquisitio Anatomica published by Nathaniel Highmore of Trinity College, Oxford in 1651.[20]

Notes

1   Levick, P. Human Bone report from Bartlemas Chapel, see ORA online archive (Chapter 4).
2   Beck 1997.
3   Glisson 1650.
4   Radbill 1974.
5   Glisson 1651.
6   Sawday 1995, 56.
7   Sinclair and Robb-Smith 1950.
8   Sawday 199.5
9   Valadez 1974.
10 Sinclair and Robb-Smith 1950, 12.
11 Ibid.
12 Sawday 1995.
13 Sinclair and Robb-Smith 1950.
14 Ibid, 12.
15 Valadez 1974.
16 Sinclair and Robb-Smith 1950, 14.
17 Ibid, 13.
18 Valadez 1974.
19 Poore et al. 2009, Munby et al. 2019..
20 In 1771, a surgeon named Samuel Glass was recorded by Oriel College as a tenant of Bartlemas Farmhouse.

Stable isotopic dietary analysis of the Bartlemas skeletons

Peter Ditchfield, Research Laboratory for Archaeology and History of Art (RLAHA), Oxford University

Stable isotopic analysis of human remains can reveal useful information about the diet of the individual and subsistence practices of past communities. The stable isotopes that are frequently used for this type of analysis are carbon 13 (C^{13}) and nitrogen 15 (N^{15}). Most carbon has an atomic mass of 12 but a small amount has an atomic mass of 13. The extra mass is because the C^{13} has an extra neutron in its atomic nucleus, however C^{13} has the same number of protons and electrons as C^{12} so it undergoes the same chemical reactions as C^{12} but the extra mass of the C^{13} means that it often reacts at a different rate to the C^{12}. This means that the products of a chemical reaction, such as photosynthesis for instance, will have a different ratio of C^{12} to C^{13} than that of the original material (atmospheric carbon dioxide in this example). This fractionation of the stable isotope ratio can be used to track many important biological processes and is widely used in many branches of environmental science.

In archaeological stable isotopic dietary analysis, the ratio of C^{12} to C^{13} can be used to give an indication of the amount of terrestrial vs marine input into the diet and the ratio of N^{14} to N^{15} can be used to give in indication of the type of protein (plant vs animal) in the diet.

To make these analyses a small sample of bone is taken from the skeleton and collagen, the main protein component of the bone, is chemically extracted. This collagen is then purified and combusted to produce nitrogen and carbon dioxide gases. These gases are then analysed in a mass spectrometer that is able to accurately detect the ratios of C^{12} to C^{13} and N^{14} to N^{15}. The collagen within bones changes throughout the life of the individual and different bones within the body turn over their collagen at different rates. This means that collagen from a fast turn over bone such as a rib may give us dietary information about the las few years of life whilst a bone with slow collagen turnover, such as a femur, might give dietary information over several decades of life. By looking at the isotopic ratio of the collagen from different bones within the skeleton we can look at changes in diet across the life span of the individual.

As collagen from modern mammalian bone has been very well characterised at a molecular level we can use the ratio of the total amount of carbon to the total amount of nitrogen to asses the amount of alteration that has taken place with in archaeological collagen. This provides some degree of quality control and helps point out samples where the collagen has been degraded by natural processes of decay within the burial environment.

Analysis of the Bartlemas Chapel skeletons

Nine of the burials were selected for analysis and these were carefully sampled during excavation. The list of which skeletons were sampled along with the specific bones that were chosen and results of the analysis are shown in table 1. Of the skeletons sampled SK 9 had bones that were so poorly preserved that they yielded no collagen at all. Another, SK 6, yielded collagen that was degraded as shown by the ratio of total amounts of carbon and nitrogen.

The carbon and nitrogen stable isotopic results for the nine samples are shown in table 1 and figure 1. Values range from ca. -22 to -18 ‰ for $\delta^{13}C$ and ca. 11 to 13 ‰ for $\delta^{15}N$. This range of values is compatible with a northern European predominantly terrestrial diet, with C3 type plants at the base of the food chain.

In order to provide a more accurate estimate of the amounts of protein from different sources within the diet stable isotopic analysis of plants and animals that were eaten by the humans would usually be required. Whilst such data is often available in the archaeological record e.g. when middens associated with settlements are excavated, in this case as it is analyses from a Christian cemetery site there are no faunal remains to provide comparative data. However, there are several other archaeological human collagen data sets from the city of Oxford for comparison. The first of these is a mass grave assemblage discovered during the construction work in the grounds of St John's College. The assemblage consists of 37 male skeletons exhibiting sever perimortem trauma buried in a single event sometime in the late tenth or early eleventh centuries AD (possibly associated with the St Brice's Day massacre, see Chapter 1). The other is an assemblage of fifty-one skeletons from a mid to late nineteenth century burial ground at the Radcliffe Infirmary, the former university medical hospital north of the city centre, which was in use between 1770 and 2007.

Although the data from the Bartlemas chapel burials falls well within the range of values that might be expected for this area, there is some interesting variation within the data. Samples from Skeleton 1 and 10 (B10, B1F and B1R0) show elevated $\delta^{13}C$ and $\delta^{15}N$ values relative to the rest of the data set such an elevation in $\delta^{13}C$ and $\delta^{15}N$ is compatible with a significant amount of marine derived protein, probably from marine fish, in the diet. Interestingly the paired rib and femur analyses from SK1 point to this becoming even more pronounced in the last few years of life as represented by the data from the rib sample which is elevated over the femoral sample from the same skeleton.

SK 2, 5, 8, 11 and 12 show a more fully terrestrial diet. However, the relatively elevated N15 values (all greater than 11) in these skeletons suggest that all these individuals had reasonable amounts of animal protein in their diets. All the data from the Bartlemas skeletons point towards a relatively well off population with access to a relatively good diet.

Notes

1   Pollard et al. 2014.
2   Draft report held at Oxford Archaeology.

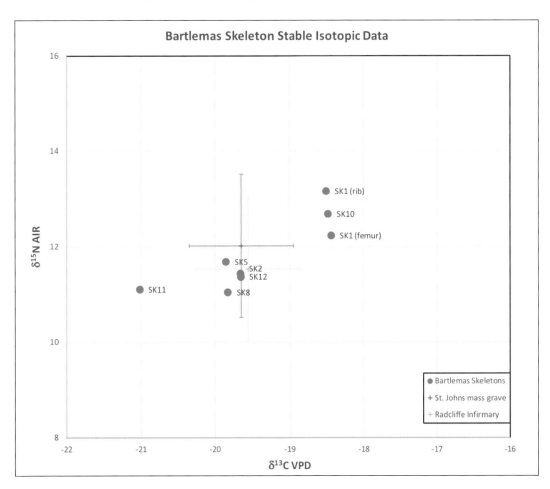

1. Carbon and Nitrogen stable isotope plot of the data obtained from the Bartlemas skeletons, with the data ranges of other comparative Oxford human collagen data sets. Note the elevated carbon and nitrogen results for SK 1 and 10 suggesting that these individuals had significant amounts of marine fish in their diets.

Bartlemas: its chapel, hospital and landscape

Graham Jones

Medieval chapels are comparatively under-investigated, not being grand like abbeys, or the centres of communities like parish churches. Across England they were diverse to a fascinating extent. There were chapels integral to hospitals (as at Bartlemas), parochial chapels serving isolated communities in large parishes; private chapels attached to manor houses; hermitage and anchorite chapels whose sites included bridges, fords, and healing springs; the chapels of small religious communities; free chapels built on the initiative of local lords, cemetery chapels; and field chapels marking minor devotional sites of many sorts.

Rural and extra-mural chapels were part of the warp and weft of local devotion. They were also a familiar feature of the Medieval landscape. This was particularly true when chapels were (as at Bartlemas) a place of pilgrimage - another common feature of past religious life which is now largely gone. While most people think of pilgrimage in terms of great destinations such as Jerusalem and Santiago de Compostela, a fair rule of thumb is that every parish community had a place outside the village or town to which an annual procession would be made: devotional and social occasions that mixed worship with festivals and saints' days. For an insight into these mostly lost traditions, the chance to excavate at a Medieval hospital chapel such as Bartlemas was a golden opportunity. However, excavation requires research aims. So certain questions were crucial: What led to the establishment of a hospital at this particular spot? Why was the apostle Bartholomew chosen as its patron saint? What was the 'afterlife' of Bartlemas, and can its remaining structures tell us anything about its lasting significance?

Chapels were integral to the landscape. Their location – particularly where pilgrimage was involved – was often influenced by, and reflected preoccupation with, cultural and spiritual interpretations of landscapes and their physical features. Water carried immense importance: for life and health, and also as a metaphorical aid for spiritual wellbeing: baptism, ritual washing, penitential cleansing, and so on. Devotional landscapes often witness to a deep past. History is balanced between change and continuity, and the former sometimes crowds out the latter. Archaeology increasingly reveals sites illustrating the longevity of ideas and practice, as well as intriguing processes of transition. This was widely evident in just a handful of examples from surviving Medieval leper and other hospitals reviewed below in in order to put Bartlemas in its historical, cultural, and geographical contexts.

The brothers, their background, and their lives at Bartlemas

It is difficult to establish much about the antecedents of the Bartlemas leper hospital and its site from the documentary record. Its fortunes following its endowment by Henry I for twelve sick persons and a chaplain *circa* 1127 are however well established.[1] From the start it was closely associated with the townspeople and scholars of Oxford. The stipends of the 'prebendary' inmates (identified as lepers in others' gifts and bequests) – a penny a day, plus five shillings a year for clothing – were paid out of the taxation due from the town of Oxford to the king's manor of Headington. The brothers' stipends compared well with those of clerks studying at Oxford. Balliol College's, for example, had eight pence a week. The generosity of the five shillings a year for clothing suggests the brothers wore livery, perhaps even royal. Indeed, given the likely difficulty in choosing between candidates from the general population of Oxford, it may be that places were restricted at first to royal servants. Otherwise the inmates were drawn from 'the infirm of Oxford', though by 1316 so many were healthy that new rules were drawn up for the king's approval. The inmates, often referred to as brothers, were reduced to eight – six infirm and two to do the farm-work – while the master/chaplain was to be helped by a clerk. Their stipends were increased from a penny a day to ninepence a week, and the master was paid four pounds a year. The hospital's smallholding was described in the thirteenth century as an 'an enclosure about their house' of six acres,[2] but this probably referred only to the arable part.

In 1161–62, some 60 shillings were spent on maintaining, or perhaps extending, the hospital buildings. At some point between 1270 and 1312 the then chaplain, warden or master built himself a house in the grounds. In 1325 the master- or warden-ship was granted for life to Adam de Brome, who had been Clerk of the Chancery under Edward II and had recently founded the House of Blessed Mary the Virgin in Oxford, better known as Oriel College.[3] In 1328 the relationship with Oriel was made permanent, and continues in part to this day (Oriel owns part of the historic chapel land outside the 'rood' possessed by the church). From 1328 onwards, the former leper hospital, now Oriel's almshouse, would serve as a place where sick members of the college 'might retire for a change of air'. The inmates – or rather servants employed by them – continued to grow garden and other produce, tend farm animals, and manage copse-wood. Apart from its smallholding at Bartlemas, by 1330 the almshouse had been given other plots of land producing £7 a year in rents.

The chapel was substantially reconstructed by Oriel in 1336, possible using some re-cycled stone features from other college buildings in the process of renewal. This might explain why the windows, whilst sharing the same gothic style, do not quite match each other.

Bartlemas: devotional life and religious context

Situated upon one of the main routes leading east out Oxford, Bartlemas was well-placed to attract pilgrims, visitors and those in search of a cure for ailments. There was a pyx – a box for worshippers' devotional offerings – at Bartlemas in the fifteenth century.[4] It seems likely that these were votive payments associated with the chapel's relics: a piece of what was claimed to be the flayed skin of Bartholomew, perhaps displayed with an image of the apostle which was itself an object of veneration; a comb of St Edmund of Abingdon; bones said to be from the body of St Stephen; and a rib-bone attributed to the apostle Andrew.[5] 'Happy [was he] that could come near either to touch or kiss them,' was Anthony Wood's comment looking back from the mid-seventeenth-century.[6]

Bartlemas was therefore far more than a refuge for lepers. Its constitution as a brotherhood, its dedication in honour of the apostle Bartholomew, its chapel and chaplain, its relics, and its association with a holy well (discussed below), made it one of a number of small religious institutions which formed part of the devotional landscape of Medieval Oxford's hinterland. Of the other suburban hospitals, only St John the Baptist outside the East Gate dated from the same century as Bartlemas. Founded *circa* 1180 to serve visitors and later the sick, it was built on what was previously the Jewish burial ground, and became part of Magdalen College in 1457. Its significance at the time of its foundation at time lies with the wave of new religious establishments springing up across Britain and in the case of Oxford the influence of its founder, Henry I.

When Henry I founded Bartlemas hospital in the 1120s, Oxford was already an established town, with parish and other principal churches inside and just outside the walls. These offered care for the sick, elderly and infirm, and lodgings for travellers. The care of lepers was a particular concern of Henry's queen Matilda, described as welcoming them to her house, washing, drying and even kissing their feet. The form of Bartholomew's martyrdom, the flaying of his skin, speaks directly to the problems of leprosy. However, although one of the nine most popular saints for leper hospitals in England, Bartholomew's total of eight pales beside the tallies of Mary Magdalene (51) and Leonard (36).[7] Thus, the association with diseased skin on its own does not adequately explain his choice as patronal saint. His cult had other sides to it: for example, St. Bartholomew's Day or Bartle Mass, August 24, slots into the pattern of Medieval account-

ing and farming dates. At Lewknor, near Watlington in South Oxfordshire, Bartle Mass was the date after which sheep were allowed on to the wheat stubble.[8] At Newbury (Berkshire) Bartholomew's feast-day was marked by the town's annual fair, so popular that election of a 'Bartlemas Mayor' survived into the nineteenth century. Many fairs in England and Wales, took place at Bartholomew-tide, including the fair at Watlington. The explanation of the choice of Bartholomew as patron is more easily sought in its royal endowment, and perhaps one other thing, the correlation between Bartholomew dedications and places with names pointing to pre- or non-Christian ritual and worship, explored below.

The site: routeways, water, and geography

The choice of site for the hospital followed the common preference for a extra-urban space where patients could benefit from fresh air, fresh water, and room for gardening, or more generously as here, land for tillage, pasture and woodland.

Bartlemas was sited less than a stone's-throw northeast of a road leading eastwards out of Oxford, continuing the line of (modern) Cowley Road through the adjacent allotments and onwards following the path now known as Barracks Lane. This route took travellers in and out of Oxford, passing Bullingdon Green further to the east (which was once a significant hundredal meeting-place), connecting to the south-eastern districts of the county beyond. Proximity to an important road afforded ease of access and a greater chance of alms from passers-by.

To the north, uphill from the chapel and its precinct, the Oxford clay meets the Corallian limestone, and at their junction is a pronounced springline, which drains southwards in small streams, one of which passes down the western boundary of Bartlemas Farmhouse.

In the thirteenth century, it was stated that the hospital's land had been taken out of 'tillage ground' called Strowell.[9] The name Strowell however incorporates the Old English term *strōd*, generally taken to signify 'marshy land overgrown with brushwood' as with Stroud, Gloucestershire.[10] So it may be that the availability of wetland was as attractive as the proximity of arable land, and another factor in the hospital's establishment was its location in a transitional tract of land where arable gave way to pasture. Certainly in the immediate topography, the term 'marsh' as in Cowley Marsh, has the meaning in Old English *mersc* of 'well-watered land'. As Margaret Gelling and Ann Cole noted, 'The common use of *mōr* and *mersc* as qualifiers in *tūn* names reflects the high value of wetland resources to early farmers.'[11] Bartlemas's elm-grove probably lay around the Strowell spring. The grove was notable but not so large that it could not be felled 'all in one day' in 1643 to deny cover to advancing Parliamentary troops.[12]

The wet clay ground of the Bartlemas site was a challenge to excavate in 2011, and it was evident from an early stage that water-courses were a feature of the Medieval landscape around, and even perhaps within the chapel, where damp was evident. Water has been an important part of the treatment of leprosy at least from Biblical times, and sacred springs were a stock feature of ancient places of healing more generally. The importance of bathing for lepers is documented, and its ritual aspect is found in *Leviticus*.[13] The origin of the Strowell spring's perception as a holy, healing well is lost to view, although intriguingly, it was also known as the Hick ('helpful') Well, pointing to its perceived beneficial properties. Nevertheless it is possible to read the Ascensiontide student procession from New College described in retrospect in 1659 as the survival of a Medieval event of communal devotion.[14] Around 1600 the service had been shortened, but chapel and well and the path between continued to be ceremonially garlanded and hymns were sung. Offerings of silver coins for the poor were put in a vessel or basin 'decked with tuttyes' [deposits of medicinal minerals, notably zinc oxide] and placed on the altar[15] or standing in the middle of the chapel.[16] Anthony Wood found an origin for the procession in the episcopal 40 days indulgence issued in 1336 for those who visited the chapel on the apostle's feast (August 24) or octave (eight days later). He also noted that the New College procession took place at Ascension because Magdalen students 'and the rabble of the town' came on May Day. This latter celebration would seem to be equally important in working out the ancient significance of Bartlemas and its spring. Wood's description of the city's youth making their way to Bartlemas on May Day with 'lords and ladies [individuals elected to preside over the festivities], garlands, fifes, flutes, and drums' aligns the custom with revels elsewhere. In Oxfordshire these were particularly associated with woodland landscapes, around the ancient forests of Wychwood and, locally, Shotover (the lower reaches of which once bordered Bartlemas to its north)

It is possible that the possession of St Edmund's comb by Bartlemas contributed to the development of an Edmundian devotional route for pilgrims, merry-makers, and others. St Edmund's Hall was established near Oxford's East Gate by 1236. There was a well of St Edmund where Magdalen School now stands, near The Plain at Magdalen Bridge. With the customs around the chapel and its spring, these suggest the possibility of a pilgrim route from Oxford separate from, and possibly predating the endowment of Henry I's hospital. The chapel's usefulness continued long after the hospital's transformation into a college retreat and almshouse. The mayor's mace-bearer was

married there in 1628,[17] and in 1657, the chapel was used for a clandestine wedding.[18] Long-surviving consciousness of Bartlemas' general reputation as a holy place may also have been a factor leading to the post-Medieval burials at Bartlemas. Only in the nineteenth century did the chapel temporarily pass out of devotional use, initially as a cholera ward during the epidemic of 1832, then as a farm building. It was restored to religious use in the twentieth century.

The chapel

The intimate setting and relationship of the chapel, farmhouse, and Bartlemas House provoke the question as to how the Medieval ward (the accommodation of the inmates), chapel, and warden's quarters were arranged. Many hospitals housed their inmates in a building whose east end was reserved for a chapel, so that those in need of care or fearing death could take comfort from its proximity. However, the first chapel at Bartlemas appeared to stand on its own, indicating that the accommodation lay separately. At St Mary's Winchester, the infirmary lies to the north of, and parallel to, the chapel.[19] At Bartlemas, the similar position of Bartlemas House (rebuilt in 1649) suggests itself as a possible successor to an earlier infirmary or accommodation building.

The excavation showed that an earlier stone-founded building underlay the standing chapel. Standard dimensions for chapels of the period around 1130 are difficult to demonstrate, though the 'golden' ratio of 2:3 seems always to have been popular. If built in stone, it would be reasonable to imagine the chapel sharing some features with the near-contemporary church of Iffley, for example a west front with processional door and round window, but on a smaller scale. In addition to evidence of small detached structures, the excavation uncovered substantial traces of what was probably a masonry structure or extension to the east end of the original chapel. Its area was partly detected by the remains of a gravel floor, the hardness of whose gritty surface of which is remembered vividly by the writer, suggesting sustained use over a long period. The associated masonry elements were bordered on their south side by the burial of the young man. Was the vanished structure an apse? The burial was clearly in a privileged position within feet of the high altar, even though outside the chapel. Even greater privilege would accrue if this structure, cut through by the reconstruction trench of the surviving building, had been a treasury for one or more of the chapels' relics. Wood reported that the hospital's relics were 'laid up in several repositories in the chapel' and on 'high and select times, especially at a general concourse of people' were 'exposed to view'.[20] A small building of indeterminate function is shown on the first ordnance survey map of the area. This structure probably reused the surviving hard-standing of the eastern extension.

If the origins of the long, oddly curving water feature which lies to the north-east of the chapel, represented on the 1840 Estate Plan (see Figs 4.6, 4.28), date to the period of the hospital, it might be interpreted as a fishpond, a laundry pool, or even a place for the bathing of patients (sadly it has been comprehensively re-landscaped including a modern ornamental garden pool). Did inmates and visitors make their way from a bathing place to the east-end annex to venerate the relics? A well-house was that incorporated under the east end of the church at St Kenelm's, Romsley (Worcestershire), where a spring that had once risen north-west of the church and been channelled through it. A damp area down the centre of the nave still caused problems in the 1990s. At Whitwell (Rutland) the eponymous 'white' or 'holy' spring rose west of the hilltop church and ran through it, excess water being channelled away through drainage stones at the base of the chancel arch pillars. San Bartolomeo on the Tiber Island, Rome, has a spring head in the sanctuary steps testifying to the accommodation of 'living water' within a church.

Antecedents

The curving nature of the area of open water as depicted in the 1840 Oriel estate plan is intriguing: this, taken together with the curve of the southern and eastern sides of the Chapel enclosure suggest that the chapel may have been deliberately built within some curving feature which had once enclosed a much earlier 'watery' site of ritual or religious significance. There is a statistically-positive spatial correlation between religious dedications honouring Barthol-omew, and places or districts whose names point to pre- or non-Christian ritual and worship, which at least allows room for such speculation. Among Bartholomew dedications elsewhere in the Oxford region are Fingest in the Chiltern Hills ('place of assembly'), and the 'shining spring' which gave its name to Brightwell Baldwin, Oxfordshire.

Notes

1   VCH Oxon, 2, 157-58, and 3, 119-31; Clark 1890, 504-19. Wood made excerpts from the muniments of the hospital in the treasury of Oriel College in August 1662: Clark 1891, 454. Charters of William II and Henry I, Sharpe 2014 (H1-Oxford-STBart-2014-1, Creative Commons)
2   Clark 1890, p. 506.
3   VCH Oxon, 3, 119-31.
4   VCH Oxon, 3, 119-31, citing Oriel College treasurers' accounts.
5   Though according to Clark 1890, 517, these were transferred to Oriel's church of St Mary the Virgin around 1400.
6   Clark 1890, 516.
7   Calculated from the tabulated data in Clay 1909.
8   VCH Oxon 8, 98-115, citing Salle Park, Norfolk, Muniments of Sir Dymoke White, B. I. 19a, b, court roll, 1594.
9   Clark 1890, 506.
10 Gelling and Cole 2000, 63; Smith 1970, 164.
11 Gelling and Cole 2000, 37. A. H. Smith translated *mersc* as 'watery land, a marsh': Smith 1970, 39. Gelling and Cole 2000 gave simply 'marsh', but noted that *mersc-tūn* settlements may have had a specialised function in relation to the marsh, or that their economy depended heavily on its products. A useful example is Moreton-in-Marsh, formerly Moreton Henmarsh (Gloucestershire).
12 Clark 1890, 517 (using the Latin term for elm-grove, *ulmetum*); Richards and Salter 1926, 297-311.
13 See for example, in comparison with East African practice: Kimuhu 2008, 383.
14 Clark 1899, 289-90 and Clark 1890, 513-16.
15 Clark 1890, 513-16.
16 Clark 1899, 289.
17 Clark 1892, 440.
18 Clark 1899, 232.
19 Roffey 2012, 225.
20 Clark 1890, 516: citing a document of 1390.

Chapter 5

Excavations at Minchery Paddock (Littlemore Priory), 2012

Jane Harrison, with Olaf Bayer, David Griffiths and Joanne Robinson

Introduction

Excavations and studies of Bartlemas Chapel (Chapter 4) established a major investigative theme in the *Archeox* project, that of looking into the history and landscapes of Medieval religious communities. As the project continued and expanded, we sought to broaden this theme, to discover yet more of the area's hidden and half-forgotten heritage. In 2012, we were granted permission by Oxford City Council to excavate in Minchery Paddock, a disused and neglected pasture on the south-eastern outskirts of Oxford, which covers part of the site of Littlemore Priory, a Benedictine nunnery founded in the mid-twelfth century. (Fig. 5.1). The name 'Minchery' comes from Old English *mynecenu*, meaning nuns or nunnery.[1] The history of the priory is known from a considerable amount of

surviving documentary evidence, and as mentioned above in Chapters 1 and 2, one part of it, the eastern dormitory range, constructed in the fifteenth century, survives as a standing building, having been used since the priory's dissolution in the 1520s as a farmhouse, and more recently as a pub. Minchery Paddock lies immediately to the west of this building, separated from it by a footpath which heads northwards towards Littlemore (Figs. 2.11, 5.2). Three trenches were excavated (Excavation code MP12, Trenches 1-3), and the fieldwork ran for six weeks from September to November 2012 (Fig. 5.3). These excavations set out to discover more about the history of Littlemore Priory, including of the buildings and the lifestyles of the nuns and the lay inhabitants, and to seek evidence for the character of its later years to compare with the

Fig. 5.1. Trench 3 from south-west, with the western façade of the surviving priory building (AerialCam).

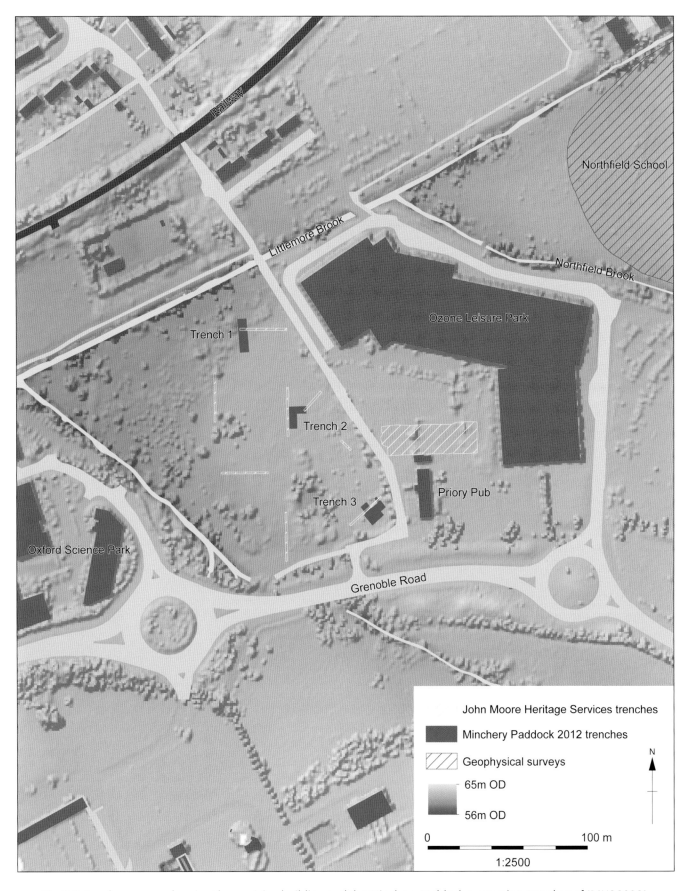

Fig. 5.2. Landscape map showing the surviving building and the Minchery Paddock excavation trenches of JMHS 2006/ 2014 and Archeox 2012 (Base mapping © Crown Copyright/database right 2012. An Ordnance Survey/EDINA supplied service. Topography © Environment Agency copyright and/or database right 2019. All rights reserved).

documentary record. We also used the opportunity of excavating in this location to identify finds and sample wetland deposits which could give us important new information on the longer environmental history of the landscape.

More than a hundred people, many of whom were local residents from Littlemore and Greater Leys, were involved directly in the excavation, and many more visited on open days or with schools and other groups. These included some of the traveller families who have lived intermittently on Minchery Paddock in recent years. This was a more challenging excavation logistically and physically than that of the previous year at Bartlemas Chapel. The areas under excavation were larger and more diverse in their technical challenges, and the location was less bucolic. Clearing the area for excavation was a big job, as the paddock was heavily overgrown with brambles, weeds and long grass, and much of it was rubbish-strewn (fly-tipping is a problem in the locality). The weather was more typically autumnal than in the previous year, and the smell of the nearby sewage farm was intermittently powerful. Trench 1, at the northern end of the paddock nearest the brook, was extremely wet and muddy, with ground-water constantly in need of pumping out. As an excavation in a somewhat run-down location on the furthest edge of the inhabited city, robust security fencing and lockable gates were considered necessary for when we were offsite, but as it turned out over the time we were working there, there were no incidents of vandalism, unauthorised entry, or indeed anti-social behaviour of any kind. Friendly information placards were put at points of

public access explaining who we were and what we were doing; passers-by expressed interest, asked questions, and were welcomed onto the site during working hours. Many of the project's volunteers achieved new levels of skill and we were delighted that the relationship with local residents was so trouble-free and positive. It felt in many ways as if the project had moved up to a yet higher level of community engagement at Minchery Paddock.

A brief history of Littlemore Priory

The Benedictine house at Littlemore was founded in the reign of Stephen (1135-1154), most likely towards the end of the reign, around 1150. After functioning as nunnery for nearly four hundred years, it was closed down by papal bull in the Little Dissolution of 1524-5, a precursor to the wider dissolution of the monasteries which followed in the 1530s. The facts of its establishment and later papal and other grants and injunctions relating to the nunnery's first centuries are well-documented,[2] and much is recorded about the priory's apparently scandalous and ill-managed final decades (see page 188). However, comparatively little has been known about the layout and history of the priory buildings before the sixteenth century, or about the ways of life of the people who lived and worked in them. The character of the archaeological remains revealed in the 2012 excavations suggested the priory's economy was flourishing until towards the end of the fourteenth century but continued to function throughout its existence. The ceramic assemblage recorded in the work supported this: for

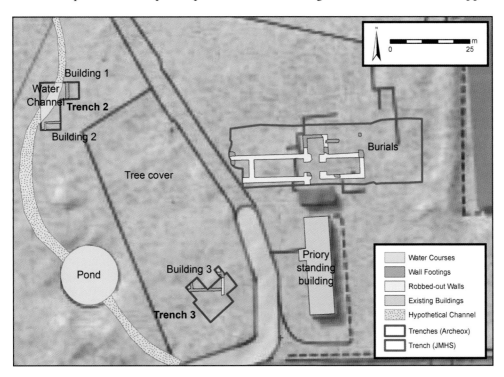

Fig. 5.3. Site map showing locations of Trenches 2 and 3 with remaining priory building.

example, the overwhelming majority of pottery in Trench 2 was later than 1150 and earlier than 1500, and dominated by wares of the thirteenth and fourteenth centuries.[3] Littlemore Priory was never a large institution but, in its heyday, it played an influential role in the local economy and society. Over the centuries, religious life in the priory was affected by outside events and politics.

The nunnery was founded by a local lordly family, the de Sandfords, principally as a place for female relatives who were unlikely to be well-married. The post of prioress provided a rare opportunity for women to exercise authority. In the case of Littlemore, after 1239 when the priory was granted by the de Sandfords to the Knights Templar, the prioress would have run the institution under an organisation famed for its effective land management. (By this time the Knights Templar had moved their preceptory from Temple Cowley to Sandford-on-Thames, a kilometre south-west of the priory). However, the Templars' suppression in 1312 must have deprived the priory of some resources and financial support. The connection with the de Sandfords was also lost not long afterwards. These unfortunate developments may have begun a long-term decline in the priory's fortunes. Later in the fourteenth century the Black Death caused population contraction and agricultural depression, and by the fifteenth century, lay charitable support for monasticism generally declined. There was some new building work at Littlemore in the fifteenth century, principally the dormitory range which survives. A visitation (inspection) in 1445 by a commissary of the Bishop of Lincoln (see page 189) was critical of the nuns' lifestyle and their administration of the priory. The main dormitory was reported as being structurally unsound, and the Bishop decreed that the nuns should sleep in separate beds; this probably led to the construction of the new dormitory range. The priory was closed following a further visitation in 1517 which was particularly damning in its criticism, making numerous accusations as to mismanagement, disobedience, and the misconduct of the last prioress, Katherine Wells, and her five nuns (see page 192). The priory was fully dissolved seven years later. Thereafter, much of it was demolished, and its remaining parts became for many centuries a farm, known as Minchery Farm.

Location and landscape context

Littlemore Priory was established on a low sandy spur of ground between the confluences of the Littlemore and Northfield brooks 150m to the north, and of Littlemore Brook with a tributary 250m to the north-west; this tributary fed the pond in Minchery Paddock and the water channel that appears to mark the western limit of the Medieval priory precinct (Fig 5.2). The site

of the priory lies at just over 60 metres above sea level, with the land falling away gently to wetter ground surrounding the brooks to the north, west and south-west. These watercourses would have provided fresh water, and as Graham Jones describes, one of the local springs may also had a reputation as a holy well (see page 194). Its wider setting was a resource-rich landscape of hay meadows, arable land, wetlands and woodland. The antiquarian Anthony Wood described the pleasant walks, fine trees, groves and fishponds of the area in the seventeenth century.[4] The priory looked across the Littlemore Brook to Littlemore Village to the north-west, through which a major Medieval routeway ran from the south towards Iffley, Church Cowley and Oxford; two kilometres to the south-west, the Thames, an artery for trade, travel and information, ran past Sandford.

In the Medieval period, the nearest larger settlements to Littlemore Priory were the village of Littlemore just under a kilometre to the north-west, and Sandford (mentioned in Domesday Book) a similar distance to the south-west.[5] In addition there were individual farms or hamlets working the surrounding land including two to the north-east in Blackbird and Greater Leys (see page 77), and others to the south and south-west, including Temple or Manor Farm just to the north-west of Sandford, now a large hotel. Temple Farm was the Sandford seat of the Knights Templar after they moved there from Temple Cowley shortly after 1240, and after their order's suppression, of the Hospitallers; elements of Medieval fabric survive there today (see Fig. 1.5). In later times the area around Minchery Farm remained undeveloped and remote from habitation, until the construction of the Oxford to Princes Risborough Railway in 1864 which passes north of the priory site (mostly closed in 1963, but the section through Littlemore to Cowley still functions as a goods line), and the Oxford main sewage plant in 1879, during which four Roman pottery kilns were discovered (see 'Roman Period' below). Housing estates, business parks, link-roads, a football stadium, and a large leisure complex 'Ozone' now crowd the skyline in the vicinity, leaving little sense of what was once a peaceful, rural place.

The archaeology of the Priory area

Prehistoric period

Although there is extensive disturbance by buildings and other activity of later periods, there is evidence that during the Neolithic and Bronze Age people were working and living in the general area. The excavations ahead of the construction of Oxford Science Park to the west of Minchery Paddock, and the Kassam Stadium to the east, produced relatively ephemeral indications of Prehistoric occupation and

Fig. 5.4. Barbed and tanged flint arrowhead of the Early Bronze Age (SF 1), just after discovery.

activity (see Fig. 1.4 for locations).[6] In all three excavation trenches in 2012, finds of worked flint dating to the earlier Neolithic through to the Early Bronze Age suggested that the margins of Littlemore brook were regularly visited, if not necessarily inhabited.[7] As well as two flint arrowheads (see page 183), one Neolithic and one Early Bronze Age (Fig. 5.4), other flint tools, some of which we re-touched, and over forty pieces of debitage (knapping waste) were discovered (see Fig. 5.33).

Roman Period

Romano-British archaeology is abundant around the priory as it sits within an area linked to the scattered settlements and industrial sites of the pottery producers. Pottery kilns and some settlement traces have been recorded in Littlemore, Iffley and Cowley to the north-west, as well as Greater Leys to the east (see page 88). In 1879, four pottery kilns were exposed, probably just to the south of Minchery Farm, during drain-digging for the construction of the new Oxford sewage plant. These were stone and tile-lined pits cut into the subsoil with much evidence of burning, and were surrounded by a substantial spread of pottery waste, with two adjacent inhumations.[8] Some fine and complete pots of local wares were

20mm

Fig. 5.5. Roman white glass fluted melon bead (SF 111).

retrieved from the site by the Oxford anatomist George Rolleston and are now in the Ashmolean Museum. In more recent times, the nearby Oxford Science Park and Kassam Stadium excavations discovered more Romano-British kilns, pottery, and pits, gullies and post-holes. Our 2012 excavations in Minchery Paddock detected no substantive Roman features, but residual Romano-British pottery was recovered from all the trenches, and from a possible Romano-British plough-soil in Trench 2. Trench 1 produced four Romano-British pottery sherds accounting for half of that trench's total pottery collection. A fine Roman white glass melon bead (SF 111) was found in Trench 2 (Fig. 5.5); it had been redeposited in a Medieval context, and its precise origin is unknown; it may have been disturbed and redeposited (possibly from a burial) or kept as a curiosity or heirloom.

Anglo-Saxon and Medieval periods

The larger area excavations at Oxford Science Park, centred about half a kilometre to the west-south-west of the priory site, uncovered the remains of an Anglo-Saxon settlement as well as possible Medieval farms (for a discussion of the wider pattern surrounding Anglo-Saxon Medieval settlement, including the village of Littlemore, see page 75). Less than 500 metres north of the priory site, on the other side of Littlemore Brook, a single early Anglo-Saxon sunken featured building, that is a small structure partially dug into the ground, was found in excavations in 2014.[9] However, no Anglo-Saxon pottery or occupation features were discovered during our 2012 excavations: if they existed, any traces had been obliterated by later buildings.

The surviving priory building

The only part of Littlemore Priory that survives above ground is a two-storey rectangular north-south aligned building, ground-plan measuring about 25 metres by nine metres, which until the mid-twentieth century was the farmhouse of Minchery Farm. This was built in the fifteenth century, and is Grade II* listed.[10] The eastern façade of the building (Fig. 5.6) presents its best-preserved aspect, which is mostly original fifteenth-century fabric. W. A. Pantin, in a seminal study of the site published in *Oxoniensia* in 1970, proposed that the nuns' dormitory had been located on the first floor with the chapter house and other rooms, perhaps including the parlour, situated on the ground floor.[11] The dormitory range and possibly other parts of the priory were refurbished in the mid-fifteenth century, less than a century before its dissolution. The new structure replaced, and was possibly rebuilt on the same site as an earlier dormitory, which was reported in 1445 to be in poor condition. The building was extensively altered at the end of the sixteenth century when it became a

Fig. 5.6. The former Priory pub, the last upstanding part of the priory, eastern façade.

farmhouse, and it lost any structural connection to the other parts of the former nunnery, most of which were demolished. Its west wall was partially rebuilt in a more domestic style, a staircase wing added and new floors and chimney stacks constructed, along with a new stone-tiled roof. Ancillary farm buildings came and went around the building throughout its working life as a farm, and its north end was heavily modified. For some time between the 1960s and 1990s, the building served as part of a music venue known as a 'country club' which had other buildings to its north which are now gone, some of them having been destroyed in a fire in 2002. Its most recent use was as a public house until 2013. As of mid-2019, it stands empty and fenced off, overshadowed by a modern business hotel built in 2014-15 over the site of the former priory church immediately to its north (see page 186).

W.A. Pantin suggested a layout for the remainder of the cloister garth extrapolating from the surviving building. His reconstruction showed a typical square and closed claustral layout (Fig. 5.7), based on an assumption that the later Medieval priory was modelled on a twelfth-thirteenth century predecessor with a small enclosed cloister. The result of *Archeox*'s 2012 excavations suggested that the layout may in fact have been both more extensive and less formal than Pantin envisaged. The excavation in 2014 by John Moore Heritage Services (JMHS) of the former priory church shows that this was located 15m to the north of where Pantin suggested and on a slightly different alignment. However, the size and alignment of Building 3 in Trench 3 (see below) does match Pantin's alignment very closely.

Other excavations in the Priory and Minchery Paddock areas

Before the *Archeox* excavations in 2012, a small amount of information had accumulated from other investigations relating to the archaeological remains of the priory.[12] Immediately around the standing pub building and east of the near north-south track, burials had been recorded north and east of the same building in the nineteenth century, with no further details provided. In 1995, a fishpond was discovered next to Grenoble Road, probably forming part of a chain of ponds including the one on the west side of Minchery Paddock, which still exists as a near-circular water feature, which is unfortunately choked with discarded car tyres and other detritus.[13] A limited archaeological investigation was carried out in 2004 by Pre-Construct Archaeology just to the north and east of the pub building, where some evidence was found for a robbed-out building on an east-west alignment north of the pub, and some grave cuts were also detected to its north-east.[14] This robbed-out structure may have been part of the church later excavated in 2014 by John Moore Heritage Services (JMHS).[15] Interestingly, the part of the burial ground uncovered in 2004 had been abandoned by the later Medieval period: it was sealed by a late Medieval surface into which pits had been cut. These pits contained later Medieval pottery and domestic waste. The reduction in size of the graveyard and its use for rubbish disposal may have been a symptom of the later decline in the priory's management. The 2014 archaeological investigations conducted ahead of the

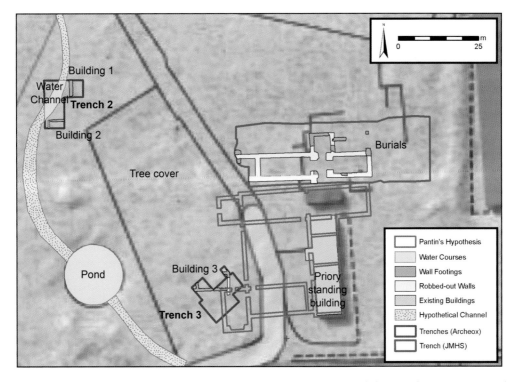

Fig. 5.7. Locations of trenches and priory building with Pantin's (1970) proposed cloister plan superimposed.

building of a hotel north of the remaining priory building revealed not only the plan of the demolished priory church but a considerable number of burials (see page 187).

Minchery Paddock

In 2006, when Minchery Paddock was being considered for housing development, John Moore Heritage Services carried out evaluation-type excavations in the paddock (long, narrow trenches part-excavated by machine which were aimed at exposing the subsurface archaeology), covering part of the area later investigated by *Archeox* in 2012 (locations, Fig. 5.2).[16] Their results were too fragmentary to draw any conclusions about the character and extent of either the cloister or the precinct, but demonstrated that elements of the priory outer complex survive in the paddock. At the southern end of the paddock, east of the pond (JMHS Trench 8), parts of thirteenth-century building remains were identified, including west-east aligned wall foundations and a spread of rubble containing some Medieval pottery. *Archeox*'s Trench 3 was located to encompass that earlier investigation and explore the possible building remains in more detail (Fig. 5.1). JMHS's Trench 4 to the north produced convincing Medieval evidence. Here a well, the edge of a possible hearth and earthen floor surfaces, with a sherds of Medieval pottery and floor tile provided indications of surviving remains of buildings to the north-west of the cloister. In 2012, our Trench 2 was positioned just intersecting the end of JMHS Trench 4, to try to define and explore these features, and also alongside JMHS's

Trench 3, which had uncovered suggestions of a ditch or channel and possible wall-lines.

EXCAVATIONS IN MINCHERY PADDOCK: TRENCHES 1, 2 AND 3

In 2012, Trenches 2 and 3 were placed in Minchery Paddock to investigate further the Medieval archaeological features detected in the 2006 John Moore Heritage Services evaluation trenches, as described above (Fig. 5.2). Two Medieval buildings within the priory precinct were discovered in Trench 2, as well as the water channel which probably defined the western edge of the nunnery precinct. Another Medieval building was uncovered in Trench 3, on the western edge of the cloister. Trench 1, at the northern end of the paddock, was intended primarily to collect environmental evidence such as peat cores from the lower-lying, wetter area close to Littlemore Brook.

Trench 1, near the brook

Olaf Bayer with Julian Stern, Adrian Parker and Gareth Preston

The northern edge of Minchery Paddock occupies low lying wet ground at the confluence of the Littlemore and Northfield brooks. Small areas of peat, formed since the latter stages of the last Ice Age, survive at the confluence of the two water courses. The peat consists of layers of plant material, which having fallen into wet and anaerobic (when air is

Fig. 5.8. Excavation conditions in Trench 1.

excluded) areas has accumulated year on year rather than rotting away. These deposits contain an important record of long-term environmental change in the surrounding landscape as seeds and pollen are trapped in the layers. The archaeological potential of these peat deposits has been known since the end of the nineteenth century, when peat containing Roman pottery and animal bones was recorded during the construction of the nearby Oxford sewage works.[17] More recently several commercial excavations close to the same brooks at Oxford Science Park and the Kassam stadium complex, as well as Test Pit 47, at Northfield School, have all revealed similar sequences of clay, peat and alluvium.

The 2012 excavations at Minchery Paddock offered another opportunity to locate, investigate and date sediments and peat deposits, and to integrate these with the results of previous investigations in the wider area.[18] Trench 1 was opened downslope from the other two trenches, close to Littlemore Brook. As much of the trench lay below the water table, working conditions were very wet and muddy (Fig 5.8). A petrol-powered pump draining water all day from a sump into the lowest corner of the trench made excavation possible, but not easy. Peat (1001) was clearly visible lower down in the section (Fig. 5.9). The deposits were investigated by means of three overlapping 50 cm monoliths (or columns of soil) to

Fig. 5.9. Peat layer exposed in south-facing section, Trench 1.

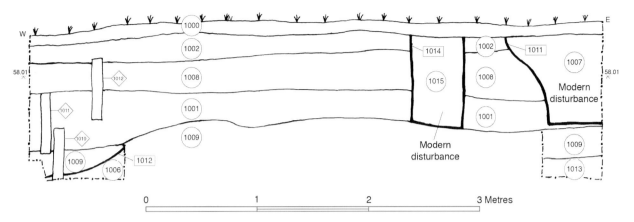

Fig. 5.10. Trench 1, south-facing section with locations of column samples marked (numbers in diamond shapes).

sample the whole sequence beneath topsoil; the locations of the monoliths are shown on Fig. 5.10.

The monolith samples were wrapped on site (Fig. 5.11) and taken away to be analysed by Professor Adrian Parker and Dr Gareth Preston of Oxford Brookes University. By examining the sediment, pollen and plant remains within the samples they were able to determine how natural and human factors had changed the surrounding landscape over time. The results were summarised in sequence of five 'zones'. Zones 1 to 3 spanned a period of climatic fluctuation between approximately 14,500-8,500BC. This lay at the end of the last Ice Age (the Devensian, marking the end of the Upper Palaeolithic period) and the start of the Mesolithic period (the beginning of the Holocene, the current climatic period). Zones 4 and 5 were more recent, probably formed from the Bronze Age c. 2000 BC onwards.

Fig. 5.11. Monolith samples wrapped and ready to be taken for laboratory analysis.

Zone 1: Clays and gravels

The lowest deposits encountered were associated with the development of the brook during the later stages of the last Ice Age, about 16,000 years ago and grouped together as Zone 1. The earliest clay and gravel deposit was found 1.55m below the ground surface, at the northern end of the trench. A depression [1012] in the surface of the clay in the north-west corner was probably the edge of a former channel of the brook cut into the gravels. The gravels were overlain by clays across the entire trench. The clay was probably carried from Oxford Clay deposits higher up in the catchment of the Littlemore and Northfield Brooks. All the Zone 1 deposits were formed by sediment washing into the stream channel during a period with sparse vegetation cover. The pollen indicated this vegetation comprised grasses and sedges with low levels of birch, pine and willow. Although no material from this deposit could be dated, by analogy with nearby sites it probably formed at around 14,500-14,000 BC during a cooler phase of the last Ice Age known as the Dimlington Stadial.

Zones 2 and 3: Peat

A layer of organic rich peat up to 0.5m thick lay over the clay described above across the northern third of the trench. The deposit was divided into two zones for environmental analysis, a lower Zone 2 and an upper Zone 3. Plant material taken from the base of Zone 2 produced a radiocarbon date of 11,521-11,449 cal BC (SUERC 53119) placing it in the Windermere Inter-stadial, a warmer period immediately following the Dimlington Stadial. Pollen from this level showed that birch-dominated woodland was developing with smaller amounts of pine, hazel, alder and willow; pollen from grasses and sedges suggested some areas of open ground nearby. A thin layer containing fragments of charcoal might have been caused by late Palaeolithic hunter-gathers burning vegetation or possibly a lightning strike.

Zone 3 although peat-based, contained more clay and silt. This may reflect the erosion of soil across a relatively open landscape. Pollen from this level indicated surroundings dominated by grasses and sedges, with areas of disturbed ground. As with Zone 2 there were signs of burning. Plant material from midway through Zone 3 gave a radiocarbon date of 10,022-9,825 cal BC (SUERC 53913). This suggested

the zone spanned the Loch Lomond Stadial, the final cold period of the last Ice Age, and the transition to the Holocene: so the start of the Mesolithic. A peak in burning evidence was probably caused by Mesolithic hunter-gathers deliberately firing vegetation; this would help account for pollen from the top of Zone 3

Fig. 5.12. Trench 2, final plan.

indicating a largely open landscape surrounded the site dominated by grasses and sedges with small amounts of alder, hazel, lime and blackthorn.

Zones 4 and 5: Alluvium

Extending across most of the trench the upper peat was sealed by thick iron-stained clay deposits of waterborne sediment or alluvium analysed as Zones 4 and 5 and laid down by repeated flooding. The upper clay deposit contained more silt and sand than the lower. A spread of limestone fragments (1004) measuring approximately 5m by 12.5m was discovered in the centre of the trench during the excavation of these upper clays. Many of the stone pieces were deliberately shaped and probably came from a wall. Tile, animal bone, brick, glass and Roman and Medieval pottery sherds were all found with the stone. The spread may have been an attempt to create a firmer surface near the brook, perhaps for cattle, for fording or fetching water.

These alluvial deposits were very different to those below and there was a chronological gap of several thousand years between samples taken from Zones 3 and 5. Charcoal at the base of Zone 5 gave an Early Bronze Age radiocarbon date of 1,972-1,884 cal BC (SUERC 53914). This gap represented either a break in sediments being laid or least a much slower rate of sedimentation during the Mesolithic and Neolithic periods. This changed in the Bronze Age: evidence from other sites in the Upper Thames Valley links the widespread clearance of woodland for pasture, grazing and cereal cultivation during this period with a rise in the water table, as well as more intense erosion and increased deposition of alluvium.

Trench 2: the outer precinct of the priory

Jane Harrison, with Will Hemmings, Steve Nicholson, Paul Rowland and Roelie Reed

Trench 2 revealed a complex group of Medieval archaeological deposits and features which had been largely undisturbed since the priory closed in 1525. The area had then become pasture and was not built upon again. Trench 2 was L-shaped: 13 metres north-south by 11 metres west-east at its maximum, with the longer north-south arm being five metres wide and the shorter west-east arm four metres wide (Figs 5.2, 5.12, 5.13). Running up the western side of Trench 2 was a silted water channel, apparently defining the western limits of the priory's precinct grounds. Building 1, a large Medieval barn or outbuilding was found in the east of the trench, and Building 2, a Medieval domestic building, in the south. Both buildings were within the area bounded by the channel and situated less than 100 metres north-west of the priory church.

The first Medieval building constructed in this area of the priory estate was Building 1, part of which was

Fig. 5.13. Trench 2, from south (AerialCam).

discovered in the eastern arm of the trench. This large outbuilding or barn was erected in the mid-twelfth century around the time the priory was founded. About sixteen metres square of the building's beaten earth floor was uncovered, and set into it was a finely constructed, large hearth formed of tiles set on end. However, as Trench 2 had been positioned to intersect with John Moore Heritage Services' 2006 evaluation Trench 4, this building's interior could also be demonstrated to have extended a little further east.[19] JMHS Trench 4 had been cut as a two metre wide strip just to the east and north-east of our Trench 2 and had uncovered a further section of the hard floor surface of Building 1, and to the north-east of that was a well with a stone surround.[20] The well may have been just within or just outside an open eastern side or entrance of the outbuilding, making Building 1 at least 11 metres long. Building 1 went through two phases of use, as described below, before being demolished, almost certainly after 1525.

A water channel, over two metres wide, ran in a south-north alignment across the western side of the trench, and may have bounded the site. This feature had been straightened, deepened and partially lined with stone, probably in the mid-twelfth century at a similar time to the raising of Building 1. Sometime not long after that, probably in the later twelfth century, Building 2 was built in stone; parts of its northern and western walls were found in the southern area of Trench 2, again within the precinct area defined by the water channel. There was probably an earlier wooden building in that location. Traces of burning indicated it had possibly been damaged by fire, before being replaced by Building 2 which then survived until the closure of the priory. Building 2 had well-built foundations, may have been furnished for at least part of its time with a tiled floor, was built in the later-twelfth century and had two phases of use, like Building 1, before it too was demolished in the earlier-sixteenth century. The archaeology suggested the second phase of activity was one during which the buildings were either relatively crudely altered and/or less well-maintained; this may have been linked to the gradual contraction and running-down of the priory before the Little Dissolution. What follows discusses in more detail the histories of the buildings and their surroundings as they were revealed in Trench 2.

Firstly, we discuss the north-eastern arm of Trench 2: from east of the water channel to the eastern end of the trench, and south as far as the small gully [2011] running west into the channel. The soils and finds west of the moat and south of the little gully were persistently different from each other and from those in the area of Building 1. All the undisturbed archaeology of this zone relates to the construction, use, alteration and demolition of Building 1 (Fig. 5.12).

Before Building 1: Prehistoric and Romano-British evidence

Fragments of flint tools and waste (debitage) from flint-working were found in this part of Trench 2, probably ranging in date between the Mesolithic Period to the Early Bronze Age. All were redeposited and residual, having moved at least once from where they were originally deposited, but testify to probable Prehistoric activity in the general area.

In the west of this part of Trench 2, and running north-east to south-west along the eastern edge of the water channel and as far south as the west-east gully, was a strip of sandy silt (2012): over a metre wide in the south but narrower in the north. This layer was caught in section in the northern [2026] and central slots [2027] across the water channel and appeared to be a plough-soil overlying the natural sandy subsoil and cut by the channel. This plough-soil had clearly developed before the channel or the structures within its ambit were constructed. This may have been the Romano-British plough-soil encountered across the wider Minchery Paddock area in the 2006 JMHS excavations, and the source of some of the residual Roman pottery found in many layers in the *Archeox* investigations. Moreover, where the Medieval earthen floors within Building 1 had disturbed this plough-soil they contained some large rim sherds of residual Roman pottery, suggesting there might have been Romano-British buildings in the near vicinity as well as fields.

Building 1: first phase: walls and post-pads and post-holes

Under the rubbly layers created in the process of dismantling this building, sufficient elements of its structure survived to demonstrate at least two phases of its use. The first version of the building seemed to be better-built and maintained, and as will be shown there was a similar sequence in Building 2 to the south. The original western end-wall foundations [2054] of Building 1, running north-south, were far better-built than the subsequent re-construction (Fig. 5.12, 5.13, upper right). The first wall was located just east of the water channel, which cut thin layers associated with building the wall. Building 1 would have occupied the whole of the eastern arm of the trench and run beyond. The foundations of the wall were 1.1m wide and built from vertically laid sub-angular rough-shaped limestone cobbles trending west-east with some horizontal north-south edging stones. A 3.5m length was revealed; the foundations may have ended with post-pad [2042] in the south of the trench, but definitely continued beyond a second post-pad [2041] and the trench-edge in the north. The post-pads were mortared into the foundations and probably intended to support a wooden and wattle and daub super-structure linked to post-holes found within Building 1. The post-pads themselves were built of rough square limestone blocks mortared together. Both bases were about 0.7 square metres in size and two-three courses of their stonework survived. A later, less-substantial north-south wall [2040] (see second phase, below) was built against, but not mortared into, the eastern side of these post-pads. The original Building 1, which sheltered a large hearth, was therefore a considerable structure with wide, well-built stone foundations and posts supporting a wooden superstructure. Its walls may not have been full height; with a large hearth within, some of the upper portions of parts of the walls at least were probably open.[21] The original floors seem to have been beaten earth (see below) and this suggests this part of the building was probably not used for grain storage, when the floors are more likely to be cobbled.

Building 1, first phase: floors and hearth

The hearth [2031] in the eastern corner of Trench 2 was beautifully built, constructed re-using ceramic

Fig. 5.14. The hearth, working shot from north-east.

roof and floor tiles laid vertically on edge, flanked to the south by six large flat hearth-flags showing signs of significant heat-damage. The broken tiles, some of them glazed, were bedded at 70° from the horizontal (Fig. 5.14); the overall shape was sub-oval, measuring 2.5m west-east and 2.4m north-south, with the fire area to the west. The most southerly flags were firmly embedded into clay (2062), which may have served as the bedding layer for both the hearth and the wall to the west. The four shaped flags to the west around the fire were heavily burnt. Within the sub-square area enclosed by these stones (slightly truncated to the south by JMHS Trench 4), layer (2056) which comprised lenses of ash and burnt sand, contained large chunks of charcoal, and burnt stones and tiles. This was clearly the centre of the fire, with the hearth working area to the east. High temperatures were being generated there for some sort of industrial use as there was environmental evidence for oak charcoal; local brushwood was also used as kindling, along with the waste from grain processing.[22]

The floor area (2036) immediately around the hearth had been much affected by the heat of the fire and contained abundant charcoal and ash. A radiocarbon date on hazel charcoal was taken from (2036), next to the hearth, and produced a range of 1151-1258 cal.AD (at 85.7% probability).[23] Thus this phase of use of Building 1 probably embraced the first century or so of the priory's existence.

The other silty layers running east of wall [2054], and below the later wall, represented the earthen floors laid within the barn while the substantial hearth was in use. Floor (2035) north of the hearth was silty and still rich in charcoal and ash lenses, but with slightly less evidence for burning than immediately around the hearth.

Building 1: second phase

Probably sometime in the fourteenth century, Building 1 was altered or perhaps repaired after a period of neglect. A three-metre length of wall was built against the internal face of the earlier and wider north-south wall [2054]. The surviving wall foundations of this second phase of building [2040] were narrow and roughly-built, using undecorated tile fragments as well as small, mostly un-faced limestone blocks. It had been constructed after the hearth to the east had gone out of use as there was no sooting on the stones' internal faces, and the ashy hearth-related deposits ran under the wall. This suggests the outbuilding was being used in a different way in this phase and perhaps also that it was no longer as well-maintained. The archaeology of this phase had also been disturbed and truncated by the demolition of Building 1, most of the floor levels had been lost and it is not really possible to suggest anything more about its character and use.

Building 1: the demolition layers and JMHS Trench 4 backfill

Above the Medieval archaeology in Trench 2 only demolition layers and disturbed topsoil were discovered; the land here had most probably been turned over to pasture after the Little Dissolution and only otherwise been marked by the modern traces (archaeology in themselves!) of the Traveller community and the evaluation work of the 2006 JMHS investigations. To the east of the moat and covering almost the entire eastern arm of the trench was a deep layer (2013; up to 0.4m deep), which sealed the Medieval layers. Three-quarters of this spread was limestone rubble – relating to the dismantling of Building 1 and perhaps other structures nearby but outside the trench. The surviving wall-lines were however discernible within this destruction layer, which also contained redeposited Medieval debris: both decorated and undecorated Medieval tile fragments; Medieval pottery sherds; oyster shell and animal bone.

Trench 2 had also caught a small triangle of the south-west side of JMHS Trench 4, which made up the remainder of this layer sealing the surviving Medieval archaeology. North-east trending strips of backfill (2014-2016) excavated across the south-east corner of this part of Trench 2 represented disturbance caused by the JMHS investigations which had halted at the undisturbed Medieval archaeology.

In layer (2003) above both (2013) and the JMHS backfill and covering the whole of this area east of the water channel it was very difficult to distinguish between the JMHS disturbance and the upper spread of demolition-related material. Medieval plaster and worked stone fragments, as well as Medieval pottery, wall and floor tiles were discovered, underlining that this was the location of dismantled buildings. Layer (2000) above (2003) was much more rubbly than the corresponding layers in other parts of the trench and, in particular, than the layer west of the moat. The rubble comprised many relatively small fragments of rough limestone building stone. The stone-content difference between the layers sealing the two Medieval buildings in Trench 2 may be explained by their differing construction. Building 1 used many more smaller and irregular limestone pieces in its wall and these would have been discarded on demolition. More of the finer stone used in the upper courses of Building 2 was probably taken away from the priory for re-use, some perhaps in St George's House in Littlemore (see page 195).

The cobbled yard and Building 2, in the south of Trench 2

The archaeology east of the water channel in the southern area of Trench 2 was dominated by the north-western corner of a Medieval stone-built structure, Building 2 (Figs 5.12, 5.13, southern area), and to the north of it, the remains of a cobbled yard associated with Building 2 (Fig 5.15) and delineated to the west by the channel and to the north by a small gully [2011].

Archaeology preceding Building 2

As elsewhere in Trench 2, residual flint tool fragments, tool-making waste and Roman pottery sherds, in this area small and worn, testified to earlier activity in the vicinity. However, the earliest *in-situ* archaeology belonged to a phase of Medieval building preceding Building 2, perhaps contemporary with the construction of Building 1 to the

Fig. 5.15. Trench 2, southern area, from south showing cobbled yard inside water channel.

Fig. 5.16. View across Building 2 later in excavation, from south-west.

north. This archaeology comprised the back-filling of a cut feature running under Building 2 and evidence for the burning of an earlier building.

The northern wall of Building 2 [2030] and a near-circular, flat stone slab feature [2053] just within the building were cut into a back-filled ditch-stretch or pits uncovered both south of the stone slabs of [2053] and north of the wall (Fig. 5.16). Only the west side of the pit or ditch was seen inside the building: 0.9m wide as excavated and over 0.65m deep. Although the cut feature clearly ran north under the slabs of [2053] and another pit-like feature [2058], albeit slightly differently filled, appeared just north of the wall, the intervening wall-line made the relationship between the pit/ditch to the north and south of the wall impossible to confirm. However, it was likely they were parts of the same feature, which may have extended further south beyond the trench. Inside the building the pit/ditch fills were very humic with the upper layer containing some finds and excellent environmental evidence; the lower layers appeared to be natural peat above natural grey clay. The feature therefore cut through natural sand and into the clay below and may have been part of a natural channel back-filled when construction work began in the area during the Medieval period.

Although the purpose of the feature was difficult to explain, it produced a radiocarbon date on hazel charcoal from the upper layer (2059) of 1152-1260 cal AD (SUERC 49309: at 90.1% probability), placing its back-filling in the first century of the priory's life.[24] The material from the back-fill – bone, pottery, ash and charcoal – also suggested people active in the vicinity before Building 2 was constructed. The fill of pit [2061] inside Building 2 contained charred grains of oats and rye, likely used as animal feed, and bread wheat, as well as oak and hazel charcoal, and a large quantity of burnt broad beans. This suggested agricultural and domestic

waste was being re-used as hearth-fuel and beans cultivated, probably in the priory gardens. The pottery sherds included an unusual Brill-Boarstall ware skillet handle and a pitcher-like jug (see Fig. 5.34), emphasising the link to cooking and domestic work, perhaps taking place in a wooden building damaged by fire and demolished before Building 2 was constructed (see below). The similar character of thin layers sealing the pit and running under the stone slabs of [2053] suggested that both the fill and those layers were material redeposited as part of the preparation of previously occupied ground for raising Building 2.

Building 2: construction and use

Building 2 was defined by its north-west corner: 4.3m of its northern west-east aligned foundations and lower courses were uncovered [2030] (Fig. 5.17). These were 0.75m wide and survived up to 0.8m in height, soundly constructed of roughly-faced Corallian rag limestone; the maximum size of stones was 0.4m by 0.25m, with most slightly smaller. Smaller stones and some tiles had been used to level courses. Seven to nine courses survived, with a well-constructed relieving arch at the eastern end built over pit [2058] outside and to the north of the wall, and pit-like feature [2061] inside and to the south (Fig. 5.18). The relieving arch would have spread the weight of the wall over the softer ground of the in-fill and was very similar in size and construction to that at Bartlemas Chapel (see page 129), and also to one which can be seen in the walls of another twelfth-century Benedictine nunnery, Godstow Abbey, north-west of Oxford beside the Thames.

The lower seven courses of Building 2 were built in one phase, a double-faced wall and foundations, with rubble and earth infill and encompassing the relieving arch. The upper two courses were built with smaller stones, included a butt joint and made heavy use of

Fig. 5.17. Wall [2030] from north.

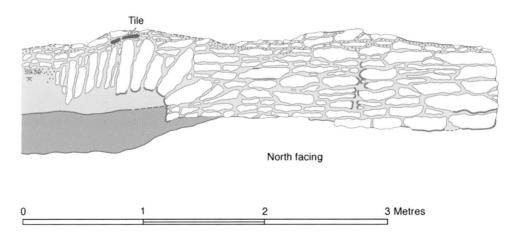

Fig. 5.18. Elevation drawing of wall [2030] showing relieving arch built over pit [2058].

mortar bonding, suggesting a second, less well-constructed phase or reconstruction/repair of Building 2. Over the pits at the eastern end, which had necessitated the use of the arch, the wall had slumped. The wall had returned to run north-south, just before the water channel to the west, but relatively little of that western wall had survived. The second phase may also have included a rebuilding of the north-south wall-return, but its traces had been largely eradicated during the demolition of Building 2. The pottery assemblage suggested that second phase likely coincided broadly with the downturn in the priory's fortunes into the fourteenth and fifteenth centuries.

Inside Building 2, an enigmatic semi-circular stone slab structure [2053] was built against the inside of the relieving arch in the north-east corner. It was around 1.4m in diameter and constructed of slabs of rough-cut limestone with three large slabs visible on the top in an outer ring, the largest being 0.6m by 0.45m, with smaller slabs filling the centre and sloping gently to

the south and east into the centre of the feature. The slabs were bonded with a rough gravelly mortar. The slabs to the north may have been partly built under the relieving arch and although this feature was difficult to interpret, it may have been part of efforts to secure the surface for construction by covering the infilled pit/ditch. Alternatively, it is possible that there was originally a well there, accessed from both sides of the wall, and the slab-stones of [2053] were part of the construction of its top. However, it seems more plausible, and stratigraphic relationships support this, that [2053] was part of the sequence of construction events linked to the building of wall [2030] and thus of Building 2.

The thin levelling layers over the pit included a charcoal and silt-rich layer (2060) that was laid just before wall [2030] was built and obviously linked to burning. The layer also spread west under the north-south return of [2030] into the edge of the water channel. West of the wall-return, the layer contained

Fig. 5.19. The bone tuning peg, SF 138.

Fig. 5.20. Silver coin of Henry III, Voided long cross, Class III, 1248-50, SF 85 (obverse and reverse views).

charcoal and also the fragmentary remains of charred timbers, possibly from a floor. This suggested that an earlier building, perhaps with a slightly different footprint to its stone successor, had been damaged by fire. Inside Building 2 three thin layers (2049, 2050 and 2052) laid over the silt of (2060) evened up the interior, preparing the area for the construction of the stone-slab feature and the floor surfaces that followed. The levelling layers were built up of fine, laminated spreads of dumped sand, ash and silt with consolidating spreads of fragments of roof and floor tiles concentrated over the fill of the pit/ditch. Layer (2052) produced one of the most evocative finds made on the site: a carved bone tuning peg for a plucked Medieval stringed instrument called a psaltery (Fig. 5.19; SF 138).

A Medieval socketed arrowhead (see Fig. 5.33) found in (2049) may have come to the priory embedded in hunted meat, possibly from deer or wild boar; it is very similar to one discovered at Bartlemas. The consolidation layers inside the building otherwise contained pottery and bone – including fish bones. It seems probable that Building 2 was constructed after the founding of the priory and perhaps as the nunnery gradually expanded to fill its precinct during the thirteenth century. The remaining layers excavated within the building related to its use (and demolition) and in particular to Building 2's floors. Establishing more precise date ranges for the origin and phases of use in Building 2 was complicated by the re-laying of the floors above this level and the concomitant disturbance and truncation of original bedding layers. A sandy bedding (2045) discovered over the levelling layers in interior may not have been the first such layer, or have been made up of repeated layers. It merged

with (2044), in the south-east corner which was a stonier, thicker layer, set to compensate for slumping over pit [2061]; it is plausible this may have been part of a later re-flooring. That stonier layer contained a couple of sherds of Medieval pottery and a silver coin (voided long cross, probably Henry III, 1248-50; SF 85, Fig. 5.20), providing a date range in the mid-later thirteenth century, after which a floor must have been laid (or re-laid). The sandy bedding layer (2045) was finds-rich suggesting that an element of midden had been incorporated into the spread. Along with Medieval pottery, both jugs and jars, fragments of tile and animal bone, including pig, were six iron objects, including a smith's punch and nails, and a fragment of a copper object (SF 87). A radiocarbon date, again on hazel charcoal from that layer gave a date range of 1297–1405 cal AD (SUERC 49314: at 95.4% probability), and together with the coin and artefactual evidence, suggested Building 2 was also in use through the fourteenth century.[25]

Spread (2029) above the sand comprised hard-core consolidation for another floor and was made up almost entirely of evenly-sized limestone rubble. The rubbly layer contained some Medieval pottery, broken tile and iron objects; it also sloped slightly towards pit [2061], now under the floor of Building 2. The uppermost surviving internal layer (2008), although much disturbed and damaged by Building 2's dismantling, had clearly also been a bedding layer for a later but not necessarily final floor. A number of decorated Stabbed Wessex-type decorated floor tiles were found in this area.

The assemblage of animal bones from floor layers in Building 2 was relatively small, but like the objects described above, and the plant remains, it testifies to a focus on food preparation and eating. Much of the primary butchery had been done elsewhere and the bone assemblage was dominated by beef, although with relatively more sheep than found in Trench 3.[26] The nature of the pottery assemblage confirmed that the only disturbance of the archaeology had been either during Medieval alterations or in the sixteenth century, probably related to the demolition: 88% of the pottery was Medieval, the remaining being residual Roman sherds. In general, the pottery, like the other finds was domestic in character – jars, jugs, bowls, skillets, chafing dishes and dripping pans –

with a few more unusual forms that suggested the dining in Building 2 was relatively refined. In the demolition layer above the building a fragment of a rare Brill-Boarstall ware zoomorphic aquamanile was discovered (see Fig. 5.34). This is part of a vessel used to pour water for hand-washing at table. Sherds of a cistern or bung-hole pitcher used for brewing ale in the same fabric were also found in the demolition layer (2009) just north of Building 2.[27]

The yard north of Building 2, within the water channel

The earliest feature found in the area outside of the building but east of the channel was pit [2058] described above. Outside Building 2 the pit was two metres wide and over 0.3m deep with sides at 45 degrees, cut into the natural sand beneath the relieving arch, and reaching under the wall to the south. The silty fill of the pit (2057) contained fresh sherds of Medieval pottery and a residual Neolithic leaf-shaped flint arrowhead (see page 184). A radiocarbon date on a charred bread wheat grain from (2057) of 1035-1186 cal AD (94.5% probability), indicated that the feature may have been back-filled in preparations before priory-related building commenced.[28] The precinct area north of the building was turned into an external yard; the earliest surface in this area (2047) had been partly consolidated with a thin silty midden spread. A collection of horse mandibles were found in this surface and the layer also yielded a good collection of mostly unabraded sherds of Medieval pottery, especially at the junction between (2047) and surface (2032) above it, and also animal bone and slag, copper alloy tweezers (SF 114) and five worked flints (see Fig. 5.33).[29]

Fig. 5.21. Silver coin, Henry II, Short cross, 1180–89, SF 81 (obverse and reverse views).

The second surface (2032), in the roughly triangular area between Building 2's west-east wall [2030], the water channel to the west, the trench side to the east and the gulley to the north had been disturbed by the later demolition. However, (2032) had clearly been a cobbled yard, well-constructed of regular limestone cobbles about 0.2m in diameter. Excavation of this yard surface produced animal bone and iron objects, including nails and some possible shears and an assemblage of Medieval (later-thirteenth to fourteenth century) pottery sherds, including some highly decorated jugs. The pottery implied that Building 2 was of some status. A third and later yard partially survived beneath demolition rubble in a patchy and truncated state. This surface may have been a gritty earth layer beaten into the cobbles below to create a cheap but practical surface and included a possible post hole lined with upright stones. Along with the indications of less well-resourced alteration or repair to Building 2's external wall and possible stripping of internal tiled flooring, this later yard also hints at an economically more challenged phase in the priory's history, perhaps into the fourteenth and fifteenth centuries. The rubbly layer (2009) above the yards had most likely resulted

Fig. 5.22. Trench 2, silted water channel from south-east prior to excavation.

from the process of demolishing priory buildings, including Building 2, carting off re-usable stone and rejecting smaller fragments. Along with building rubble not worth retrieving for re-use, the demolition layer contained fragments of floor and roof tile, pottery (all fourteenth or fifteenth-century), animal bone and oyster shell, iron nails and a worn silver penny (Henry II short cross, 1180 to 1189; SF81, Fig. 5.21).

The water channel

It was not uncommon for nunneries to be encircled, protected and set apart by a water-filled ditch which functioned like a moat. The Benedictine nunnery at Little Marlow, about 50 km south-east of Minchery was also encircled by water: 'The priory [at Little Marlow] was a small and never wealthy house of Benedictine nuns… with a plan of somewhat irregular setting out on level and marshy ground by the river. It was surrounded by streams watered by the springs that rise to the east and west.'[30]

The water channel that curved around the precinct in the west was clearly visible beneath the upper top-soil related layers as a band of ditch-fill (Figs 5.12, 5.13, 5.22). While the ditch may have started life as a natural feature cutting down through bedrock, it had clearly been deliberately deepened and straightened. The consistently near-vertical sides, remnants of stone lining, and traces of wooden features indicated a channel modified and managed for a purpose. The stretch revealed in Trench 2 was 11 metres long, ran SSW-NNE, was 2.5m wide on average and over 1.2m deep, at which depth both the water table and the natural silting fill of the channel were reached. This water channel probably flowed from the fish-pond discovered south of the Minchery

Paddock site in earlier archaeological work ahead of the building of the sewage farm, north-west through the fish pond which survives west of Trench 3, and then probably continued to the NNE to join the Littlemore Brook (Fig. 5.3).

Three sections were excavated across the water channel. The northern one [2026] was the only one to reveal the full profile and depth to the natural silting layer (Fig. 5.23). A later cut into the western ditch-side seen in that section was related to a rubble spread and possible building to the west of the moat, outside the priory's precinct. The sandy clay matrix (2022) for the rubble had been very disturbed by mole-runs so it was difficult to interpret what the building may have been.

The first deliberate fill of this part of the ditch, over the natural silt accumulation (2039) was dark silt influenced by the rise and fall of the water-table; the deposit was marked by sand and clay lenses and iron panning, but also contained a small amount of abraded Medieval pottery and tile. Two possible stake holes were observed hammered down the east side of the ditch. Tip-lines were very visible in this layer and the one above, suggesting that the ditch had been filled in from the west side. The layer above, (2025) also contained Medieval, and some Romano-British, pottery as well as Medieval tile, bone and worked flint. The fill was very mixed but much stonier than the one below, with large 0.3m long stones as well as an assortment of slightly smaller limestone chunks. These fills both seemed to comprise demolition rubble and debris collected from Medieval buildings and surfaces and then dumped into the ditch. The upper ditch fill (2018) contained very large limestone boulders. The pottery however was still Medieval or residual Romano-British, and there were more tiles

Fig. 5.23. Section dug across water channel.

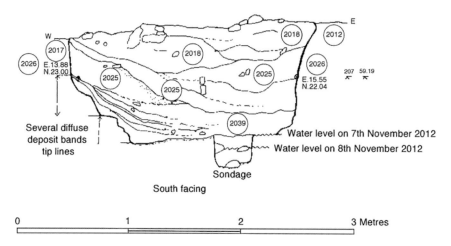

Fig. 5.24. Section dug across water channel (drawing).

and bone. The channel at this point had near-vertical sides; it was cut through the underlying natural sand, then limestone bedrock and finally into the clay beneath that (Fig. 5.24)

The central section [2027] excavated across the ditch, slightly wider at 2.7m, was extended from eastern to western trench-edge to obtain an extended profile through the layers on either side of the channel. These layers were completely different to the east and the west of the ditch, demonstrating that it had acted as a boundary between the precinct and outside throughout the Medieval period. The slot for this section was excavated until undisturbed natural layers were reached on either side of the channel and so was only 0.4m deep. The sandy silty fill of the ditch (2019) had very few large stones, unlike the other upper ditch fills excavated to the north and south, but contained fourteenth to fifteenth century Medieval pottery and tile. The layers to the west, outside the channel, (2017) and (2043), were notable for their lack of stone and rubble. (2017), a homogenous humic silt, contained Medieval domestic debris including animal bone and pottery along with a Medieval buckle-plate (SF 59). (2017) gradually merged into a similar but less humic and finds-rich layer (2043). (2043) in turn merged into (2046), an increasingly sandy layer containing very few finds, which gradually diffused into the natural sand below (appearing across the site at 59.12–59.17m OD). These three layers together were only about 0.3m deep. There was Medieval activity west of the water channel but it is difficult to characterise it otherwise than as a broadly domestic or agricultural spread, from the small area excavated.

The southern section across the channel and across gully [2011]

The southern section [2028] showed only the eastern side of the ditch as the western one was beyond the trench. The slot for this was excavated to a depth of 1.2m, when the water table was reached. A very large

stone, 0.8m long, was wedged against the eastern side and 19 other large (over 0.3m long) stones were removed from the fill, concentrated in the east of the ditch. These stones were from a range of local geological sources and, while some were very similar to stones in wall-foundation [2030] and the associated relieving arch, others were larger than seen in the structural elements that remained on site. They may have been from the upper courses of walls rather than foundations. The lower fills of the ditch in this slot were varied and marked by tip lines confirming that the ditch had been filled in from the east side here unlike further north. The uppermost layer (2020) filled the ditch at a level where there may have been a stone lining, at least on the eastern side. (2033) below contained many large stones and produced Medieval pottery, tile and bone. Several of the large stones removed looked from their position as if they may originally have come from a lining, while others were unwanted structural stones, thrown into the ditch, presumably during the demolition process. A small gully [2011] fed into the large ditch from the east and its profile was visible cut into the side of the moat in this slot. The narrow, shallow gully was U-shaped, with straight sides; the base sloped to the south-west towards the moat. A 2.25m stretch was revealed, 0.5m wide and 0.4m deep. The layers north and south of the gully were different indicating it was a boundary separating the areas around Buildings 1 and 2. It may have supported a fence; the fill (2010) suggested an ephemeral line of stake holes against the southern edge of the gully. The gully fill was very mixed, with areas of silt and clay, and contained a few sherds of Medieval pottery.

Archaeological layers above the buildings, features and demolition layers

The uppermost archaeological layers in Trench 2 post-dated the levelling of the Medieval site but yielded clues to what lay buried beneath them. All these upper layers yielded residual (disturbed from their original location) animal bone, iron fragments and objects, including a lever lock key and carpenter's gouge, Medieval floor and roof tile, including glazed tiles, Medieval and Roman pottery, and a number of worked flints. The upper layer of the in-filled water channel was also apparent as a wide pale stripe running NE-SW through the trench (Fig. 5.22).[31] North-west of the channel the upper soil spread was dark, even and contained little stone (2004); the corresponding layer east of the channel and in the south of the trench was relatively rubble-free (2005) but the surviving wall-line [2030] was already clearly visible running west-east across it. In the eastern arm of the trench layer (2003) was very stony and rubbly, obscuring the line of the surviving walls beneath. There was a relatively small amount of more modern disturbance in these layers, but what there was testified to an interesting chapter in the site's more recent past. The uppermost layers in the north of Trench 2 contained some shallow pits or scrapes used to bury small car parts and debris (wing mirrors etc.), while deep ruts and dips around a huge stone dumped in the centre of the trench had been levelled with modern pea-grit, probably where a heavy vehicle had churned up the ground. This modern debris and ground-churning may be linked to the use of the site by Traveller families and the subsequent tidying up of the site by the Council after they had left.

Trench 3: claustral buildings and kitchen midden

Joanne Robinson, with Jane Harrison and Nathalie Garfunkle

Trench 3 was located closer to the heart of the Medieval priory, almost within reach of the surviving standing building which stands 25m to the east. As described above, in 1970 W. A. Pantin published a conjectural layout of the Littlemore Priory's cloister, based on a study of the surviving priory building, then known as Minchery Farm, using analogies from other English nunneries.[32] His suggested plan showed a central cloister garth with a church to the north and kitchen and refectory or dining hall to the south (see Fig. 5.7). Pantin's projected position of the nave of the priory church was 15 metres south of the position confirmed by the JMHS 2014 excavations (see page 186), and the earlier JMHS archaeological evaluation conducted in Minchery Paddock in 2006 had detected stone walls of Medieval buildings in the area later covered by *Archeox* Trench 3, but beyond Pantin's layout. This hinted to us that Pantin's projected plan was too tightly-defined and had under-estimated the extent of the buildings forming the priory complex.

The 2012 Excavation: Trench 3

It was obvious that the Medieval structures in the area west of the priory cloister and within Minchery Paddock had been impacted differently in the past to those in Trench 2 and that this had greatly affected the character of the archaeology. In Trench 2 to the north, two Medieval buildings had been demolished down to ground level with the remains buried beneath pasture land and then lying undisturbed until archaeological investigations of the twenty-first century. After the Little Dissolution, what was not demolished of the priory became a farm. In the area around Trench 3, some elements of priory structures had been thoroughly dismantled, down to and including their foundations, whereas other buildings were repurposed rather than immediately levelled; the Medieval archaeology was therefore disturbed by later re-use and alteration of structures throughout the history of the farm. The south-west area of the trench had also been landscaped in the later nineteenth century as a garden. As surface neglect of the paddock took hold in more recent times, root spreads from rampant tree growth had eaten into the archaeology.

Trench 3 was 13 metres wide SW-NE by 13 metres NW-SW. JMHS 2006 Evaluation Trench 8 ran SW-NE across parts of the northern extent of the trench (see Fig. 5.2). The surrounding dense vegetation meant the shape of the trench had to be designed to avoid large trees, and the area actually excavated was considerably less than a 13 metre square (Figs 5.25, 5.26). The archaeology in the south-west quadrant had been almost entirely obliterated by later landscaping. The accumulated disturbance meant that under the topsoil was a confusing spread of rubble, but beneath this emerged the clear and substantial foundations of a west-east aligned stone-built structure (Building 3). Building 3 lay parallel to Pantin's projected southern claustral range and at right-angles to the standing building, so was perhaps situated just beyond the western cloister passage. There was also evidence for a possible kitchen area in the south-east of the trench with an associated midden.

Pre-Medieval archaeology and previous excavation, JMHS 2006

As in Trench 2, the topsoil across Trench 3, and many other contexts, contained occasional residual sherds of Roman pottery and worked flints, indicating activity from earlier periods. The considerably more disturbed character of the archaeology in Trench 3 was evident in the topsoil with Roman, Medieval and post-Medieval pottery mixed with a range of more modern material; the vast majority of the pottery dated from between 1850 and 1900.[33] The 2006 JMHS evaluation (JMHS Trench 8) had identified elements of what was interpreted as a thirteenth-century building, including west-east aligned wall foundations and a spread of rubble containing some Medieval pottery. Trench 3 was located so as to encompass that earlier investigation and explore the possible building in more detail; however, it could not be extended north-west to trace the northern side of the building because of large trees. JMHS had also located a north-south possible boundary ditch just to the west of the building, perhaps intended to separate the central buildings from the pond a little down-slope to the west.[34]

The construction and use of Building 3

The stone foundations of the southern and eastern walls of Building 3 were discovered in the north-west of the trench (Fig. 5.26), obscured by disturbed and truncated layers of rubble left by its final demolition. All the worked building stone and any window traceries had clearly been taken away for reuse elsewhere, perhaps for repairing the still-standing buildings or in the construction of houses in Little-more village (see page 195). The foundations survived as three rough courses mapping a structure 10m west-east internally, as revealed in the trench, with an internal north-south wall [3032] breaking it into a eight metre long section with a further element to the west of unknown length. The building was four metres wide north-south internally, with a possible extension to the north; the foundations were 0.8m

wide, without bonding, of rough-hewn stone and rubble. The south-east corner of the building had been robbed out, but there was a suggestion of an external staircase, porch or buttress, which may have been added in the Medieval period. Inside there were traces of mortared floors (3044-3045-3046) laid over hard core and undisturbed subsoil; the fragments of floor tile discovered in the demolition rubbish suggested that these floors may have been finished with glazed and decorated tiles. The tiles, as in other religious institutions in the Oxford area, including Godstow Abbey, were mostly of the Stabbed Wessex type (see page 181). A later and less sophisticated internal floor, layer (3031), survived as patches of degraded compacted soil and fine rubble, but this had been very badly disturbed by nineteenth-century building and landscaping in that area of the trench.

The eastern wall of Building 3 [3042] was in very poor condition, much of the foundations having been dug away by later activity. Building 3 may also have had an extension added to the east, possibly in the thirteenth century and possibly linking the building to the cloister, which extension was later refashioned for agricultural use in connection with Minchery Farm before being finally demolished (see below). That area of extension and/or rebuilding was defined by post-Medieval levelling layers of mixed domestic rubbish and other waste material (3037-3038): the post-priory structures may have reused floor areas and building material rather than the actual Medieval

Fig. 5.25. Trench 3 at the end of excavation, from south-east (AerialCam)

wall-lines. However, those levelling/floor layers provided good evidence for priory-related activity as all the material used to consolidate the post-Medieval floor foundations was redeposited, Medieval in origin and included a notable collection of cooking ware sherds, including jars, jugs and pipkins.[35]

The kitchen midden

The Medieval kitchen midden (3007/3017) discovered just to the south of Building 3 was a deep spread of refuse which yielded important evidence for the priory inhabitants' diet and their access to resources, including cereal grains, game and fish. Such evidence is rare and important from a Medieval nunnery site (Roberta Gilchrist, pers. comm.) The midden was dominated by material from the final phase of the priory from about 1350-1525, but its upper layers included later sixteenth-century additions. A radiocarbon date on charred wheat grain from a

midden deposit returned as 1413-1467 cal AD.[36] The midden was reached along a herringbone cobble pathway [3012], almost two metres of which were uncovered in the south of the trench running west to east and cut through by a completely robbed out post-Medieval wall. The silty organic midden itself extended over six square metres and contained large quantities of oyster shell, animal bone and pottery: a collection of domestic waste typical of kitchen and cooking refuse. The western side of the midden had been truncated by the excavation of a large pit perhaps to create another farm pond sometime during or after the seventeenth century.

The Medieval midden layers were full of oak-dominated charcoal and range of charred grain seeds, as seen in Trench 2, but in a much more degraded state of preservation. Archaeobotanical specialist Dr. Diane Alldritt suggested that agricultural waste could first have been used as fuel for the hearth in Building 2 and

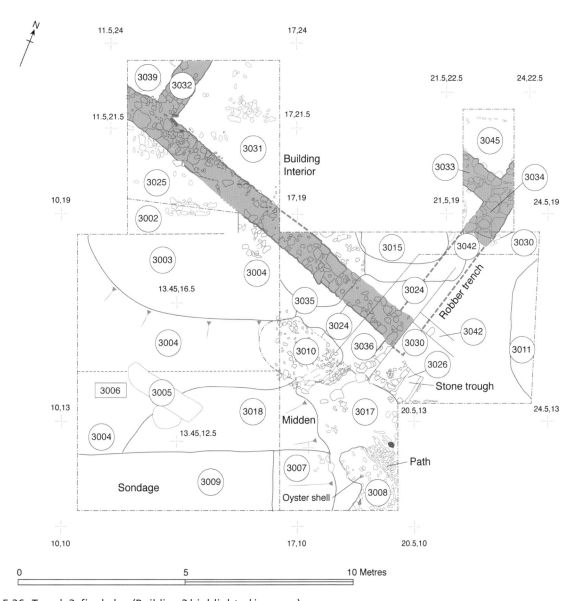

Fig. 5.26. Trench 3, final plan (Building 3 highlighted in green).

then the ash disposed of to quell smells in the midden in Trench 3.[37] Archaeobotanical evidence sieved from soil samples taken from the Trench 3 midden confirmed that the nuns were cultivating on their own land, or bringing in, wheat and barley and growing broad beans. The animal bone, other seeds and shell also revealed they were importing large dried cod, eating oysters and growing or acquiring apples and cherries. Archaeozoologist Julie Hamilton's analysis of animal bone retrieved from the midden layers shows that the inhabitants of the priory were consuming beef. Cattle bones dominated the assemblage, but they were also dining on mutton, pork and venison, as well as domestic fowl, rabbit and hare, duck and goose.[38] Cattle and sheep may have been reared at the Manor of Sandford under the Templars and Hospitallers, and the nuns are likely to have been the recipients of hunted deer and smaller game, probably shot and trapped in Shotover Forest or in wetland areas around the Thames. It was of course essential that a monastery

should have a regular supply of fish, with the cod most probably coming in as dried stockfish, with oysters supplied up the Thames from fish markets in London, and it is almost certain that the nuns kept their own rabbits, chickens and other domesticated fowl within the priory's grounds.

The Trench 3 pit

A pit [3043], most likely dug in the sixteenth century was found alongside the south-west wall- of Building 3, and appeared to be linked to the disposal of material from the demolition work at the priory after 1525. The pit was filled with rubble and soil including some small fragments of much degraded painted plaster and of fine glass, as well as a short section of window came or leading still holding green window glass (Fig. 5.27; SF38).[39] Such glass began to be used in religious buildings in the thirteenth century and was probably discarded from the priory church when it was demolished.

55mm

Fig. 5.27. Leaded window came with green glass (SF 38).

125mm

Fig. 5.28. Green-glazed roof ridge tile fragments from Trench 3.

The larger fragments of tile found in the upper spit of this pit and other demolition-related layers in Trench 3 were perhaps more likely to have come from Building 3. The tile assemblage was dominated by glazed flat roof tiles. The glaze would have imparted a copper-like sheen to the roof and the use of flanged tiles suggested the building would have had a pitch of at least forty percent. Stone roof-tiles, of the kind that can still be seen on the surviving building, were actually more expensive than the ceramic equivalent in the Medieval period, but it appears that Building 3's tile roof may have been given a final touch of class with the addition of green-glazed ridge tiles (Fig 5.28), pieces of which were found in Trench 3.[40] Comparing tile fabrics from across the site, Gwilym Williams suggested the tiled roofs in the priory complex had been patched and repaired over time with tiles that came from just one long-curated original order of roof tiles from perhaps the thirteenth century. He also noted the absence of Penn tiles, which dominated trade in the later fourteenth century; perhaps the priory was not in a financial position to afford new roof tiles at that time.

Almost half of the pottery found in Trench 3 was Medieval in date, although often mixed in disturbed layers with post-Medieval material. The Medieval assemblage comprised jars, cooking pots, jugs, bowls, bottles, dripping pans and a Brill-Boarstall lamp. These were the same forms as in Trench 2 and similar both to contemporary, ordinary domestic assemblages found in central Oxford and to the pottery at Bartlemas Chapel (Chapter 4). The only exotic item in Trench 3 was a small jug in south Netherlands majolica, in use during the final years of priory (see Fig. 5.35). John Cotter noted that on Medieval religious sites jugs normally dominate even in the eleventh to thirteenth century period, during which time jars and cooking pots predominated in secular contexts. However, at Littlemore Priory jugs and jars were evenly matched throughout Medieval period across Trenches 2 and 3, implying a domestic character predominated. The pottery collection also suggested that Building 3 was perhaps put up slightly later than Trench 2 Building 2, with a peak of activity in the thirteenth-fourteenth centuries.[41] Finds in undisturbed, midden-mixed wall-fill implied the core of the building went up after the late-twelfth century and the date ranges of pottery within the floor deposits in the western part of the building (3039) suggested that part was in use between 1250 and 1400. This may fit with other evidence for a second phase of building and re-building after 1400.

This evidence demonstrates that Building 3 was probably a domestic building, perhaps used for a range of purposes over its lifetime; it could have been used as a refectory, as a considerable amount of food preparation and cooking as well as eating went on in its immediate vicinity, and it may also have been used as a guest house. To its south, close to the midden, there may have been a kitchen, as Pantin proposed. There was a phase of extension and renovation, including work on Building 3 in the thirteenth century. We know from documentary sources that the priory received donations in 1214 to carry out repairs to a number of its buildings that had become somewhat dilapidated.[42]

The demolition of the cloister

Some of the priory buildings were used as farm buildings after the dissolution of the priory in 1524-25, but as discussed above there was clear evidence for demolition and robbing out of much of Building 3. In the west of the trench, demolition rubble (3025) contained large quantities of fragmentary roof tile. Rubble layer (3014) in the east overlay priory walls and early floor surfaces. This layer contained some intrusive material, but the pottery largely consisted of Medieval sherds, supporting the idea that demolition happened soon after dissolution. Further evidence for Medieval demolition was provided by feature [3041], the void for the third wall of the building [3034]. All the pottery found in the backfill of the robber trench was Medieval.

After the dissolution, parts of the original buildings, or areas of floor were re-used within farm buildings before much of the trench area was landscaped for a garden in the nineteenth century. A number of features identified in Trench 3 were likely to date to these periods. There were ground-levelling layers containing sixteenth and seventeenth-century pottery and later rubble spreads relating to the demolition of farm

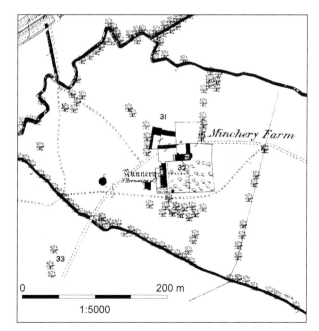

Fig. 5.29. Minchery Farm with ancillary buildings, 1876 Ordnance Survey 6 inch to the mile First Edition (© Crown Copyright and Landmark Information Group Limited 2014).

buildings. Stony spreads, incidentally containing clay pipe fragments and nineteenth-century pottery, were perhaps laid to improve the uneven ground before the pub garden was created.

The 1876 Ordnance First Edition one to six inch map (Berkshire Series) depicts a small square building, possibly an outhouse, just west of the current standing priory remains (Fig. 5.29). Some evidence for this building was identified in Trench 3. Removal of rubble (3013) had revealed a well-worked stone ridge tile [3029] of substantial size (c. 0.4m long). The stone was lying along the alignment for the western wall of a later building and was probably re-used in its drainage system: upside down it looked like a trough. The line of the robbed-out wall cut through the herringbone cobble pathway. To the east of the robbed-out wall were two floor surfaces (3022) and (3023) bedded into a layer sealing Medieval floors discussed above.

Trench 3: Modern Activity

Although the site was very disturbed, there were some instances of more defined modern activity in Trench 3. A British Geological Survey trench [3006] measuring 2.25m long by 0.5m wide had cut through a number of deposits on the western side of the

trench. Further modern intrusion was discovered in feature [3048]: a poorly defined, roughly circular pit measuring approximately 1m in diameter. The lowest fill, (3021) was a slump of rubble from Medieval wall-foundations [3027], which had slipped into the cut during the digging work. The feature had been backfilled with a mix of heavily disturbed midden deposit, probably dug from the buried midden spread (3017) to the east, and large amounts of more modern material including nineteenth-century clay pipe and pottery.

Discussion: the life of the priory

The economic life of Littlemore Priory would have run very much like any secular manor of similar size. Plans and descriptions of other nunneries suggest that their layout was smaller and developed more organically than their male monastic equivalents. This seemed to have been the case here, and the complex within the encircling water channel, ponds and brook would thus have presented a busy and workaday scene (Fig. 5.30). The most distinctive feature of the priory was the priory church, the plan and position of which was revealed in the JMHS excavations in 2014 (see page 186).[43] As discussed above (see page 169), the

Fig. 5.30. Conjectured reconstruction of life at Littlemore Priory, from west. Artwork by Helen Ganly.

Fig. 5.31. Blocked-up dormitory cinquefoil window, priory building, eastern façade.

surviving standing building from the neighbouring claustral range probably had the chapter house and parlour downstairs, with the nuns' dormitory upstairs consisting of small individual cells each with their own small, narrow window (Fig. 5.31). It remains unclear as to whether the cloister was fully completed in quadrangular form as suggested by W.A. Pantin.[44] The 2012 excavations found a building (Building 3), possibly a refectory or guest house, built in line with the western side of Pantin's cloister garth, with a probable kitchen area to the south. The central sector of the cloister, between the surviving range and the excavation area of Trench 3 lies under the public path, so was not available for investigation, but remains a potential future opportunity for archaeologists (see Fig.5.3).

The priory would almost certainly have cultivated vegetable gardens and tended fruit trees within its precinct, as there was archaeobotanical evidence in the midden layers for broad beans, apple and cherry as well as hazelnuts being consumed.[45] The nuns probably kept poultry and pigs. The Prioress managed the assets granted to the nunnery, including pasture, arable, and woodland where the pigs foraged and servants gathered firewood. The nuns also had access to oak timber, dried stockfish, venison, and grants of extra hay and grain. Building 2 (Trench 2) was a large barn or outbuilding discovered next to a well in the north-west of the precinct, where industrial-type work requiring a high-temperature hearth was also carried out. This may have included small-scale

smithing. Strands of untwisted copper wire and completed knot-head copper veil or shroud pins (e.g. Fig. 5.33; SF 40) found across the site suggested the nuns were making their own veil pins, if not also producing some for other people. In the area between Trench 2 and Trench 3, inaccessible today beneath thick tree growth and scrub, may have been stables, animal pens and other outbuildings as well parts of the gardens and orchards.

There was also evidence for dining and entertaining, particularly in relation to Buildings 2 and 3. Building 3 may also have housed boarders, sheltered travellers, or harboured the poor or sick, perhaps people for whom the nuns were caring. Analysis of the skeletons found buried around and within the church in the JMHS excavations in 2014 supported the idea that the priory took in a range of people, as old and young, male and female were discovered (see page 186). Despite all this activity, the priory remained at its heart a religious institution and the nuns would have been expected to spend much of their time in church at prayer, and following the Benedictine ideals of study and of dutiful work. The survival of the Littlemore Book or Psalter (see page 188) and the discovery of the tuning peg for a stringed musical instrument (Fig. 5.20) testify to the literate and musical culture of the nuns' lives.

The priory must have had considerable local social and economic importance, providing a home for women not destined for marriage, as well as work and succour to the local people of Littlemore, Sandford, and their surrounding farms. It was both a consumer and a source of produce and possibly craftwork. It also lay within the outer ambit of Medieval Oxford, had social and political connections to its colleges, and was thus influenced by outside events. The priory's fortunes were linked to those of the wider Catholic Church in England. Whilst for example, Pope Innocent IV's encouragement for the building of the church in the 1240s was welcome, the subsequent suppression of the Knights Templar in the early 1300s would have had a more negative impact, as must have the dreadful famines and plagues of the fourteenth century.

There is clear evidence for contraction and a decline in building standards in parts of the precinct in the fourteenth to fifteenth centuries. Perhaps the site was contracting, or scarce resources were being diverted towards the new dormitory range. Building 1 in Trench 2 was altered, perhaps partially rebuilt and shortened, in the later-fourteenth century, but in a somewhat slapdash fashion, and this coincided with the large, well-constructed hearth inside it being abandoned. Building 2 to the south may also have been altered, perhaps in the mid-late fifteenth century, again to less exacting standards. There is the possibility neither building was fully-used in the final years of the priory, before all the buildings in the Trench 2 area were thoroughly dismantled, presumably in the wake of Little Dissolution.

Summary of the finds

David Griffiths, with Olaf Bayer and Chris Turley

There is a greater range and quantity of finds from Minchery Paddock than from the previous year's excavation at Bartlemas Chapel, reflecting the larger size of the three excavation trenches in 2012 and the richness of their deposits. Most of the finds come from the period between the twelfth and sixteenth centuries when Littlemore Priory was in existence, although there are also some from earlier and later times. Only the finds from the 2012 excavations are summarised here: material from the site evaluation of Minchery Paddock in 2006, and the excavation of the priory church in 2014, have been reported upon by John Moore Heritage Services, the organisation which undertook the work.[46] (A summary of the 2014 priory church excavation is provided below).

The finds from the 2012 excavations fall into three main period groupings: items which originated before the priory was established in the mid-twelfth century; Medieval material from the period of the priory; and thirdly, finds from after the priory was closed in the early sixteenth century and its surviving buildings became a farm. The range of Medieval material is impressive, with much of it coming from the prosperous heyday of the priory in the twelfth and thirteenth centuries. Nearly all of the Medieval finds come from Trenches 2 and 3, with the emphasis on architectural ceramics in Trench 3, which was located in closer proximity to the central buildings of the priory. Trench 1, which is located much further away from the priory, produced by far the fewest finds, with only 19 sherds of pottery among a total of 2706 from all three trenches.

A general scatter of lithic artefacts was found in the three trenches, comprising 59 pieces of struck flint ranging in date between the Mesolithic Period and the Early Bronze Age (Fig. 5.33). As a background scatter, most of these are small-sized flakes and blades, similar to material found in nearby excavations at the Kassam Stadium and Oxford Science Park. However, outstanding among this earliest group of finds are two flint arrowheads, one Neolithic in date and one from the Early Bronze Age (Fig. 5.32; see note by Olaf Bayer, p. 183). These were both found in Trench 2, and had been redeposited in Medieval layers dating to three or more millennia after they were made. Their appearance was initially greeted with surprise, as we were not expecting to find Prehistoric artefacts among the remains of a twelfth to sixteenth-century priory! The two competing theories aired among the team after the discovery of these very ancient objects were that they had been (unknowingly) redeposited among rubble as a result of Medieval disturbance and digging up of nearby prehistoric remains, which given the background presence of over forty pieces of flint debitage (manufacturing debris from flint tool-making) does seem possible, or that, perhaps more excitingly, one or both of them had been kept and curated as a special object at a much later time. The discovery of Prehistoric flint weapons such as axes and arrowheads at Medieval ecclesiastical sites is rare but not unknown, and finds have occurred in church contexts at Kilwinning Abbey, Ayrshire, and Raunds, Northamptonshire. They have also been found in Medieval domestic contexts in Britain and Scandinavia. Known to some as 'elf shot', such objects may have been kept as curios, or in the belief that they protected against thunder or evil spirits. Some were copied in metal to be worn as amulets. As Roberta Gilchrist has shown, practice and belief in magical and unbiblical superstitions was far from unusual in Medieval times.[47]

A fine white glass Romano-British 'melon' bead in Trench 2 (Fig. 5.5) was also an unusual and surprising find. These, are as the name suggests, somewhat watermelon-like in shape, they have fluted, convex sides, and are normally made of blue or yellow glass, although white examples are known, including a near-

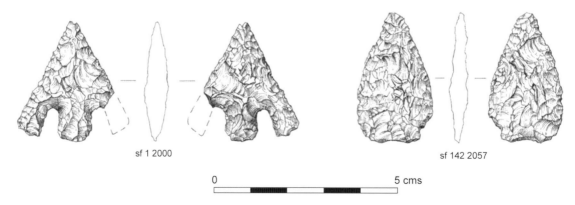

sf 1 2000   sf 142 2057

0   5 cms

Fig. 5.32. Flint barbed and tanged arrowhead, Early Bronze Age (SF 1); Flint leaf-shaped arrowhead, Neolithic (SF 142), see page 183. Drawn by J. Wallis.

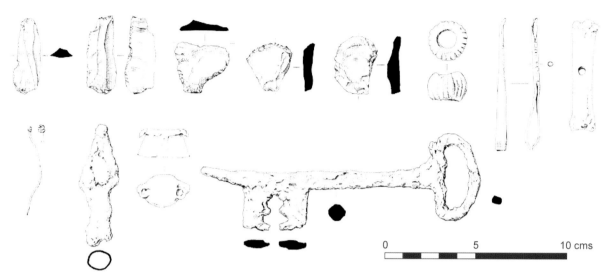

Fig. 5.33. **Upper row:** Five struck flint tools, all from Trench 2, blade (SF 5), retouched blade (SF 60), date: Mesolithic or Early Neolithic; Notched flake (SF 4), scraper fragment (SF 7) and end scraper (SF13), date: Neolithic or Early Bronze Age; Roman white glass melon bead (SF 111); Copper-alloy pair of tweezers with ear-scoop terminal, date 1270-1400 (SF 114), Bone toggle, pierced pig metatarsal (SF 137); **Lower row:** Copper-alloy wire pin with drawn shaft and wound-wire head, probably intended as a shroud pin, date 1300-1600 (SF 140); Socketed iron arrowhead, Date: 1100-1400; Type 2 in *Museum of London Medieval Catalogue.*[61] ; Cast lead cap from powder holder or measure, with two small opposed pierced lugs, date 1600-1700 (SF 12); Iron lever lock key with solid stem and kidney-shaped bow with two mirror-image bits (SF 132). Drawn by J. Wallis.

identical one from the Roman town of Wroxeter (Shropshire) now in Shrewsbury Museum. A scatter of 126 abraded Romano-British pottery sherds was also found across the excavation areas, from what we interpreted as a Roman ploughsoil layer. These were mainly of local cream and orange-buff wares from the Oxfordshire pottery industry (see page 86). The presence of the melon bead raises similar questions to the flint arrowheads. Was the bead kept deliberately, or did it become accidentally mixed up with Medieval remains associated with the priory? If so, did it come from a Roman site (perhaps a burial) at or near this location, or was it brought in from elsewhere? Despite the nearby presence of several Roman pottery kilns between Blackbird Leys and Sandford, as demonstrated in previous excavations,[48] the three trenches at Minchery Paddock did not reveal any substantive physical traces of Roman industry or occupation. Once again, we must leave the matter open, until future research produces a clearer link to Roman activity in the vicinity.

A single sherd of Thetford Ware later Anglo-Saxon (or Anglo-Scandinavian) pottery dating to between 850 and 1100 is all that we have for the period between the Romans and the foundation of the priory in the mid-twelfth century: it was found in a later context and therefore tells us little or nothing about what was happening here (if anything) between the fifth and twelfth centuries. It seems that this site did not attract the attention of the Anglo-Saxons or Normans, despite being located between Anglo-Saxon settlement remains found during the excavations at Oxford

Science Park and in Minchery Farm allotments, just north of Northfield Brook. However, the subsequent period of nearly four hundred years between the foundation and closure of the priory is closely reflected in the ceramic finds; among the 2850 sherds of pottery discovered in the excavations, around two thirds date to between its foundation in the twelfth century and its closure in the sixteenth century. The post-Medieval pottery from Minchery Paddock reflects the change in character of the site after the end of the priory. Fewer in number and more restricted in range and status, the post-Medieval assemblage nevertheless includes some interesting early pieces of Cistercian Ware and Frechen stoneware (the latter paralleled at Bartlemas) but is dominated numerically by relatively common red earthenwares, English tin-glazed earthenware, stonewares, clay pipe fragments, and broken Staffordshire china. Some of these items probably reflect the more humdrum domestic material culture of the farm in the post-priory period, but much of the post-Medieval pottery was from upper dump deposits in Trench 3, and was probably therefore brought onto the site already broken and discarded, as part of general rubble scattered on muddy surfaces.

The Medieval pottery (Figs 5.34, 5.35) is an important collection from a relatively isolated site on the distant eastern periphery of Oxford. It is nevertheless relatively typical of an Oxford urban assemblage of this period, showing the priory's close links with the city and its religious and scholarly communities. The assemblage is dominated by Brill/Boarstall wares from western Buckinghamshire, dating to between 1175 and

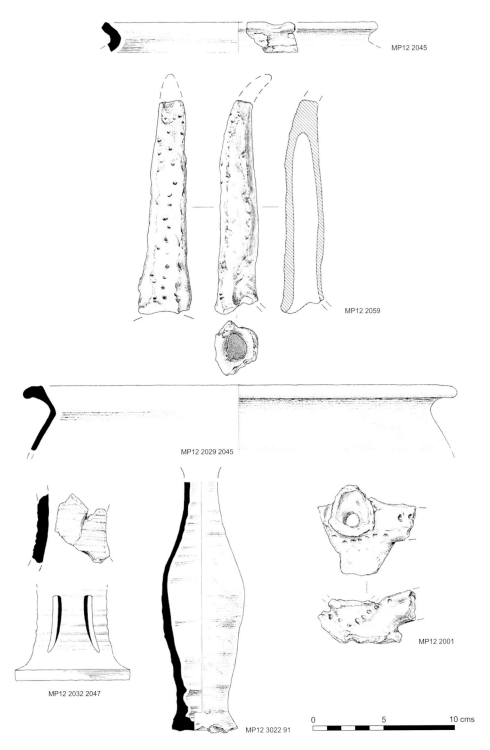

Fig. 5.34 **Top:** Jar/cooking pot rim with trace of vertical thumbed strip on shoulder. Light grey externally with red-brown core. Probably Thetford-type ware (East Anglia, probably Ipswich). Date: c. 1250-1400. Trench 2, Context (2045), construction layer for walls of southern building. **Upper, centre:** Medieval Oxford ware pot handle. Unusual hollow skillet or pipkin handle attached to trace of (deformed) rim. Length 14.5 cm. Date: 1250-1325. Trench 2, Context (2059), fill of pit and under walls, southern building. **Lower, centre:** Early Brill/Boarstall ware jar or cooking pot. Rim diam 31 cm. Thin-walled (only 3.5mm thick at shoulder). Trench 2, (2029, rims), (2045, base), rubble/ construction layers. **Bottom, left:** Early Brill/Boarstall ware, joining sherds from hollow pedestal base of a chafing dish with vertical knife-cut slots (traces of 2 surviving, probably 3 or 4 originally). Diam in middle c. 0.5 cm. Date: 1250-1350. Trench 2 (2032) and (2047). **Bottom, middle:** Brill/Boarstall ware bottle. Near-complete profile (minus rim). Six fresh sherds including complete splayed flat base (diam c 4.6 cm). Height c. 17cm. Crudely made/slightly warped. Date 1250-1400. Context (3022), residual in 19c context. **Bottom, right:** Brill/Boarstall ware zoomorphic aquamanile (water ewer). Fragment for the upper/rear end. Pale cream-buff fabric with bright copper-green glaze. Length of surviving sherd 7.3 cm. Trench 2, Context (2001), residual in 19c context. Drawn by J. Wallis.

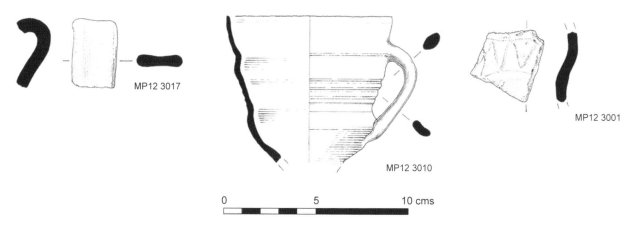

MP12 3017

MP12 3010

MP12 3001

0   5   10 cms

Fig. 5.35. **Left:** South Netherlands maiolica jug handle. Length 3.6 cm; width 2.4 cm. Fine sandy yellow fabric. Fairly fresh. Date c. 1480-1575. Trench 3 (3017), midden.   **Middle:** Cistercian-type ware (mainly Brill). Thin-walled cup with flaring rim. Glossy orange-brown glaze. Date: probably 16c. Trench 3, Context (3010), residual in 19c context. **Right:** Brill/Boarstall ware jug neck sherd with applied scale decoration and vertical red strip. Length 4.2 cm. Trench 3, Context (3001), residual in 19c context. Drawn by J. Wallis.

1550, with a smaller number of later Brill/Boarstall wares extending to the early seventeenth century. From the earlier period of the priory are 47 sherds of Medieval Oxford Ware, dating to before 1300, and 300 sherds of East Wiltshire ware dating to between 1150 and 1350. Smaller numbers of Cotswold-type Ware, Nuneaton, Olney Hyde and Minety-type wares, and 47 sherds of Ashampstead-type wares from Berkshire, confirm the regional distribution stretching from Warwickshire to Wiltshire. From later in the Medieval period, between 1350 and 1550, are Coarse Border wares and Tudor Green Ware from Surrey and Hampshire, together with copies of Tudor Green ware made at Brill/Boarstall. From more distant origins are a jug handle in Southern Netherlands Majolica ware dating to 1480-1575, together with six sherds of Raeren stoneware drinking mugs from Germany, from roughly the same period (these are paralleled at Bartlemas). Much of the Medieval pottery consists of cooking and dining vessels, with sherds from cooking pots, jugs, pitchers, bowls and cups and bottles found in quantity. More unusual items consistent with this theme include a skillet (frying pan) or pipkin (saucepan) handles, a dripping pan, and a cistern bunghole, probably from an ale vessel. Some of the discarded and broken vessels point to the presence of a refined or high-status dining culture, perhaps associated with the prioress and her immediate circle in the heyday of the priory in the twelfth and thirteenth centuries. A zoomorphic aquamanile fragment was found in Trench 2. These were elaborately-decorated showy vessels for dispensing water at table, made in this case at Brill/Boarstall. From the same period, also from Trench 2, is an unusual pedestal from a chafing dish (or plate warmer), which is also likely to have been a prestigious dining table item. The strong cooking and dining theme probably reflects the areas of the priory complex which Trenches 2 and 3 investigated, the proximity

of the kitchen and its midden in Trench 3 are clearly influential.

The wealth of the priory in its twelfth to fourteenth-century heyday is reflected in the metal and bone finds. Most of these came from Trench 2, with a smaller number from Trench 3. Two silver coins include an broken short cross penny of Henry II (Fig. 5.21), minted between 1180 and 1189, by the moneyer Osber (mint uncertain as this part of the inscription is missing, although a moneyer named Osber is known from the London Mint); and a voided long cross penny of Henry III (Fig. 5.20), Class III, minted 1248-50; it is too worn to be able to discern either mint or moneyer. A pair of tweezers with an ear-scoop terminal (Fig. 5.33), dating to between 1270 and 1400, is a valuable personal grooming item, undamaged, so probably an accidental loss.[49] A simple dress accessory, a bone toggle, consists of a pierced pig metatarsal. As at Bartlemas, there is a much finer worked bone object (Fig. 5.19), which is probably part of a musical instrument, a tuning peg of Lawson's Type B.[50] The hole for the string is in the head of the peg, a feature which suggests the instrument in question was a type of box zither known as a psaltery.[51] At a site on the west side of St Aldates, Oxford, eight similar examples were found in a fifteenth-century context, which led the excavators to suggest the site had been an instrument-making workshop.[52] Perhaps the tuning peg is indicative of contacts with central Oxford, but more likely to have been made at Littlemore Priory itself is a dress or shroud pin found in Trench 3; this is a drawn copper alloy example with a wound wire head, and dates to between 1300 and 1600. Several more of these were found in burials in the priory church excavation in 2014. An incomplete pin from Trench 2 is probably a dress or brooch pin dating to between 1400 and 1700.

Other finds, notably among the iron objects, reflect the working life of the extended priory community, which must have included servants and artisans as well as the nuns themselves. A socketed arrowhead from Trench 2 (Fig. 5.33) implies that somebody from the priory community went out hunting into nearby Shotover Forest. A long-lived and simple form of arrowhead it is part of a multipurpose type dated to between the eleventh and the fifteenth centuries. Tools such as a smith's punch, part of a tanged carpenter's gouge, a fire rake, nails, staples, a spring probably from a pair of shears, a figure-of-eight hasp and a lever lock key show the extent of craft and repair going on at the site, and emphasise the location of Trench 2 in particular as part of the working outbuildings of the priory. A long side bar from a bridle with curb bit, and several fragments of iron harness buckles indicate the presence of horses, so stabling was probably located nearby.

Some melted lead was found in Trench 2, so it is unsurprising that a fine piece of lead window-came was found during the excavations, in this case from Trench 3 (Fig. 5.27). Representing a corner of a stained glass window (with green glass in situ), and probably dating to around 1200, it is tempting to believe this came from the priory church itself, being broken and discarded when it was demolished. Lead was widely used in alloys such as pewter or lead-tin for vessels, and we have fragment of a small gilded pewter bell from Trench 3 (Fig. 5.40). It may have had a religious use, or may possibly have been used to summon servants to table. An interesting lead object is a squashed cast lead cap with two small lugs (Fig. 5.33), from a powder holder (see note by Chris Turley below); this is one of very few items from this site that imply weaponry of any kind (but like the iron arrowhead, it may be for hunting rather than fighting). A much less elegantly-made, but no less necessary, item is a section of lead pipe, which in providing water was no doubt a necessary adjunct to cooking or craft-working. A simple 'tombac' (brass alloy) button and several clay pipe fragments (Figs 5.41, 5.42) give a glimpse of the everyday apparel and pastimes of the farm's inhabitants in the three centuries after the priory closed.

In contrast to Bartlemas, a large amount of architectural ceramics in the form of various types of tile was retrieved from the Minchery Paddock excavations (1192 fragments, weighing 86 kg), with the preponderance favouring Trench 3, in closest proximity to the claustral range of the priory. Trench 2 produced more modest amounts, with Trench 1 producing very little, perhaps unsurprisingly given its distance from the priory buildings. The material divides into three categories: roof tile, ridge tile and floor tile. Most of the tile was Medieval in date, with some modern pieces (broken land drains etc.). Two

fragments of Roman *tegulae* (roof tile) were present in Trench 3. These are relatively common finds in the Oxfordshire countryside, and given their small number probably do not reflect the *in situ* presence of a Roman building. Like the Roman pottery mentioned above they probably came onto the site with rubble or other redeposited materials.

The Medieval flat roof tile consisted of 1043 fragments weighing 76.8 kg, so was by far the largest component of the tile groups, although much was residual. Ridge tile, of which there were 34 fragments (Fig. 5.28), was far smaller in number but comparable in fabric to the roof tile, indicating a similar place of production. Where catalogued separately at other monastic sites, such as Rewley Abbey, Oxford, ridge tile usually forms a much lower percentage of the finds than flat tile, possibly indicating it was valuable enough to be re-used when buildings were demolished after the reformation. Roof tile fabric groups among the Minchery Paddock material were identified in study work-shops involving volunteers, some of which were present in both Trenches 2 and 3, implying there was probably a common style across the priory buildings, with the glaze on the tile adding a copper-like sheen to the priory's roofscape. Gwilym Williams notes that none of the flat roof tiles were of a flanged style, implying that the roof had a pitch of at least 40°, and the absence of any in a hipped style suggests the roof structures were relatively open with gable ends. Tile was cheaper than stone, locally it was made at Brill, Buckinghamshire, with major production centres in London and Northamptonshire producing bulk volumes for sale. The surviving upstanding building from the priory, the fifteenth-century nuns' dormitory (later the pub), is roofed with limestone slabs, so does not match the Medieval evidence from the excavations. Either the new dormitory block was roofed differently to some of the older priory buildings when it was constructed, or re-roofed in stone at a later point after the priory closed.

Most eye-catching among the tile assemblage are the floor tiles, in particular the decorated floor tiles (Figs 5.36-5.39). These objects are familiar finds from Medieval monastic sites, and were used extensively to floor churches and other important interior spaces. Many excavations at sites in central Oxford have produced these, as has another twelfth-century Benedictine nunnery, Godstow, beside the Thames north-west of the city. Like ridge tile, floor tile is highly portable and can easily be re-used, so it is not surprising that relatively little remained intact, most of it was worn or broken, and none of it was still *in situ*. The floor tile assemblage from Minchery Paddock is dominated by a decorated type known as 'Stabbed Wessex' (12 fragments from trenches 2 and

71mm

Fig. 5.36. Decorated floor-tile of 'Stabbed Wessex' type, with Griffin facing right, incomplete. SF 47, Trench 2, Context (2005), mixed silty layer with many finds in southern part of trench.

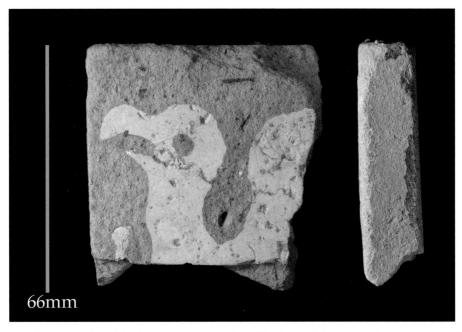

66mm

Fig. 5.37. Decorated floor-tile of 'Stabbed Wessex' type, with Griffin facing left, incomplete. SF 73, Trench 2, Context (2005), mixed silty layer with many finds in southern part of trench.

3), together with six pieces of thicker, plain floor tile from Trench 3. 'Stabbed Wessex' tile is usually dated to between 1280 and 1330, although there are suggestions that its use in Oxford may date to as early as the 1260s. The type-name comes from the technique of 'stabbing' the backs of the tiles (normally with a round implement) to provide a better grip for the mortar holding them in place, or possibly also to make their firing easier. They were made in several locations in Berkshire and Oxfordshire, with Medieval kilns at Bagley Wood, south-west of Oxford, being a possible local source.[54] Normally measuring between 19 and 21 cm square,

and between 1.7 and 2.2 cm thick, they are decorated in a variety of stamped, slipped and glazed heraldic designs and laid in complex patterns forming pavements. The floor tiles from Trenches 2 and 3 conform to three design groups, all recognisable within a scheme published by Loyd Haberly in 1937.[55] It is clear from these finds, and other examples found in the 2006 evaluation trenches by John Moore Heritage Services, that Littlemore Priory must have once had at least one impressively tiled floor, which from the general date of these types was most probably constructed in the mid to late thirteenth century, when we know the priory was

Fig. 5.38. Decorated floor-tile of 'Stabbed Wessex' type, with studded circle design, incomplete. SF 125, Trench 2, Context (2005), mixed silty layer with many finds in southern part of trench.

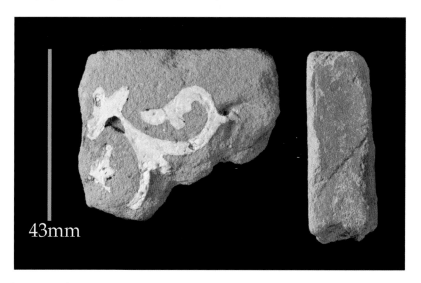

Fig. 5.39. Decorated floor-tile of 'Stabbed Wessex' type, with fleur-de-lys forming corner design, incomplete. SF 95, Trench 3, Context (3017), disturbed midden spread.

Fig. 5.40. Fragment of gilded pewter bell. Diam c. 6cm. Date: 16-18c. SF 129, Trench 3, Context (3015), fill of pit.

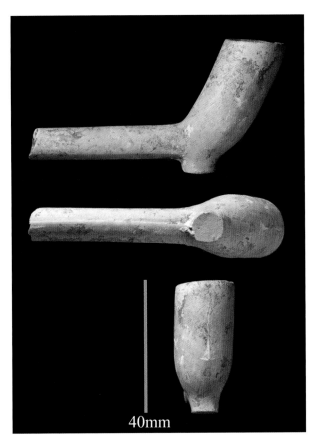

40mm

Fig. 5.41. Clay pipe bowl, undecorated with part of stem. Date: 1700-1770. SF 105, Trench 1, Context (1003), fill of shallow cut.

partially rebuilt following a papal bull of Innocent IV in 1245 which aided the work. One is most likely to have been located within the chancel of the church itself, and must have been removed after the priory closed in the early sixteenth century (although 60 individual examples of Stabbed Wessex floor tiles were found during the excavation of the church in 2014, none were *in situ*). We may therefore assume that after the closure of the priory, floor tiles and other similar fittings which were retrieved in reasonable condition were taken away or sold, and the rest were discarded, many into a stock of general mixed rubble which was used for spreading on surfaces and filling holes during demolition or the subsequent life of Minchery Farm.

The flint arrowheads

Olaf Bayer

Two flint arrowheads were found during the 2012 excavations, both in Trench 2. The first is a beautiful barbed and tanged arrowhead dating to between 2500 and 2000 BC, the Beaker Period, between the Neolithic Period and the Early Bronze Age. It was discovered early in the excavation, when in the gloom of a 7am start during a live broadcast for BBC Radio Oxford, it was unexpectedly found from a layer overlying a Medieval cobbled surface. Measuring 30mm long by 27mm wide by 6mm thick, and weighing 3.2g, it is delicately shaped from a distinctive translucent orangey brown flint by the removal of shallow invasive flakes over its entire surface. Although missing its tip and most of one of its barbs, when handled, the arrowhead feels symmetrical, balanced and light. At this point in time, when the first metals are being introduced to this country, the overall quality of flint working would soon begin to decline. Only a very limited range of artefacts display anything more than a functional, expedient approach to making stone tools. The exceptional quality of the flint-working demonstrated by the arrowhead and the deliberate selection of a striking raw material raises questions about the original purpose of this artefact. It is suggested that large, and or finely made barbed and tanged arrowheads, such this example, were created for ceremonial purposes rather than for hunting.[56] Morphologically the arrowhead fits most closely with the 'Conygar Hill' type,[57] and comparisons can be drawn with those found with high status Beaker burials such as the Amesbury Archer from near Stonehenge.[58]

The other arrowhead is older, a leaf-shaped arrowhead dating to the Early Neolithic between 4000 and 3500 BC and used by some of the earliest farming communities. The discovery of this artefact was also a surprise. After the excavations had been completed and the trenches back-filled, the arrowhead came to light whilst soil samples collected during the excavation were being processed at Oxford Archaeology.

32mm

Fig. 5.42. 'Tombac' button, brass alloy. Thickness 5 mm. Date: 18c–early 19c. SF 104, Trench 3, Context (3040), fill of drainage channel.

Fig. 5.43a: Flint barbed and tanged arrowhead, Early Bronze Age (SF 1); 5.43b: Flint leaf-shaped arrowhead, Neolithic (SF 142); photographed by Ian Cartwright.

Undiscovered during the excavation, the arrowhead came from a soil sample taken from a Medieval pit. Measuring 33mm long, by 20mm wide, by 2mm thick and weighs 2.7g, it is finely flaked from a translucent dark grey flint. The tip of the arrowhead is missing, as is one of the corners of the base. It is most similar in form to Green's class 3A.[59] This artefact probably has a more mundane status and purpose than the barbed and tanged arrowhead, and was probably a hunting projectile.

Questions remain as to how these very ancient artefacts came to be discovered in deposits associated with a Medieval priory. The most straightforward and perhaps unexciting answer is that they belong to a broad spread of Prehistoric lithic finds discovered here and at excavations on neighbouring sites, which in these cases must have been disturbed from their original contexts and redeposited (possibly unknowingly) during the life of the priory. A second, more interesting possibility (see above), is that the arrowheads were recognised in Medieval times as ancient and possibly superstitious or magical artefacts,[60] so were deliberately collected and kept, before being discarded or lost, thus finding their way into the deposits in which we found them.

A Civil War powder cap

Chris Turley

Whilst washing finds from the 2012 excavation, volunteer archaeologists Mandy Bellamy and Chris Turley came upon this object (Fig. 5.33, SF 12, lower row; Fig. 5.44). At first it looked most like a squashed bottle top, but seemed to be made of lead. The working was very fine, with metal loops soldered to the top, and it was small: 25 by 15mm. Anni Byard, the Finds Liaison Officer for Oxfordshire, identified the object. It is a cap from an English Civil War powder charger or flask, also known as an Apostle, as there were usually twelve of them, and dates to between 1642 and 1646. Civil War musketeers wore a bandolier from shoulder to hip, holding a row of powder flasks, each with enough powder to prime one lead shot for his musket. Twine was threaded through the loops so the little cap did not usually get lost. Each day the musketeer would refill the flasks and refit each cap. Both the Royalist and Parliamentarian armies had musketeers, and a number of Civil War skirmishes were fought in and around Oxford. Either a Royalist or a Roundhead could have lost this cap.

One of the more famous Roundhead (Parliamentarian) commanders during the sieges of Oxford was Sir Robert Devereux, third Earl of Essex. It is recorded that in May 1644 his troops crossed the Thames at Sandford, so it is possible one of his soldiers dropped the cap at Minchery Farm. At the parliamentary garrisons, probably at Bullingdon Green or at Abingdon, camp followers supported the army with supplies, craft-working, and heavy horse-drawn wagons and carts. These carried equipment, such as pikes, and food and fodder for men and horses. Important among the army's supporters were the tinkers. The tinker was a metalworker and probably would have made the flask and caps. They would also been responsible for making lead shot. Known as itinerant casual workers, tinkers travelled from village to village sharing their skills with anyone who could pay. The name tinker apparently arose from the tinkling noise which their metallic possessions made as they travelled the bumpy roads.

Fig. 5.44: Lead Civil War powder cap (SF 12).

Conclusion

At the time of the 'Little Dissolution' there were probably around 150 nunneries in Britain and only a handful have been excavated to any great extent.[62] Together the various excavations around Littlemore Priory provide an insight into the life of one modest-sized but, for much of its existence, relatively prosperous female religious institution. It was founded during the peak period for the initiation of Benedictine nunneries in England. Female monasteries were often sited in isolated locations compared to their male equivalents. Littlemore Priory, despite being remote from the city, was nevertheless near enough to villages and farms to have ready access to labourers and craftspeople.[63] The church may also have been shared at times with the parochial congregation of Littlemore for worship and burial; the priory seems to have been relatively integrated with the local community.

Cloisters in nunneries often fulfilled a number of functions, including kitchen spaces and domestic rooms, and this may have been the case at Littlemore as seen in Trench 3, where a building plan was uncovered which aligns with the surviving standing part of the priory. Otherwise, there are few indications that the plan of cloister or outer precinct followed a regular model. Many smaller nunneries developed irregular building plans within the precinct and cloister. Evidence of sickness, including leprosy, among the burials found in the JMHS 2014 excavation of the demolished priory church, suggests that the nuns were probably caring for the sick and afflicted as part of their resident community.[64] Accommodating these people may have prompted further deviations from a standard plan. At the nearby nunnery of Godstow, west of Oxford, the nuns were recorded in the fifteenth century as living in a number of separate households, within the precinct but out of the main claustral range; it is not impossible that such arrangements may have occurred at times at Littlemore.[65] Evidence from JMHS 2006 trenches and Trench 2 in Minchery Paddock shows that the priory complex is more extensive than had hitherto been assumed. The nunnery was well-supplied with water, there was a well close to Trench 2, and there may have been a holy well or spring nearby (see page 194).

Excavations to date have, however, only touched upon a small proportion of the area of Littlemore Priory. Many elements of the nunnery probably still survive in the parts of Minchery Paddock which are currently inaccessible to excavation due to tree growth between Trenches 2 and 3; these might include peripheral domestic buildings, more barns, as well as stables, and a bakehouse, brewhouse and dairy, set around gardens, fish-ponds and orchards. Further potential for detecting fresh archaeological evidence also exists around the eastern, southern and western sides of the surviving building, including the possibility of identifying traces of its predecessor as the dormitory range. Opportunities may well arise in the future to explore further the archaeology of the priory, but research so far, as summarised here, has generated a vibrant and important picture of Medieval female monastic life, which is now available for comparison with that of other religious houses associated with Oxford. The priory site is of high importance to Oxford's heritage; its remains, both above and below-ground, should be protected, better-known and valued.

Notes

1 VCH Oxon 5, 267.
2 VCH Oxon 2, 75–77.
3 Reports on lithics by Olaf Bayer, Archaeobotanical remains by Diane Alldritt, Palaeoenvironmental analysis by Adrian Parker and Gareth Preston, Animal Bone by Julie Hamilton, Pottery by John Cotter, Metalwork by Anni Byard, and Tile by Gwilym Williams, can be found under Chapter 5 in the ORA data archive.
4 Clark 1899, 404.
5 VCH Oxon 2, 75–77.
6 RPS Consultants 2001; Moore 2001 (Science Park): very few Iron Age discoveries have been made near the priory.
7 Olaf Bayer, report on ORA.
8 May 1922.
9 McNicoll-Norbury 2014.
10 Pevsner 1974, 689. Listing: https://historicengland.org.uk/listing/the-list/list-entry/1047672
11 Pantin 1970, 19.
12 Beckley and Radford 2012 (several periods).
13 Booth 1995.
14 PCA 2014.
15 Murray 2015.
15 Williams 2006: evaluation trenches detect and confirm the presence of archaeology but do not excavate further to establish details.
17 Cobbold 1880, 319; May 1922.
18 Adrian Parker and Gareth Preston, report on ORA.
19 Williams 2006.
20 Unfortunately, in the 2006 the well was uncovered but not investigated further. We made a deliberate decision not to excavate the well, due to the safety challenges it may have posed. It remains for future archaeologists.
21 Diane Alldritt, report on ORA.
22 Diane Alldritt, report on ORA.
23 SUERC-49305 (GU32059).
24 SUERC-49309 (GU32063).
25 SUERC-49314 (GU32065).
26 Julie Hamilton, 2013 report on ORA.
27 John Cotter, 2013 report on ORA.
28 SUERC-49308 (GU32062).
29 Olaf Bayer, report on ORA.

30   VCH Oxon 3, 77-84.

31   Covered by stratigraphic grouping [2024].

32   Pantin 1970

33   John Cotter, report on ORA.

34   The *Archeox* investigations demonstrated that, in the Medieval period, the land had dropped away more steeply from the headland on which the cloister and church were situated down to the west and to the pond.

35   John Cotter, 2013 report on ORA.

36   SUERC-49313 (GU32064)

37   Diane Alldritt, report on ORA.

38   Julie Hamilton, report on ORA.

39   Anni Byard, report on ORA.

40   Gwilym Williams, report on ORA.

41   John Cotter, report on ORA.

42   VCH Oxon 5, 267-275.

43   Murray 2015.

44   Pantin 1970, pp. 19-22.

45   Diane Alldritt, report on ORA.

46   JMHS 2006; JMHS 2014; Murray 2015.

47   Gilchrist 2012, 247.

48   Booth and Edgeley-Long 2003; Moore 2001, 165-6.

49   Egan and Pritchard 1991, see 380-82 for examples.

50   Lawson 1990.

51   Egan 1998, 286.

52   Durham 1977, 163-6.

53   Wood 1994, 294.

54   Mellor 1994, 79.

55   Haberley 1937.

56   Devaney 2005.

57   Green 1980, 123.

58   Fitzpatrick 2013

59   Green 1980, 71.

60   Gilchrist 2008.

61   Ward-Perkins 1940, 66.

62   Gilchrist and Sloane 2005.

63   Bond 2003.

64   Murray 2015, 327.

65   Ganz 1972.

Excavation of the Priory church, 2014

Jane Harrison

In 2014, John Moore Heritage Services (JMHS) carried out archaeological excavations, paid for by the developer, before a new hotel was built on derelict land immediately to the north of the former pub, which is the last remaining building of Littlemore Priory. Shells of burnt-out buildings and a large amount of hard-core were removed from the site before the dig could go ahead. The excavation revealed the plan of the demolished priory church with burials located inside, and outside to its east and south (Fig. 1).[1] The discovery of the burials provided insights into the lives of those linked to the nunnery.

The excavations discovered very slight evidence for an earlier church, perhaps one built at the establishment of the priory in the mid-twelfth century. A larger church with choir, nave, crossing tower and belfry was built on the site, probably in the mid-thirteenth century, around the time that the priory was granted to the Knights Templar. The foundations indicate that the church was just over forty metres long, with an 8 metre wide nave and built of dressed limestone. A pit at its western end may have been used for casting bells. Unfortunately, later construction on the site after the church's dismantling, including of the twentieth-century country club, had left the church's foundations in a degraded state and thus difficult to interpret. During its lifetime, alterations had been made to the northern side of the choir, but the fragmentary condition of the foundations meant it was difficult to be sure about the sequence and overall character of the changes made to the church. The finds were dominated by glazed floor tiles, almost all of the Stabbed Wessex type familiar from the tile assemblage associated with the precinct buildings (see page 180).

The burials

Ninety-two burials were excavated with six more uncovered but left in the ground as their locations were undisturbed by the new hotel building. Fifty-two of the burials were packed into a small area outside and east of the church so graves were often inter-cut. The sex of twenty-nine of the skeletons could not be determined and, although thirty-five of the remainder were women, twenty-eight were men. Inside the priory church, the most distinguished burial was in a limestone cist of a woman over forty-five years old, probably one of the prioresses, located in the centre of the church at the crossing of nave and transepts. Other burials inside the church included a new-born baby and a young woman, buried face down. This relatively unusual posture may have been deliberate, an indication she had committed some egregious sin for which she was being marked out. Finding an infant among the church burials may add credence to the reports of the nuns' immorality, but may also reflect the nuns' nursing role, as the woman may have been in their care when she died in childbirth along with her baby.

The oldest people interred were over sixty: indeed thirty-two of the burials were of people over forty-five years old. This age-profile would fit with a priory population of nuns, chaplains and other retainers and workers. While most of the remaining identifiable burials were of adults over sixteen, there were fifteen

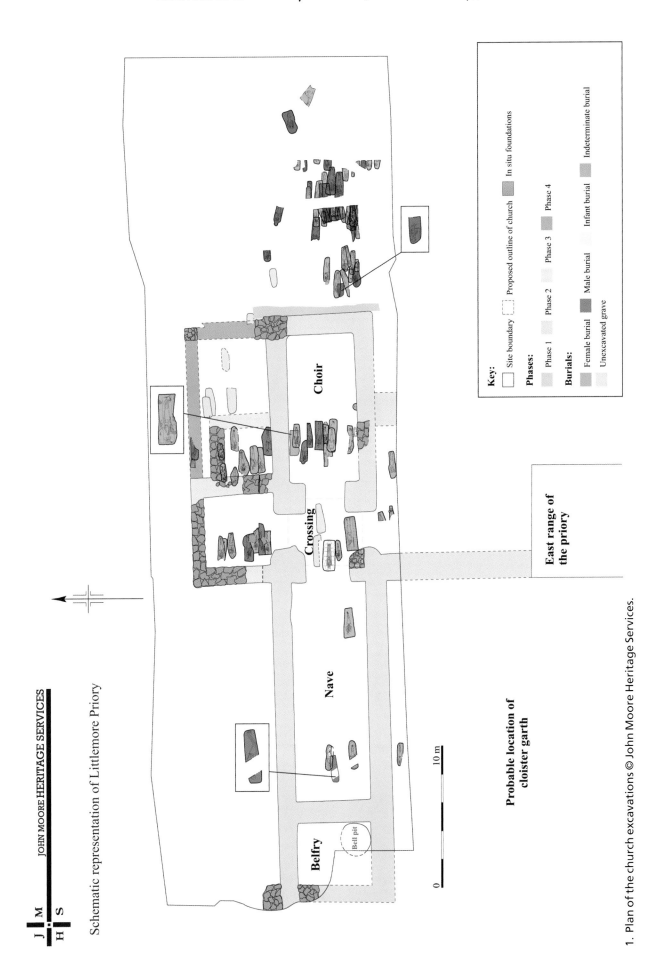

JOHN MOORE HERITAGE SERVICES

Schematic representation of Littlemore Priory

Key:

Site boundary [ ] Proposed outline of church [ ] In situ foundations

Phases:

Phase 1 Phase 2 Phase 3 Phase 4

Burials:

Female burial Male burial Infant burial Indeterminate burial

Unexcavated grave

Choir

Crossing

Nave

Belfry

Bell pit

East range of the priory

Probable location of cloister garth

0   10 m

1. Plan of the church excavations © John Moore Heritage Services.

children, some as young as three or four. These young children may have been boarders at the priory or perhaps the offspring of more important villagers. The *Archeox* excavations in 2012 discovered that the nuns may have been making their own copper alloy veil and shroud pins (see page 179) and such shroud pins were found with three of the burials.

Skeletons identified with pathologies, relating to injury and disease, provided further evidence that the nuns may have been caring for ailing individuals. Two of the children with traces of disease on their skeletons had suffered developmental problems and would have limped badly. Interestingly, one of the adults had leprosy and been sheltered by the nuns. As discussed in relation to Bartlemas, the fear of the disease was lessened by the belief that lepers were effective spiritual intercessors for the living. Overall, examination of the

skeletons revealed a population that had relatively wholesome diets and healthy living conditions. There was no striking difference between those buried inside or outside the church.

After the dissolution of the priory, its church may have served the inhabitants of Littlemore for some time, as there is no certain evidence for a church in the village pre-dating the present one, which was instigated by John Henry Newman and finished in 1836. However its fabric was evidently too valuable to be left unattended for long, and its demolition provided building stone and other materials for buildings in the area (see page 195).

Note

1   This summary is based on a report in *Medieval Archaeology*, Murray 2015.

The Littlemore Priory Book

Katie Hambrook

One book survives which belonged to Littlemore Priory and is now in the Bodleian Library (MS. Auct. D. 2. 6.). The book consists of three separate manuscripts which were written around the middle of the twelfth century and bound together. It is likely that this collection of texts was originally commissioned for a nun at Harrold Priory in Bedfordshire but there are indications that it reached Littlemore Priory at some point in the thirteenth century, perhaps as a gift from a nun at Harrold to someone at Littlemore.

One of the three manuscripts was a calendar: it was common for religious houses to own calendars to help them keep track of saints' days and other religious feast days. It has little illustrations of the signs of the Zodiac

2. Prayers of St Anselm: nun with a book kneeling before the Virgin and Child © Bodleian Libraries, Oxford.

and illuminated initials showing typical activities for each month (Fig. 1 and back cover). The second manuscript was a psalter with three large illuminated initials; psalters were essential for nuns' daily singing of the psalms. The final manuscript was a collection of the prayers of St Anselm; this has beautiful illustrations, which often include figures of nuns (Fig. 2).

The acquisition of a book including the St Anselm prayers may suggest the level of literacy among the nuns at Littlemore in the thirteenth century and that they were reading prayers written in Latin. However, an annotation reveals that in the fifteenth or sixteenth century the book was valued more for the silver clasp that fastened it: at this time one of the Littlemore prioresses pawned the book for two pounds. Katherine Wells, the last Prioress of Littlemore, was accused of pawning the priory's silver, so it is quite possible that this book with its silver clasp was one of

1. Calendar: July/August, man with scythe © Bodleian Libraries, Oxford.

the items referred to. By the seventeenth century the book belonged to an Exeter College fellow who donated it to the Bodleian Library.

Nuns' voices: Littlemore Priory

Katie Hambrook

Littlemore Priory was East Oxford's local nunnery, founded by the de Sandford family around AD 1150. They gave some of their land in Sandford, where the nunnery could be built, and they endowed the nunnery with other property to provide it with an income. The early grants explain some of the reasons why they founded the nunnery. Robert de Sandford granted land to the nuns so that there would always be prayers said 'for the souls of the Empress Matilda and King Henry her son, who gave the land to him for his service, and for the souls of his father and mother, and for the health of his own soul, and the souls of his parents and friends.'[1] The de Sandford family could have given a donation to an existing religious house, but founding their own was more prestigious. However, it was cheaper to found a nunnery than a monastery and at this time a number of knightly families, like the de Sandfords, chose to found small nunneries. Some nunneries were founded to satisfy

1: The Virgin holding a book (from the manuscript of St Anselm's prayers owned by Littlemore Priory).

Images from the Littlemore Book illustrate this feature, the following feature (Nuns' Voices), together with Chapter 6.

the religious vocations of women in the founding family; these women often became nuns in their family's nunnery. Robert de Sandford's daughter Christine became a nun at Littlemore.[2]

Nuns were committed to the core purpose of monastic life: they spent many hours a day praying and singing psalms and other sacred music. They served the local community, both living and dead, by praying for their souls. Over the years, Littlemore Priory received further gifts and bequests, mostly from local people. The early records of the priory are mostly financial documents, showing that the priory flourished alongside the de Sandford family in the thirteenth century. This was a time when the de Sandford men were prominent Templars and gave the manor of Sandford to the order; two de Sandford women became prioresses later in the century. In the early years of the fourteenth century the priory was deprived of its wealthier local supporters: the descendants of the de Sandfords lost their connection to the area and in 1312 the Templars were suppressed by the Pope. Nevertheless, the priory continued.

Records of bishops' visitations

In the documents of the fifteenth and sixteenth centuries the inhabitants of the priory come alive, speaking in their own voices about their concerns and particularly about the troubled final years of the convent. These records were written by male clerics and they highlight clerical anxieties about female sexuality – but we can read through the preoccupations of these texts and come to know the nuns of Littlemore. These documents illuminate the archaeological picture: a 1445 visitation includes an unusual example of clerical anxieties about female homosexuality and records from 1517 to 1524 tell the story of the last prioress, the defiant, dictatorial Katherine Wells.

The key documents for Littlemore Priory are the surviving records of the bishop's visitations. Most nunneries and monasteries were accountable to their local bishop and he was expected to go around his diocese every few years inspecting them. Littlemore Priory was in the very large Diocese of Lincoln. The standard procedure for the Bishop of Lincoln was that he would stay in Oxford and would undertake in person the visitations of the many religious houses there. He would delegate the visitation of Littlemore to a 'commissary', one of his assistant priests or a priest from an Oxford college. The commissary would go to

Littlemore and meet with all the nuns in their chapter-house. The prioress was expected to present him with the financial accounts. Then the commissary would meet with each nun separately, in order of seniority, and ask them a number of questions. The answers were written down and taken back to the Bishop, and the commissary would report on what he had seen at the nunnery. The Bishop would then set down a series of injunctions for the nuns, asking them to amend their ways in particular aspects. Either the nuns' answers may survive, or the Bishop's injunctions, or both sets of records.

The questions and the injunctions relate to the rules governing the nuns' way of life, specifically the Rule of St Benedict, relevant papal legislation and injunctions set out by previous Bishops. They often reflect the preoccupations of the current Bishop and his views of what was appropriate for nuns. But the nuns' answers often reveal different priorities and indeed the nuns did not always agree with each other. So the visitation records need to be read carefully, thinking about why a question was being asked and why a particular nun might reply as she did.

Littlemore Priory in 1445

On the 1st of June 1445, when William Alnwick, Bishop of Lincoln, was visiting Oxford, he sent his assistant, John Derby, to inspect Littlemore. From the nuns' answers we can list some of the inhabitants of the priory. Alice Wakely was the prioress and Agnes Piddington was the sub-prioress. The other five nuns, probably in descending order of age, were: Alice Byllesdone, Joan Maynard, Isabel Sydnale, Christine Cordberde, and Agnes Marcham, who was 28 years old. Most of the nuns came from Oxfordshire or Berkshire. Agnes, a retired servant, was boarding with the prioress and there were two girl boarders. There would have been female servants, perhaps as many as there were nuns, but only the male cook is mentioned. John Somerset, the parish chaplain of Sandford, was living in the priory and probably acting as the priory's priest. The priory also had a steward, John fitz Aleyn, to help look after its estates.[3]

Most of the nuns were happy and had no complaints about how the Priory was run. However, they did have a problem with Agnes Marcham. She had entered the nunnery at the age of thirteen and for the last thirteen years she had been refusing to become a fully professed nun. She was both unhappy and stubbornly resistant to the authority of the older nuns. In her interview with the Bishop's commissary, she excused her disobedience by counterattacking with accusations about the prioress and Joan Maynard. She did not go as far as saying they were guilty of sexual misconduct but accused them of allowing local clerics too much access to their rooms. Agnes may have had some hope that the Bishop might get her transferred

to another nunnery. There were a couple of references to the state of the priory finances and buildings. Agnes Marcham complained of the slenderness of the priory's revenues and the prioress claimed that the dormitory was in a ruinous state.

Bishop Alnwick's concerns about the priory

The Bishop's injunctions, and the questions his commissary asked the nuns, showed a completely different set of priorities. The commissary had discovered that the prioress and Christine Cordberde were sharing a bed, as were the sub-prioress and Isabel Sydnale. In ordinary domestic, non-monastic life, sharing beds was completely usual and expected. However, monastic rules like the Rule of St Benedict had different expectations:

'Let each one sleep in a separate bed… If possible let all sleep in one place; but if the number does not allow this, let them take their rest by tens or twenties with the seniors who have charge of them. A candle shall be kept burning in the room until morning.'[4]

This is one of the many early monastic rules intended to prevent homosexual activity among monks; throughout the history of male monasticism there were monks writing about the wickedness of sodomy and the need to prevent homosexual behaviour in monasteries. Bishop Alnwick had punished a case of homosexual activity in a male religious house a few years before. Although much of medieval writing about 'unnatural sex' was about male sodomy, there was also clerical literature about

2: Priest celebrating mass and two female worshippers (from the manuscript of St Anselm's prayers owned by Littlemore Priory)

sex between women. Alnwick took the issue of the Littlemore nuns sharing beds very seriously – it was the first injunction (ahead of any concerns about the nuns having too much access to male clerics). The language used in this injunction is much more emphatic than in other injunctions: 'we charge, enioyne commaunde yow and yche one of yow undere payne of the grete curse'. He refers to sharing beds as being against 'the rule of your ordere and also the commune lawe', perhaps hinting at activity which he would have seen as being against the law of nature.[5] Even if Alnwick had suspected the nuns of having sexual relationships with each other, he might have wanted to be discreet in how he dealt with this. A lot of the clerical writings for confessors cautioned not to speak too clearly to lay people about acts of unnatural sex – in case it gave them ideas.

Given the reluctance to speak about same-sex relations, it is not clear what the nuns would have made of this injunction. Did they understand the reason for prescribing separate beds? Monastic rules and injunctions also stressed the need to avoid close friendships that would unbalance the life of the community – the nuns may have seen the rule and the injunction in this light. The prioress certainly felt the need to defend herself and her sisters when the commissary started asking questions about their sharing beds. It was at this point that she claimed that they did so because they were afraid to sleep in the dormitory, which was in a ruinous state. The Bishop seems to have thought she was exaggerating about the dormitory – 'as it is saide is in plyte to falle.' He asked her to make sure that there was a bed for each of the nuns, whether they were in the dormitory or some other room in the nunnery.[6]

The Bishop's other injunctions reflected further anxieties about preserving the purity of the nuns' lives and reputations and keeping them separate from the secular world. The prioress was forbidden to have male visitors and she was to supervise the nuns' contacts with men. The nuns were not to have women boarders sleeping in the nuns' rooms; they were to ask the Bishop's permission to allow adults to board at the priory. Following this visitation, the prioress seems to have been successful in fundraising to pay for the rebuilding of the dormitory (however necessary or not this was). It is this latest building which is the surviving part of the priory (subsequently used as a farmhouse, it was most recently a pub until 2013, and is currently empty, see Fig. 5.6).

The last prioress

By the time of the next surviving visitation records, the priory buildings were in a poor condition, and the nuns were suffering the abusive rule of the last prioress, Katherine Wells. Katherine was elected prioress by her fellow nuns sometime before AD1507.[7] At the time of her election there were very few nuns at Littlemore, and apart from her they were all elderly or very young. Katherine was herself probably fairly young (though she would have been at least 21 when she was elected) and she may have seemed full of youthful energy.[8] There are also signs that she was an effective administrator of the priory, making the most of limited opportunities to maximise the nunnery's income. She was certainly successful in recruiting three or four young girls to enter the nunnery. She secured a legacy from Sir John Cottesmore of Brightwell Baldwin and negotiated tax exemptions for the priory. She made arrangements to pay an annuity to a Cowley man in return for his house and land. Later accusations of financial impropriety may have arisen partly because of disagreements over her methods of raising money: letting out tenements on a twenty-year lease, dealings with an unpopular local landowner.[9]

Meanwhile something far more problematic was going on at the priory – Katherine was having a relationship with the priory chaplain, Richard Hewes. Richard was an Oxford student who had got a degree in church law in 1508 and was continuing to study for his doctorate.[10] In 1510 Katherine gave birth to a baby girl and nursed her child in the priory. She seems to have made arrangements with a local landowner for fostering her daughter, but the child died aged about three years old. At some point around this time, Katherine had her first visitation. It is not clear exactly when this visitation was held and Bishop Smith's injunctions only survive in a later summary. This suggests that a humbly penitent Katherine admitted only a brief lapse, a limited relationship with Richard Hewes. She may have told the nuns not to say anything (as she did at a later visitation). The injunctions required the prioress to keep continent and chaste, and not to allow Richard Hewes into the nunnery in future.

The injunctions had absolutely no effect and Katherine continued her relationship with Richard – he wrote to her and visited two or three times a year, spending the nights in her bed. He gained his doctorate in 1516 and when he left Oxford to take up a living in Kent, she gave or lent him a feather bed and bolster, a pair of sheets, a surplice and a silver cup. There is something touching about Katherine helping her lover to set up his new home. Perhaps Katherine saw herself as the heroine of a romance – when the nuns tried to persuade her to stop seeing Richard Hewes, she replied 'I don't want to – whatever anyone says, I love him and I always will.'[11] The nuns may at first have tried to protect the reputation of the priory and tried to prevent people gossiping about Katherine's lover and child. But when a prospective novice came to stay, she discovered what was going on, left in disgust, and spread the news around.

Katherine and Bishop Atwater

In the summer of 1517 a new bishop, William Atwater, went on a visitation to Oxford. He chose as his commissary Edmund Horde, a fellow of All Souls; the records of this visitation survive and give a vivid picture of life in Littlemore Priory. There were six nuns: Katherine; an older nun, Juliana Bechamp; four younger nuns, Anna Willye, and three sisters or cousins from Iffley, Juliana, Joanna and Elizabeth Wynter. Katherine had threatened the nuns with punishment if they told the commissary anything but, led by Juliana Bechamp, they gave Edmund Horde a detailed account of the prioress's behaviour.

Katherine ruled the priory with threats, punishment and violence. In a world where hierarchy and authority were all-important, a prioress had every right to punish her nuns – but she was expected to do this with some sort of decorum and solemnity. Katherine had set up stocks in the parlour of the priory and used them to imprison any nun who displeased her, in one case for as long as a month. This was very unusual – the stocks were normally part of official judicial procedures and were intended to be a public punishment. There is no record of anything like this in any other monastery or nunnery. This punishment did not lead to good order and discipline. Katherine herself would walk around in the fields and into Oxford, accompanied only by one of the boy boarders. One of the Wynter girls, Juliana, had a relationship with a male priory servant and had recently had a child.

3: St Anselm gives books to Countess Mathilda of Tuscany and to monks (from the manuscript of St Anselm's prayers owned by Littlemore Priory).

The nuns also complained about the prioress's handling of the nunnery finances. In these sorts of circumstances there would have been resentment at any preferential provision of food and accommodation for the prioress and there were suspicions that she was using priory property to benefit her child and her lover. Both the nuns and the prioress agreed that the priory buildings were falling into ruin. At the end of their evidence to Edmund Horde the nuns stressed their main concern: without immediate help they would leave the nunnery for fear of the punishment the prioress would inflict if she heard that they had informed on her. When Edmund Horde and Bishop Atwater heard the nuns' evidence they were horrified by Katherine's sexual behaviour – they were less worried about the plight of the other nuns. At the end of six months the Bishop had summoned Katherine to appear before him and Edmund Horde accompanied her on the journey from Oxford to a special court hearing at the Bishop's manor at Woburn.

Katherine was charged with sexual and financial misconduct and was questioned for two days. She showed an impressive defiance in the face of the authority of the Bishop and his staff and denied everything she thought she could get away with. So she admitted the relationship with Richard Hewes and having a child, but she claimed that he had only been her lover for six months. She claimed that she had never been reprimanded by the previous Bishop for having a child and she had excuses for not being able to produce her copy of Bishop Smith's injunctions. When she was accused of allowing the priory buildings to fall into ruin, she denied this and added 'It would take more than a hundred pounds to repair the Priory.'[12]

Bishop Atwater was deeply shocked by her sexual relationship and her bringing up her child in the nunnery. The court record contains extra comments in his own handwriting ('the worst example of evil living').[13] At the end of the court proceedings he found her guilty of the charges against her and solemnly deprived her of her post as prioress. However, this sentence was immediately suspended and Katherine was allowed to continue to act as prioress under special supervision. Edmund Horde was to inspect the priory finances and Katherine would have to follow his advice. She was to obtain agreement from two senior nuns for every financial transaction. Finally, there was some recognition of the nuns' concerns: the Bishop ruled that she was not to punish any of her sisters without the approval of two senior nuns. It is curious that Katherine escaped so lightly and was allowed to remain as prioress. It is possible that she had friends in Oxford who argued for her to be shown mercy. It is likely that there was no one else capable of being prioress; the other nuns were too old, too young or in some other way unsuitable. Bishop Atwater personally inspected Littlemore the following year and this visitation record shows how much more difficult life had become at the priory. Katherine kept verbally abusing the sisters for informing on her at the previous visitation, she also complained of the younger nuns' behaviour, saying that they were disobedient and giggled in church.

Richard Hewes had visited again just after Easter. After he left, the prioress found Elizabeth Wynter playing in the cloister with the boy boarders. Katherine shouted at her, knocked her down and kicked her; then she locked Elizabeth in the stocks. This was the last straw for the younger nuns – they freed Elizabeth, burnt the stocks in the parlour fireplace and refused to let the prioress into the parlour. That night they broke a window, climbed out and ran off to stay at a friend's house for three weeks.

It is not clear how the nuns returned to the priory; perhaps relatives and friends were involved in promoting some sort of reconciliation between the prioress and the nuns. After the visitation, the Bishop yet again left the priory in Katherine's hands. It is possible that he temporarily transferred some of the nuns to other nunneries: the 1520 Godstow Abbey visitation records the presence of three young nuns who had no funds to pay for their maintenance and clothing.[14] Life may have been grim for any nuns remaining at Littlemore under Katherine's despotic rule. After Edmund Horde left Oxford in 1520 and Bishop Atwater died in 1521, there was no one left with an interest in supervising Katherine.

The last days of the priory

Katherine continued to run the priory and its estates. In the early 1520s she would have been aware of Cardinal Wolsey's plans to close down St Frideswide's Priory in Oxford to build his new Oxford College. She may also heard that the Cardinal's agents were looking out for other religious houses which could be dissolved so that their properties could be added to the new college's estate. Littlemore had a number of advantages for Wolsey's agents. Although it was poor, it owned land conveniently close to Oxford. It also had no influential patrons or nuns to argue against its closure. And it may also have been convenient for Katherine; she negotiated a good severance package for herself: an annual pension of £6 13s 4d (there is also a record of other nuns receiving a limited pension). By the summer of 1524 Littlemore Priory was on Wolsey's list of religious houses to dissolve. The following February, his agents turned up at Littlemore to accept the prioress's surrender of the priory and its estates.[15] The first 350 years of the priory's history are known through records that tell us little about the devotion of the nuns and the ordered running of their lives. The surviving records give us a vivid, but untypical, picture of the troubled last years.

Notes

1 Turner 1878, 293.
2 Thompson 1991, 179.
3 Thompson 1918, 217-218.
4 Order of St Benedict, chapter 22.
5 Thompson 1918, 218.
6 Thompson 1918, 218.
7 Turner 1878, 293.
8 Information about the Priory for the period 1507–1518 comes mostly from Thompson 1947, 8-12 and Bowker 1967, 46-51.
9 Weaver and Beardwood 1958, 100; Turner 1878, 293; Hamilton Thompson 1947, 10.
10 Foster 1891, 762.
11 Thompson 1947, 10, author's translation.
12 Bowker 1967, 48, author's translation.
13 Bowker 1967, 51, author's translation.
14 Thompson 1944, 154.
15 O'Sullivan 2006, 227-58; Brewer 1875, 502; Caley 1821, 337.

The patronage of SS Mary, Edmund and Nicholas at Littlemore Priory

Graham Jones

Littlemore's Benedictine nunnery was founded 'in a pasture called Cherleyham pertaining to the manor [and in the parish] of Sandford',[1] late in the reign of Stephen (1135-54).[2] It was described circa 1160 as dedicated in honour of SS Mary, Edmund and Nicholas.[3] Dedication of twelfth-century religious houses to Mary was customary,[4] her feast day in August coincided with the harvest and with meadowland's most productive season; Benedict's rule enjoined work, after all, including in Mary's gardens.[5] It was the saints who accompanied her who filled out the devotional tone, and were chosen for what they represented to the community.[6] Dedications to St Edmund, King of East Anglia, martyred in 869,[7] and St Nicholas, fourth-century bishop of Myra in Asia Minor, together proclaim, I argue, the nuns' and their benefactors' indebtedness to Abingdon Abbey.

Abingdon Abbey's Domesday lands included 15 hides at Sandford,[8] and the priory's founder Robert de Sandford was mesne lord of that portion held from the abbey in return for knight service.[9] Littlemore Priory's homage to Benedictine Abingdon and its endowment by Robert and others holding land from the abbey is an example of how small religious houses at this period were founded and organised by local families concerned to reflect the interests of overlords.[10] Among the Abingdon monks' relics were pieces 'of the bloodstained shirt of St Edmund, worn by him at the hour of his passion, and of his coffin'.[11] I. G. Thomas thought it possible that they were brought to Abingdon by Spearheafoc, a monk of St Edmundsbury and renowned gold- and silversmith who became abbot of Abingdon in 1048.[12] Powerful saint that he was, Edmund is mentioned as a patron of Littlemore Priory only once. Thereafter, for example in 1177[13] and again in the Hundred Rolls of 1279/80, patronage of the religious house is said to come from Nicholas alone.[14] His importance for Abingdon, where a hand reliquary of the saint was venerated,[15] was as titular of the monks' church which stood at the abbey's gateway from the marketplace (below). Coincidentally, Edmund and Nicholas' joint commemoration gave Littlemore Priory a short festive season spanning the start of Advent, for Edmund's feast day is November 20 while Nicholas is celebrated on December 6.

Littlemore Priory church, situated to the north of the remaining building, was marked by coffins discovered in 1661[16] and fully revealed in more recent excavations in 2014 (see page 186). The priory was endowed with six virgates (one-and-a-half hides) of arable and four acres of pasture at 'that place which was called *Chirleham* and is now called *Chaldewelle*'.[17] Robert's charter of *circa* 1160 refers to the land and church of 'Cherley' as if there was a settlement there, and though the priory church is meant it remains a possibility that 'Cherleyham' was the site of a church or field chapel before the foundation of the priory.[18] If such a church or chapel had been (re)consecrated in the second half of the eleventh century, some portion of Abingdon's relics of St Edmund, recently arrived, could well have been installed in its altar. It is easy to imagine the free tenant (Old English *ceorl*), established on his 'island' (*ēg*) between converging streams, wishing to express his allegiance to Abingdon.

'Chaldewelle' spring is probably that shown at Ordnance Survey grid reference SP 5470 0261 (350m north-north-east of the priory within Littlemore parish, underneath modern-day Falcon Close) on large-scale mapping from 1876.[19] The multiple water-source ('Choswell Springs' in 1819)[20] was known as 'Chawdwell' in 1512,[21] reached by 'Chowleswell lane' in 1605,[22] later 'Chose-well', and by 1850 'Chosel' or 'Chosler',[23] and gave its name to a curving area of rising ground in Sandford parish, 'Caldewelhoc', *circa* 1240.[24] Furlongs in Lake Field, one of the open fields east of Littlemore village and lying by the stream flowing south into Northfield Brook, were named after Chose-well Lane, modern Spring Lane, now truncated just north of the nineteenth-century railway. Another path led from Littlemore village past this, or another spring across Northfield Brook to the site of the priory, just within Sandford parish.[25] A William de Chalderwelle was taxed at Littlemore in 1316 and 1327.[26]

The naming looks like a normal progression in local pronunciation from an original ceald wella, 'cold well/stream'. In West Saxon Old English ceald (pronounced with an initial 'ch') was the counterpart of Anglian cald, ancestor of the modern word 'cold'. Cold wells have been considered curative.[27] Thus John Warburton, writing about Paulinus' Well in Northumberland, in his history of the county circa 1715, wrote of 'water very cold, and clear as christall, and if cleaned out would be a most comodious cold bath and perhaps effect several cures without a marvell'.[28] Some midland Chadwells have been misconstrued as 'holy' wells of St Chad. A nearby water supply considered curative could well attract a small religious foundation or a chapel, perhaps with a hermit as custodian. Indeed, some functional association with the 'Coldwell' springs could explain the adoption of their name in place of 'Cherleyham'.

The west end of the monks' church of St Nicholas at Abingdon, first mentioned in the late twelfth century,[29] overlooks the market place, a frequent location for Nicholas churches[30] resonating with his legend.[31] Usually interpreted as a sailors' saint, Nicholas is best seen as role-model for generous and merciful merchants.[32] Cures attributed to Nicholas were often credited to the 'miraculous' oil said to flow from his shrine; his episcopal city was Myra on the southern coast of modern Turkey, eponymous production centre of myrrh. A *Life* and an account of his miracles, written in Naples in the third quarter of the ninth century, sparked interest in Nicholas across western Europe.[33] It was said that William the Conqueror had cried out to Nicholas for help when his invasion fleet was caught by a Channel storm.[34] However, existing interest was dwarfed by the surge of popularity after Nicholas's remains were stolen from Myra in 1087 and taken to Bari on Italy's Adriatic coast. Bari had recently fallen to Robert Guiscard, an adventurer from Normandy. At the time of the foundation of Littlemore Priory Nicholas was fast becoming one of the pre-eminent patronal saints of English churches and hospitals, doubtless benefitting from the Norman connection.

Another attractive explanation for the dedication of the priory and its church in Nicholas's honour may lie in the legend of the Three Balls, bags of gold thrown in by Bishop Nicholas through the window of a merchant whose three daughters were without dowry as a result of his commercial misfortunes. Nunneries were not only the preserve of pious women who dedicated their lives to God. They were also refuges for women who, for whatever reason, needed a haven. When Robert of Sandford founded Littlemore Priory, his daughter Christine became a nun there.[35] The foundation of the priory may therefore have been Christine's own dowry in that she was married to Christ in place of an earthly spouse, thus also creating a refuge for women with no such wealthy advantage.

Notes

1   *Rotuli Hundredorum* 2, 1818, 723.

2   Stevenson 1858, 2, 60 for the adulthood of its founder Robert of Sandford by 1111 and the earliest materials in the Pipe Rolls of Henry II for his succession by his son Jordan.

3   Oxford, Bodleian Library, MS Charter Oxfordshire 4, summarised in Turner 1878, 297, with the 53 Littlemore charters and confirmations discussed on pp. v-vi.

4   Binns 1989.

5   Mary's feasts on August 15 (Assumption) and September 8 (Nativity) were popularly known as 'Mary' and 'Little Mary' 'in Summer' (Jones 2006, 80-81). Flowers and herbs were blessed in churches at Assumption and kept as curative and protective charms; Marian associations with flowers and gardens are of long-standing (Warner 1976, 99-100).

6   Motives behind dedication choices were varied but non-random (Jones 2007).

7   Not the local St Edmund, Archbishop of Canterbury, born at Abingdon in *circa* 1177, canonised in 1246 shortly after his death.

8   Domesday Book, Oxon 9, 3-5.

9   *Rotuli Hundredorum* 2, 1818, 723.

10 Postles 2002. The term 'honor' applies to extensive territorial overlordships.

11 Stevenson 1858, 2, 157.

12 Thomas 1974, 154; Thorpe 1878, 1, 201n.

13 Turner 1878, 293, Oxford, Bodleian Library, MSS Charters Oxfordshire, 6*, 8, 10.

14 *Rotuli Hundredorum* 2, 1818, 723.

15 Stevenson 1858, 2, 157.

16 VCH Oxon 5, 268.

17 *Rotuli Hundredorum* 2, 1818, 723.

18 For the place-names 'Cherley' and 'Cherleyham' see Gelling 1953, 187.

19 County Series 1:2500, First Edition.

20 Gelling and Stenton 1953-4, 180, citing Littlemore Enclosure Award.

21 VCH Oxon 5, 207, citing Oxford, Bodleian MS. Christ Church College, c. 320, ff. 2, 4-5.

22 Probably marked as such on Thomas Langdon's map of 1605, Oxford, Christ Church College Muniments.

23 Lobel 1957, 268, footnote 60, citing Oxford, Bodleian MS. Top. Oxon, c. 78 (W. Plowman Collections), f. 198.

24 Leys 1941, 1, 20, No. 20; Gelling 1953, 187.

25 VCH Oxon 5, 207.

26 CH Oxon 5, 207, citing TNA, E 179/161/8, 9.

27 Harte 2008, 2, 286.

28 Harte 2008, 2, 180.

29 VCH Berks 4, 430-51.

30 Jones 2006, 73-88, esp. 79-81.

31 Jones 2006, esp. 79-81.

32 Jones 2006, 82-88.

33 Jones 2006, 75 fn. 11.

34 Chibnall 1969-80, 2, 208-09.

35 Leys 1941, 1, 16, fn. 6.

Religion and rebuilding at St. George's House, Cowley Road, Littlemore

Philip Salmon FRHistS

Located mid-way along Cowley Road in Littlemore stands a large stone farmhouse flanked by high stone walls. Traditionally dated to 1611, St George's, as it came to be known in the Victorian period, has a number of well-documented religious associations (Fig. 1).[1] During the later seventeenth to early eighteenth centuries it was home to at least three generations of the Kimber family, staunch Catholics and noted members of Littlemore's recusant community.[2] A century later St George's became the last private house that John Henry Newman lived in before retreating to his monastic college, where he famously converted to Catholicism in 1845. During the two years that he kept rooms at St George's, between 1840 and 1842, Newman is said to have used the east-facing first floor room looking out on to Cowley Road as his prayer room or oratory.[3]

Most of what has been written so far about St George's House and its religious associations has focused on the building's residents.[4] The location and

structure of the house itself, by contrast, have never really been considered. Some work on Newman has hinted at possible lines of inquiry: the way Newman used to be able to see the remains of Littlemore Priory from his bedroom window, for instance, or his interest in the building's history, as suggested by an account of his signing (and possible preservation) of a late Tudor stained-glass window during alteration works (Fig 2).[5]

More recently, it has become apparent that St George's is situated exactly 1,000 yards (914m) from the archaeological remains of the Medieval church at the Priory. This distance is perhaps significant, since it is the Biblical maximum of 2,000 cubits that an observant could travel on the Sabbath. Although the priory was dissolved in 1525, long before St George's was built, there was probably an earlier house on this site, as suggested by domestic pottery finds from the twelfth century, and surviving timber-frame elements within the stone structure.[6] Dating this timber has so far proved impossible: most of the accessible material is elm and lacks a sufficient number of rings.

Some of the distinctive stone used in the construction of St George's, however, points to two intriguing possibilities. Either material was reused from an earlier stone building on the site – one that featured finely carved and cut masonry. Or, and

1. St George's House, Cowley Road, Littlemore, eastern range.

probably more likely, the farmhouse was constructed with stone and rubble robbed from the ruins of nearby Littlemore Priory. Both scenarios suggest another religious dimension to the history of this house. Recent excavation work at the priory has revealed most of the buildings had been comprehensively demolished. The removal and reuse of building material from this site fits neatly with the general pattern of 'great rebuilding' that occurred locally at that time, while evidence for late Tudor features at St George's, such as the 'Newman window', indicates that the construction of this farmhouse probably started earlier than 1611.

St George's House is now made up of two ranges arranged in a T-shape. The eastern range facing the Cowley Road was built before the western range,

located towards the rear, and with more attention to the appearance of its stonework.[7] Most of the publicly-visible external walls of this range have alternating thin and thick courses of limestone squared on all four sides. This contrasts with the rest of the property, which is predominantly built from rubble and more roughly-squared stone. It is the internal walls, however, which are most revealing, especially the load-bearing elements around fireplaces and their infills. Scattered throughout these structures are fragments of possible tracery, mullions and other shaped stone features. Mostly still in situ, their apparently random placement suggests these walls were never intended to be seen, and instead would have been covered by lime plaster or hidden behind other fireplace structures (Fig. 3).

2. A late Tudor stained-glass window, allegedly signed by J. H. Newman (panel since removed).

3. The rear wall of this inglenook contains fragments of a chamfered lintel and socketed stones.

4. Carved sandstone fragments from the rubble internal walls of an inglenook.

5. Shaped stone from an inglenook infill: possibly part of a slab used in a brass memorial.

Some of these worked stones are so oddly shaped that it has proved impossible to put them back during the course of lime repointing and routine repairs (Figs 4-6). Loose fragments in the builder's hole of one inglenook included pieces of finely carved sandstone, part of what might have been a monumental brass slab and a decorated, almost Romanesque, stone lintel or upright.

Further work needs be done at St George's to establish the building phases and the materials used. Some link with re-use of stone from Littlemore Priory, however, now appears to be very likely, adding to our understanding of vernacular rebuilding in this area. The seventeenth-century stone property across the road, 28 Cowley Road, for instance, may well have been rebuilt along similar lines.

Newman's well-documented journey towards monastic life, it would seem, occurred whilst staying in a farmhouse built from the ruins of a priory which he looked at daily. In April 1842, he left St George's and moved 100 yards down the road into his own monastic college, constructed, perhaps rather appropriately, from former farm buildings.[8]

6. Decorated upright or lintel from the rear rubble wall of an inglenook.

Notes

1 VCH Oxon 5, 206.
2 Payne 1886, 215; Coombs 2012, 3; Basset 1987, 32.
3 Tracey 1995, 326, 405; and 1999, xxiv; Anthony Hill, son of Captain James Hill, (pers. comm.), 2010.
4 Other noted residents include Professor Charles Upton (1831-1920), a 19th century theologian, and the artist Louis Davis (1860-1941), described by Nikolaus Pevsner as the 'last of the pre-Raphaelites'.
5 Taylor nd; Basset 1987, 33; Hill (pers. comm.), 2010.
6 East Oxford Archaeology Project, TP 60, 15, 16 June 2013.
7 Gill 2007.
8 Basset 1987, 32-35.

Chapter 6

Place-names and the historic landscape of East Oxford

Peter Finn and Katie Hambrook, with Jane Harrison

On first acquaintance, many of East Oxford's place-names seem baffling or downright odd. Even major names like *Iffley* and *Blackbird Leys* seem to defy straightforward explanation. What's an *Iff-* – or a *ley* for that matter? And why were there blackbirds on the leys – and what are *leys* anyway? What do *The Kidneys* have to do with a bodily organ? Why is a street in Cowley called *The Grates*? And to which bear did *Bear's Hedge* belong? When you start looking at old field-names they seem to get no less baffling, but sometimes even a bit uncomplimentary or just plain rude. Would anyone want to own a field called *Shitten Corner*, or *Broad Arse*? What is one to make of these names? The answer is: hopefully, quite a lot – and if you would like to know what we think the above names mean, read on.

Until about 150 years ago East Oxford was still almost entirely rural, and almost every feature of that landscape of fields, meadows, marsh and woodland bore a name. Many older names have survived into modern times, at least in some form. Archaeology attempts to describe and explain aspects of human activity in the past, typically by interpreting physical evidence in the landscape. However, one way in which we can really 'get into the heads' of earlier inhabitants is through the study of place-names. Place-names can tell us how people saw the landscape, what was important to them, even in some cases what their attitudes were. Studying place-names can augment our understanding of the earlier physical environment, as well as how the land was used and governed. Personal names (often denoting ownership) are evident in place-names, as are terms for topographic features such as hills or marshes, and resources such as livestock, pasture, woodland and meadows. The names of the some of the core settlements of East Oxford, *Cowley*, *Iffley* and *Littlemore* originate in the Old English language of around 1000 years ago, and sum up the character of the area in the Anglo-Saxon period.

In this chapter we look at place-name evidence for the ways in which the Anglo-Saxon inhabitants of East Oxford viewed and used the landscape – concentrating on names referring to landscape features or names that are more likely to be of Pre-Norman origin, derived from Old English words (see Fig 6.1 the for the locations of these names). Then we go on to look at what place-names can reveal of the Medieval and later development of the area.

The place-names of East Oxford were investigated by a group of *Archeox* volunteers, with expert guidance.[1] In our research, we concentrated on names that we could locate on the ground, using the maps of nineteenth century tithe and enclosure (or 'inclosure') records. We consulted the records of Oxford colleges relating to the property they held in East Oxford, especially the estate maps and the terriers that listed the land colleges held in each field. The earliest source we used was an Anglo-Saxon charter of AD1004 written at the royal estate of Headington, which describes the boundaries of Cowley (which is presented in more detail below, see page 214). We also used title deeds listed in the cartularies of Medieval religious houses around Oxford. Using the earliest record we could find for each name, we considered whether the form of the name suggested an origin from Old English names or words, or whether it was more likely to be a recent name. Some names clearly derive from words or names that have not themselves been recorded, but can be reconstructed from early forms of the place-name. These unrecorded words and names are indicated by an asterisk (e.g. **Hocc*, an unrecorded Anglo-Saxon personal name, as in Hockmore).

Woodland resources

In both *Cowley* and *Iffley* the second element is clearly Old English lēah 'wood-pasture' – woodland used as pasture for livestock, probably mostly for pigs. This sort of woodland would have been fairly open, depending on how intensively it was grazed. *Lēah* areas often have settlements which have developed from scattered farmsteads or small hamlets, rather than a clearly defined centre.

The first element of the name *Cowley* appears to be the Old English man's name *Cufa*. The earliest form of this place-name, *Couelea* (recorded in the 1004 charter), allows us to make this judgement; in the study of place-names, the earlier a name was recorded, the more sure we can be of the derivation from a particular Old English word or name.[2] The first element of *Iffley* is more of a puzzle (given as *Gifete* in 1004). Earlier scholars have suggested that it comes from an otherwise unrecorded Old English word for a plover or lapwing, but since plovers and lapwings prefer more open country than wood-pasture, the first element

may be a different unrecorded word or personal name.[3]

Other local wood-pasture names include Cowley's *Leye Hill*, evidently containing Old English *lēah* in dative singular form (*lēage* '[land] at the wood pasture'),[4] and the Iffley field-name *Bear Wood*, the main element evidently 'swine-pasture' (Old English *bǣr*). A *bǣr* was often an outlying area of an estate – so the name *Bear Wood* might hint at a time when this part of Iffley was a peripheral portion of a larger estate.[5]

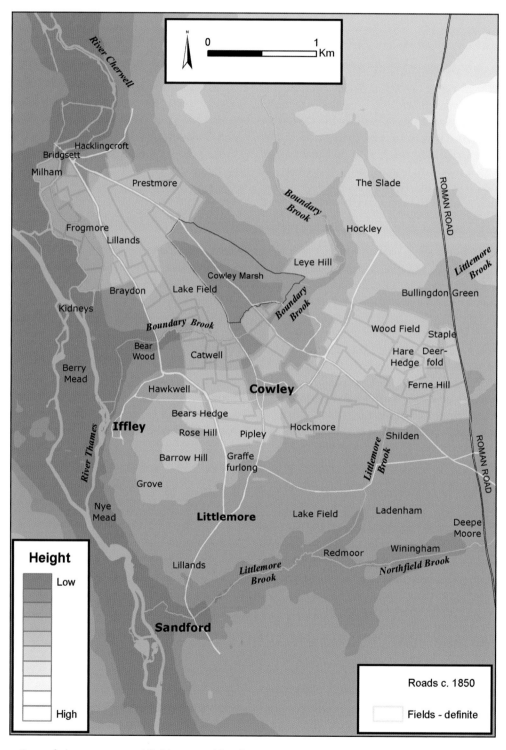

Fig. 6.1. Locations of place-names and field-names: Map 1.

Fig. 6.2. Wood pasture (from the twelfth- century calendar owned by Littlemore Priory) © Bodleian Libraries, Oxford.

A name that might reflect settlement dispersed within patches of woodland and scrubby clearings is *Burbushe* – 'a copse of bushes with a cottage'.[6]

A different use of woodland resource is represented by Iffley's *Grove*.[7] In Anglo-Saxon and medieval times a 'grove' was an intensively managed wood, maintained for wood and timber and not used for pasture. Groves were often enclosed by ditches or fences. Another grove in our area was *Bulendesgrave*, presumably a grove near Bullingdon Green.[8] Just north-east of our area was the royal forest of Shotover, where woodland was important for hunting. A thirteenth-century field-name in Cowley, *Derefolde*, records the presence of an enclosure for deer, which is likely to have been associated with hunting in the forest.[9]

Early estates and landholders

Occurrences of Anglo-Saxon personal names may give hints of earlier estates and landholdings. The two settlements of Cowley and Iffley may represent a division of the area into two estates, possibly both associated with founders such as *Cufa*.

The related names **Hocc* and *Hocca* may occur locally up to four times, suggesting landholdings centred on what became Church Cowley – bounded on the south by *Hockmore*, possibly 'Hocca's boundary';[10] incorporating *Hawkwell* 'Hocc's spring', in Iffley, to the

west;[11] possibly extending as far east as Old Horspath, with *Hockawell*, probably 'Hocca's spring';[12] and possibly reaching as far north as the later Cowley–Headington boundary, where we have a *Hockley*, conceivably 'Hocc or Hocca's wood-pasture'.[13]

Just to the west of Hockmore, the Medieval field-names *Puppelowe* and *Pippelewe* (later *Pipley Furlong*) show that the Cowley–Iffley–Littlemore boundary junction was marked by a barrow. The second element is from Old English *hlæw*, a word used for pagan Anglo Saxon burial barrows: the first element was a male personal name something like **Pyppa*.[14] The individual involved may be the same man as that commemorated in *(on) pippan lege* '(at) Pyppa's wood-pasture' at Arncott, eight miles away, in AD 983.[15]

Another Old English personal name, *Wine* ('friend'), may occur not only in Littlemore, in a field known as *Winingham* or *Winingale* (probably alternative names for 'Wine's river-meadow'), but also in Cowley, in *Winsimor*, 'Wine's marsh'.[16] Ownership by a religious institution may be indicated in *Prestemore* 'priest's marsh', perhaps alluding to land in Cowley that was part of the St Frideswide's estate.[17]

Hills and valleys

The most basic names in any landscape describe major topographical features – the 'lie of the land'; many of these names are likely to have Old English origins. Given East Oxford's topography, it's not surprising that many local names are for hills, valleys, watercourses and wetlands.

Old English had a number of different words for 'hill', some of them referring to very specific hill shapes, including *dūn*, used for a low, fairly level hill, suitable for settlement. This word may occur in a field-name recorded in the seventeenth century, *Braydon Close*, and in a name for a nearby hedge, *Bradon Hedge* (1723).[18] This is where the land slopes up quite steeply from the Thames; the Iffley Road runs along the top of this slope, which dips down again at the Boundary Brook. *Braydon* could possibly be a relic of a very early name for this ridge: a Celtic–English 'hill-hill' tautological compound containing British **bre* 'hill' plus an explanatory Old English *dūn*. Such a doublet name would be of interest not only because it would constitute a rare Celtic survivor in our area, but also because it might relate to the adjacent probable Romano-British settlement at Fairacres Convent discovered by test-pitting (see Chapter 3, Part 1). However, other examples of *bre-dūn* hills are much larger and it is difficult to be certain about the origin of *Braydon* without earlier forms of the name.

The field *Braydon Close* had an alternative name recorded earlier, in the thirteenth century: *Hertesheved*. The second element may come from another word for a hill, Old English *hēafod* 'head', 'small hill, projecting piece of land'. The first element is evidently Old English *heorot* 'hart, male deer' or a Middle English personal name *Hert* (i.e. *Hart*) or the like from the same source (such a name was indeed borne by a Medieval Cowley landholding family). It seems unlikely that a hill so close to settlements would have been frequented by deer and named for this, so perhaps a medieval 'Hert's hill' is more probable. It might also be possible to take *hēafod* literally as 'stag's head', an animal head stuck up on a post to mark a boundary, a meeting place or even a ritual site.[19]

North of Braydon and south of Cowley Road the land rises. The field here was called *Longe Hill* in 1605,[20] and *Ridge Field* in the eighteenth century, either referring to the ridge and furrow of the ploughed field, or to the ridge of land here.[21] The prominent *Rose Hill* was apparently so named only in the nineteenth century, after a house.[22] It may earlier have been called *Barrow Hill*, with *Barrow* probably coming from the Old English word *beorg*.[23] *Beorg* does sometimes mean barrow and the name may refer to a lost prehistoric barrow somewhere on the hill. But *beorg* is also used of hills with a continuously rounded profile – exactly the shape of *Rose Hill*. So this may have been another 'hill-hill' name, rather like Braydon above. It is also possible that the name came from a different Old English word, *bearu*, 'small wood' which would refer to the woodland resources of this area. East of Temple Cowley the land rises to form the lower slopes of Shotover Hill. Here there were names that may reflect a wood-pasture landscape: *Ferne Hill* 'hill overgrown with ferns' (Old English *fearn* + *hyll*)[24] and *Swalewnenhulle* 'hill frequented by swallows' (now *Brasenose Wood*).[25]

One of the most important local names was the name of a valley. *Bullingdon* is the name of the local hundred – from Anglo-Saxon times until the nineteenth century English shires were divided into hundreds, each comprising several parishes. In each hundred would be a place or places where the men of the hundred would assemble to hold open-air meetings and courts. The earliest form of the name *Bullingdon* is *Bulesden*, refering to a *denu*, the Old English word for a narrow valley or dene. This was either 'the bull's dene' or 'the dene of a man called *Bula* 'The Bull''.[26] The name of the hundred was transferred to *Bullingdon Green*, an area of high ground extending from the north-east of Cowley into Horspath, shared as common pasture between those parishes and Iffley.[27] There are records of thirteenth century hundred meetings at Bullingdon Green and it is likely that this was a traditional meeting place for the hundred.

The location of the original *Bullingdon* valley is unclear and it is possible that it was elsewhere in Bullingdon Hundred. It may have been one of the valleys close to Bullingdon Green, such as the valley where the upper section of the Boundary Brook runs.

This is joined by the smaller *Lye Valley*, which may have originally been called *The Slade*, from Old English *slæd* 'valley, usually a small side valley, often wet,' with the name *Slade* later transferred to a common and a road above the valley.[28] Finally, there are names referring to the flatness of a landscape: the first element of the field-names *Sheldon* and *Shilden* probably comes from *scylf* 'shelf,' describing the rather flat, level land around the eastern boundary between Cowley and Littlemore.[29]

Rivers, streams and springs

East Oxford abounds in names for watercourses, ranging from major rivers to minor springs or streams and the numerous Old English and later terms for specific types of watercourses are well represented in our area.

Thames is one of the oldest recorded names in the entire British Isles, cited by the Greek geographer Ptolemy around 150 BC; it may even be a pre-Celtic name. It is also probably our longest-attested name locally, if the Celtic personal name *TAMESUBUGUS* – recovered from a third century (AD) potsherd found in Headington – really does mean 'Thames-dweller' or the like.[30]

The 1004 Cowley charter bounds give a sense of how the Anglo-Saxon inhabitants saw the area, and marked its boundaries, in terms of different watercourses (see below for more details of the charter). The bounds start at the Cherwell and go along its stream until the *rīþig*, 'small stream'. Later the bounds hit another *rīþig* and twice follow part of the Boundary Brook before re-joining the Cherwell.[31]

The *Boundary Brook* rises in Headington and runs southwards through Cowley to join the Thames at the northern end of Iffley. This important local stream was given the name after it was used to mark the new parliamentary and city boundary of Oxford in the nineteenth century. Earlier it was known variously as *Moor Ditch*, *Marsh Brook* or simply *The Brook*.[32] The Old English word *brōc* was used specifically for more muddy streams that were flowing over clay and alluvium – which would fit the lower reaches of the Boundary Brook.

The *Northfield* and *Littlemore* brooks also formed a boundary, in this case between Littlemore and Sandford, and we have records of older names for the Littlemore Brook. In a 1050 charter it is called the *lacu* of Sandford; *lacu* is an Old English word sometimes used for the tributary of a river, in this case the Thames.[33] An alternative name was recorded in 1605: *Lidginge Well*.[34]

Many other local watercourses are named using the element -*well* (Old English *welle* 'spring or stream'); the most significant and earliest recorded of these is the Cherwell. Some evoke the landscape around Cowley

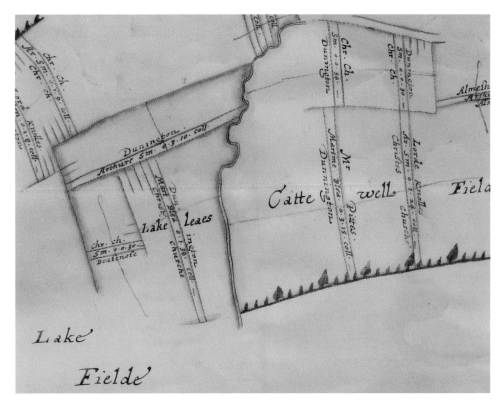

Fig. 6.3. Lake Field and Catwell Field. Langdon map, Cowley, Corpus Christi College MS 533, 19.

Marsh: *Crowell*, 'crow spring/stream' (Old English *crāwe* + *welle*),[35] and *Strowell*, 'spring in brush-covered marsh' (Southern Old English *strōd* 'marshy land overgrown with brushwood' + *welle*).[36] Just north-west of Church Cowley was *Catwell*, which was possibly 'spring/stream frequented by cats'.[37] Cats in Oxfordshire are not likely to have been wildcats but semi-domesticated or feral cats, living near people; their presence suggests that there may have been an early settlement near the spring. Alternatively, the spring might have been associated with a man called *Catta*, 'The Cat'.

Whole open fields were characterised by small streams called *lakes*, a word derived from the Old English word lacu (which sometimes meant 'small, slow moving stream'). So we have a *Lake Field* in both Cowley and Littlemore, as well as *Lake Furlong* and *Lake Ditch Furlong* in neighbouring fields.[38] The level of water in these streams would have varied seasonally – as it did with *Winterbrook* 'stream dry except in winter' (Old English *winter* + *brōc*), probably one of the intermittent streams near Bartlemas.[39]

Some watercourses were seen as having religious significance or healing powers: a stream running through Iffley meadow was called *Halibroc*, the 'holy brook'.[40] Strowell was later associated with the leper hospital at Bartlemas and in the 16th century a service was held at the spring each year on Ascension Day.

Yet more terms for watercourses are recorded in *Pill Furlong* (*pyll*, Old English, 'small stream'), *Sichefurlong* (*sīc*, Old English, 'very small stream') and *Eaffurlong*

(grandiosely using the Old English word *ēa*, 'river', for a field near the Boundary Brook).[41] Alongside these streams grew willows, giving rise to names like *Selleby* (possibly from Old English *sealh* 'willow' + *byge* 'ring) and *Worgs Path* (dialect *wergs* 'willows').[42]

Marshes, meadows and islands

All these springs and streams created a marshy landscape. *Mersc* is the Old English word that gives us modern 'marsh' and was used in East Oxford for *The Marsh* that dominated central Cowley, as well as for Iffley's *Litlemersh* 'little marsh' and *Michelmersh* 'great marsh'.[43] The word mōr tended to be used for marshy land running alongside the rivers, such as *Littlemore*, the 'small marsh' running along the Thames and the Littlemore Brook.[44] This was perhaps contrasted with *Deepe Moore*, next to the Northfield Brook further east.[45] Some of the *mōr* names evoke the sights and sounds of this landscape: near the Cherwell was *Frogmore* 'marsh populated by frogs', and *Redmoor*, probably 'reedy marsh', was next to the Northfield Brook.[46] These marshes would have been used as seasonal pasture.

Even more valued were meadows, riverside land where hay could be grown for winter fodder. The general Old English word for 'meadow' was *mæd*, and a couple of the meadows have particularly descriptive names. *Lagmead* includes the dialect word 'lag', 'a long, narrow, marshy meadow, usually by the side of a stream' – the meadow indeed ran along a little stream

Fig. 6.4. Marshy land in Littlemore. Langdon map, Cowley, Corpus Christi College MS 533, 19.

in Littlemore.[47] Next to the Littlemore Brook was *Wig Mead*, 'meadow infested with beetles'.[48] The only reference to the hay crop itself in our area is *Heyford Hill*, named after a nearby ford across the Thames, presumably used at the hay harvest.[49]

Riverside meadows were often described using the Old English term *hamm* 'river-meadow', such as for Cowley, *Sidenham* 'wide river-meadow' and *Milham* by the mill.[50] *Ladenham* in Littlemore covered much of what is now the circular centre of Blackbird Leys. *Hamm* here may have had an alternative meaning: 'land on a promontory hemmed in by water or marsh', referring to the streams to the west and south. The first part of the name might be an old name for one of the streams or a personal name.[51]

Many of the meadows were on islands or semi-islands in the Thames, called by the Old English term *ēg*. These include in Littlemore, *Nye Mead* '(land) at the river-island', and in Iffley, *Great and Little Kidney* 'river-islands frequented by kites'.[52] Little Kidney in fact forms the northern extremity of the large island called *Berige*

in about AD 950, and later *Berry Mead*. The island's earlier name means 'barley island', suggesting in this case that the land was earlier used for growing barley and only later for meadow.[53] The island was the subject of a tenth-century dispute between Abingdon Abbey and Oxfordshire, reputedly resolved by floating a shield bearing a taper (representing Abingdon) and a wheatsheaf (representing Oxfordshire) upriver of Berry Mead; it duly followed the eastern stream, confirming that the island belonged to Abingdon and Berkshire.[54] An alternative name for Little Kidney, *Almondbury*, recorded in the eighteenth century, suggests that this part of Berry Mead belonged to an Anglo-Saxon man called Ealhmund (perhaps an Oxfordshire man who managed to acquire the land from Abingdon Abbey).[55]

Arable farming

It is likely that arable farming expanded in our area to some extent over the Anglo-Saxon period. By the

Fig. 6.5. Harvest (from the twelfth-century calendar owned by Littlemore Priory). © Bodleian Libraries, Oxford.

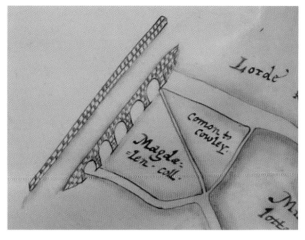

Fig. 6.6. Magdalen Bridge. Langdon map, Cowley, Corpus Christi College MS 533, 19.

Cowley charter bounds as *Hacklingcroft*, 'enclosure where flax was combed or heckled'.[60]

Routeways, bridges and fords

Probably the most important local routeway was the Roman road that connected Dorchester-on-Thames in the south to Alchester in the north and formed the multiple parish boundary to the east. The oldest bridge in our area was the forerunner of *Magdalen Bridge*, over the Cherwell: a *Cerewillanbrycg* 'Cherwell bridge' is recorded in the 1004 Cowley charter bounds.[61] There appears to have been a bridgehead settlement there at the same time, known as *Bridgsett* 'bridge settlement' (Old English *brycg* + *(ge)set*). This later became known as *St Clement's* but the earlier name expresses better the Oxford-focused, suburban character of this place.[62]

The earliest recorded ford name in our area is Sandford, described in a 1050 charter.[63] A more basic crossing was provided by the log bridge referred to in the Iffley field-name *Runforlonge* (from Old English *hruna* 'tree trunk, often used for a log bridge').[64]

Boundaries and meeting places

Anglo-Saxon estates, shires and hundreds used existing features to mark boundaries where they could, such as the Roman road or local rivers. Other boundary markers could be used, both for these areas and for smaller areas like fields or groves.

Hedges were used to create boundaries and in the 1004 Cowley charter we seem to have a reference to a hedge called 'boundary hedge', **Mær-hecg*, possibly marking what later became the Cowley/Headington parish boundary.[65] *Harehedge* in Temple Cowley probably comes from the Old English *hār*, a word used for things with a greenish grey colour and a textured surface (like lichen).[66] The hedge (still partly visible on the 1605 Corpus map) may have marked an earlier

time of the 1004 charter, there were enough arable fields in the area for them to appear in the bounds. There were fields described as furlongs: *ofranfurlang* 'upper furlong', and (to) *hwet furlanges heafda* '(as far as) the headland of the wheat furlong'. The mention of furlongs implies some form of open field farming. There is also a reference to acres, meaning 'cultivated pieces of land' rather than an exact land measurement: *(to) den acre* '(as far as) the valley acres'.[56]

Craft and industry

An increase in arable farming went with the development of mills and there were two in East Oxford in 1086. One was *Temple Mill* (though the name is medieval, see below).[57] The other was *Boy Mill* (1106-7) 'mill of a man named Boia'. An alternative meaning might be 'the rogue's mill', reflecting the common low regard in which millers were held.[58] As well as cereal crops there were also fields growing flax – two separate fields called *Lillands* in Cowley and Littlemore (from Old English *līn* 'flax' + lands).[59] To produce workable fibres, flax needs to be left in water ('retting'), which would commonly be done in dammed streams or ponds. Processing of the flax took place in a field by the Cherwell in St Clement's, – mentioned in the 1004

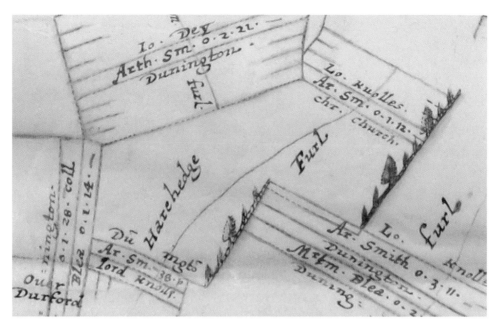

Fig. 6.7. Harehedge. Langdon map, Cowley, Corpus Christi College MS 533, 19.

boundary of Shotover Forest. This otherwise rare hedge-name also occurs in two other places around Shotover Forest: on the Horspath/Garsington border and near the Beckley/Stowood border.[67] Later the Cowley Harehedge may have divided the open fields Wood Field and Far Field from each other.

Bears Hedge, running east-west across Rose Hill, probably contains the Middle English *berse*, a word that means 'fence made of osiers or stakes, associated with woodland management'.[68] It is possible that this is a later name for an earlier hedge; the hedge may have marked an earlier edge of Iffley's Grove, or protected arable fields from livestock in an area of wood-pasture.

Boundaries and meeting places could be indicated by point-markers such as trees, standing stones or posts (and later crosses), hills or barrows. *Hār* stones are particularly common across the country as boundary markers and we have a *hore stone* marking part of the Cowley–Iffley border.[69] There was a Cowley field called **agayn þe stone* (c. 1220) 'opposite the stone', possibly an earlier standing stone and perhaps the same field as *Ston furlong* (1605).[70] The post in *Staple Furlong* (Old English *stapol*, post or pillar) may have marked a hundred meeting place for Bullingdon Hundred.[71] The field was enclosed by Bullingdon Green, Bullington Furlong and Bullington Slade, and was close to a point where the parishes of Headington, Cowley and Horspath converge.

Place-names and Medieval land use

Changes and intensifications in land use, resulting both from the estate management practices of the local religious houses and from population growth, are clearly shown in the field-names of East Oxford

(for the locations of names in the following section, see Fig 6.8).

A significant change appears to be from wood-pasture to arable – suggested by several medieval names from the northern and eastern parts of Cowley, including the open field name *Wood Field*, *Newland* (unlocated, but in Wood Field)[72] , as well as fields called *Broken Furlong* 'broken-in furlong' in the east of both Cowley and Littlemore.[73] A field next to the Garsington Road was called *Broad Arse* (derived from the Old English *ersc* 'newly broken-in land').[74] Clearance evidently occurred in Iffley also, where we have names such as *Rodehende* ('field at the end of a clearing') and *The Breach* (Middle English *breche* 'broken-in land').[75]

However, other names incorporating *breche* evidently refer to conversion of marshland that had once been part of Cowley Marsh; these include *Langebrich* (1207), *Middebrech* (c. 1210) and *Schorte-broch'* (c. 1240) ('long', 'middle' and 'short breach or piece of newly broken-in land') and *Alesbreach*, probably originally 'Neil's breach', referring to the local landowning *FitzNiel* family.[76]

Field systems – open fields and common land

Medieval references to field-names in East Oxford are usually to the furlong name and the parish or manor, and rarely to open field names. It looks as if open fields were originally less relevant, at least as a way of classifying or locating furlongs. The field systems of East Oxford were affected by complicated parish arrangements and the presence of multiple manors and estates.

The township of Littlemore (split between the parishes of Iffley and St Mary the Virgin, Oxford), had, by the 17th century, the following open fields: *West Field*, *Graffe Furlong*, *Broad Field*, *Lake Field*, *Little Field*, and *Ladenham Field*.[77] There were meadows around the Littlemore Brook and the Thames, and common land in the far south east of the township.

The township of Iffley (at least at the time of the Enclosure Award) had a *Lower Field* and an *Upper Field*; there was also a small field, *Hawkwell*, and there were meadows, especially *Iffley Meadow*.[78]

Cowley contained three settlements: *Church Cowley*, *Temple Cowley* and *Hockmore Street*[79] (which was part of Iffley manor). Cowley fields contained sections and strips that belonged to the parishes of Iffley and St Clements. The open fields had a variety of alternative names and ways of grouping furlongs. The earlier names for the open fields include *Houvere Mulne* ('over the mills', *Campus Field*, 'compost' in the late 16th century), *Bartholomews Field* (1605), *West Field* (early 16th century), *Wood Field* (c. 1240), *East Field* (1605,

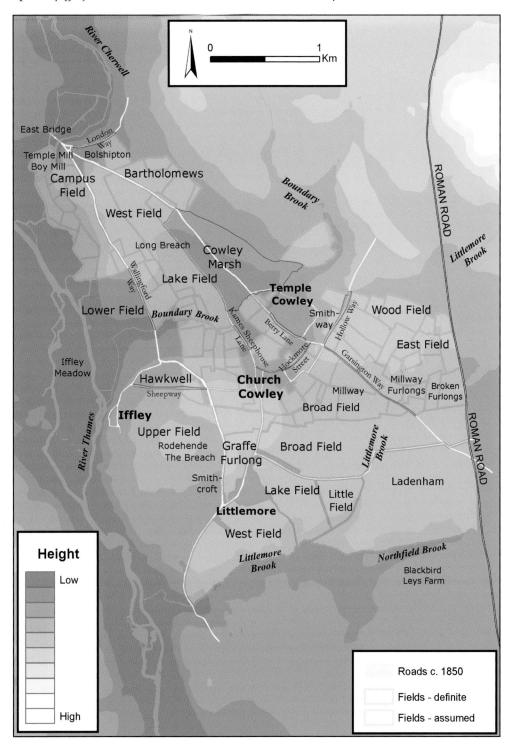

Fig. 6.8. Locations of place-names and field-names: Map 2.

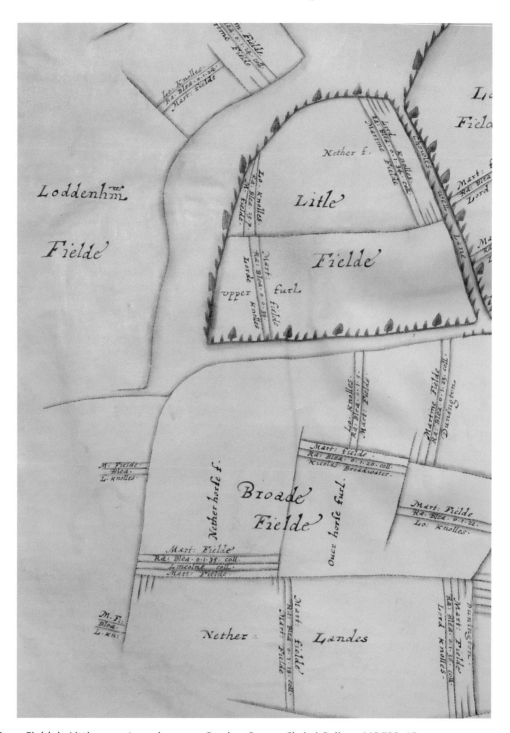

Fig. 6.9. Open Fields in Littlemore. Langdon map, Cowley, Corpus Christi College MS 533, 19.

later recorded as *Far Field*), *Lake Field* (1605), and *South Field* (1512, *Broad Field* from 1605).[80]

Cowley had meadows along the Cherwell and a large amount of common pasture, partly in Cowley Marsh, but also on Bullingdon Green, and in land close to Shotover Forest (including extra-parochial land shared with other parishes).

Soil and weeds

Many fields have names that describe their position or shape (see the open field names above) but there are also names that more closely reflect the concerns of those who worked the land. Soil type is indicated in Cowley names like *The Grates* 'gravel' and *Chisliforlong* (the Old English word cisel is used in place-names for soil containing lots of smallish pebbles or flints).[81] There are also Iffley names like *Rychifurlong* (1338) 'rich or productive furlong' and *Witelong* (c. 1250) 'long strip of land with a white surface'.[82] Littlemore in particular has a number of names referring to plants that would be unwelcome in an arable field: *Ferny Furlong*, *Scrubb Furlong* ('brushwood') and *Fursson Furlong* ('gorse').[83]

Fig. 6.10. Shearing sheep (from the twelfth-century calendar owned by Littlemore Priory) © Bodleian Libraries, Oxford.

Livestock

Sheep, cattle and horses were all still important in the local agricultural economy and leys from Old English *lǣs* 'pasture, meadow' was a common element in names of fields for livestock, for example in Iffley's *Horse Leys* (1613).[84] Some later arable field-names show previous use as pasture, for example, Littlemore's *Nether* and *Over Horse* furlongs (1605).[85]

There are names referring to the housing of livestock. A prominent name at St Clements was *Bolshipton* (1358),[86] the 'shippon or cattle-shed' of the Bolles family (Fig. 6.11) a convenient location to keep cattle handy to supply to Oxford (and a name that gave rise to the neighbouring field *Shitten Corner*).[87] Today's Rymers Lane in Cowley was earlier *Kames Sheephouse Lane* (1605), with the sheephouse perhaps among farm buildings to the south of Church Cowley owned by Oseney Abbey, and near the pasture on Cowley Marsh.[88] *Sheepway* in Iffley records an older name for Tree Lane, and a droveway for sheep that may have linked Iffley to the pastures below Shotover.[89]

Industry and craft

Several watermills are recorded, *Boy Mill* (see above) and *Temple Mill* 'mill owned by the Knights Templar'[90], on the Cherwell, and Iffley Mill, on the Thames.[91] There was a pathway called *Millway*, going east from Church Cowley, possibly to the windmill in Garsington.[92] There also seems to have been a mill in Wood Field in the early sixteenth century, bearing the Norman name *Henere mille* 'Henry's mill' – presumably another windmill.[93] Another industrial activity that seems to have taken place in Wood Field is the bleaching of cloth, in *Bleach Furlong*.[94]

Smithing is referenced directly in *Smith way furlong* next to Temple Cowley, and indirectly in *Smithcroft* 'Smith's enclosure' – the latter was next to Littlemore's medieval *Smithsplace*, home of the local *Smith* family who, though originally smiths, became yeoman farmers.[95]

Manor and estate centres

Names deriving from Old English *burh* often refer to the centre of an estate, a hall or manor house originally surrounded by some form of fortification (which could be earthworks or fencing). Sometimes these names refer to the estate or manor more generally, which may originally have also been surrounded by a fence or ditch. *Westbury* was a name used to refer to a substantial part of Church Cowley and probably meant 'the west *burh* or estate', as opposed to the east *burh*, the estate that became Temple Cowley when it was given to the Templars.[96] *Berrie Wall* and *Berry Lane* marked a boundary of the *burh* of Temple Cowley, along the Cowley Road.[97]

Hallcroft may have been a field attached to the hall of the little manor of Hockmore Street.[98] *Court Close* was a field at the western end of Temple Cowley, named for its association with the *courte*, the Norman French word for a manorial house.[99]

Routeways, fords and bridges

The roads of the area have early names that alternate between local connections and references to destinations further afield. Routes to London are reflected in road names around St Clements: *Londonysschestrete* (1325), and *London Way*.[100] Today's Iffley Road is evidenced in the form of *Wallingford Way*.[101]

The routeway linking St Clements with Bartlemas and Cowley, and eventually Horspath and London, necessitated the building of a causeway across Cowley Marsh for the first segment – today's *Cowley Road*. It seems the main causeway section was referred to as 'the Causeway' (cauce in 1340).[102] However, the segment near Bartlemas was evidently also commonly referred to as *St Bartholomew's Way* (in the sixteenth and seventeenth centuries).[103] As mentioned above, the part of the road by Temple Cowley was known as *Berry Lane*. In 1385 this part of the road was *le Pygelesweyze*, the way by the 'pightles' – a collection of small enclosed fields or crofts that might have looked a little like modern allotments.[104] Beyond Temple Cowley the routeway changes its name to *Garsington Road*, earlier *Garsington Way* and earlier still *Gærshāmstrǣt*, all referring to the destination, Garsington.[105]

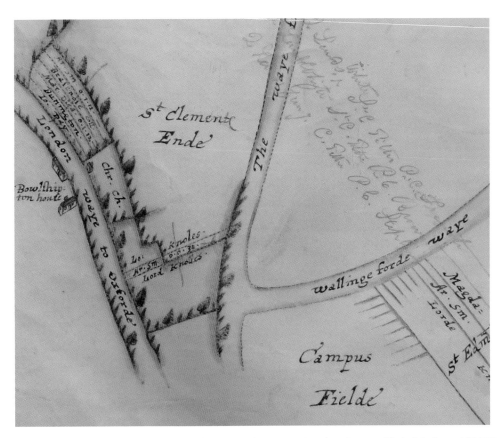

Fig. 6.11. Routes leading east from Magdalen Bridge. Langdon map, Cowley, Corpus Christi College MS 533, 19.

Within Cowley routeways included *Mud Lane* (possibly a spur of the Roman road), *The Holloway* (perhaps also known as *Wodewey* 'wood way', referring to the woods on Shotover), and *Millway*, a pathway from Church Cowley also known as *Thameway*, presumably ultimately leading to the River Thame, 6.5 km to the east.[106]

Earlier in the Middle Ages Magdalen Bridge was usually known by the French term *Petipont* 'small bridge', in contrast to *Grandpont* 'great bridge', the bridge that bore the main road into Oxford city from the south.[107] In the thirteenth century it seems the bridge was more often called East Bridge (again in contrast to *South Bridge*, an alternative name for Grandpont), perhaps to some extent a sign of the resurgence of English.[108] Nearby was *Milham Ford*, a crossing on the Cherwell, via the island there called *Milham*, just downstream of the Magdalen Bridge crossing.[109] This was for long an alternative crossing point, at times involving another bridge.

Finally, we come to a crossing point on the Northfield Brook which has generated the name of the largest council estate in Oxford: *Blackbird Leys*. Originally there was a ford where the Roman road crossed the Brook, called *Blackford* for the colour of the soil there. Once a bridge was built, the name of the nearby farm and meadows (the *leys*) varied between *Blackford Leys* and *Blackbridge Leys*. By 1840 the farm was known as Blackbird Leys.[110]

Conclusion

The place-names and field-names of East Oxford allow us to build up a detailed picture of the area in the Anglo-Saxon period: people and their flocks and herds in a landscape of wooded hills, river meadows and marshy pasture. We can trace ancient boundaries and traditional meeting places; we even have names of landholders and founding fathers of local estates.

The field-names add to the other evidence for the development of East Oxford in the medieval period, showing how the marshes and woods were cleared to create more fields. Altogether the names enable us to strip away the modern buildings and see the lost fields through the eyes of the earlier inhabitants of East Oxford.

Notes

1   Thanks to the members of the *Archeox* Place Names Group for their research and discussions about East Oxford and the area's names: Christopher Lewis, Nina Curtis, Anita Martin, Maggie Willis, Jan Greenough, Anne Grimm, Joan Coleman, Jane Darke, Margaret Moss, David Manners. Acknowledgements are due to Jane Harrison, Leigh Mellor, Graham Jones, James Bond and Judy Webb; to staff of the college archives and the Oxfordshire History Centre; to Kelly Kilpatrick, leading place-name scholars Ann Cole and Jayne Carroll, as well as other members of the Society for Name Studies in

Britain and Ireland. Our research was underpinned by the work of Margaret Gelling in her *Place-names of Oxfordshire* [Gelling 1953] and we made much use of the Victoria County History volume for Bullingdon Hundred [VCH Oxon 5, 1957].

2 Cowley, *Couelea* 1004, [Cowley Charter L909.3.00, LangScape]. 'Cufa's wood-pasture' from Old English male personal name *Cufa* + *lēah*.

3 Iffley, *Gifete lea* 1004, [Cowley Charter L909.3.00, LangScape]. 'Wood pasture' from Old English *lēah*.

4 *Leye Hill* 1605, [Langdon map, Headington, Corpus Christi College MS 533, 17]. 'Wood pasture' from Old English *lēage* dative singular, + *hyll*.

5 Bear Wood, *Bare Wood* 1706, [Manor of Iffley court rolls, Oxfordshire History Centre DH I/4]. Probably 'swine-pasture' from Old English *bǣr*.

6 *Burbushe furl.*1605, [Langdon map, Cowley, Corpus Christi College MS 533, 18]. 'A copse of bushes with a cottage' from Old English *būr* 'cottage' + *bysc* 'bush'.

7 *Grove Close* 1830 [Iffley Enclosure Award, Oxfordshire History Centre OSD/A Vol. E, 212-259]; *gravam de Yiftele* c.1250 [Leys 1938, 62], assuming '*granam*' is a mistranscription of '*gravam*'. 'Grove' from Old English *grāf*.

8 *Bulendesgrave* c.1240 [Leys 1938, 54]. *Bullingdon* see below + 'grove' from Old English *grāf*.

9 *Derefolde* c.1210 [Leys 1938, 52]; *Dorfolde/Lytell dorefolde* c.1532 [Temple Cowley terrier, Corpus Christi College, A2 cap. 7 Ev. 51]; *Upper/Lower Darvall* 1777 [Chapman map of Cowley, Christ Church College].

10 Hockmore, *(into) hocce mǣre* 1004, [Cowley Charter L909.3.00, LangScape]. Possibly from Old English personal names *Hocca/*Hocc* + *(ge)mǣre* 'boundary'; alternatively, 'boundary marked by mallow, *Malva sylvestris*' from Old English *hocc* 'mallow'.

11 Hawkwell, *Hockeswell* 1278–9 [Record Commission 1812-18, Vol. 2, 713]. 'Spring, stream of a man named *Hocc* from Old English *Hocc* + *welle*.

12 *Hockawell Furlong* 1849 [Horspath Tithe Award, Oxfordshire History Centre, Acc 4922]. Possibly 'spring, stream of a man named Hocca' from Old English *Hoccan-welle*.

13 *Hockley-in-the-hole* 1666 [Merrett, quoted in Druce 1886, 177]; *Hockley* [Plot 1677, 146]. Possibly 'Hocca's/*Hocc's wood-pasture' from Old English *Hocc/Hocca* + *lēah*.

14 *Pipley Furl.*1605 [Langdon map, Cowley, Corpus Christi College MS 533, 18]; *Puppelowe, Pippelewe* c.1240–50 [Leys 1938, 64-65]. '*Pyppa's burial mound' from Old English *Pyppa* + *hlǣw*.

15 *(on) pippan lege* 983 [Kelly 2000, 462], '(at) *Pyppa's wood-pasture' from Old English *Pyppa* + *lēah*.

16 *Winingham* 1605 [Langdon map, Littlemore, Corpus Christi College MS 533, 21]; *Winingale* 1674 [Littlemore terrier, Lincoln College, Z/IFL/5], from Old English *Wine* + *hamm* 'river-meadow' or + *halh* 'a nook of land' or sometimes 'river-meadow';

Winsimor 1220 [Leys 1938, 41], 'Wine's marsh' from Old English *Wine* + *mōr*.

17 *Prestemore* 1605 [Langdon map, Cowley, Corpus Christi College MS 533, 19]; *prestmare* c1532 [Temple Cowley terrier, Corpus Christi College, A2 cap. 7 Ev. 51]. 'Priest's marsh' from Old English *prēost* + *mōr*.

18 *Braydon Close* 1613 [Terrier, Magdalen College, EP/148/40]; *Bradon Hedge* 1723 [Manor of Iffley court rolls, Oxfordshire History Centre DH I/3]. Possibly from British **bre* 'hill' + Old English *dūn* 'low, fairly level hill, suitable for settlement'.

19 *Hertesheuid* 1201 [Leys 1938, 51], from a Middle English surname *Hert* [Leys 1938, 54] or Old English *heorot* 'stag' + *hēafod* 'head; hill, projecting piece of land'.

20 *Longe Hill* 1605 [Langdon map, Cowley, Corpus Christi College MS 533, 19].

21 *Ridge Field* 1777 [Chapman map of Cowley, Christ Church College].

22 *Rose Hill* 1806 ['Advertisements & Notices' *Jackson's Oxford Journal*, 19 July 1806, Issue 2777, 3]

23 *Barrow hill* 1706 [Manor of Iffley court rolls, Oxfordshire History Centre DH I/3], from Old English *beorg* 'barrow; rounded hill', or *bearu* 'small wood'.

24 *Upper Ferne hill* 1605 [Langdon map, Cowley, Corpus Christi College MS 533, 18].

25 *Swalewnenhulle* 1337 [Salter 1930 *Boarstall Cartulary*, 172], from Old English *swalwe* + *hyll* 'swallow hill'; alternatively, the first element may refer to a swallow-hole or sink-hole.

26 *Bulesden'* 1179-91 [Gelling 1953, 159], from Old English *bula* + *denu*, 'bull's valley'.

27 Bullingdon Green, *Bulandenesgrene* 13th c. [VCH Oxon 5, 79].

28 *The Slade* 1802 [Headington Enclosure Award, Oxfordshire History Centre, PAR126/16/H/2], from Old English *slæd* 'valley, usually a small side valley'.

29 *Shorte Sheldon* 1605 [Langdon map, Cowley, Corpus Christi College MS 533, 18], possibly related to *scheldrey* c.1532 [Temple Cowley terrier, Corpus Christi College, A2 cap. 7 Ev. 51]; *Nether and Upper Shilden* 1605 [Langdon map, Littlemore, Corpus Christi College MS 533, 20]. Probably from Old English *scylf, scelf* 'level ground'; the second element is uncertain.

30 Ptolemy, *Geographia*, section 3; Coates 2000, 266-267; Finn 2012.

31 Cowley Charter L909.3.00, LangScape.

32 *Marsh Brook* 1893 [Great Britain. Royal Commission on Metropolitan Water Supply, 91]; *Moor Ditch* 1887 [Ordnance Survey, Oxfordshire XXXIII]; *into þam broce* 1004 [Cowley Charter L909.3.00, LangScape], 'to the brook'.

33 *Sandfordes lǣce* 1050 [Kelly 2000, 560], 'Sandford + Old English *lacu* 'tributary'.

34 *Lidginge well* 1605 [Langdon map, Littlemore,

Corpus Christi College MS 533, 20], possibly 'ambling stream' from Old English *līdiande* + *welle*.

35 *Crawell'* 1154-66 [Leys 1938, 53], from Old English *crāwe* + *welle*, 'crow spring/stream'.

36 *Strowell* 1661-6 [Wood 1889-99, 514], probably from Old English *strōd* 'brushwood' + *welle* 'spring/stream'.

37 *Catwell'* c. 1240 [Leys 1938, 55], from Old English *catt* 'cat' or personal name *Catta*, + *welle* 'spring/stream'.

38 *Lake Fielde* 1605 [Langdon map, Cowley, Corpus Christi College MS 533, 19]; *Lake Fielde, Lake furl* 1605 [Langdon map, Littlemore, Corpus Christi College MS 533, 20]; *Lakes ditch Furlong* 1674 [Littlemore terrier, Lincoln College, Z/IFL/5]. From Old English *lacu* 'small, slow-moving stream'.

39 *Wynterbrok* 1225 [Wigram 1885-96, Vol. 2, 31] from Old English *winter* + *brōc* 'brook, stream'.

40 *Halibroc* 1350-1360 [VCH Oxon 5, 190].

41 *Pill furlong* 1605 [Langdon map, Cowley, Corpus Christi College MS 533, 18], from Old English *pyll*, 'small stream'; *Sichefurlange* c. 1207 [Salter 1930 *Feet of fines*, 37], from Old English *sīc* 'very small stream'; *Eaffurlag* c. 1230-40 [Iffley deed 2, Magdalen College], from Old English *ēa*, 'river'.

42 *Selleby* 1278–9 [Record Commission 1812-18, Vol. 2, 712], possibly from Old English *sealh* 'willow' + *byge* 'ring'; *Worgs Path* 1847 [Hockmore Street Tithe award, Oxfordshire History Centre, 227/A], possibly from dialect *wergs* 'willows'.

43 Cowley Marsh, *Merse* 1207 [Salter 1930 *Feet of fines*, 37], from Old English *mersc*, 'marsh'; *Litlemersh* and *Michelmersh* 14th c. [VCH Oxon 5, 190].

44 Littlemore, *Luthlemoria* c. 1130 [Gelling 1953, 180], from Old English *lītla* 'little' + *mōr* 'marsh'.

45 *Deepe Moore* 1605 [Langdon map, Littlemore, Corpus Christi College MS 533, 21].

46 *ffrogmore* c.1460 [Clark 1907, 21], from Old English *frogga* 'frog' + *mōr* 'marsh'; *Redmoore* 1605 [Langdon map, Littlemore, Corpus Christi College MS 533, 21], from Old English *hrēod* 'reed' + *mōr* 'marsh'.

47 *Lagmead* 1819 [Littlemore Enclosure Award, Oxfordshire History Centre, QSD/A Vol. D], from dialect *lag* 'a long, narrow, marshy meadow, usually by the side of a stream'.

48 *Wig mead* 1674 [Littlemore terrier, Lincoln College, Z/IFL/5], from Old English *wicga* 'beetle or similar insect' + *mǣd* 'meadow'.

49 Heyford Hill *Eyford Ait* 1634-1733 [Kennington deeds, Berkshire Record Office, D/EX 75/T/15] from Old English *hēg* 'hay' + *ford*.

50 *Sidenham* c. 1460 [Clark 1907, 21], probably from Old English *(æt þǣm) sīdan hamme* '(at the) broad river-meadow'; Milham, *Milhamforde* 1512, [Rental of Templars' lands, Corpus Christi College, MS 320], from Old English *myln* 'mill' + *hamm* 'river-meadow'.

51 *Loddenham Fielde* 1605 [Langdon map, Littlemore, Corpus Christi College MS 533, 21]; *Ladnum* 1674 [Littlemore terrier, Lincoln College, Z/IFL/5];

second element from Old English *hamm* 'land on a promontory hemmed in by water or marsh'.

52 *Nighe meade* 1605 [Langdon map, Littlemore, Corpus Christi College MS 533, 20], from Middle English *atten eye* 'at the island'; the Kidneys, *cytan igge* 956 [Kelly 2000, 251], Old English 'kite island'.

53 Berry Mead, *Berige* 955 [Kelly 2000, 251], from Old English *bere* 'barley' + *ēg* 'island'.

54 Stevenson 1858, 89.

55 *Almondbury* 1744-1787 [Leases, Berkshire Record Office, D/EPT/T36/25/1-13]; possibly from *Ealhmund* + *bere* + *ēg*, 'Ealhmund's barley island'.

56 Cowley Charter L909.3.00, LangScape.

57 *Templemullham* 1302-3 [Salter 1914-17, Vol 1, 5], 'meadow by Temple Mill'.

58 *Boiemylna* 1106-7 [Stevenson 1858, 106], from Old English man's name *Boia*, (or possibly from Middle English boy 'young man, servant; bordar; knave, rogue, wretch') + *myln* 'mill'.

59 *Lillands furlong* 1777 [Chapman map of Cowley, Christ Church College]; *Lillians* 1725 [Terrier of Alice Smith's Charity's lands, Oxfordshire History Centre, MS DD Par Iffley 654]; in from Old English *līn* 'flax' + *lands*.

60 Hacklingcroft, *hacel-inges crofte* 1004 [Cowley Charter L909.3.00, LangScape], 'enclosure where flax was combed or heckled'.

61 Cowley Charter L909.3.00, LangScape.

62 *Ecclesia sancti Clementis de Bruggeshete* 1261 [Jobson 2006, 454], 'church of St Clement's of Bridgsett' from Old English *brycg* 'bridge' + *(ge)set* 'settlement'.

63 *(æt) Sandforda* 1050 [Kelly 2000, 560], from Old English *sand* + *ford* 'sandy ford'.

64 *Runforlonge* late 13th c. [Iffley deed, Lincoln College, D/IFF/1], from Old English *hruna*, 'tree trunk, log used as a footbridge'.

65 **Mær-hecg*, possible reading of *mer higte* 1004 [Cowley Charter L909.3.00, LangScape], from *(ge)mǣre* + *hecg*, 'boundary hedge'.

66 *Hare hedge* c. 1532 [Temple Cowley terrier, Corpus Christi College, A2 cap. 7 Ev. 51], possibly from Old English *hār*, 'greenish grey'.

67 Horspath Tithe Award, 1849, Oxfordshire History Centre, Acc 4922; Beckley Enclosure Award, 1831, Oxfordshire History Centre, QS/D/A/book 7, page 13.

68 Bears Hedge, *berys hedge* c. 1532 [Temple Cowley terrier, Corpus Christi College, A2 cap. 7 Ev. 51], probably from Middle English *berse*, 'fence made of osiers or stakes, associated with woodland management'.

69 *hore stone* 1614 [Terrier, Magdalen College, EP/148/40], from Old English *hār*, 'greenish grey'.

70 *ogayn þe stone* c. 1220 [Leys 1938, 46], 'opposite the stone'; *Ston furlong* 1605 [Langdon map, Cowley, Corpus Christi College MS 533, 18].

71 *Staple Furlong* 1777 [Chapman map of Cowley, Christ Church College], from Old English *stapol*, 'post or pillar'.

72　Wood Field, *Wodefeld'* c. 1240 [Leys 1938, 46]; *new lande* c. 1532 [Temple Cowley terrier, Corpus Christi College, A2 cap. 7 Ev. 51].

73　*Longe broken furl* 1605 [Langdon map, Cowley, Corpus Christi College MS 533, 18]; *Short Broken Furlong* 1777 [Chapman map of Cowley, Christ Church College]; *Long Broken Furlong, Short Broken Furlong* 17th c. [Littlemore terrier, Lincoln College Z/IFL/6].

74　*Broad Arse acre* 1783 [Chapman collection lease, Oxfordshire History Centre, Chap/IV/i/1], from Old English *ersc, ærsc* 'ploughed field, especially newly broken-in land'.

75　*Rodehende* late 13th c. [Iffley deed, Lincoln College,D/IFF/1], from Old English *rod*, 'a clearing' + *ende* 'end'; *the breach* 1706 [Manor of Iffley court rolls, Oxfordshire History Centre DH I/4], from Middle English *breche* 'broken-in land'

76　*Langebriche* 1207 [Salter 1930 *Feet of fines*, 37]; *Middebrech* 1210-19 [Leys 1938, 44]; *Schortebroch'* 1240-50 [Leys 1938, 65]; 'long', 'middle' and 'short breach or piece of newly broken-in land'; *Alesbreach* 1605 [Langdon map, Cowley, Corpus Christi College MS 533, 18], *Nelesbrech* c. 1220 [Leys 1938, 49], probably 'newly broken-in land associated with the (Fitz)Niel family'.

77　*Weste Fielde, Graffe Furlong, Broade Fielde, Lake Fielde, Litle Fielde, Loddenham Fielde* 1605 [Langdon map, Littlemore, Corpus Christi College MS 533, 20].

78　Lower Field 1745 [Manor of Iffley court rolls, Oxfordshire History Centre DH I/57]; *Upper Field* 1830 [Iffley Inclosure Award, Oxfordshire History Centre OSD/A Vol. E, 212-259]; Hawkwell, surname *Hockeswelle* 1279 [Record Commission 1812-18, Vol. 2, 713], field-name *hakewell* 1706 [Manor of Iffley court rolls, Oxfordshire History Centre DH I/4]; Iffley Meadow, e.g. *Eifeleye Meadow* 1605 [Langdon map, Cowley, Corpus Christi College MS 533, 19].

79　Church Cowley, *Chirchcouele* c. 1250 [Leys 1938, 62], the settlement around the church; *Temple Couele* 1200 [Leys 1938, 62], the manor owned by the Templars; *Hockemore Streete* 1605 [Langdon map, Cowley, Corpus Christi College MS 533, 18], settlement on the street leading to Hockmore.

80　*Houvere Mulne* Medieval period [Lobel 1957, 79], 'over the mills'; *Campus Fields* late 16th c. [Woolgar 1981, 94-8], 'compost'; *Bartholmewes Fielde* 1605 [Langdon map, Cowley, Corpus Christi College MS 533, 19]; West Field, *campo occident* early 16th c. [Terrier, Magdalen College, EP/148/8]; Wood Field, see above; *Easte Fielde* 1605 [Langdon map, Cowley, Corpus Christi College MS 533, 18], *Furr Field* 1777 [Chapman map of Cowley, Christ Church College], 'far field'; Lake Field see above; *South felde* 1512 [Rental of Templars' lands, Corpus Christi College, MS 320], *Broade Fielde* 1605 [Langdon map, Cowley,

Corpus Christi College MS 533, 18].

81　*the Grates* 1847 [Hockmore Street Tithe award, Oxfordshire History Centre, 227/A], from Old English *grēot* 'gravel' or dialect *grate* 'finely pulverised soil'; *Chisliforlong* early 16th c. [Terrier, Magdalen College, EP/148/8], from Old English *cisel* 'gravel'.

82　*Rychiforlong* 1338 [Gelling 1953, 33] from Old English *rīc* 'rich'; *le Witelong* c. 1250 [Leys 1938, 62] from Middle English *wite* 'white' + *lang* 'long strip of land'.

83　*Fearny Furlong* 17th c. [Littlemore terrier, Lincoln College, Z/IFL/6]; *Shrubs furlong*, 'brushwood'; *fursons furlong* 'gorse'; 1674 [Littlemore terrier, Lincoln College, Z/IFL/5].

84　*the horse lease* 1613 [Terrier, Magdalen College, EP/148/40], lease 'pasture, meadow'.

85　*Nether* and *Over Horse furlongs* 1605 [Langdon map, Littlemore, Corpus Christi College MS 533, 20].

86　Bolshipton House lay on the north side of St Clement's Street, approximately opposite the Black Horse Inn (see Fig. 6.11). It was destroyed in 1643 during the Civil War. Bolleslees was an enclosure lying between Bolshipton and the original church. It combines the *Bolles* family name with Old English *læs* 'pasture'.

87　*Bolles Shypeyn* 1358 [Wigram 1895, 472], the 'shippon or cattle-shed of the Bolles family'; *Shitten Corner* 1777 [Chapman map of Cowley, Christ Church College].

88　*Kames Sheephouse Lane* 1605 [Langdon map, Cowley, Corpus Christi College MS 533, 18].

89　*Lower Sheepway* 1706 [Manor of Iffley court rolls, Oxfordshire History Centre DH I/4].

90　*Templemullham* 1302-3 [Salter 1914-17, Vol 1, 5], 'meadow by the Templars' Mill'.

91　*Hyftele Mill* 1284–5 [Iffley deed, Lincoln College, D/IFF/].

92　*Mylle wey* c. 1532 [Temple Cowley terrier, Corpus Christi College, A2 cap. 7 Ev. 51].

93　*Henere mille* early 16th c. [Terrier, Magdalen College, EP/148/8], 'Henry's mill'.

94　*Blechesfeldforlong* 1347–8 [Cowley deed, Lincoln College, D/IFL/1], 'land on which cloth was bleached'; otherwise 'land with pale soil'.

95　Smith Way Furlong, *Smett wey* c. 1532 [Temple Cowley terrier, Corpus Christi College, A2 cap. 7 Ev. 51]; *smith croft* 1702 [Manor of Iffley court rolls, Oxfordshire History Centre DH I/3]; *Smithsplace* 1370 [VCH Oxon 5, 209].

96　*Westbury* 1512, [Rental of Templars' lands, Corpus Christi College, MS 320].

97　*Berrye Lane, Berrie wall* 1605 [Langdon map, Cowley, Corpus Christi College MS 533, 18], from Old English *byrig* 'at the estate/manor centre'.

98　*Hallecroft* c. 1250 [Leys 1938, 58]

99　*Courte Close* 1605 [Langdon map, Cowley, Corpus Christi College MS 533, 18], from Old

French/Middle English *courte* 'manorial house'.

100 *Londonysschestrete* 1325 [Salter 1929-36, Vol. 2, 192]; *london way* late 16th c. [Woolgar 1981, 94-8].

101 *wallingforde hie way* late 16th c. [Woolgar 1981, 94-8].

102 The Causeway, *cauce* 1340 [Sharpe 1889, 452-465].

103 *Bartlemews way* late 16th c. [Woolgar 1981, 94-8].

104 *le Pyghelesweyze* 1385 [Gelling 1953, 29]; the adjacent field was *Pytlesforlong* c1250 [Leys 1938, 57], later *Pye hille* 1605 [Langdon map, Cowley, Corpus Christi College MS 533, 18], from Middle English *pightel* 'small enclosure'.

105 Garsington Road; *garsone wey* c. 1532 [Temple Cowley terrier, Corpus Christi College, A2 cap. 7 Ev. 51]; *Gersham-Streete* 13th c. [Wood 1890, 507], perhaps showing an alternative name for Garsington, for example, from Old English *gærs* + *hām*, 'grassy village/homestead'.

106 *Mud Lane* 1886 [Druce 1886, 232]; Hollow Way, *Holweye* c. 1220 [Leys 1938, 46], from Old English *hol* + *weg* 'hollow way'; *Wodeweya(m)* 1142 [Leys 1938, 35], from Old English *wudu* + *weg* 'wood way'; *mylle wey* (see above); *Thame Way* 18th c. [VCH Oxon 5, 78].

107 Petipont, *Petitpund* [Gelling 1953, 35], 'small bridge'; Grandpont, *Grantpunt* 1180-4 [Gelling 1953, 21].

108 East Bridge *Astbrugestrete* 1256-60 [Wigram 1895-96, Vol. 1, 459]; South Bridge, *Suthbriggestrete* c. 1225 [Gelling 1953, 35].

109 *Milhamforde* 1512, [Rental of Templars' lands, Corpus Christi College, MS 320].

110 *Blackbird Leys Farm* 1840 [Advertisements & Notices, *Jackson's Oxford Journal* November 7, 1840; Issue 4567, 2]; *Blackbridge Lease* 1751 [Deed, Oxfordshire History Centre K/36/1e]; *Blackford Lays* 1797 [Davis 1797].

The boundaries of Cowley in AD 1004

Katie Hambrook

The early eleventh-century Cowley charter bounds are the earliest recorded description of East Oxford. Bounds (boundaries in modern parlance) are typical features of Anglo-Saxon charters, providing a written description of the boundary of the piece of land (or estate) being granted in the charter (this being long before the introduction of estate maps), but the Cowley bounds are a bit of a puzzle. They are described in in a charter of AD 1004, dated 7th December, which was drawn up as part of a renewal of privileges for St Frideswide's Priory, Oxford, by King Æthelred II 'The Unready' (who reigned from 978 to 1016).[1] It was written by order of the King at the royal estate at Headington, and confirmed the priory's ownership of four estates, at Winchendon (Bucks) and Whitehill, Cowley and Cutteslowe (Oxon) following the loss of the Priory's records (these had been burnt in its church along with the persecuted Danish population of Oxford in the St Brice's Day Massacre of 13 November 1002, see Chapter 1). The charter included bounds in Old English for each of the four estates. For the other three estates, the bounds can be identified and traced on a modern map. However, the Cowley bounds contain some confusing details which make it more difficult to follow the boundary described (see below).

There are differences between the AD 1004 charter and Domesday Book's description of the ownership of the area in AD 1086. The AD 1004 charter bounds suggest that St Frideswide's owned most of Cowley. Domesday describes land in St Clements (owned by St Frideswide's) and land in Cowley (with none owned by St Frideswide's). Perhaps the Priory had lost its Cowley

holdings in the redistribution of land following the Norman Conquest? The identifiable points in the AD1004 Cowley bounds seem to enclose St Clements and most of Cowley; the charter describes this landholding as three hides. However, in 1086, the holdings in St Clements and the whole of Cowley added up to over 15 hides. There is thus a discrepancy between the amount of land described in the Cowley bounds and its measurement of 3 hides.

However, we can still trace the bounds on the map in some places (Fig. 1) and we can see what they tell us about East Oxford in the time of Æthelred the Unready. (The sentences in quotation marks are modern versions of the boundary section of the charter):

> 'These are the boundaries of the three hides in Cowley.
> From Cherwell Bridge along the stream to the streamlet.'

The map shows the current Magdalen Bridge across the Cherwell; the original crossing may have been a little further south. The boundary goes along the Cherwell and turns inland near Hacklingcroft, a meadow which is the site of the present St Clement's Church. The boundary proceeds from Hacklingcroft to the Boundary Brook:

> 'Near Hacklingcroft straight along eastward until it comes to the upper furlong
> From there it runs up northward to the headland of the wheat furlong.
> From the headland to the streamlet, eastwards to the (?) boundary hedge.
> From the (?) hedge to the brook.'

The detail in the description of the boundary's route around the edge of the fields suggests that this part of the boundary may have been disputed or new. It is not

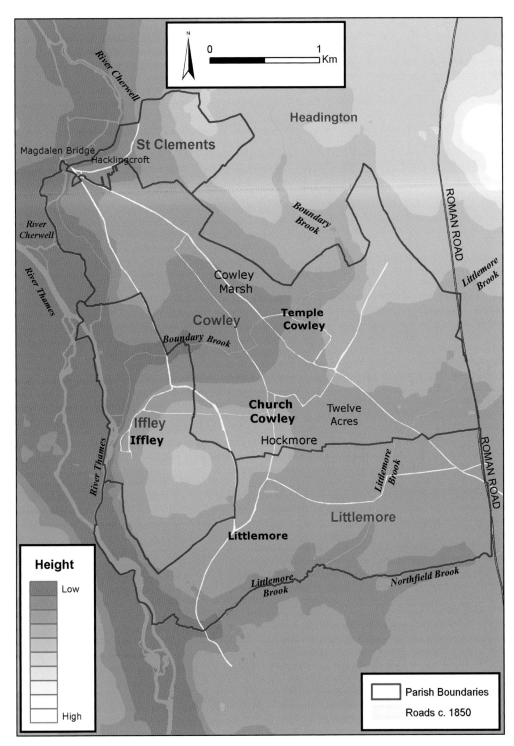

1. Places referred to in text.

clear how far east or north to take the projection of the boundary between Hacklingcroft and Boundary Brook, and the location of the streamlet is lost. 'Boundary hedge' is a suggestion making sense of a garbled part of the text. If correct, it might imply a return to a more established boundary – perhaps between Headington and Cowley (or between what was to become Temple and Church Cowley). The boundary then continues from the Boundary Brook to a valley containing small fields.

'From the brook to the cultivated acres in the valley; from the acres to Hockmore.'

There might possibly be a link with the field-name Twelve Acres, recorded in 1605, although this is not in a valley but in the saddle of land between Temple and Church Cowley. Hockmore is on the border between Cowley and Littlemore, perhaps specifically at the point on that border where Hockmore Cottages were situated in later times.

'From the boundary to Iffley.'

The bounds now become less descriptive and evidently relate to established boundaries, here taking the borders of Iffley, crossing the point where Boundary Brook flows into the Thames, and then back upstream to the Cherwell:

> 'From Iffley to the brook; from the brook back to the Cherwell.'

Thus the features selected to mark the bounds start with a reference to the road connections via the bridge to Oxford and elsewhere. Then they go on to suggest a landscape cut by little streams and rivers, watering areas of cultivated fields.

Notes

1   A translation in modern English of the 1004 charter may be found in Whitelock 1979, 590-93.

Domesday Book and the Normans in East Oxford

Jane Harrison, with David Griffiths

Domesday Book was completed in 1086, in the aftermath of the Norman Conquest, following an inquest (survey) of each county by William the Conqueror's officials. It was an extraordinary venture: the new king needed to discover who owned what, what it was worth, and therefore what he could command in taxes, rent, renders and dues. For historians it is a marvellous resource, a 'snapshot' of wealth and ownership in England between moments of major change. Domesday entries usually tell us who owned or held manors and land in the time of Edward the Confessor (TRE 'in the time of King Edward' or 1066), and then who owned or tenanted them in 1086 after the Conquest.[1] It tells us very little, however, about many of the things that archaeologists are interested in: exactly where and how people lived, their allegiances or beliefs, their daily life, or their possessions. Only owners, assets and productive workers (free or unfree) were recorded: of others in the community such as wives, children and the elderly or infirm, it says nothing.

Many lands and assets changed hands between Anglo-Saxon lords and Normans between 1066 and 1086, whereas in other cases we can see the pre-Conquest lords and tenants surviving. We can chart those manors held by the king, his tenants-in-chief and others who held land from them, as well as land held in demesne (for the owner's individual use), including arable land, fisheries, mills, meadows and woodland. The value of a manor was assessed on the number of ploughs or ploughlands (arable land) and on the manor's access to wood pasture, meadow, or greens, and on the value of any mills, fisheries or groves. Ten pounds indicated a relatively rich manor, up to five pounds a fairly modest estate, four shillings was a meagre holding. A well set-up villein might farm 15–30 acres (6–12 hectares); bordars (or cottagers), who would occupy a small cottage with a garden or yard, were fortunate to hold five acres (two hectares). Many places saw changes in value between

1066 and 1086, such as Roger d'Ivry's holdings at Cowley which were worth 60 shillings at the Conquest but only 40 shillings by 1086. Earl Aubrey's holding at Iffley had also decreased in value. The upheavals of the Conquest may explain these changes, although not all landholdings were affected, and some rose in value. Oxfordshire escaped their worst effects; in northern counties of England, 'waste' (land which was worthless by 1086) was much more widespread.

Headington

Headington, which also gave its name to the larger land-unit known as the Hundred, had been a royal manor since long before the Norman Conquest. The king continued to hold it with ten hides[2] in demesne, with six ploughlands (an area of arable land to be ploughed in a year by a team of eight plough-pulling oxen). The 20 villagers and 24 smallholders rented or owned a further 14 ploughlands. Two mills, five fisheries, meadow land and pasture are also mentioned and altogether the estate rendered £60 in dues, rents, and taxes. Shotover is recorded as one of the royal forests in the county, along with four others: its exact extent and boundaries at the time are not given.

Cowley

In 1086 the Norman magnate Roger d'Ivry held land in (Church) Cowley from Odo, Bishop of Bayeux, half-brother of King William. This land comprised only two hides and a third of a virgate (a quarter of a hide); providing two ploughlands, both in demesne, with meadow and pasture worth 40 shillings. There is no mention of an earlier owner so it is possible this may have been a manor newly created out of a previous 'multiple' estate (a large land-holding encompassing several farms). Count Eustace of Boulogne had three hides in (Temple) Cowley from the King, and Roger d'Ivry held them of him. This was a more substantial holding than the first and again no previous tenant is given. These hides yielded five ploughlands, five acres of meadow, a grove and a mill, which must have been down by the Thames, and were again worth 40s. Toli also held land in Cowley from Miles Crispin (a major Norman landowner closely associated with building Wallingford Castle, who also held properties within

1. Iffley Parish Church, from south-west.

the Borough (city) of Oxford, and land around Appleton Manor to the west of Oxford). These one and a half hides included one ploughland, meadowland and a grove three acres square valued together at 20s. Toli was probably the tenant in 1066. Leofwine (of Nuneham), a surviving landowner from before the Conquest, held land in Cowley from the king, which he had prior to 1066, of four and a half hides with ten ploughlands. So his was a more productive holding than those of Roger d'Ivry; not only was there a greater proportion of arable land but also two fisheries, one mill, meadow land and grove. Leofwine's land was valued at 100s. The two mills and two fisheries recorded for Cowley were all royal holdings so quite possibly were those granted fifty years later to the Templars in 1136 with the package of land from Queen Matilda.

Iffley

In Iffley, Earl Aubrey was granted royal land previously held in 1066 by Azor. This single record for Iffley details four hides with six ploughlands, only 20 peasants (villeins and cottars) but one fishery, meadow, pasture and a grove of two square acres, worth together £4. There is an interesting contrast between the single relatively valuable holding of Iffley and the four more modest holdings in Cowley, of which three may have been newly created estates. In Cowley, a larger pre-Conquest estate had probably been broken up in re-planning by the new Norman regime. This fragmentation was partially reversed with the royal grant of land to the Knights Templars, but the organisation of Cowley was still dominated by two manors: Church Cowley, and the Knights' manor of Temple Cowley. Breaking up the pattern of ownership in Cowley yet further, the hamlet of Hockmore Street was held from the mid-twelfth century by the parish of Iffley. Iffley's relative wealth in the post-Conquest period is reflected in its parish church, St Mary the Virgin, built by Robert de St Remy around 1170, which is famed as one of the finest late Norman or Romanesque churches in England.

Notes

1   Information from VCH Oxon, Phillimore Domesday Series, and Open Domesday https://opendomesday.org/

2   A hide was land of between about 40-120 acres, supposed to be sufficient to support one family and so inevitably varied in area according to the quality and potential of the land.

Improvement and enclosure in East Oxford

Graeme L. Salmon

Prior to the great changes brought about by the Oxford Improvement Act of 1771,[1] Magdalen Bridge, or East Bridge as it was known in the seventeenth century, was barely half its present width. The old East Gate in the city wall still stood over the High Street. East of the bridge stood old St Clement's Church on what is now the roundabout called The Plain. The small parish of St Clements was a mere cluster of houses near the church. Beyond the houses grazing land stretched east up the slopes of Headington Hill. The visible ridge and furrow strips in South Park and also in Headington Hill Park show the land's history as open fields (see page 98). To the south was Cowley Field, a large open ploughed field, meadow and marsh stretching for 4.5 km to beyond the villages of Church Cowley and Iffley.

Most of the pre-seventeenth century houses of St Clements had been demolished during the English Civil War including the manor house, Bolshipton House (see Fig. 6.11), which stood on St Clement's Street. A star fort and other defences had been thrown up near the bridge in 1642–3 as shown in De Gomme's map of the defences (see page 102).[2] After the war, Loggan's map of 1675 shows houses being built along St Clement's Street, but a square earthwork survives a short distance south of the church, which is identifiable as one of the bastions of the fort shown on de Gomme's plan. The same feature appears in a view of Oxford from the east of 1669 (Fig. 1) and was said to have been still visible in gardens next to Iffley Road in the 1930s.[3] The drawing was made by the artist Pier Maria Baldi (c. 1630–1686) who accompanied Cosimo de Medici (later Cosimo III) on his grand tours to the cities of Europe. From the position of the towers in the drawing, the fortification mound depicted would be on or next to Iffley Road (as sketched by Loggan and confirmed by the 1930 remnant); the artist's viewpoint would be where modern Marston Street joins Iffley Road.

The Mileways Act of 1576 had compelled inhabitants living within five miles of the city to contribute to the maintenance of roads out to one mile from the city boundary – the mileways. Then the Oxford Improvement Act of 1771 set up a Paving Commission to improve the mileways and bridges, to supervise the paving of streets, to keep the roads in good repair and to supervise cleansing, lighting, and general improvements. It provided for re-building Magdalen Bridge, turnpiking St Clements Street and raising income for those projects through toll-gates at Magdalen Bridge. Widespread demolition in the city was proposed to encourage traffic and trade: the East Gate and North Gate were removed together with nearby houses (the south and west gates had gone in the early-seventeenth century). Magdalen Bridge was declared dangerous and was to be widened. Buildings were cleared away on

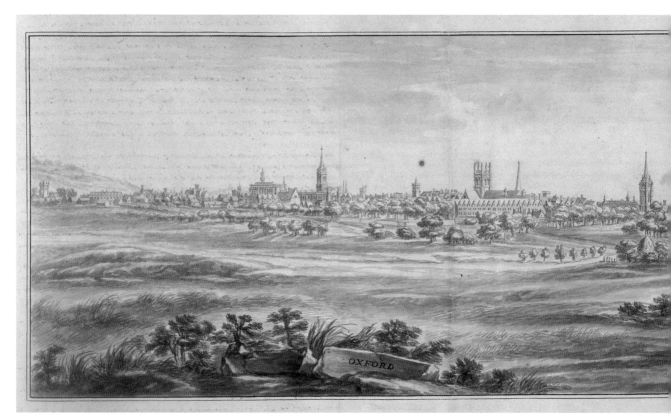

1. View of Oxford from the East, 1669 by Pier Maria Baldi, reproduced with permission © Laurentian Library, Florence.

the approach roads and by the bridge itself. During the rebuilding of Magdalen Bridge in 1771–9 temporary wooden bridges were built to cross Milham Meadow, 200m to the south, on the site of older stone bridges built or, more likely, rebuilt by Wolsey during the building of Christ Church (Cardinal College) to provide more direct access to his college from the Headington quarries. Wolsey's bridges were damaged in the Civil War and do not feature on maps of that period. The temporary bridge across the western branch of the Cherwell onto Milham Meadow is shown in a drawing by J.B. Malchair.[4] The temporary bridge across the eastern branch still stood in 1861 when it was photographed by Charles Dodgson (Lewis Carroll) (Fig. 2). By 1876 this bridge had gone but the central supporting pillar remained in the middle of the river.[5]

The old road to Henley and Iffley skirted around old St Clement's Church at the Plain to join Cowley Road,

2. Magdalen Bridge photographed by Charles Dodgson, 1861.

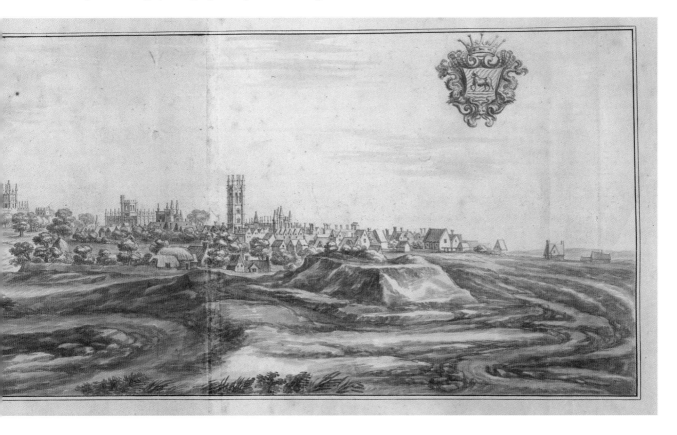

branching off this road near modern Circus Street. The largest scale demolition occurred in St Clements to create a new straight road to Henley, completed by 1778 and now the part of Iffley Road nearest to Magdalen Bridge. The old roads to Cowley branched near St. Bartholomew's Leper Hospital, commonly called Bartlemas. One road, now called Barracks Lane, skirted the north side of Cowley Marsh and led to Bullingdon Green, a large open space partly in Cowley and partly in Horspath parish that was used for field sports in the eighteenth century. The southern branch, Cowley Road, was raised as a causeway across the marsh and led to Temple Cowley. East of Boundary Brook it is now called Oxford Road but was known at least until 1853 as 'Berry Lane' and as 'Pile Road' in 1922. The old route from Oxford to London through High Wycombe and Uxbridge was by way of St Clements. Halfway up Headington Hill this road turned into Cheney Lane, then joined Old Road next to the site of the future Warneford Hospital and continued over the top of Shotover Hill to Stoken-church via Wheatley.

Enclosure

At the beginning of the eighteenth century large areas of the country including East Oxford were farmed in open fields as they had been for centuries, each farmer cultivating many separate ridge and furrow strips scattered widely throughout the large common fields. No building development could take place in an open field without violating the common rights to pasture animals after the harvest on the open field stubble, and the complex intermixture of holdings in Cowley Field before enclosure made building impossible there. In the early nineteenth century development took place either in the confined area of St Clements or further from the city in Iffley or Headington.

The process of enclosure saw the land of the open fields rearranged into compact farmsteads with smaller fields enclosed by hedges of fences which created the agricultural landscapes we still see today. From the mid-sixteenth century early enclosure had taken place in the parishes of Marston and St Clements. In the latter parish, pasture on either side of Headington Hill was enclosed in 1565. Following a parliamentary act of 1802 Headington parish was enclosed in 1804[6] and Iffley was enclosed in 1830.[7] But Cowley parish remained unenclosed and strip-farmed in large open fields until 1853.[8] Early enclosure was by mutual agreement of the parties involved but from the mid- eighteenth century the need to feed a growing population encouraged enclosure for greater product-ivity and profit. Acts of parliament appointed comm-issioners whose job it was to prepare an Enclosure Award, distributing the land in proportion to the common rights previously enjoyed in the open fields. The Cowley Award covered a vast area: 1685 tithe

strips were exchanged for 183 allotments of land. Cowley Field was common to the three parishes, Cowley, Iffley and St Clements and the Award defined the allotments that formed detached parts of each parish. It distinguished Temple Cowley from Church Cowley, although both were parts of Cowley Parish. Figure 3 shows the boundary of Cowley Field in red. The detached parts of the parishes are coloured pink for Church Cowley, green for Temple Cowley, yellow for Iffley and blue for St Clements and the boundaries of individual allotments shown in red. The underlying map is an early O.S. map.

The major landowners at enclosure were Christ Church in Church Cowley as Lords of the Manor of Church Cowley, Donnington Hospital (outside Newbury) as Lords of the Manor of Iffley, and the Hurst family of farmers in Temple Cowley. Most of the Christ Church allotments became detached parts of Cowley Parish and identified with Church Cowley. Most of the Hurst's allotments became detached parts of Cowley Parish and identified with Temple Cowley. Donnington Hospital allotments became detached parts of Iffley Parish, mostly in the region of Hock-more Street. Detached parishes were abolished after the Detached Parishes Act of 1882. Exact definitions of the parishes were important because social services at the time were provided on the basis of the parish.

The Award also created some new roads, in particular Cross Road, now Magdalen Road. Public watercourse No. 2 was designed to drain Cowley Marsh, an area of marshland on either side of Cowley Road which stretched from Magdalen Road to Boundary Brook. Public Watercourse No. 1 is the present straight stretch of Boundary Brook and Cross Footway the path running beside it.

The Hursts who were awarded most of the allot-ments from The Plain to Magdalen Road, between Iffley and Cowley Roads, were the first to sell from 1853 and there was much building here in the 1860s. With the rapid growth of East Oxford following enclosure, Father Richard Meux Benson (1824–1915), vicar of Cowley, built a temporary iron church of St. James in Stockmore Street to serve the rapidly growing population. In 1868 he was instrumental in the creation of the new parish of Cowley St. John[9] and with his wealth, inherited by his wife Elizabeth Meux whose father owned the London Meux brewery, he financed the building of the Marston Street Mission House for the Cowley Fathers, St Mary and John Church, St John the Evangelist Church, schools and other institutions in the area.[10]

When Cowley St. John ecclesiastical parish separated from Cowley parish in 1868, the new parish was a rapidly expanding suburb of Oxford, but the old villages of Church and Temple Cowley remained largely unchanged. Then in 1864 the British Land Company bought land at Temple Cowley and laid

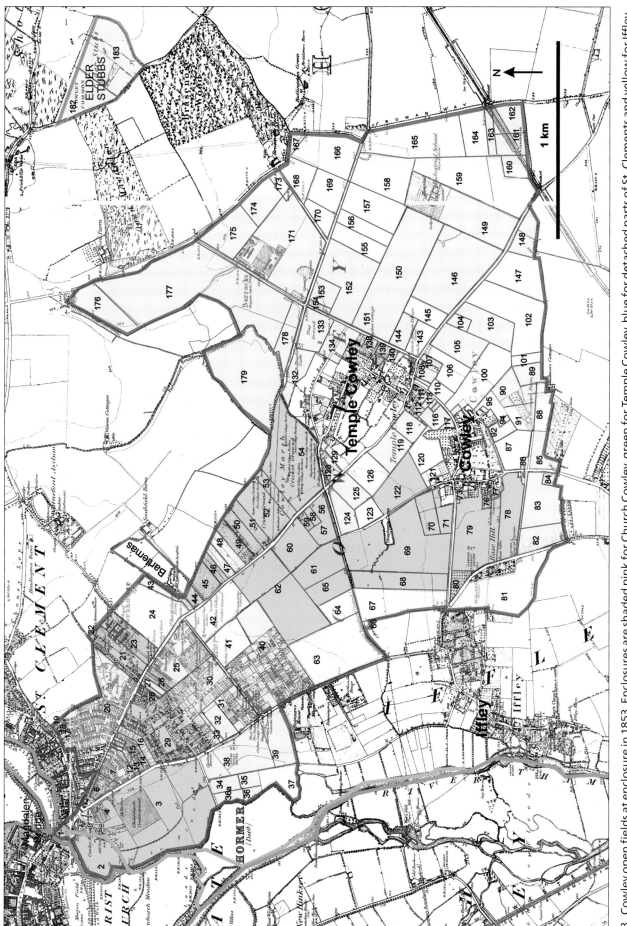

3. Cowley open fields at enclosure in 1853. Enclosures are shaded pink for Church Cowley, green for Temple Cowley, blue for detached parts of St. Clements and yellow for Iffley. The Bartlemas Estate is shown by a blue outline. Base Map: first edition Ordnance Survey 6 inch to the mile (© Crown Copyright and Landmark Information Group Limited 2014).

out Crescent Road. Freehold building plots were auctioned from 1866 but building there was slow.

Before Cowley Marsh was drained in the 1860s, Cowley Road still crossed the marsh on a causeway supported by wooden piles which led on to Temple Cowley. The smooth turf of the Marsh had never been ploughed and provided a good surface for recreation. The Magdalen College Cricket Ground was laid out on Cowley Marsh in the 1820s by Magdalen College School who used it until 1893, when they obtained a lease from Christ Church for their present ground on Milham Meadow near Magdalen Bridge. At enclosure the University bought the Magdalen Cricket Ground for the Oxford University Cricket Club and the western part of the Cowley Marsh Cricket Ground further out on the marsh for the use of the college clubs.

Up the hill from Bartlemas was Southfield Farm on the former South Field of Headington Parish. It was sold in 1874 and during the following fifty years subdivided by further sales. Part became housing,

part farmland for the Warneford Mental Hospital, and later the Churchill Hospital site, and the rest became golf course, playing fields and school. Fig. 3 shows the boundary of the farm with its early field subdivisions.

Notes

1 Salmon 2010, 5.
2 Lattey et al. 1936, Plate 22.
3 Lattey et al. 1936, 168.
4 Corpus Christi College Archives, *Malchair* vol.III, f.52, October 1, 1772.
4 Henry Taunt photo, Oxford History Centre, HT83
6 Headington Enclosure Award, Oxford History Centre, QSD/AF.
7 Iffley Enclosure Award, Oxford History Centre, QSD/AE.
8 Cowley Enclosure Award, Oxford History Centre, QSD/A/book24.
9 London Gazette 4 August 1868, 4312.
10 Smith 1980.

The Bath Street baths, St Clements, 1827–1879

Martin Murphy

In the early nineteenth century, deaths of bathers by drowning in Oxford's rivers were not uncommon. In 1827, to try to rectify this situation, a local entrepreneur, Andrew Richardson, opened a 'school of natation' in St Clements, at the bottom of what came to be called Bath Street. His promotional brochure, illustrated with views by Nathaniel Whittock, 'lithographist to the University of Oxford', declared that 'it was to prevent a recurrence of fatal accidents and to encourage the exhilarating pleasures of bathing, which are in great measure prevented by the publicity of the walk near the rivers, that first suggested the idea of this establishment.'[1] (Fig. 1)

Mr Richardson's new bath offered the advantages of safety and privacy, but its situation, on the less salubrious eastern side of Magdalen Bridge, was unlikely to attract the select clientele he had in mind, and it is surprising that he did not take this into account. The population of St Clements had doubled from 770 to 1,412 in the three years following 1820, and largely due to the influx of poor families dispossessed by slum clearance in central Oxford.[2] A glimpse of their condition is to be found in the diaries of John Henry Newman, then the parish curate. Apart from that, the world beyond Magdalen Bridge was outside the ambit of many undergraduates, though Mr Richardson argued that the walk from the city would offer them an oppor-

tunity for 'gentle exercise both before and after their immersion'.

The grandiose complex included a large open-air unheated swimming pool, lined with Bath Stone, measuring 83 by 44 feet, 18 dressing rooms, two screened recesses (one for the use of 'timid or juvenile bathers', the other for use as a plunging bath), private hot and cold baths, a tower containing the reservoir and pumping machinery, a reading room, and a salon or lounge. The whole magnificent structure was designed in 'Greek Revival' style by Thomas Greenshields, later the architect of the neo-classical front of what is now St Peter's College. His designs (reproduced in Whittock's brochure) are remarkably similar to those of John Lethbridge's baths at Southernhay, Exeter, opened in 1821, and to those at Edinburgh (1825-28) and Liverpool (1826-29).[3] It is possible, however, that some of the features illustrated by Whittock – notably the imposing frontage on Bath Street – never made it from the drawing board to reality.

According to the Oxford and University City Guide of 1828 the swimming bath contained 120,000 gallons 'of the most pellucid water.' This contradicted the facts. Far from being 'pellucid', the Cherwell was notorious for its contamination. St Clements was one of the districts most affected by the cholera outbreak of 1832, and even though the authorities had yet to make a connection between the spread of the disease and the quality of the water supply, the official report of the 1832 outbreak drew attention to the state of the Cherwell which 'runs, if it may be said to run, along the bottom of St Clements. As the drains of this populous district discharge themselves into this branch of the river, which, since the removal of the mill above [the King's Mill], has ceased to flow, the lodgements in these stagnant waters are in summertime dangerously offensive to the inhabitants.'[4]

Some of Whittock's plates feature undergraduates in academic dress, but this was wishful thinking. Oxford, dominated by a clerical establishment which was vigilant in supervising undergraduate morals, was not a fashionable health resort. The dons are likely to have been suspicious of Mr Richardson's salon and library ('supplied with morning and evening papers') as places conducive to idling and dissipation. Yet undergraduates were the only section of local society able to afford the fees for membership (one guinea per annum) or swimming lessons (one shilling per session). There are indications that the venture soon ran into financial difficulty. In May 1828 Jackson's Oxford Journal carried an advertisement for an instructor: 'He must be of good character, and perfectly master of swimming. Apply immediately.' Gradually what had been exclusively a 'school of natation' was adapted for wider use. By about 1842 the property was 'furnished with ground for the performance of gymnastic exercises

and other sports,'[5] but even this did not ward off decline. Jackson's Oxford Journal of 15 November 1851 announced the 'peremptory sale of the university baths, gymnastic room and tennis court, St Clement's, erected and fitted up at a cost of nearly £8000 … for many years conducted by Mr Richardson.' By then the gymnasium occupied what had been the salon, and the tennis court seems to have been installed in the area adjoining Bath Street. The proprietor soon had to face strong competition from the purpose-built and popular gymnasium opened in 1858 by Archibald McClaren in a central situation on the corner of Alfred Street and Bear Lane. In 1866 the new proprietor of the Bath Street premises, Job Tolley, seized a new opportunity by opening 'Turkish Baths and Fives Courts'. The fashion for hot-air 'Turkish' baths was then at its height.[6] Again he had to face competition. Oxford's first indoor swimming pool opened in Merton Street in 1869, and in 1873 'University Turkish Baths' were advertised at 54 Cornmarket Street. The end of the ill-fated Bath Street venture came in 1879, when Jackson's Oxford Journal of 2 August carried notice of the sale by auction of the property 'of the late Job Tolley'. The new owner then demolished the baths to make way for a

OXFORD BATHS
Swimming School

1. The Swimming School. To the left, the front of the saloon, engraving by N. Whittock.

housing development (Bath Place). That in its turn was pulled down in 1971 to be replaced by post-graduate accommodation for St Catherine's College.

Acknowledgments

Especial thanks are due to John Ashdown for his stimulus and generous sharing of information.

Notes

1   Richardson 1827.
2   Salmon 2010, 12-13.
3   Binney 1982, 2.
4   Thomas 1835, x.
5   Dewe, c. 1842, 27.
6   Mount 2010, Chapter 1.

Henry Taunt: a Victorian photographer in East Oxford

Helena Clennett

To the casual observer 393 Cowley Road does not appear to be a place of particular interest, sitting as it currently does, surrounded by more modern buildings along one of the busiest main roads in East Oxford (Fig. 1). In its various recent guises as a bus company depot and offices there was once nothing to suggest that the building had once been the home and workplace of a figure as important to our cultural heritage as Henry Taunt (Fig. 2), a well-known photographer, author, publisher and entertainer. His life has been the subject of a biography by Malcolm Graham.[1] A blue plaque commemorating Taunt was unveiled on his former home in 2008 (Fig. 3), which perhaps as a result of this historical connection has since miraculously escaped demolition, and has now become part of a student residence.

Taunt was born in Pensons Gardens, St. Ebbes, Oxford, on June 14th, 1842. He began his career as a photographer in 1856 aged 14, when he went to work

2. Henry Taunt, studio portrait, circa 1910 (CC56 743: © Historic England).

1. 'Rivera', Henry Taunt's former home at 393 Cowley Road, East Oxford.

for Edward Bracher, the 'pioneer of photography in Oxford'. Taunt set up his own photographic business at 9-10 Broad Street, Oxford in 1874, having worked at photographic studios in High Street and Cornmarket previously. Moving to East Oxford in 1889 after a period of bankruptcy, Taunt leased a red-brick detached house at 393 Cowley Road, where he established a photographic studio and printing works.

Taunt's lifetime was a period of historic change and growth in Oxford and the population grew from 11,921 in 1801 to 49,336 in 1901. The Cowley Marsh area of East Oxford offered new, spacious homes to residents moving from poorer areas in central Oxford. It had a reputation for being unhealthy due to the wet clay subsoil but this was rectified with sufficient drainage.[2] Taunt was known to have enjoyed walking on Cowley Marsh indulging his love of botany, and his photographs show that the Cowley Road area of his day was quiet and rural compared with today (Fig. 4).

Taunt had been involved in local politics from 1880. As the son of a plumber/glazier from St. Ebbes, principles rooted in his own humble origins meant that he regularly campaigned against injustices in East Oxford. In a letter to the council in 1908 he complained about the '...unhealthy practise...of putting Snow and Muck from the City, on the Children's Recreation Ground on the Cowley Road...' and states that he has done what he can to stop it.

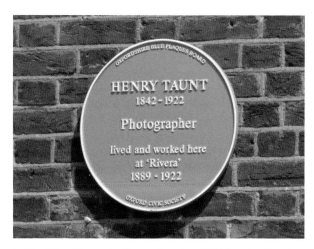

3. The Blue Plaque to Henry Taunt on 393 Cowley Road.

Around the time of arrival in East Oxford, Taunt began to focus more on writing and map production and entrusted his later photographs to his assistants. He is known to have produced books on myriad subjects from the history of St. Giles Fair to Comets, but his great love seems to have been the River Thames, after which he named 393 Cowley Road 'Rivera'.

In 1859 Taunt took a trip up the Thames to Cricklade, a venture that is thought to have inspired the guidebooks and maps that he later produced, such as the first guide book of the Thames to be illustrated with photographs. He is known to have played a role in promoting the use of the river for recreational

4. A view looking north towards 'Rivera', taken by Taunt around 1901 (HT 8054:© Oxfordshire History Centre).

activities after the Thames lost freight traffic due to the development of the rail network. After the 1872 publication of 'A New Map of the River Thames' Taunt produced many maps and guidebooks of Oxford and the surrounding areas aimed at tourists, but it was from 1900-1914 that his writing was at its peak, The *New York Times* considered his work on the Thames 'as essential as the boat for a successful journey'.

Henry Taunt died in 1922 and is buried in Rose Hill Cemetery. Taunt's historical leanings encouraged him to photograph scenes, streets and buildings which might otherwise have been forgotten. His work might also have been forgotten if it hadn't been saved by the City librarian E.E. Skuce, who bought the collection after learning it was being systematically destroyed by a builder who had bought 'Rivera' after Taunt's death. Taunt himself is quoted as saying 'All photographs have some limited historical value; those taken today, many of them will be much wanted in fifty years' time.'[3] This statement is still true a century later. Photographs illustrate history in a way that words cannot, and for that reason Henry Taunt's work will remain valuable forever.

Notes

1   Graham 1973.
2   Graham and Waters 2002.
3   www.sandersofoxford.com

Chapter 7

A changing landscape and community

David Griffiths and Jane Harrison

It is inevitably difficult to summarise, reflect upon, and conclude a varied and long-term research project, when so many new connections, ideas and thought-provoking discoveries have emerged. Archaeology is an open-ended process. Unlike the 'hard' sciences, it very rarely produces definitive advances which change the world in one fell swoop. Perhaps that is one reason why there is no Nobel Prize for Archaeology. With sound method and good fortune, however, it can produce exciting discoveries, robustly recorded, which can alter our view of a period, or a site, contributing to a bigger picture. Mostly its contribution lies in the 'middle ground' of partial advances, when new data and interpretations dispense with some old theories or misconceptions, but produce yet more questions, ideas, possibilities and ways forward. This is perhaps its greatest strength, the sense that archaeological research is fundamentally a debate, and that our search for new evidence is not an exercise in filling storage boxes, but in populating ideas with fresh impetus. Throughout, it is important to retain a sense of continuity and change across time. No period should be studied in isolation, as demonstrated by the finds of our two most impressive and intriguing Prehistoric artefacts: the two flint arrowheads from Minchery Paddock, which came to light amidst the abandoned structural remains of a Medieval nunnery.

Any archaeological investigation has to proceed in reverse, in that it tackles the most modern first, and usually the most ancient last. The upper layers of most archaeological excavations are often seen as 'contaminated' with modern material, and something to get out of the way as quickly as possible to reveal the 'undamaged' archaeology below. This attitude can be mistaken. Traces of activity from the near-present day, or the relatively recent past, can tell us a great deal about how people lived in a place in more distant times from our own. Topsoil, as witnessed in our test-pits and excavations is often the richest layer for artefacts, even though these may have been displaced from below. Archaeology connects to the present day, and a dump of Victorian bottles and earthenware vessels from a chemists' shop, found in an old allotment at Boundary Brook Nature Park, has the power to inspire some of today's residents with an interest in the lives of previous generations.

The modern suburban townscape is the framework for understanding more ancient landscapes. The formerly rural character of East Oxford is preserved in a myriad of small ways, from street patterns which echo the shapes of former open fields, to the continued use of names for byways, slopes and watercourses. An evocative glimpse of a quieter, more rural East Oxford was captured by renowned local photographer Henry Taunt at the end of the nineteenth century. The map studies included here show the richness of the information present in nineteenth-century tithe maps, and how these reflect the more ancient lay-out of the fields and roads of the area before widespread suburban development. The study of South Park (Chapter 3) has shown the value of careful and repeated surface observation and map studies. A combination of tithe and early Ordnance Survey maps allowed us to perceive the historic lay-out of this surviving sliver of rural East Oxford. The boundaries of the formerly enclosed fields captured by the creation of the park in 1932 are still detectable, and the swathe of well-preserved ridge and furrow across the lower reaches of the park has been subject to intensive Lidar, surface and geophysical survey. The study of South Park interested us in particular because of its connection to the siege of Oxford during the English Civil War.

The place-name studies presented here in Chapter 6 have shown the depth of history attached to the names and boundaries of the area. As a result of the painstaking archival detective work of the *Archeox* research group which concentrated on maps and place-names, the landscapes of the Medieval and Anglo-Saxon periods come alive. Forgotten places reappear, such as Puppelowe, a field named after a barrow or burial mound at or near the junction of the boundaries of Cowley, Iffley and Littlemore, and Hacklingcroft, a meadow beside the Cherwell where flax was combed or heckled. Great care is however required when studying and interpreting place-names. Much is not as it might seem. The evocative names Cowley, Bear Wood, Kidneys and Broad Arse, for example, are all of very different origin to how they may appear to the uninitiated: no cow, bear, nephritic organ, or rump, forms any part of their original derivation. The pattern of place-names across East Oxford can be traced back as far as the Later Anglo-Saxon period, aided by the remarkable survival of the AD 1004 Headington Charter which gives the bounds of the estate of Cowley. Beyond that time, it becomes harder to perceive the detail of the structure of the landscape through place-names and documents, but Roman roads, watercourses and springs give us hints as to the main enduring divisions. How therefore was the landscape perceived, owned, and contested in the much more distant past?

A connected landscape

Under the busy and built-up clutter of the modern day, the physical form and nature of the ancient landscape remains largely intact. The rivers Thames and Cherwell, their waters now guided, managed and bounded by human-made structures, occupy the verdant, flooding valley-bottoms which still remain the main dividing landscape features between areas of occupation. Small streams, little-noticed and partly culverted, are still the same watercourses which provided sustenance to the first human settlers in the area, and around which the earliest traces of human occupation are mostly to be found. The low-lying wetland area known as Cowley Marsh is now drained, and extensively built-upon, but less than two centuries ago it remained an impediment to permanent occupation. Roads skirted its edges, in a pattern still detectable today. Between the marshes and watercourses, gravel terraces form low spurs and ridges which attracted settlement activity throughout the history of human inhabitation. In this respect, the gravel areas of East Oxford are contiguous to and little different from those in the broader Thames Valley. People used the river valley corridors for fishing, wildfowling and transport, and they functioned as conduits for ideas and innovation. As permanent settlements began to take shape in Neolithic times, the surrounding resources of the landscape began to be exploited in different and more intensive ways. Woodlands on the hillslopes, previously exploited in their natural state for hunting and gathering, began to be cleared for agriculture or managed for grazing. As tree cover gradually diminished over time, soil erosion on the hills accelerated and choked the fast-flowing streams with alluvium, slowing them down and causing yet more deposition in the valleys. The landscape became flatter, and a little tamer.

The lives of people in such distant times are visible to us only through the most fortunate glimpses. The collections of the Ashmolean and Pitt Rivers museums gave us opportunities to study and record finds from the earliest periods of human occupation, and to connect them once again to the living landscape. The 1881 discovery of a hoard of Bronze Age weapons from Leopold Street, off Cowley Road, was brought out of obscurity and studied afresh, as was a stone hand-axe from Chester Street. Both were deposited between the edges of gravel terraces and wetlands or watery places. Much of the Neolithic and Bronze Age material collected by A. M. Bell in the 1890s came from along the gravel ridge which today underlies Iffley Fields, so this encouraged us to concentrate test-pits and geophysical surveys in this vicinity. The 2013 excavation at Donnington Recreation Ground was a direct consequence of geophysical survey, when a cluster of pit-like anomalies was detected. Its proximity to Bell's discoveries was an added incentive, and by excavating we were able to demonstrate stratified contexts and radiocarbon dates for a new body of data.

The Roman and early Anglo-Saxon material found at Donnington was more of a surprise, and gave useful insights into continued use of these river margins close to the Thames. The rivers remained important, but connections to the wider world were reinforced as new power and economic impetus affected the area. The Romans introduced new roads and river-crossings, perhaps in some cases making use of older trackways and fords. These created new patterns of access, and the increased ability to transport goods in bulk allowed the exploitation of another natural advantage: clay. Alongside wood and water, this was the key to the rapid emergence of a major pottery industry, the products of which spread out over most of Roman Britain and beyond. Christopher Young's summary of nearly fifty years' worth of research on the Roman pottery kilns lays out a key research challenge, to find out where the people lived who worked in this productive industry. The test-pit campaign described above in Chapter 3, together with all three of the more extensive excavations undertaken by the project, found scatters of Roman pottery sherds, mainly in the topsoil. This is perhaps unsurprising given the proximity of the many kilns in the area. However, we found that the spread of Roman pottery is far from uniform across East Oxford, and some definite clusters were detected. Two such were the quantity of material found in test pits at Fairacres Convent, on the gravel terrace near Iffley Road, and in a cluster of test pits at Greater and Blackbird Leys. Geophysical survey struggled amidst the background noise of later activity to locate demonstrable traces of activity from the Roman period, but coupled with studies of the existing archaeological record, such as the development-related archaeological work undertaken at Blackbird Leys in the 1990s, we can now point to some of the probable locations of Roman rural settlement with more confidence than before. The landscape was busy and evidently well-populated. Yet we do not know by what name the general area was known, or what local identity its inhabitants adopted. In the Roman period and indeed for some centuries after it, the city of Oxford did not yet exist. The urban story was to follow.

An urban hinterland

Oxford was evidently not a central place in the early Anglo-Saxon Period, but a scatter of finds and one or two burials suggest that the area was far from depopulated. Movement and change there certainly must have been after the Roman pottery industry declined, but some groups remained rooted in the area. It is almost certain that descendants of the communities created during the hey-day of the pottery industry remained living in the landscape, although there may have been changed to the balance between pasture and cultivated land. People continued to occupy the river gravels and slopes. *Archeox*'s test-pit campaign, together with the excavation at Donnington Recreation Ground, was successful in finding new clusters of early to middle Anglo-Saxon pottery across the area. Test Pit 1 at Stanley Road, Test pit 65 at Church Cowley, and the Donnington Recreation Ground excavation hint at an Anglo-Saxon settlement presence on the gravel terrace underlying Iffley Road, even if, due to the small scale of the areas studied, confirmation of structural evidence was elusive (which had it been detectable would most probably have been in the form of sunken-featured buildings such as those found by developer-funded archaeological projects at Oxford Science Park and East Minchery Farm Allotments in Littlemore).

The major change in the area during the post-Roman period came somewhat later than the immediate aftermath of the end of Roman Britain, with the development of Oxford as an urban centre. Beginning with a monastic presence around AD 700, situated at what later became Christ Church College, Oxford's presence as a centre of population and its influence over its rural hinterland began to grow. This received a major new stimulus around 900 when the burh was founded by Alfred the Great, expanding yet again in the eleventh century. The growth of the early city was not a smooth process. There were set-backs, such as the massacre of the Danes on St Brice's Day in in 1002, and the burh was attacked by avenging Danish armies in 1009 and 1013. It is to this turbulent period that we may attribute the find of a decorated pair of Viking stirrups on the banks of the Cherwell near the strategic crossing at Magdalen Bridge. Around this crossing, the first urban community in east Oxford began to grow, initially a Danish garrison settlement with the characteristic church dedication to St Clement, the area later became an important manor and hospital site in the Middle Ages. The roads that fanned out eastwards from Magdalen Bridge became the spines along which later Medieval settlements congregated.

Test pit clusters in Church Cowley, Iffley and Greater Leys, produced evidence for later Anglo-Saxon settlement as well as Medieval and later Medieval wares. These closely reflect the types of pottery found in numerous excavations in the city centre. As the city increased in size and economic influence, its rural environs increasingly fulfilled the role of a hinterland, providing resources and services to the growing urban community. Agricultural produce, wood, clay, sand and limestone from East Oxford fed and built the growing city. The roads linking the countryside to the city became a means of social and cultural contact, and the fortunes of the secular and religious communities east of the city were determined in part by their connections with Oxford. The ebb and flow of the city's political and economic fortunes: the growth of learning, epidemics, the reformation, and civil wars, had a direct impact on its rural hinterland which is reflected in its archaeology. Tensions familiar in East Oxford's modern identity – a periphery to Oxford, intermediate between town and country, but also retaining a sense of being a separate and distinctive place – must surely have become recognisable in the Middle Ages.

This sense of an historic city's hinterland acquiring a distinct identity is reflected in the growth and contraction of the settlements of East Oxford both before and after the Norman Conquest. An archetypal trajectory around this period for village development in an agriculturally productive region would see the creation of nucleated villages with housing, gardens and paddocks clustered around a manor and church. This coalescing of settlement freed up land to lay out large and efficient open fields farmed in strips by the villagers and landowners. East Oxford however did not spawn these classic open field villages, rather generating a more individual and mixed settlement landscape.

In many areas of the Midlands clustered villages with their attendant open fields were already establishing in the later Anglo-Saxon period; there was little evidence for this happening in the *Archeox* study area, with the notable exception of Church Cowley and perhaps relatively limited beginnings in Iffley (Chapter 3, Ceramic Phase 4, see page 70). Church Cowley was distinctive, the test pit evidence suggesting a place that had always been a favoured location for human activity and then settlement from early Prehistory, becoming a nucleated village in the later Anglo-Saxon period. In topographical and geological aspects Iffley, Fairacres and Temple Cowley would have been as likely candidates for continuing human interest, but there was clearly something significant about the Church Cowley area, plausibly linked to the location of burial mounds and intersecting routeways and boundaries. Elsewhere in the area the settlement pattern in the pre-Norman period continued to be dominated by farms and hamlets.

After the mid-eleventh century, big changes in the character and arrangement of settlement are clearly evident in the archaeology of East Oxford. New communities were growing around the religious institutions at Bartlemas, Temple Cowley and Littlemore Priory, all founded in the early-mid twelfth century. The village at Temple Cowley developed rapidly in Ceramic Phase 5 (1050-1400), Iffley village expanded and Church Cowley continued strongly. The arrival of the nuns and the construction of the priory seems to have attracted more people to the community of Littlemore, although like Iffley, Littlemore emerged as a poly-focal, rather than strongly nucleated village. However, not everyone was drawn to village life and there is plenty of evidence for the continuation of individual farms or hamlets in the East Oxford landscape after the Norman Conquest, in Greater Leys, Fairacres and the margins of Cowley Marsh. As discussed in Chapter 3, this varied settlement landscape of villages of different forms, religious establishments, hamlets and farms, probably reflected a varied agricultural economy, with some open fields (for example in Iffley Fields, see Chapter 6) laid out amidst pasture, orchard and managed woodland. Supporting the nunnery, preceptory and leper hospital, and responding to the demands of the burgeoning city, generated a different landscape to that of nucleated villages. This understanding of Medieval East Oxford thus establishes a distinct character for an urban hinterland and underlines the value of exploring the archaeology of the suburbs.

In the later Medieval period, after 1400, the villages, both those of clustered and poly-focal lay-outs, experienced varied fortunes. There is, in the test pit evidence a generalised drop-off in quantities of pottery, perhaps a reflection of the impact of the famines and plagues of the fourteenth century, but the decline seen at Temple Cowley and Littlemore may have begun with the loss of the Templars' preceptory and the nunnery respectively. However, Iffley is settled and even expanded, stretched across the mid-slopes of Rose Hill and Church Cowley, if perhaps slightly contracted, also persists. However, the overall pattern of settlement remained little-changed until the nineteenth century. The greatest change in the test pit evidence for the settlement landscape, before that period of rapid suburbanisation, is in the seventeenth and eighteenth centuries when it is clear from the considerable decrease in pottery amounts that people were disposing of their rubbish differently, perhaps in landfill sites documented along the Thames.

In addition to its broad landscape investigations, *Archeox* was fortunate to have the opportunity to undertake excavations at East Oxford's two most important Medieval religious sites, Bartlemas Chapel, and Littlemore Priory. Both have surviving Medieval buildings, but despite some limited previous archaeological investigation, many aspects of their extent, plan and economy remained little-understood. In both cases, our knowledge of these has improved considerably. At Bartlemas Chapel, we were able to document

the northern and eastern walls of the earlier structure, which we interpreted as the first stone chapel on the site, very probably dating back to the twelfth-century foundation of the leper hospital. The probable lay-out of the leper hospital has come more into focus. Ancillary buildings and a possible bell-tower were discovered. Recent excavations at the leper hospital of St Mary's, Winchester, show the chapel and the infirmary, which was a longer, narrower building, on much the same east-west alignment. It is not difficult to envisage a similar arrangement here, where Bartlemas House, a seventeenth-century rebuild on a long, narrow east-west plan, occupies almost exactly the probable site of the Medieval infirmary; indeed parts of its fabric may include it. We made some progress in mapping and understanding the role of minor watercourses in bounding, supplying and draining the Bartlemas site; these were clearly important to the Medieval hospital, yet the precise location of the holy well remains in question.

The Bartlemas excavations provided a fascinating insight into the hospital community. Although it was strongly anticipated that the surroundings of the chapel had functioned as a burial ground, these were the first inhumations to be confirmed archaeologically. An interesting range of age, sex and apparent social status was observed among the burials. The charnel deposits included Medieval bones, several of which gave the first confirmed identification of leprosy at Bartlemas, and rickets was also noted. The charnel pits themselves were extremely interesting. Human and animal bone was mixed up in parts of them, implying a rushed and ill-considered process of reburial, in part probably relating to the use of the site during the Civil War. Some of the bones showed evidence of surgical drilling, probably for display. The finds from the site suggest that the Medieval community at Bartlemas was far from poor or isolated, with a silver coin and imported pottery demonstrating a material connection with the wider world, but particularly with Oxford. In the post-Medieval period, by now an almshouse, the site saw varying fortunes, with the disruptions of the Civil War requiring a substantive renovation in 1649-51. Thereafter Bartlemas functioned essentially as a tiny rural hamlet on the edge of the city, much as it appears today.

Littlemore Priory (known locally as the 'Minchery') was founded in the mid-twelfth century, shortly after St Bartholomew's Hospital. Like Bartlemas, part of it remains as a standing structure, in the form of the fifteenth-century dormitory range. However unlike the cared-for and much-loved chapel at Bartlemas, the remaining priory building (most recently used as a pub) is currently in private ownership, inaccessible and in poor superficial condition. Its surroundings could not offer a greater contrast to the bucolic charms of Bartlemas. Overshadowed by boxy modern hotel and retail developments, the Medieval building stands isolated at the edge of a sea of car-parks, near to waste ground and the aromatic presence of Oxford's main sewage treatment plant. To its west is the overgrown wooded area known as Minchery Paddock, where *Archeox* excavated three trenches in 2012. Trench 1 succeeded in establishing a profile through peat layers extending up to 16,000 years ago, which was radio-carbon dated to as far back as thirteen thousand years ago (11,500 years BC). This was also a glimpse of the agricultural use of landscape beyond the priory precinct, which revealed itself in more detail in trenches 2 and 3. Trench 2 showed partial evidence for the remains of two buildings, and within the north-eastern building was an impressive hearth constructed from tile. The evidence points towards these outer buildings in Trench 2 being part of an artisanal area, with workshops, food preparation and craft activities, which is more likely to have been frequented by servants or local labourers than by the nuns themselves. By contrast, Trench 3, located much closer to the central zone of the priory, produced evidence of more formal architecture, probably related to the claustral range. Extensive animal bone remains from the adjoining midden did indeed appear to confirm W.A. Pantin's prediction that the nunnery's kitchen was located here. The remains had been disturbed by later activity and dumping, but the connection to the nuns' domestic lives was far more tangible in this part of the site. Finds from trenches 2 and 3 of Medieval pottery, tile, coins, personal and domestic implements show the material culture of the priory was well-provided for, particularly in the thirteenth and fourteenth centuries. An aquamanile, pitchers and a chafing (warming) dish indicate that a fine dining culture was present at the priory, perhaps associated with the prioress's own table. A distant echo of the music of a stringed instrument is conveyed by a bone tuning peg.

Littlemore Priory benefited from acts of royal favour in its earlier years, but later on acquired a bad reputation, perhaps somewhat undeservedly, as a result of the visitations or inspections made in 1445 and 1517 by commissaries of the Bishop of Lincoln. One of the accusations made by the 1445 visitor, Dr John Derby, that the nuns broke their rule by eating flesh every day in the refectory, does seem to chime with our discovery of beef, mutton, pork, venison and poultry bones in the Trench 3 kitchen midden. The 1517 visitation was even more damning in its criticism. Historical study of the nuns' lives undertaken by Katie Hambrook has nevertheless gone some way to redress the balance in favour of a small community of religious women whose dedication to their mission managed to survive for nearly four centuries. The visitations, particularly the second in 1517, appear to have had an ulterior motive in discrediting the nuns so that the priory could more easily be closed, taken over, and asset-stripped. Behind this development lurks the

figure of Cardinal Wolsey, whose college in Oxford (Cardinal College, later Christ Church) was the benefi-ciary of some of the priory's wealth. In this sense, the close connections of the priory to Oxford, which had been an advantage for much of its existence, turned out in the end to be a fatal vulnerability. We were fortunate in that commercial excavations by John Moore Heritage Services in 2014, undertaken ahead of the construction of a business hotel north of the surviving Medieval building, revealed most of the plan of the priory church, contributing a great deal more to our knowledge of the priory lay-out. 92 burials were recorded, and some impressive individual graves survived, notably a stone cist on the central crossing of the church, containing a middle-aged female skeleton who seems very likely to have been one of the prioresses. What was also striking about the 2014 excavation was how little of the fabric of the church building had survived *in situ*. It was evidently stripped of its fittings and construction materials with great efficiency, and studies of buildings in Littlemore Village, such as St George's House, indicate that some of the priory's stonework was re-used locally.

The 2012 and 2014 excavations at Littlemore Priory are an example of how the results of volunteer-led archaeology and those of the commercial profession can be productively combined, casting new light on an overlooked and neglected site, together representing a nationally-important case-study of a Medieval nunnery. There is considerably more archaeological potential in and around the site, notably in Minchery Paddock, where *Archeox*'s trenches touched only a tiny part of what could be achieved in terms of excavation. Set against this is the currently overgrown and neglected state of the area. It would probably take a major clear-ance operation, such as would only be feasible in advance of development, to expose larger areas for excavation. Given its known archaeological content, and its relatively low-lying and wet state, we may yet hope that it could be spared the destructive attentions of the bulldozers, instead remaining as an open space for nature between the encroaching residential areas on all sides.

People and their heritage

From the start, the *Archeox* project sought to include all of its participants as equals in a conversation. The project leaders went about their roles principally as local residents, friends, neighbours, and parents, at least as much as academics. This stance helped to create a relatively level platform upon which the project community interacted. Formal titles, univer-sity status, hierarchies, and any delusions of self-importance were dispensed with from the beginning. Everyone was on first-name terms, without exception. An open encouragement to participate was broadcast to all who were prepared to hear and respond to it. There came together a cross-section of people with varied lives, age, health, professional and educational backgrounds. Throughout, the project sought to focus dialogue and mutual support upon what united us, our interest in the past and the heritage of our area, not upon what otherwise may have divided us.

From the perspective of 2019, it is possible to look back with satisfaction and pleasure at the range of people, places and interests which converged within this project. The investment in training paid off principally in the short-term, as volunteers engaged with research and other aspects of the project whilst its activity plan continued in its staffed and funded form until 2015. However it has had more long-term implications as well. As described above in Chapter 2, many people were stimulated and encouraged to develop their own higher education as a result of participating. Several local societies, in Iffley, Littlemore, and in Cherwell District, were reinvigorated or started afresh as a result of *Archeox*. Volunteers have assisted the City Archaeologist in his work, and during major excavations by Oxford Archaeology at the Westgate shopping centre redevelopment in central Oxford, under the guidance of Dr Jane Harrison they put together and fronted an influential and much-praised archaeological outreach initiative in the form of a 'pop-up shop'. Jane has also been influential in the aftermath by recruiting *Archeox* volunteers to new field projects in neighbouring areas of Oxfordshire, including the excavation of an Anglo-Saxon hall at Long Wittenham, and an ongoing multi-strand landscape investigation project at Appleton. The research base and part-time studies courses offered at Continuing Education in Oxford have benefitted in many ways from the insights and experiences gained working within the community in East Oxford, and these have changed (for the better) as a result. *Archeox* is very far from being in the past!

Meet some of the team

Chris Turley

I found archaeology late in life – but not too late! I was born and grew up in Oxford, one of the last babies born before the NHS began. I was an only child and had a happy and secure childhood. I left my all-girls' school at age 15. In my teenage years I joined the Oxford Youth Theatre and this gave me the confidence to run my own business, in upholstery and soft furnishing, based in North Oxford.

By the time I retired in 2008 I had been through a few careers and done courses to catch up on my basic education. I found archaeology, by a chance through attending a talk given by Jane Harrison at the Museum of Oxford about what lay under the ground of East Oxford. That one afternoon changed the direction of my retirement. I love to find odd things – the powder cap from Minchery Paddock was one of these as it kept asking me questions (see page 184): what am I, what did I do, where did I come from? I really enjoyed identifying the objects found during the digging, washing and sorting process. It feels very special to find something that was lost hundreds of years ago and to know that my hands, trowel and eyes were the first to see the object since it was lost. I have since founded an archaeology group in my own area (Cherwell).

Chris (left) and her friend Mandy Bellamy excavating at Minchery Paddock.

Christopher laying out trenches at Minchery Paddock with Roelie Reed.

David (centre) speaking to a group on the project launch day at Bartlemas Chapel (Gail Anderson).

Christopher Lewis

As someone completely new to archaeology I enjoyed the practical experience I gained on the *Archeox* project, in particular excavation and finds processing. Also important were the supportive and friendly group dynamics, and working with colleagues within a structure and with a serious purpose. It was great the project unfolded on my doorstep, rooted locally and providing a wider context for my own family history research.

I was delighted to find a decorated floor-tile at the Minchery Paddock excavation, especially as it was discovered where we didn't necessarily expect it! At Bartlemas, my first major excavation, it was great to have charge of my own area of the dig: the corner of one of the buttress foundations. I did everything: all the digging, recording, even the drawing – which was quite a challenge!

David Griffiths

I am a resident of East Oxford, to which I moved in 1993. I am originally from the Wirral, in north-west England, where as a youngster I developed a love of local history and landscape. After university, I worked in commercial archaeology for a while, and since 1999 I have been a member of the teaching staff at Oxford University Department for Continuing Education (OUDCE), where I am responsible for leading the Archaeology programme. I believe people thrive best when they know their own community and some of its history, and since arriving in East Oxford, the area has fascinated me. Walking across the ridge and furrow earthworks in South Park or up the narrow lane to Bartlemas is a powerful stimulus to the imagination.

East Oxford is a special place, and it has its own strong identity within the city. I have been responsible for other research projects some distance from home, so it was exciting to start something new and innovative which was very much on the doorstep and I could talk to my neighbours about. We initiated the *Archeox* project to try find out more about the area's past, and also to build more bridges and connections between the academic side of Oxford and community. Helped by having a brilliant team led by the indomitable Jane, this project has been utterly transformative of the way I see the value of archaeology and heritage. We have discovered a wealth of fascinating new evidence, changing perceptions of the area's history. I have met an unbelievable number of interesting, kind and enthusiastic people, and it has been a wonderful experience throughout. I feel very blessed.

Graham Jones

As a landscape historian with an additional interest in patterns of popular religious devotion, I grabbed the chance to take part in the project, notably in the dig at

Graham excavating Skeleton 1 at Bartlemas Chapel.

Bartlemas Chapel. I was already enjoying doing my bit for the project as a whole, as an East Oxford resident and Councillor for St Clements Ward representing the City Council on the project steering committee, so getting down to it at the sharp end revealed the practical value to the community of what the project was aiming for.

It was also, frankly, great fun to have a trowel and a brush in hand again, and to learn the rather more rigorous techniques than those which prevailed in the Seventies when my wife and I spent happy weekends and summer breaks as volunteer diggers. No free beer money nowadays, but the comradeship of the trenches is just as strong. To cap it all, I had the good fortune to be assigned to the trench along the east end of the chapel. Here was the devotionally most sensitive part of the site, closest to the altar. Spatial relationships are highly significant where the veneration of

holy objects is concerned. The chapel's dedication to the apostle Bartholomew fed into a long interest I have in devotion to this saint.

It was a huge privilege and pleasure to learn new skills within the project team and from fellow volunteers. Hurrah for Continuing Education! The project convinced me afresh that public investment in community archaeology pays dividends. It proved the worth of working across disciplinary boundaries, something I learned as a doctoral student in the Department of English Local History at Leicester, and hopefully put to good use as Lecturer in English Topography there, and in my current affiliation to the School of Geography at Oxford. Our project's work on East Oxford was greatly enhanced by the important historical contributions from fellow volunteers on place-names, land-use, and early cartography. It has been altogether an exceptional experience!

Greg Owen

I am a qualified architect who has, unfortunately been suffering from a clinical depression and anxiety for some years. I have lived on the Greater Leys estate for nearly 20 years and was always curious about The Priory pub, as it is the oldest building in the area and in my profession I always preferred working with historic buildings. I became involved in *Archeox* after the team gave a talk at a local community centre which piqued my interest. I had recovered enough to be able to take part in the Minchery Paddock dig. It helped me a great deal that the team running the project were sensitive to my problems, very supportive and patient in their teaching, which all built my confidence. I was

Greg (left) at work at Donnington Recreation Ground.

able to work and learn at my own pace and develop a new skill set in field archaeology, as well as discovering that I had transferable skills from architecture. Thus a passion from my childhood was reawakened.

I continued to be involved in *Archeox* activities including the Donnington Recreation Ground dig on a Prehistoric site. I get a tangible thrill from uncovering objects and features from the past. More recently I was lucky enough to be invited to work on a commercial dig, excavating the church of Littlemore Priory, so I continued my link with this important local site. I have gained both physically, mentally and socially from being part of this amazing project.

Jane Harrison

I have lived in East Oxford for over 20 years with my family. I grew up mostly in the north-east of England where I learnt to appreciate the power of community and a strong sense of belonging to a place. Archaeology can contribute to both. My career has been varied; after working on excavations and taking history at university I came back into archaeology through study at Oxford University Department for Continuing Education (OUDCE). I have now been teaching at OUDCE since 2008 and, as well as running community archaeology projects, have excavated in Orkney, Oxfordshire and the north-east.

All archaeology projects should reach out to the locals; some of the most inspiring and significant results come from those ventures driven by and actively involving people living in the area. Our aim was to draw people into discovering their own past and this project showed me just how exciting that

process can be. East Oxford is such a diverse and vibrant area and given the opportunity so many dedicated, supportive and fun people gave their time to a collaborative effort in recreating the area's past landscapes. The photo accompanying this piece captures a tea-break discussion about archaeology at Minchery Paddock, and the delight I felt at being part of the team working there. We have now taken the legacy of *Archeox* forward into new projects and groups, bringing even more people into archaeology.

Jeff Wallis

I was born and brought up in East Oxford, a five-minute bus trip from some of Britain's finest collections of archaeological and geological material in the Ashmolean Museum, so it is no surprise that I fell into the archaeology trap, encouraged by my parents and avid reading of *Knowledge Magazine*. I was entranced by the discovery of a fine example of a 'Neolithic Celt' (a form of axe), found just round the corner from where I lived. The museum label read "found in Chester Street" (see page 21).

I began to investigate East Oxford's archaeology, perusing a tatty old copy of *Early Man of Oxfordshire*, part of the 'Victoria County History'. Thumbing through for my favourite periods, the Neolithic, Bronze Age and Iron Age, I read about the Leopold Street Hoard (see page 22). This hoard was inextricably linked with the Burgess Meadow hoard found on Port Meadow, a favourite childhood bike-ride to pay homage to Old Father Thames. (Burgess Meadow is at the southern end of Port Meadow.) I passed down Leopold Street many times, wondering about the

Jane (right) with Leigh Mellor and Steve Nicholson at Minchery Paddock.

Jeff (right, furthest from camera) leads a drawing training session at Rewley House.

hoard find-spot, frustrated at not being able to find out more of the history of this group of artefacts. Cue the arrival of the *Archeox* project and my initiation into the Ashmolean Museum Antiquities Study Room. I was invited by the Project to draw and study artefacts (and most of the finds illustrations in this book are my work). Now I could satisfy my addiction to looking ever more closely at collections preserved in this holy shrine, and request from the endlessly helpful Alison Roberts permission to conjure up other artefacts from enticing storage boxes. Here at last I was fortunate enough to observe and draw the Leopold Street hoard at first-hand.

Jennifer Laird and Mark Viggers

Jenni: I have been very fortunate to be involved with *Archeox* from the beginning. I now have experience in planning test pits, digging, levelling, geophysics, finds washing and the paperwork that goes with it all. Sometimes I can't do the more physical aspects of the volunteering as I have Multiple Sclerosis, but the project and the team allow for this and there is always something more sedate, but equally as important to do.

The *Archeox* project has brought history and archaeology to life for me, including the work with the Ashmolean Museum. The opportunity to spend afternoons in the Ashmolean study room with artefacts, whether packing, photographing or being taught about them, was something I could not refuse! The object biography idea was fascinating. As I am heavily involved in Anglo-Saxon re-enactment, I just had to choose to concentrate on the shield boss and Viking stirrups from Magdalen Bridge (see page 26). I brought Mark Viggers onboard for this as he portrays a warrior in our group, *Wulfheodenas*, and had previously enjoyed helping at *Archeox* events. It has been a very rewarding, interesting and enjoyable few years being an *Archeox* volunteer and I've made some great new friends. I hope we can carry on our volunteering, in some way, in the future.

Mark: I have had a lifelong interest in history and became involved in early medieval re-enactment seven years ago. My focus soon narrowed onto the early Anglo-Saxon migration and settlement periods. Jennifer Laird and myself are members of the early Anglo-Saxon period group *Wulfheodenas* (Wolfheads), a group that portrays the social elite and mead-hall culture of the sixth and seventh centuries. The aim is to represent, as accurately as possible, aspects of the Germanic culture that lead us to become the people we are today. This involves years of research, months of recreation and many a day wearing wool, linen and very shiny bling, while interacting with and hopefully educating the public. As members of this group we have been fortunate to

Jenni and Mark interpreting a sixth century Anglo-Saxon warrior and high-status woman: Mark is holding the re-created shield and boss. Photo: Nigel Ferris.

work with a number of museums, including several museums in Sweden.

I have been fortunate to handle artefacts that only a handful of people have ever seen, row a longboat up the River Thames, fight against the Norman invaders on Senlac ridge and, on one special winter's night, having just celebrated Yule in an Anglo-Saxon hall, we stood in the snow under a bright full moon and listened to a pack of wolves howling. More recently, Jennifer Laird introduced me to the members of *Archeox*, and we became involved by providing a display of a warrior and his lady at the Cowley Carnival in South Park, at Oxford Castle and at Ashmolean Museum events.

Joanne Robinson

I joined the project part way through on a Council for British Archaeology Community Archaeology Training Placement, or CATP, a slightly snappier title. I was unemployed when I applied for one of the community archaeology bursaries, and feeling very disenchanted with my chosen career. Archaeology can be an infuriating choice: it's hard to get a step on the elusive ladder, and once you do, you soon realise that your ladder is only a short lease and in three months – six months if you're lucky – you're back at the bottom. I was no stranger to volunteering when I applied for the bursary. I had volunteered in various roles myself, largely trying to improve my skills and experience while I was between jobs, but also for fun. I love archaeology and missed it while I was working in various non-heritage related roles. You know you're addicted when you're willing to do it for free!

I knew I would really enjoy working professionally within community archaeology, and had some experience in supervising volunteers. What I didn't know was how to turn that into a full-time job. I spotted the Council for British Archaeology's CATPs on an archaeology job website, and applied. I was completely overwhelmed when I found out I had been successful!

The bursary project was funded by the Heritage Lottery Fund's Skills for the Future programme, and designed to train a cohort of community archaeologists, giving them both the practical and soft skills needed to work with voluntary groups and communities. The basis of the placements was that each post holder was placed with a host experienced in working successfully with communities, so able to help develop skills necessary to deliver community archaeology projects through hands on experience (otherwise known as dropping you in the deep end).

I was nervous when I first started: I didn't know Oxfordshire well geographically, let alone have any great understanding of the demographics of the community I would be working with. I thought I had a good general idea of the types of people that the project would be engaging with, which of course turned out to be completely wrong. Oxford, as it turned out, is home to more than just students and university professors. And there is actually archaeology beyond the famous core of the city.

Finding my feet

One of my earliest memories of working on the project was finding myself in a cold, wet, environmental processing shed, with a small contingency of *Archeox* volunteers, feeling somewhat out of my depth. I had never processed an environmental sample before, let alone shown someone else how to do it, and glancing around at the equipment for inspiration left me more bewildered. There is something very disconcerting about not being able to answer one of your volunteer's questions, when you know your role is to support and inspire confidence, and so I endeavoured to absorb every detail of the introductory demonstration by professional environmental archaeologist, Sharon Cook. Once I got into the task, I felt myself falling into the role of community archaeologist for the first time. Take a group of inexperienced volunteers, add a great challenge and some professional instruction, and you get a successful and satisfying afternoon (actually two weeks as it turned out).

What you don't get in community archaeology, is production line speed. Of course there are volunteers who become, or may already be very efficient, but community archaeology, it soon became apparent, was about the experience and learning, not just the end result; about enjoying the task, feeling comfortable asking lots of questions and having a laugh and working with your fellow project members. That's what people enjoyed and what kept them coming back, and after all, isn't that what inspired us professionals to pick up a trowel: that passion for knowledge and enjoyment of the, sometimes downright dirty, tasks involved in archaeology? The *Archeox* project reminded me why I hadn't given up on archaeology – I enjoy it too much. Once you accept the slower paced but thorough archaeological process, you see the group is achieving professional standard results, it just takes longer.

It was made clear to me from the offset that we didn't 'play' at archaeology in East Oxford: it was real archaeology, with real responsibility. Whilst that may sound obvious to many, I have heard ideas of 'mock digs' banded around as a plausible activity for volunteers at professional conferences. Insisting that volunteers work on real archaeology, is what makes it truly engaging community project. I think that involving people in simulated archaeological tasks has little value, especially in terms of the benefits to the archaeological record. If it isn't real, it doesn't add to our understanding of the local historic landscape.

While community archaeology was quickly revitalising my passion for the profession, it wasn't without

oxfordmail.co.uk/news   OXFORD MAIL

Delving into what's under your garden

EAST Oxford residents will soon get a glimpse into what was happening in their gardens 800 years ago.

And if past finds are anything to go by the picture may not be all rosy.

Archeox, the East Oxford archaeology and history project, is carrying out two mini-excavations in Temple Cowley on Saturday and Sunday.

The team is inviting residents in Temple Road, St Christopher's Place, Don Bosco Close, Junction Road and Crescent Road to help them uncover the secrets buried in their gardens.

With the help of residents, they will square off a metre of land and carefully dig down, sifting soil in the hope of finding evidence of the area's past.

The team has carried out two major East Oxford excavations, in Bartlemas and Minchery Farm, but is using the smaller digs to hone skills and enthuse volunteers.

For the last three years they have been building up a picture of life in the 12th century around East Oxford from its days as a Roman settlement.

■ **Mark Taylor**
mtaylor@oxfordmail.co.uk

Alongside the Romano-British pottery industry they have uncovered prehistoric sites, a medieval leper hospital and civil war defences.

Archeox archaeologist Jane Harrison said: "We've leafleted the entire area and have about 600 volunteers, so it will be a case of walking up to someone's house, knocking on their door and asking if we can dig in their garden. It is a very careful and delicate process. We take photographs of everything, but anything that is found belongs to the householder or landowner."

Mrs Harrison added: "We know the crusading monks the Knights Templar had a manor around this area in the 12th century and we'll be looking for evidence of that. There was a medieval village in Temple Cowley, we have even found prehistoric artefacts in that area, so it is a very exciting place for us to search."

● To take part, email jane@archeox.net

■ **DIG IN:** Jane Harrison, *left*, and Jo Robinson from Archeox   Picture: OX60066 Ed Nix

Jo (foreground) and Jane Harrison (background) in an *Oxford Mail* report, 2013.

its challenges. Being part of a community archaeology project is no 9–5. Many a weekend was given up to digging test pits in gardens all across East Oxford, come rain or shine, and many an evening spent at talks and presentations or attempting to make a dent in the mountains of unwashed pottery sherds which lurked in our project shed. The role itself was similarly changeable; sometimes at talks for example, I would find myself event organiser, lead speaker, teacher or simply 'coffee-maker', and so one of the most challenging aspects of the job was being able to fall in to the role most needed that day.

Developing my role within the team

One of the most enjoyable parts of my role was the freedom and encouragement to be creative. I remember back in my interview for the post, cringing (visibly not just metaphorically!) as I used the phrase 'think outside of the box', but for a large portion of time on the project, that's exactly what I was encouraged to do. One of the responsibilities of my post was to broaden the project's outreach and engage a wider audience. The term 'non-self-selecting' is a very clinical way to refer to those who haven't previously shown interest in archaeology and heritage, or those that have perceived barriers to engaging with it.

I thought about people within the Oxfordshire community who might be described as non-self-selecting, and tried to envisage a way I could encourage their involvement with the project. It had become clear to me that Oxfordshire has a considerable homeless community, something I hadn't fully anticipated.

I thought that it would be a real shame not to include a community which has an identifiable presence within Oxford. A huge part of the resulting successful relationship with a number of homeless people, was a fortuitous partnership with a charity called Julian Housing, who happened to be located in East Oxford. I knew I didn't yet have the experience, or the understanding of the complex needs of this particular group of people, to know where to start. So, with the support of my project colleagues, I looked up local homeless charities and found Julian Housing. I contacted them, and was in a meeting room with one of their team, Kris Scott, before I'd had chance to blink. Kris was extremely enthusiastic and had plenty of ideas, so together we worked up a plan of suitable activities, which dealt not only with issues such as kit provision and activity location, but also the more sensitive subject of how to make the participants feel comfortable and welcome.

We concluded that the events would need to be, at least initially, held on Julian Housing premises, and in an atmosphere that enabled plenty of chatting, and like all archaeology sessions, plenty of tea drinking! I knew straight away that this called for the community archaeologist's secret weapon – pot washing. It never fails as an introductory task: it is real archaeology, pursued in a relaxed environment, introduces people to artefacts – and very little can go wrong. I was told to expect a small turn-out, and that a number of those that did come would probably leave before then end. Well, every bowl was in use, and stayed in use until it came to packing up, which everybody helped with, while making encouraging noises about doing more activities in the near future. I felt very pleased with the results of our first session.

Over the coming weeks, a number of people from Julian Housing took part in finds washing sessions, geophysical survey in the parks of East Oxford, and even the ever so pleasant task of environmental processing. (I always seemed to be the one who got banished to the shed… I tried not to take it personally.) While our time with Julian Housing was relatively short, I think it demonstrated successfully that even groups who may at first seem beyond the reach of community archaeology, can be engaged, and can in turn enrich projects, by giving another fresh perspective, and enabling the project to be as all-encompassing as possible.

Arty archaeology

I had previously dabbled in arts and crafts, and they always remained a passion of mine, so when I was asked to develop some more alternative approaches to outreach, I jumped at the chance to mix in my favourite things. I looked for art projects and groups, preferably within East Oxford, who looked like they would be open to trying something different. Following from the success of Julian Housing my lucky streak continued and I found *Artscape*, an art project for Oxford Health NHS Foundation Trust, who work in Oxfordshire and Buckinghamshire, and had a group currently working out of the Fusion Arts centre in East Oxford. The *Artscape* class is for people with dementia, as well as those who care for them, and the members work with different artists in order to create unique and original pieces with a distinctive theme.

I decided to contact the project co-ordinator Tom Cox, and asked if he thought there would be scope for us to work together. In all honesty, at this point I still wasn't exactly sure what we could work on, but inspiration wasn't far away. It was at this time that we were also excavating the Minchery Paddock monastic site (Chapter 5). I was trying to think of a way to merge the two, the art project and the excavation, and to keep it relevant, when one of the volunteers discovered a Medieval decorative tile. I suddenly realised that we could work on something relating to Medieval art, specifically tile designs, and that this would link the group's artwork with the excavations that were currently happening, despite the people being unable to participate on site. I contacted an artist who lived locally (three doors down from me), who just so happened to have a kiln in her back garden, and asked for some help and advice on tile making. I also discussed it with Tom, and so another project took shape.

A brief reflection on my time with the project

I learnt a lot during my training placement, and developed some extremely valuable skills. In terms of a community archaeology project model, I learnt that some things work and others don't. Pretty obvious, but completely true. What didn't work as well on this project might be extremely successful within a different community and vice versa. As communities, we are too individual for 'one size fits all', that's what gives us our unique identities, and understanding those identities fuels a project's success. There are of course, more general approaches that I would adopt into any future projects: allowing more time, drawing the volunteers further into guiding the project, and taking more time to identify pre-existing groups that may be interested in engaging with the project in weird and wonderful ways.

One of the most memorable parts of the East Oxford Project for me was being part of the community that it created. People from East Oxford, but also from other parts of the county, of all ages, all abilities, and each with a differing interest, all came together under one project, to create a community within a community.

Katie Hambrook

I enjoy how archaeology and the study of place-names both allow me to reconstruct in my mind past landscapes and buildings. Now, because of my involvement with the project, wherever I go in East Oxford I can imagine the fields and settlements that existed there in the Middle Ages. One of my roles in the project was to lead the work of the Place-Names Group. This was a small group of volunteers who researched the old field names of the area. Apart from Peter Finn, who acted as our linguistic expert, none of the others had studied field names before.

Katie on Magdalen Bridge, Oxford.

I enjoyed introducing the members of the group to methods of studying field names and helping them to use local and College archives for their research. We had fascinating meetings where we shared our research and discussed what the field names told us about East Oxford in the past. The other part of the Project that meant a lot to me was the Minchery Paddock excavation. I have a longstanding interest in Medieval nunneries, and particularly in Littlemore Priory. I loved seeing the remains of the buildings being gradually revealed, and looking at and handling objects that the nuns had used.

Leigh and Gill Mellor

When we moved to Oxford from London in 2010, both of us were retired and decided to turn our armchair archaeology into something more practical. Searching online, we found a reference to 'The East Oxford Archaeology and History Project' which was just starting and sent off our names as volunteers. For the last five years, we have learnt how to dig ('clean up your loose', 'no sitting on the edge of the trench', 'sharp, straight edges', 'have you read and signed the health and safety?', 'are those context sheets *fully* filled-in?') and have taken part in all of the major digs at Bartlemas, Minchery Paddock (Littlemore Priory) and Donnington Recreation Ground, as well as many small test-pits. We have learnt to recognise different types of pottery, bones and other finds and how to clean, sort and mark them. Then there were sessions (involving lots of water) handling environmental samples, looking for tiny finds, seeds, bones and other environmental evidence, in the shed at Oxford Archaeology. The resulting finds when dried were examined under a microscope. Alongside all this, there was plenty of research to be done into old maps and records. Leigh has done a lot of work on mapping and Gill has concentrated on finds.

Everyone in Oxford has been very helpful and supportive: the Project team, staff at the Ashmolean, various Colleges, the Bodleian, the City and County Archaeologists and staff of commercial archaeology units, Oxford Archaeology and Thames Valley Archaeological Services. Along the way there have been teaching sessions, workshops, dig open days, social events and art projects. We have enjoyed every minute and made some very good friends.

Leslie Wilkinson

Archeox has been a wonderful experience for me all around. From providing me with opportunities in charnel pit excavation at Bartlemas Chapel to the analysis of test pits, I was able confirm my passion in archaeology. This has encouraged me to pursue further study in the discipline. As a result, I have undertaken an MA in Maritime Archaeology at the University of Southampton.

I was very lucky to have heard about *Archeox* through a reporter from the *Oxford Mail*. With *Archeox*, I was provided with free training within an on-going and long-term project. The excavation at Bartlemas was very exciting. This included sensitively lifting human bones to understand these past peoples in relationship to the site, as well as extending knowledge in the greater context of Medieval people and leper hospitals. I learnt to record context sheets, create detailed drawings (plans and sections), measure and record small finds, identify bones, prepare soil samples and process them using flotation. Not only was I given excellent training, but I was provided with the experience of working with a great team in an area that was too long overlooked as a result of its relationship with Oxford city centre.

I want to use my experience and knowledge to work in the archaeological field both on land and in water. Most of all, I hope to use my background as a teacher

Gill and Leigh processing finds at Ark-T Centre.

Leslie, having recently excavated this piece of human pelvis from the charnel pit at Bartlemas (David Manners).

to provide opportunities and encourage a passion for archaeology amongst all ages and backgrounds.

Louise Bailey

My time with the *Archeox* project has been full of invaluable and memorable experiences. I can honestly say that I loved every single minute of it; from excavating in seemingly endless rain, to staring down a microscope attempting to distinguish between a piece of grit and a fish bone; from supervising and directing a mechanical digger in a fluorescent yellow jacket, to carefully inking in trench drawings trying not to smudge the lines; and from uncovering my first ever small find (a Civil War clay pipe) to learning how to record 3D co-ordinates. I have learnt more about archaeology than I even knew existed and I got the chance to have a direct physical connection with the past – my local history – and I will never forget that. Alongside all of this (as if it wasn't enough) I have met the most amazing and genuinely nice people from all walks of life; individuals with many skills and talents that I have been able to learn from and with whom I shared these unforgettable experiences with.

Mandy Bellamy

My name is actually Maraleen and my four sisters are Maureen, Kathleen, Sharleen and Rosealeen; we also have three brothers. I was born in 1948 in the Churchill Hospital but my siblings were all born in our family home in Spencer Crescent, Rose Hill, in East Oxford.

It was in 2010 that I developed an interest in archaeology, after listening to an interesting talk given by

Louise fronts a stall at a Blackbird Leys family fun day.

Neil Stevenson. Neil was the Community Engagement Partnership Officer at The Museum of Oxford. I was inspired to join the archaeology workshops at the Museum. At one of these workshops Jane Harrison gave a talk and later we heard from her about the East Oxford History and Archaeology project. I had always wanted to learn more about the history of East Oxford. It was by coincidence that Chris Turley and I

Mandy at work at Bartlemas Chapel.

both decided to join. Chris and I had been friends for over 25 years before we lost touch. Renewing our friendship by working together learning the many aspects of archaeology was a joy. We dug together at both Bartlemas and Minchery Paddock, and my favourite moment was at Minchery (Trench 2) when, side by side, we started uncovering what turned out to be a hearth made of tile from Medieval times.

Marcus Cooper with Charlie Cooper

In 2009 I began a part-time Undergraduate Certificate in Archaeology at the University of Oxford Department for Continuing Education, and it was there in 2011 during a lecture given by Dr David Griffiths that I heard about the *Archeox* project. I thought it would be a great opportunity to put into practice some of the things I had learnt on the Certificate course training excavation earlier that year, to learn new skills and gain some additional experience. I was also happy to learn that my son Charlie, who was only seven at the time, would be welcome to take part in the project too.

The Bartlemas Chapel dig was the beginning of our involvement with the project, and it holds special memories for both myself and Charlie. We had a lovely time over the three weekends we spent there and the weather was unseasonably good too. I couldn't think of a better way to spend weekends than digging with my son in such a spot with some lovely people. The learning environment was great too: although we worked hard the atmosphere was relaxed, trying our hands at many different jobs. It wasn't long before Jane Harrison gave Charlie the very responsible position of chief staff-wielder during levelling operations, a role he

Charlie and Marcus working at Bartlemas: T-shirts in October!

was very proud of; but I think his favourite position was that of meeting and greeting at the gate on Open Day. Welcoming people in and armed with a smile, Charlie was in his element. Charlie and I returned later to dig on the Minchery Paddock excavation, reuniting with some familiar faces and meeting new ones, Charlie teaming up with his pals Paul and Alfie. Charlie often talks about his time on the project with a smile, and he still asks me if the tile he found at Bartlemas is in a museum with his name under it yet.

Molly Storey, with Leo and Nell

At a time when I was feeling my life was rushing by without my being able to do things that interested me, I happened to see an *Archeox* pamphlet. I joined and expressed my interested in taking part in the Minchery dig. As a parent with three young children, it was important that anything I did was something that the children could also participate in. The first Sunday we arrived at Minchery we were greeted warmly by Jane Harrison, who accommodated us in Trench 3 with Jo. We all set to work with relish – scraping, finding, learning about the objects we found, emptying buckets and, from time-to-time, when the children fancied a change, sieving soil. Everyone was friendly and welcoming, and Jo was remarkably patient with children.

My two older children – Leo and Nell (8 and 6 at the time) – were completely enthralled. Nell was the first to find something, which greatly pleased her! She found a piece of medieval pot with a deep glossy green glaze and a criss-cross pattern incised into it. Shortly afterwards Leo found a piece of medieval pot with a light yellowish green mottled glaze. I remember finding pieces of very fine wire, I put them in my finds tray and later, at an architectural exhibition of display designs for our finds. I found out that they were pins for nuns' wimples – fascinating, I would never have guessed!

Later that same day, Leo found something which looked very much a like a stick. When he showed it to Jo, she told him it was a bone. There were small scratches and gnaw marks in it, so it seemed likely that it had been moved from somewhere else by an animal. This was the icing on the cake for Leo, who went around telling everyone he knew about it for the next two weeks. By the end of the day we had uncovered the foundations of two walls meeting at a corner. In other areas of the trench, we heard exclamations about all the oyster shells that were being dug up in the midden area. Jo also found the most elegant piece of roof tile; its points and curves were so stylistically medieval. They reminded me of a court jester's attire.

The next Sunday saw us positioned in Trench 2 with Jane. The excitement continued. We found pieces of Medieval and Roman pottery, and a piece of boar tusk! Every find left us feeling elated, it was lovely to see the children so fascinated and absorbed. My most memorable moment was when I uncovered something pale green. It was small, elongated and pressed flat into the soil. Jane told me that it was the end of a saddle strap or belt. On closer inspection it was possible to see the most exquisite entwining leaf pattern decorating the metal: I imagined the person it had belonged to and what their life would have entailed.

We continued to take part in all the subsequent digs that were available to us: I also took some days off work to help with the excavation at Donnington. It was refreshing to meet people from so many different walks of life. Not only did I enjoy learning about archaeological processes, I also really enjoyed the sense of companionship and community that the project evoked in all those that took part. It was lovely to share stories, knowledge and experiences over a cup of tea and a biscuit.

When asking Leo and Nell what they liked best about the project, they both said they liked finding things and then finding out about the things that they had found. Nell liked finds washing as she got to look at and handle finds in detail. Both children still count archaeology as one of the main things they'd like to do when they grow up. For my part, the whole *Archeox* experience, from lectures, to sessions on specialist areas, to finds washing and sorting, to inking archaeological drawings, to looking at soil samples under microscopes, has been completely fulfilling. I found myself eagerly awaiting each new opportunity offered. I've always been interested in archaeology, but had never had the opportunity to try it. I now know that archaeology makes the past become tangible. It's tactile and visual as opposed to bookish. I feel indebted to the *Archeox* project: it brought our local area's past to life and has given us experiences together as a family that we will cherish.

Northfield School and the Minchery Paddock excavation

Stella Collier: I became involved with *Archeox* with my son Greg, and took part in different activities, which we both found very interesting. The whole process of learning how to actually participate in a dig and to record finds is fascinating and was very professionally done by a friendly team. It was easy to become a part of the team no matter how little experience you had at the beginning.

As I work at Northfield School I thought that the students would gain a lot from taking part in something they would not normally be involved with. The site is situated close to the school. This was the first time any of the boys has taken part in any type of archaeology: they attended the dig one day a week over a number of weeks. The students were able to participate in all areas of the dig and worked as part of the team with members of the public and the *Archeox* team: this helped the students with their social skills.

The work the students did was also linked to many parts of the curriculum for example, history, maths,

Molly and children (centre) with other volunteers at Minchery Paddock.

science and art. The students were drawn into the history of Littlemore Priory and how the finds showed what kind of life was led there. All the students were taught how to take part in a dig with professionalism and were amazed themselves to uncover interesting objects, such as a pig's lower jaw, oyster shells, Medieval roof tiles and much more. It was a fantastic opportunity for both the students and myself, and really brought history to life for us.

Northfield School is a Special School for students aged 11–18 years, with Social, Emotional, and Mental Health Needs. The school is situated in Blackbird Leys, Oxford, and accepts students from across Oxfordshire. https://northfieldschool.co.uk/

Olaf Bayer

I worked as an *Archeox* project Officer for 2 years from April 2012. At the time I had just completed a PhD in Prehistoric landscape archaeology, and before that I had worked on commercial and academic archaeological research projects since the mid-1990s. Although I had lived in East Oxford on and off since 2001, and during that time had worked from Cornwall to Lancashire, I had never really considered the past on my own doorstep, archaeology was always something that happened elsewhere. The project offered me an amazing opportunity to discover the archaeology of my home landscape whilst sharing my archaeological skills and knowledge.

I now have a far deeper understanding of how East Oxford came to be as it is, and made some lasting

friendships along the way. The project was particularly interesting as we had to adapt the normally rural techniques of landscape archaeology to suburban context. Highlights for me were: recording earthworks by gaffer taping the project's survey grade GPS to one of the city council's tractors as it cut the grass in Southpark; and combining lidar data and geophysical survey to discover previously unknown prehistoric features next to the football pitch on Donnington Recreation Ground. After the project finished I worked briefly for Oxford Archaeology, spent a year as a departmental lecturer at OUDCE, and I now combine my day job as an archaeological investigator for Historic England with occasional teaching at OUDCE.

Peter Finn

Originally from Zimbabwe, I've lived in the UK since 1988, and in Temple Cowley, with my wife Jackie, for several years. I have a long-standing interest in archaeology, history and language and the interfaces between these – especially, how the study of language can inform the study of history and prehistory, in areas such as place-name analysis – and I have taught and researched in the field of English sociohistorical linguistics at various UK universities. I would have loved to have got my hands dirty in East

Olaf (left) with the Trench 1 team at Minchery Paddock (David Pinches, Julian Stern and Will Hemmings).

Oxford – I've previously volunteered on excavations at Crickley Hill (Gloucestershire), Guildford Castle (Surrey) and Beedon (Oxfordshire) – but my day job as a digital development editor at the Open University in Milton Keynes precluded this, so I opted to focus on another area where I felt I could contribute. I have greatly enjoyed working with the other volunteers in the place-names group as well as more widely.

Phil Price

I have always had a strong interest in local history and how previous generations managed to live and develop their environment. When I decided to consider 'early retirement' one of the key activities I was hoping to embrace was archaeology. My academic background was in Chemistry and Material Sciences and my career had been in the pharmaceutical industry. I found out very quickly that there was a common link between the pharmaceutical industry and archaeology in that accurate recording and complete traceability was a key activity.

I became a volunteer for the project after visiting the magical Bartlemas site. I quickly discovered it was 'the digging, finding and recording' aspect that I enjoyed the most, along with the teamwork and general camaraderie. Once I had become familiar with the excavation process, and the terminology such as 'clean up your loose' before tea break and 'mattocking', it become almost a joy to spend four-six hours on my knees sifting earth and looking for artefacts which could help define how the site had been

used! Bartlemas was a fascinating introduction to archaeology. There was not only the existing building and foundations of previous structures but also the burial ground. The mass of finds, some of which dated from the twelfth century, added more interest to each day. Landscapes and sites were assessed using earlier archaeological reports and evaluations, old maps and techniques such as geophysics. I was subsequently involved in various test pits in the Iffley and Rose Hill areas and major excavations at Minchery Paddock and Donnington Recreation Ground. The best finds for me must be the prehistoric flint arrowhead and the fire-hearth in Trench 2, Minchery Paddock.

Roelie Reed

To me, this project has been a real eye-opener, not only archaeologically, but more importantly in the discovery of quiet places in the busy suburbs of Oxford. One of the first events I attended was a walk along the Boundary Brook from the urban nature reserve to Cowley Marsh, the Golf Club, Warneford Meadow and back to the nature reserve. We 'visited' a whole range of periods on this single walk: from Bronze Age and Iron Age to Romano British, Medieval and modern times, all within a couple of miles. Another amazing experience was the discovery of Bartlemas Chapel, up its peaceful lane just off the noisy Cowley Road. The cottages, the multi-period farm house, the chapel and the seventeenth century almshouse take you away from the modern hustle and

Phil (left) and Mark Franks planning at Bartlemas Chapel.

Roelie excavating at Minchery Paddock.

bustle straight back to a much earlier age. It looks like time has stood still in this tranquil corner.

The excavation at the Minchery Paddock turned out to be another revelation, this time in a part of Oxford not known for its tranquillity. The area west of the then public house, very overgrown and covered in brambles, was once part of Littlemore Priory, but the lay-out of the buildings had been lost. Local people using the public footpath next to the excavation site regularly came for a chat as we worked and were keen to hear about their area's history. The project was not just the excavations and discovery of new places, it was also about meeting new people, many of whom had never held a trowel but became very good excavators; about the visiting school children, keen to learn about the history and having a go at archaeology – several came back after school to help out. They all contributed to making the project an unforgettable experience.

Steve Nicholson

I'm now retired, but among my varied jobs I've been a navy signalman, a car factory computer operator and had a successful but brief stint as a driving instructor.

Steve recording a test pit.

I was also a volunteer at a city-funded IT project to help people use computers, but I had finished that and was looking around for a new role when I saw an *Archeox* article calling for volunteers in the *Oxford Mail* at the end of 2010.

At one of the first sessions Jane said we could be as involved as little or as much as we liked, which I realised was exactly what I wanted to hear. Initially I was only interested in the digging side of archaeology and was not at all interested in pottery washing, or finds sorting, or drawing or measuring … but as time went on I wanted to know more about the stuff I was digging up, which meant I was drawn more and more into those activities that had not initially interested me. I remember in the early days of my digging career finding an amazing dinosaur-like long, vicious tooth, and held it up for acclaim, only to be told the long pointy item was in fact a root. What a let-down....

I have also helped out at lots of the mini-digs known as test pits in people's back gardens, as well as the several large digs lasting weeks. I still enjoy digging and finding things the most enjoyable, but adding knowledge through all those other activities improves the digging experience. Some of the things we dug up were researched further, as I did with an arrowhead I found at Bartlemas Chapel, which is very interesting and enjoyable.

Tim Lee

Like many people, I've had a lifelong interest in history and in particular archaeology but had always thought of it as the province of academics and young students. I therefore leapt at the opportunity presented by the *Archeox* project when it was first publicised. Having lived and worked in East Oxford for the last thirty years, being able to join digs in my own home area seemed like a dream come true. I was able to join a number of test pits in various back gardens, and the householders clearly loved the opportunity to find out more about the history which was, quite literally, on their doorstep! I particularly enjoyed the Bartlemas dig, revealing as it did so much about the history of East Oxford. The story of the leper hospital, royal patronage, civil war and agricultural landscapes was brought to life by the evidence dug out of the ground. That, for me, is the fascination of archaeology – every new excavation and every scrape of the trowel or mattock reveals something new which had remained hidden for generations.

As well as the digs I learnt a lot from all of the technical work which is now an essential part of archaeology – the geophysical surveys, GPS calculations and systematic recording methods provided an opportunity to learn new skills and stretch my intellect. However, one of the memories which will stay with me is very different: the sight of enthusiastic young volunteers from Northfield School up to their knees in mud at Minchery Paddock, digging in waterlogged Trench 1. Now that's what I call commitment to the pursuit of knowledge!

Thomas Matthews-Boehmer

My interest in archaeology was first stimulated by visiting a number of historic and archaeologically significant places around Oxford and the Chilterns. The East Oxford Project helped encourage my interest, and has offered a way to keep up with the significant local discoveries made in archaeology I have mainly been involved in the project in two ways: first as it gave me the chance to carry out a professional geophysical survey while I was still at school. Secondly, I had the opportunity to work on a dig at Minchery Paddock and so was given the chance to investigate periods with which I hadn't come into contact.

Both of these involvements have been very important in helping me develop the skills and insights to make my own way in archaeological study after school. I went on to study Ancient History and Classical Archaeology at Warwick University. On a less personal level, the project is having a great impact in increasing people's exposure to archaeology around Oxford through relating it to their daily life in their area. I very much hope that this continues as the world needs to deepen its understanding of the distant past which, despite surface appearances, continues to inform life today.

Valeria Cambule

The time spent with the project has been an important phase of my life. When I moved to Oxford from Italy, I looked for a way which would allow me to learn quickly about the local surroundings. Then, talking with people I heard about a community project which organised activities relating to the history and archaeology of Oxford and was accessible to all.

Having always been interested in historical subjects I started to volunteer with the *Archeox* project, which allowed me to partake in many activities and interact with people who shared common interests. In this period, one of the events that I still remember clearly was the Chapel service for the reburial of human remains from the Bartlemas excavation. A religious celebration surrounded by sermons and sung with a medieval flavour that certainly enchanted all who attended, myself included: a respectful reinternment that hopefully was appreciated by the unfortunate souls. The *Archeox* project taught everyone interested in archaeology and history many new skills, such as finds sorting, recording and object handling and it let them enjoy archeological sites, lectures and workshops. These were activities in which volunteers had the opportunity to increase their knowledge about different subjects and to build friendly relationships with the project coordinators and other local people. (see page 21 for my study of the Chester Street Neolithic hand-axe).

These experiences allow the community to appreciate how much time and effort goes into preserving

Thomas excavating at Minchery Paddock.

Valeria at the location of the discovery of the hand-axe which she researched.

our past, and how crucial the work of the *Archeox* project has been to fully engage the community participation and to involve local people in discovering more about the past city of Oxford.

Will Hemmings

Archaeology has been in me since childhood. I remember with affection digs in my youth at Hascombe hillfort, Barnsley Park and Wroxeter, but no practical archaeological experience was as important as the one at Minchery Paddock. This dig marked a return to archaeological excavation after thirty-five years. It was through a friend that I read an article in the local *Leys News* which described the excavation, inviting public involvement. Here was something new: archaeology was being marketed as an important community asset. Another change I discovered, also for the better, was the standardisation of methods for recording data. The potential now existed for enthusiasts like myself to make significant contributions in the field. So, praise be! I was trusted. I learned to throw aside my unorthodox recording methods and apply contemporary techniques, and was encouraged to dig on.

So what was it like? To say it was the most enjoyable dig I have worked on would be selling the reader short of the facts. The experience cannot be summed up by attempting to communicate the excitement of uncovering features such as the intricately laid hearth or the ambivalently thrown dump of tiles, because the experience represented so much more than that. Likewise, any description of the thrill of unearthing artefacts such as the conjoined pot fragments or a tiny, beautifully crafted bead would also be insufficient. For me, the revelation was that for the archaeological process to be valid, one must trowel with one hand and think with the other, and I had the very

Will Hemmings excavating at Minchery Paddock.

good fortune to be working in areas for a sustained period of time, which focuses this process perfectly. There is no joy quite like the one attached to watching successive phases come and go as the layers are stripped away, like a silent, time-lapsed visit through the generations, now quiet with the restfulness of a pastoral landscape, now furtive with the flowing of rapid waters, here alive and clamouring with the burning waste of industrial processes, there decaying in the twisted metalwork and rubble of abandoned buildings. To see it, smell it, and feel it, as I have done during the excavations at Minchery Paddock is the essence of archaeology, and I am immensely satisfied and extremely privileged to have experienced and been part of it.

Bibliography

Allen, I. M., D. Britton, and H.H. Coghlan (1970) *Metallurgical Reports on British and Irish Bronze Age: Implements and Weapons in the Pitt Rivers Museum*, (Occasional paper on Technology, 10) Oxford: Oxford University Press.

Andonova, E. and B. Wyatt (2015) *Impact Evaluation Report on the East Oxford Archaeology and History Project (Archeox)*, Oxford: OUDCE and Isis Innovation. See ORA project archive

Arkell, W.J. (1947) *Oxford Stone*. London: Faber and Faber.

Atkins, R. and E. S. Popescu (2003) 'Excavations at the Hospital of St Mary Magdalen, Partney, Lincolnshire', *Medieval Archaeology* 54(1), 204-270.

Atkinson, R. and A. McKenzie (1946-7) 'Archaeological Notes and News' *Oxoniensia* 11-12, 163.

Atkinson, R.J.C., C.M. Piggott and N.K. Sandars (1951) *Excavations at Dorchester on Thames, Oxon, first report. Sites I, II, IV, V, and VI with a chapter on henge monuments*, Oxford: Ashmolean Museum.

Aston, M. and C. Gerrard (2012) *Interpreting the English Village: Landscape and Community at Shapwick, Somerset*, Macclesfield: Windgather Press.

Attlee, J. (2007) *Isolarion, A Different Oxford Journey*, London: Black Swan.

Barton, R. N. E., P.J. Berridge, M.J.C. Walker and R.E. Bevins (1995) 'Persistent Places in the Mesolithic Landscape: an Example from the Black Mountain Uplands of South Wales' *Proceedings of the Prehistoric Society* 61, 81-116.

Basset, B. (1987) *Newman at Littlemore*, reprinted 2019, Leominster: Gracewing.

Beck, S.V. (1997) 'Rickets: Where the Sun Doesn't Shine' in Kiple, K.F. (ed), 130-35.

Beckley, R. and D. Radford (2012) *Oxford Archaeological Resource Assessment 2011: Palaeolithic to Mesolithic (500,000–4000 BC); Neolithic and Bronze Age (4000–800 BC); The Iron Age (800 BC–43 AD); Roman Oxford (43–410 AD); Anglo-Saxon and Viking Oxford (410–1066); Norman Oxford (1066-1205); Medieval Oxford (1205–15400; Post-Medieval Oxford (1540–1800); Modern Oxford (1800–1950)*, Oxford City Council. Available online at: https://www.oxford.gov.uk/downloads/20200/archaeology

Benedict, Order of St, 'Rule of Benedict, Chapter 22': http://www.osb.org/rb/text/rbefjo3.html#22 (accessed 29/5/14).

Benson, D. and D. Miles, D. (1974) *The Upper Thames Valley, An Archaeological survey of the River Gravels*, Oxford: Oxford Archaeological Unit.

Binney, M. (1982) *Taking the Plunge: The Architecture of Bathing*, London: Save Britain's Heritage.

Binns, A. (1989) *Dedications of Monastic Houses in England and Wales, 1066–1216*, Woodbridge: Boydell Press.

Blair, J. (1994) *Anglo-Saxon Oxfordshire*, Stroud: Alan Sutton.

Blair, J. and B. Crawford (1997) 'A Late-Viking Burial at Magdalen Bridge, Oxford?' *Oxoniensia* 62, 135-144.

Bond, J. (2003) 'English Medieval Nunneries: Buildings, Precincts and Estates,' in D. Wood, (ed.) *Women and Religion in Medieval England*, Oxford: Oxbow Books, 46-90.

Booth, P. (1995) 'Blackbird Leys Peripheral Road,' *Oxford Archaeological Watching Brief*, Oxford Archaeology: unpublished report.

Booth, P., A. Dodd, M. Robinson and A. Smith (2007) *The Thames through Time, The Archaeology of the Gravel terraces of the Upper and Middle Thames, The Early Historical Period AD 1–1000*, Oxford: Thames Valley Landscapes Monograph 27.

Booth, P., and G. Edgeley-Long (2003) 'Prehistoric settlement and Roman pottery production at Blackbird Leys, Oxford' *Oxoniensia* 68, 201-63.

Boston, C. (2004) '2 Stephen's Road, Headington' *South Midlands Archaeology* 34, 70.

Bowker, M. (ed.) (1967) *An episcopal court book for the diocese of Lincoln: 1514-1520*, Lincoln: Lincoln Record Society.

Bradley, R. and M. Edmonds (1993) *Interpreting the axe trade: production and exchange in Neolithic Britain*, Cambridge: Cambridge University Press.

Brewer, J.S. (ed.) (1875) *Letters and Papers, Foreign and Domestic, of the reign of Henry VIII, Volume 4: 1524–1530*, London: HMSO.

Burton, J. (1994) *Monastic and Religious Orders in Britain 1000–1300*, Cambridge: Cambridge University Press.

Caley, J. (ed.) (1821) *Valor ecclesiasticus temp. Henr. VIII. Vol. 4*, Record Commission, London: Eyre and Spottiswoode.

Carver, M, A. Sanmark and S. Semple (eds) (2010) *Signals of Belief in Early England: Anglo-Saxon Paganism Revisited*, Oxford: Oxbow.

Case, H. (1953) 'Mesolithic finds in the Oxford area', *Oxoniensia*, 17-18, 1-13.

Challis, C. (2005) 'Iron Age and Roman Features at Eastfield House, Brasenose Driftway, Oxford' *Oxoniensia* 70, 97-113.

Cherry, J. (1991) 'Pottery and Tile' in J. Blair and N. Ramsay (eds) *English Medieval Industries*, London: Hambledon Press, 189-209.

Chibnall, M (ed.) (1969-1980) (6 vols) *The Ecclesiastical History of Orderic Vitalis*, Oxford: Clarendon Press.

Christie, N., O. Creighton, M. Edgeworth and H. Hamerow (2013) *Transforming Townscapes: From burh to borough: the archaeology of Wallingford, AD 800-1400*, Society for Medieval Archaeology Monograph 35, Leeds: Maney.

Clark, A. (ed.) (1889) *Survey of the Antiquities of the City of Oxford, composed in 1661-6 by Anthony Wood, Vol. I, the City and Suburbs*, Oxford: Clarendon Press.

Clark, A. (ed.) (1890) *Survey of the Antiquities of the City of Oxford, composed in 1661-6 by Anthony Wood, Vol. II, Churches and Religious Houses*, Oxford: Clarendon Press.

Clark, A. (ed.) (1891-1900) (5 vols) 'The Life and Times of Anthony Wood, Antiquary, of Oxford, 1632–1695, Described by Himself', *Oxford Historical Society* 19, 21, 26, 30, 40: Oxford: Clarendon Press.

Clark, A. (ed.) (1907) *The English Register of Oseney Abbey, Part 1,* London: Kegan Paul.

Clay, R.M. (1909) *The Medieval Hospitals of England,* reprinted 1966. London: Frank Cass.

Coates R., and A. Breeze (2000) *Celtic Voices, English places: studies of the Celtic impact on place-names in England,* Stamford: Shaun Tyas.

Cobbold, E.S. (1880) 'Notes on the strata exposed in laying out the Oxford sewerage works at Sandford on Thames' *Quarterly Journal of the Geological Society* 36, 314-20.

Coombs, D. (ed.) (2012) *Roman Catholicism in Littlemore*, Littlemore Local History Society Pamphlet.

Coppock, G.A., B.M. Hill and E.A Greening-Lamborn (1933) *Headington Quarry and Shotover, A History compiled on behalf of the Quarry Womens' Institute,* Oxford: Oxford University Press.

Crawford, B. (2008) *The Churches dedicated to St Clement in Medieval England, a hagio-geography of the seafarers' saint in 11th century north Europe,* St Petersburg, Axioma.

Day, P. (1991) 'Post-Glacial Vegetational History of the Oxford Region' *New Phytology cxix*: 445-70.

Davis, R. (1797) *A new map of the County of Oxford,* London: J. Cary.

Debus, A.G. (ed.) (1974) *Medicine in 17th Century England,* Berkeley: University of California Press.

Devaney, R. (2005) 'Ceremonial and domestic flint arrowheads' *Lithics: The Journal of the Lithic Studies Society* 26: 9–22.

Dewe, J. (c.1842) *A Handbook for Oxford,* Oxford.

Dey, H. W. (2008) '*Diaconiae, xenodochia, hospitalia* and monasteries: 'social security' and the meaning of monasticism in early medieval Rome' *Early Medieval Europe* 16.4, 398-422.

Dickinson, T.M. and H. Härke (1992) *Early Anglo Saxon Shields.* London: Society of Antiquaries of London.

Dodd, A. (ed.) (2003) *Oxford before the University,* Oxford: Thames Valley Landscapes Monograph 17.

Druce, G. C. (1886) *The flora of Oxfordshire,* Oxford: Parker and Co.

Durham, B. (1977) 'Archaeological Investigations in St. Aldates, Oxford' *Oxoniensia* 42, 83-203.

Durham, B. (1984) 'The Thames Crossing at Oxford, Archaeological Studies 1979-82' *Oxoniensia* 49, 57-100.

Durham, B. (1990) 'Bartlemas House and Chapel', *The Quarterly Newsletter of the Oxford Archaeological Unit 18(2),* 21-2.

Egan, G. and F. Pritchard (1991) *Dress Accessories c.1150–c.1450,* Medieval finds from excavations in London 3, London: Museum of London/HMSO.

Egan, G. (1998) *The Medieval Household: Daily Living c.1150–c.1450,* Medieval finds from excavations in London 6, London: Museum of London/Boydell.

Egan, G. (2005) *Material culture in London in an age of transition, Tudor and Stuart period finds from excavations at riverside sites in Southwark,* MoLAS Monograph 19, London: Museum of London/English Heritage.

Ekwall, E. (1964) *The Concise Oxford Dictionary of English Place-Names* 4th ed, Oxford: Clarendon Press.

Fitzpatrick, A. (2012) *The Amesbury Archer and the Boscombe Bowmen: Bell Beaker burials at Boscombe Down, Amesbury, Wiltshire.* Salisbury: The Trust for Wessex Archaeology.

Ford, S. (2005) *Temple Cowley Middle School, Cowley, Oxford; an Archaeological Evaluation,* unpublished report for Thames Valley Archaeological Services Ltd.

Foster, J. (1891) *Alumni Oxonienses: the members of the University of Oxford, 1500-1714, Vol. 2,* London: Parker & Co.

Gaffney, C. and J. Gater (2003) *Revealing the Buried Past: Geophysics for Archaeologists*, Stroud: Tempus.

Ganz, D. (1972) 'The Buildings of Godstow Nunnery' *Oxoniensia* 37, 150-57.

Gee, E.A. (1953) 'Oxford Masons 1370–1530', *The Archaeological Journal* 109, 53-131.

Gelling, M and D.M. Stenton (1953–4) *The Place-Names of Oxfordshire*, English Place-Name Society (2 Vols), Cambridge: Cambridge University Press.

Gelling, M. and A. Cole, (2000) *The Landscape of Place-Names*, Stamford: Shaun Tyas.

Gerrard, C. and M. Aston (2007) *The Shapwick Project, Somerset: A Rural Landscape Explored*, Society for Medieval Archaeology Monograph 25, Leeds: Maney.

Gibson, A. (1992) 'Possible Timber Circles at Dorchester-on-Thames' *Oxford Journal of Archaeology* 11 (1), 85-91.

Gilchrist, R. (1995) *Contemplation and Action: The Other Monasticism*, Leicester: Leicester University Press.

Gilchrist, R. (2008) 'Magic for the Dead? The Archaeology of Magic in Later Medieval Burials' *Medieval Archaeology* 52, 119-159.

Gilchrist, R. (2012) *Medieval Life, Archaeology and the Life Course*, Woodbridge: Boydell.

Gilchrist, R. and B. Sloane (2005) *Requiem: the Medieval Monastic Cemetery in Britain*. London: Museum of London Archaeology Service.

Gill, J. (2007) *St. George's House, Littlemore, Assessment of historic significance of staircase*, Oxford: Oxford Archaeology Report 3554.

Glisson, F. (1650) *De Rachitide Sive Morbo Puerili, Qui Vulgo the Rickets Dicitur*, London: Dugard.

Glisson, F., G. Bate and A. Regemorter (1651) *A Treatise of Rickets being a Disease Common to Children*, London: Cole.

Goldman, L. (1995) *Dons and Workers, Oxford and Adult Education since 1850*, Oxford: Oxford University Press.

Graham, M (1973) *Henry Taunt of Oxford: A Victorian Photographer*, Yeovil: The Oxford Illustrated Press.

Graham, M. and L. Waters (2002) *Cowley and East Oxford: Past and Present*, Stroud: Sutton Publishing.

Graham-Campbell, J. (1991) 'Anglo-Scandinavian equestrian equipment in eleventh-century England' *Anglo-Norman Studies* 14, 77-89.

Green, H. S. (1980) *The flint arrowheads of the British Isles*. Oxford: British Archaeological Reports (British Series No.75).

Green, S. (1983) 'The Roman Pottery-Manufacturing Site at Between Towns Road, Cowley, Oxford' *Oxoniensia* 48, 1-13.

Haberly, L. (1937) *Medieval English Paving Tiles*, Oxford: Basil Blackwell.

Harden, D.B. (1936) 'Two Romano-British Potters'-Fields near Oxford' *Oxoniensia* 1, 81-102.

Harte, J. (2008) *English Holy Wells: A Sourcebook*, Loughborough: Heart of Albion.

Heaney, M (ed.) (2017) *Percy Manning, the man who collected Oxfordshire*, Oxford: Archaeopress.

Hey, G., P. Garwood, M. Robinson, A. Barclay and P. Bradley (2011) *The Thames through Time, The Archaeology of the Gravel Terraces of the Upper and Middle Thames, Early Prehistory to 1500 BC*, Oxford: Thames Valley Landscapes Monograph 32.

Hicks, D. and A. Stevenson (2013) *World Archaeology at the Pitt Rivers Museum, A Characterisation*, Oxford: Archaeopress.

Holgate, R. (1988) *Neolithic Settlement of the Thames Basin*. Oxford: British Archaeological Reports (British Series No. 194).

Jahn, M. (1916) *Die Bewaffnung der Germanen in der alteren Eisenzeit etwa von 700 vor Christ bis 200 nach Christ*. Würzberg: Kurt Kabitsch.

JMHS (2002) *Bernwood First school, North way, Barton, Oxford*, Beckley: John Moore Heritage Services.

JMHS (2006) *An Archaeological Evaluation at Minchery Farm Paddock, on behalf of Oxford City Council*, Beckley: John Moore Heritage Services.

JMHS (2008) *Archaeological Watching Brief at Emmaus Community, 169 Oxford Road, Cowley, Oxford*, Beckley: John Moore Heritage Services.

JMHS (2011) *An Archaeological Watching brief at the Site of the former King of Prussia, 76 Rose Hill, Oxford*, Report to Midcounties Co-operative, Beckley: John Moore Heritage Services.

JMHS (2016) *Littlemore Priory, Grenoble Road, Littlemore, Oxford, Archaeological Excavation report on behalf of The Firoka Group*, Beckley: John Moore Heritage Services.

Jobson, A. L. (2006) 'The Oxfordshire Eyre Roll of 1261', Unpublished PhD thesis, King's College, London.

Jones, G. (2006) 'St Nicholas, icon of mercantile virtues: transition and continuity of a European myth', in R. Littlejohns and S. Soncini (eds), *Myths of Europe in Transition*, Amsterdam: Rodope, 73-88.

Jones, R. (2005) 'Signatures in the Soil: the Use of Pottery in Manure Scatters in the Identification of Medieval Arable Farming Regimes' *Archaeological Journal* 161, 159-188.

Jones, R. and M. Page (2006) *Medieval Villages in an English Landscape: Beginnings and Ends*, Macclesfield: Windgather Press.

Keevill, G. and T. Durden (1997) 'Archaeological Work at the Rover Plant Site, Cowley, Oxford' *Oxoniensia* 62, 87-100.

Kelly, S. E. (ed.) (2000-01) *Charters of Abingdon Abbey part 2,* Oxford: Oxford University Press.

Kimuhu, J. M. (2008) *Leviticus: the priestly laws and prohibitions from the perspective of ancient Near East and Africa,* Studies in Biblical Literature 115, New York: Peter Lang.

Kiple, K.F. (ed.) (1997) *Plague, Pestilence and Disease,* London: Weidenfeld and Nicholson.

Kirk, J.R. and E.T. Leeds (1952-53) 'Three Early Saxon Graves from Dorchester' *Oxoniensia* 17/18, 63-78.

Knowles, D. and R.N. Hadcock (1953) *Medieval Religious Houses: England and Wales,* London: Longman.

Lambrick, G. and M. Robinson (2009) *The Thames through Time,* The *Archaeology of the Gravel Terraces of the Upper and Middle Thames, Early Prehistory to 1500 BC,* Oxford: Thames Valley Landscapes Monograph 29.

LangScape: No date. The Language of Landscape: Reading the Anglo-Saxon Countryside: http://langscape.org.uk

Lattey, R.T, E.J.S. Parsons and I.G. Phillip (1936) 'A Contemporary map of the defences of Oxford in 1644' *Oxoniensia* 1, 161-72.

Lawson, G. (1990) 'Pieces from Stringed instruments' in M. Biddle, *Object and Economy in Medieval Winchester: the arts, crafts, industries and daily life of Medieval Winchester,* Winchester Studies 7: Artefacts from Medieval Winchester, Part 2. Oxford: Clarendon Press, 711-18.

Leeds, E. T. (1916) 'A paper on two Bronze Age hoards from Oxford' *Proceedings of the Society of Antiquaries of London* 2nd ser., 28, 147-52.

Lewis, C. (2007) 'New Avenues for the Investigation of Currently Occupied Medieval Rural Settlements: Preliminary Observations from the Higher Education Field Academy' *Medieval Archaeology* 51, 133-162.

Lewis, C. (2019) 'Test pit excavation within currently occupied rural settlements: results of the English CORS project in 2016' *Medieval Settlement Research* 32, 70-78.

Lewis, J. (2009) *An archaeological evaluation at Bayards Hill Primary School, Waynflete Road, Headington, Oxford,* Thames Valley Archaeology Services Ltd. http://archaeologydataservice.ac.uk/archives/view/greylit/details.cfm?id=7939

Leys, A.M.S. (1938-1941) (2 vols) *The Sandford Cartulary,* Oxford: Oxfordshire Record Society.

Linington, R.E. (1959) 'The Roman Road from Alchester to Dorchester' *Oxoniensia* 24, 103–5.

Lobel, M. D. (ed.) 1957 'Parishes: Little Marlow' *VCH Bucks 3,* 77-84.

Lobel, M. D. (ed.) (1957) 'Parishes: Sandford on Thames' *VCH Oxon 5, Bullingdon Hundred,* 267-275.

Lund, J. (2010) 'At the Water's edge' in M. Carver, A. Sanmark and S. Semple (eds) *Signals of Belief in Early England: Anglo-Saxon Paganism Revisited,* Oxford: Oxbow, 49-66.

Magilton, J., F. Lee and A. Boylston (eds) (2008) *'Lepers outside the Gate': Excavations at the Cemetery of the Hospital of St James and St Mary Magdalene, Chichester, 1986-87 and 1993,* Chichester Excavations vol. 10, York: Council for British Archaeology.

Mallet, E. (1924) *A History of the University of Oxford,* 3 Vols, London: Methuen.

Manchester, K. (1984) 'Tuberculosis and Leprosy in Antiquity: an Interpretation' *Medical History* 28, 162-73.

Manchester, K. and C.A. Roberts (1989) 'The Palaeopathology of Leprosy in Britain: a Review' *World Archaeology* 21, 265-72.

Manning, P. and E.T. Leeds (1921) 'An Archaeological Survey of Oxfordshire' *Archaeologia* 71, 227-65.

May, T. (1922) 'On the pottery from the waste heap discovered at Sandford, near Littlemore, Oxon, in 1879' *Archaeologia* 72 (New Series 22), 225-42.

McNicoll-Norbury, J. (2014) *Minchery Farm allotments, Littlemore, Priory Road, Oxford,* Thames Valley Archaeological Service, unpublished report.

Mellor, M. (1994) 'Oxfordshire Pottery, a synthesis of middle and late Saxon pottery, medieval and early post-medieval pottery in the Oxford Region' *Oxoniensia* 59, 17-217.

Millson, C. (1985) *The History of Donnington Hospital: a family charity,* Newbury: Countryside Books.

Moore, J. (2001) 'Excavations at Oxford Science Park, Littlemore, Oxford' *Oxoniensia* 66, 163–220.

Monk, E. (1999) *Keys: Their History and Collection.* Shire Publications. Great Britain.

Morris, J. (1978) *Domesday Book, Oxfordshire,* Chichester: Phillimore.

Mount, F. (2010) *Full Circle: How the Classical World came back to us,* London: Simon and Schuster.

Mudd, A. and M. Brett (2013) 'Anglo-Saxon and Prehistoric Remains at Oxford Academy, Littlemore, Oxford: Excavations in 2009' *Oxoniensia* 78, 175-88.

Muir, J., Newell, K. and R. Kinchin-Smith (1999) 'Excavations and Building Survey at the former Nuffield Press, Temple Cowley, Oxfordshire (Site of Temple Cowley Manor House)', *Oxoniensia* 64, 297-300.

Munby, J., A. Norton, D. Poore and A. Dodd (2019) *Excavations at Oxford Castle, 1999-2009*, Oxford: Oxford University School of Archaeology.

Murray, P. (2015) 'Littlemore Priory: Medieval Burials at 'One of the Worst Nunneries…' *Medieval Archaeology* 59. 322-7.

Nicholas, M. and D. Hicks (2013). 'Oxfordshire' in D. Hicks and A. Stevenson (eds.) *World Archaeology at the Pitt Rivers Museum: a characterization*, Oxford: Archaeopress, 279-30.

Norton, A. and D. Thomason (2005) 'Excavations at St Hilda's College, Cowley Place, Oxford' *Oxoniensia* 70, 333-6.

Orme, N. and M. Webster (1995) *The English Medieval Hospital 1070-1570*, London & New Haven: Yale University Press.

Ortner, D. (2008) 'Skeletal Manifestations of Leprosy' in J. Magilton, F. Lee and A. Boylston (eds) (2008) *'Lepers outside the Gate': Excavations at the Cemetery of the Hospital of St James and St Mary Magdalene, Chichester, 1986-87 and 1993, Chichester Excavations vol. 10*, York: Council for British Archaeology, 198-207.

O' Sullivan, D. (2006) 'The 'Little Dissolution' of the 1520s' *Post-Medieval Archaeology* 40 (2), 227–58.

Oxford City Council (2013) *Oxford Archaeological Action Plan, 2013-2018, Building a world-class city for everyone*, Oxford, Oxford City Council.

Pantin, W. A. (1970) 'Minchery Farm, Littlemore' *Oxoniensia* 35, 9-27.

Parker, A. (1996) 'A note on the peat deposits at Minchery Farm, Littlemore, Oxford, and their implications for palaeo-environmental reconstruction', *Proceedings of the Cotswold Naturalists Field Club* 41: 1: 129-38.

Parker, A. and A.S. Goudie (2007) 'Late Quaternary Environmental Change in the Limestone regions of Britain', in Goudie, A.S. and J. Klavoda (eds) *Geomorphological Variations*, Prague: Nakladatelství P3K, 157-82.

Palmer, R. (1982) 'The church, leprosy and plague in medieval and early modern Europe', in W. J. Sheils (ed.) *The Church and Healing: vol. 19 of Studies in Church History*, Oxford: Blackwell, 79-99.

Payne, J. (1886), *The English Non-Catholic Jurors of 1715*, New York: Paulist Press.

PCA (Pre-Construct Archaeology) (2014) *An Archaeological Evaluation at Land Adjoining the Priory Public House, Kassam Stadium, Grenoble Road, Littlemore, Oxford*, Unpublished Report

Peake, A.E. (1913) 'An account of a flint factory, with some new types of flints, excavated at Peppard Common, Oxon' *Archaeological Journal* 70, 33-68.

Pevsner, N. (1974) *The Buildings of England: Oxfordshire*, London: Penguin.

Plot, R. (1677) *The Natural History of Oxfordshire*, Oxford: At the Theater.

Pollard, A.M., P. Ditchfield, E. Piva, S. Wallis, C. Falys and S. Ford (2012) 'Sprouted like Cockle amongst the Wheat; The St Brice's Day Massacre and Isotopic Analysis of Human Bones from St John's College, Oxford' *Oxford Journal of Archaeology*, 31 (1), 83-102.

Pollard, J. (1999) 'These Places have Their Moments: Thoughts on Settlement Practices in the British Neolithic' in J. Bruck, and M. Goodman (eds) *Making Places in the Prehistoric World: Themes in Settlement Archaeology*, London: UCL Press, 76-93.

Pollington, S. (1996) *The English Warrior from the earliest times to 1066*, Hockwald-cum-Wilton: Anglo-Saxon Books.

Poore, D., A. Norton and A. Dodd (2009). 'Excavations at Oxford Castle: Oxford's Western Quarter from the Mid-Saxon Period to the Late Eighteenth Century' *Oxoniensia* 74 1-18.

Postles, D. (2002) 'Religious houses and the laity in eleventh- to thirteenth-century England: An overview', *The Haskins Society Journal* 12, 1-14.

Radbill, S.X. (1974) 'Pediatrics' in A.G. Debus (ed) (1974) *Medicine in 17th Century England*, Berkeley: University of California Press, 237-82.

Rawcliffe, C. (2006) *Leprosy in Medieval England*, Woodbridge: Boydell Press.

Reader, R. (1974) 'New Evidence for the Antiquity of Leprosy in Early Britain' *Journal of Archaeological Sciences* 1, 205-7.

Richards, J.D. (1991) *Viking Age England*, English Heritage, London: Batsford.

Richards, P. (1977) *The Medieval Leper and his Northern Heirs*. Woodbridge: D.S. Brewer.

Richards, G. C. and H. E. Salter (1926), *The Dean's Register of Oriel, 1446–1661*, Oxford Historical Society 84, Oxford: Clarendon Press.

Richardson, A.H. (1827) *A Description of the Oxford Baths and School of Natation*, Oxford: Bartlett and Hinton.

Roffey, S. (2012) 'Medieval Leper Hospitals in England: An Archaeological Perspective' *Medieval Archaeology* 56, 203-33.

Rotuli Hundredorum (1818) = *Rotuli Hundredorum, temp. Henr. III. & Edw. I.: in turr' Lond' et in curia receptæ scaccarij Westm. asservati. Vol. II*, London: Printed by command of His Majesty.

Royal Commission on Metropolitan Water Supply (1893) *Report of the Royal Commission Appointed to Inquire Into the Water Supply of the Metropolis:*

Appendices to minutes of evidence, London: HMSO.

RPS Consultants (2001) *Oxford United Football Stadium, Minchery Farm,* Archaeological Assessment report (unpublished), held by Oxford City Council.

Russell, M. (2000) *Flint Mines in Neolithic Britain,* Stroud: Tempus.

Salmon, G.L. (2010) *Beyond Magdalen Bridge: the Growth of East Oxford,* Oxford: East Oxford Archaeology and History Project.

Salter, H. E. (ed.) (1914-17) *Cartulary of the Hospital of St. John the Baptist,* Oxford: Clarendon Press.

Salter, H. E. (ed.) (1929-36) *Cartulary of Oseney Abbey,* Oxford: Clarendon Press.

Salter, H. E. (ed.) (1930) *The Boarstall Cartulary,* Oxford: Clarendon Press.

Salter, H. E. (ed.) (1930) *The Feet of Fines for Oxfordshire, 1195-1291,* Oxford: Oxfordshire Record Society.

Sandford, K. S. and E. T. Leeds (1939) *Early Man of Oxfordshire,* reprinted from the *Victoria County History of Oxfordshire Vol. 1,* London: Institute of Historical Research, 223-372.

Satchell, M. (1998) *The Emergence of Leper-houses in Medieval England, 1100-1250,* Unpublished D.Phil thesis, University of Oxford.

Sawday, J. (1995) *The Body Emblazoned.* London: Routledge.

Seaby, W.A. (1950) 'Late Dark Age finds from the Cherwell and Ray 1876-1886' *Oxoniensia* 15, 30-32.

Sharpe, R. (2014) *Oxford, St Bartholomew's Hospital,* Charters of William II and Henry I, University of Oxfordhttps://actswilliam2henry1.files.wordpress.com/2013/04/h1-oxford-stbart-2014-1.pdf

Sharpe, R.R., ed. (1889) *Calendar of Wills Proved and Enrolled in the Court of Husting, London: Part 1, 1258-1358,* London: John C. Francis.

Sinclair, H.M. and A.H.T. Robb-Smith (1950) *A History of the Teaching of Anatomy in Oxford,* Oxford: Oxford University Press.

Skinner, A. (2005) *Cowley Road, A History,* Oxford: Signal Books.

Smith A. H. (1970) *The Place-Name Elements, 2, The Elements Jafn-Ytri,* English Place-Name Society 26, Cambridge: Cambridge University Press.

Smith, M. L. (ed.) (1980) *Benson of Cowley,* Oxford: Oxford University Press.

Stevenson, J. (ed.) (1858) *Chronicon Monasterii de Abingdon,* London: Longman, Brown, Green, Longmans and Roberts.

Surman, P. (1992) *Pride of the Morning, an Oxford Childhood,* Stroud: Alan Sutton.

Tannahill, R and V. Diez (2008) 'Iron Age and Medieval Quarrying at Barracks Lane, Cowley,

Oxford' *Oxoniensia* 73, 195-7.

Taylor, P. (no date) *Newman and Littlemore,* Littlemore Parish Council Pamphlet, 4.

Thomas, I.G. (1974) *The Cult of Saints' Relics in Medieval England,* Unpublished Ph.D thesis, University of London.

Thomas, V. (1835) *Memorials of the Malignant Cholera at Oxford,* 1832, Oxford: W. Baxter.

Thompson, A. H. (ed.) (1918) *Visitations of religious houses in the Diocese of Lincoln, Volume II, Part I,* Horncastle: Lincoln Record Society.

Thompson, A. H. (ed.) (1944) *Visitations in the Diocese of Lincoln, 1517-1531, Vol. 2,* Hereford: Lincoln Record Society.

Thompson, A. H. (ed.) (1947) *Visitations in the Diocese of Lincoln, 1517-1531, Vol. 3,* Hereford: Lincoln Record Society.

Thompson, S. (1991) *Women religious: the founding of English nunneries after the Norman Conquest,* Oxford: Clarendon Press.

Thorpe, B. (ed.) (1878), *Florentii Wigorniensis monachi Chronicon ex chronicis,* London: English Historical Society.

Tiller, K and G. Darkes (eds) (2010) *An Historical Atlas of Oxfordshire,* Finstock: Oxfordshire Record Society.

Tracey, G. (1995) *The Letters and Diaries of John Henry Newman,* vii. and (1999) viii, Oxford: Clarendon Press.

Turner, W. H. (ed.) (1878) *Calendar of Charters and Rolls Preserved in the Bodleian Library,* Oxford: Clarendon Press.

Valadez, F. (1974) 'Anatomical Studies in Oxford and Cambridge' in A.G. Debus (ed.), 393-420.

VCH Berks 4: W. Page and P. H. Ditchfield (eds.) (1924) *The Victoria History of the Counties of England, A History of the County of Berkshire: Volume 4,* London; Victoria County History. https://www.british-history.ac.uk/vch/berks/vol4

VCH Bucks 3: W. Page (ed.) (1925) The Victoria History of the Counties of England, A History of Buckinghamshire, Volume 3, London, Victoria County History. https://www.britishhistory.ac.uk/vch/bucks/vol3

VCH Oxon 1: L. F. Salzman (ed.) (1939) *The Victoria History of the Counties of England, A History of the County of Oxford: Volume 1.* London: Victoria County History. https://www.british-history.ac.uk/vch/oxon/vol1

VCH Oxon 2: W. Page (ed.) (1907) *The Victoria History of the Counties of England, A History of the County of Oxford: Volume 2: Religious Houses.* London: Victoria County History. https://www.british-history.ac.uk/vch/oxon/vol 2

VCH Oxon 3: Salter, H.E. and M. D. Lobel (eds.) (1954) *The Victoria History of the Counties of*

England, A History of the County of Oxford: Volume 3, The University of Oxford, London. http://www.british-history.ac.uk/vch/oxon/vol3

VCH Oxon 4: A. Crossley and C.R. Elrington (eds.) (1979), *The Victoria History of the Counties of England, A History of the County of Oxford, Volume 4, The City of Oxford,* Oxford: Oxford University Press. https://www.britishhistory.ac.uk/vch/oxon/vol4

VCH Oxon 5: M. D Lobel (ed.) (1957) *The Victoria History of the Counties of England, A History of the County of Oxford: Volume 5, Bullingdon Hundred,* London. http://www.britishhistory.ac.uk/vch/oxon/vol5

Ward-Perkins, J.B. (1940) *London Museum Medieval Catalogue,* London: The London Museum (reprinted in 1993, Ipswich: Anglia Publishing).

Warner, M. (1976) *Alone of All Her Sex: The Myth and the Cult of the Virgin Mary,* London: Weidenfeld and Nicolson.

Watson, S. (2006) 'The origins of the English hospital', *Transactions of the Royal Historical Society* 16, 75-94.

Weaver, J.R.H. and A. Beardwood, A., (eds) (1958), *Some Oxfordshire wills proved in the Prerogative Court of Canterbury, 1393-151,* Oxford: Oxfordshire Record Society.

Whitelock, D. (1979) *English Historical Documents Volume 1, c 500-1042,* London: Eyre Methuen.

Wigram, S. R. (ed) (1895-96) *The Cartulary of the Monastery of St. Frideswide at Oxford,* Oxford: Oxford Historical Society.

Wood, M. (1994) *The English Mediaeval House,* London: Studio Editions.

Woolgar, C. M. (1981) 'A Late Sixteenth Century Map of St Clement's, Oxford' *Oxoniensia* 46, 94-8.

Yates, D. and R. Bradley (2010) 'The Siting of Metalwork Hoards in the Bronze Age of South-East England' *Antiquaries Journal* 90, 41-72.

Young, C. J. (1973) 'The Roman Kiln Site at St. Luke's Road, Cowley, Oxford' *Oxoniensia* 38, 215-252.

Young, C.J. (1977) *The Roman Pottery Industry of the Oxford Region,* Oxford: British Archaeological Reports (British Series No. 43).

Young, C.J. (2000) *The Roman Pottery Industry of the Oxford Region,* Oxford: Archaeopress (updated second edition of Young 1977).

Index

Abingdon Abbey 184, 193-5, 204

Adult Education 37-8

Æthelred II, King 12, 30, 214

Alchester 10, 88, 205

Alldritt, Diane 175

Alnwick, William 190-191

Amesbury Archer 183

Annesley Road 10, 67

Anglo-Saxon Period 11-12, 59, 68, 88-9, 107, 199-216, 227-9

Animal bone 53, 85-86, 126, 165, 169, 171-2, 231

Anatomy, dissection 140-2

Appleton 217, 232

Archaeobotanical remains 125, 171-2, 175

'Archeox', abbreviation explained 39

Ark-T Centre, Cowley 40, 47, 52, 67, 68, 70, 77

Arncott 201

Arnold Road 8, 18

Arrowheads (Prehistoric) 19-20, 153, 176, 183-4

Arrowheads (Medieval) 109, 126, 134-5, 180

Ashmole, Elias 4

Ashmolean Museum 4, 8, 21, 22-26, 26-32, 40, 47, 52, 54, 88, 224, 236

Aston, Mick 6, 41

Atwater, William 192-3

Bagley Wood 181

Baldi, Pier Maria 218

Balfour, Henry 4

Balliol College 144

Barracks Lane 74, 116, 145, 220

Barton 10, 36

Barton Court Farm, Abingdon 11

Bartlemas (St Bartholomew's Chapel) 4, 13, 15, 16-17, 40, 43-7, 50, 52, 67, 70, 72, 83, 90, 121-43, 146-7, 218, 220, 230-1, 233, 240

Bartlemas excavation (2011) 45-46, 121-43, 230-1, 240, 242, 246

Bath Street, St Clements 15, 47, 222-4

Bayswater Hill, Barton 10

Bead, Melon (Roman) 153, 176

Beaker period 183

Bell, A.M. 4, 8-9, 16, 18-20, 22, 54, 228

Bells 135-6, 180, 182

Bell towers 125, 230

Benson, Richard Meux 220

Bernwood First School, Barton 9

Bidford-on-Avon 26

Black Death 139

Blackbird / Greater Leys 1, 6, 9, 10, 33, 36, 41, 51, 67-8, 70, 76-7, 81, 82, 84, 88, 90, 152, 210, 228, 229, 234

Blair, John 12, 28-30

Bodleian Library 47, 189-90

Boar's Hill 3

Bolshipton House 209-210, 218

Bond, C. James 6, 210

Boxgrove 8

Boundary Brook 10, 19-20, 39, 69, 110, 201, 202, 215-16, 245

Boundary Book Nature Park 38-9, 57-8

Brasenose Wood 93-4, 202

Bradley, Richard xv, 47

Brightwell Baldwin 147, 191

Brill 180

British Geological Survey 174

Brome, Adam de 117, 144

Bronze Age 8-9, 19-20, 22-6, 134, 152-3, 157, 159-60, 183, 224

Bullingdon Green 10, 14, 145, 184, 206, 208

Burgess's Meadow (Hoard) 22-6, 235

Burials (Human) 10-11, 45-6, 118, 126-33, 138-44, 175, 186-8, 230-1

Carfax 1

Charles I, King 14, 141

Charters 16, 28, 73, 111, 137, 199-216

Cheney Lane 13, 101, 220

Cheney School 38

Cherwell, River 1, 3, 4, 8-9, 11, 22, 47, 99, 202-5, 208, 214-6, 218

Chester Street 9, 21-2, 235, 247

Chichester 137

Chislet 25

Cholera epidemic, 1832 14, 118, 222

Christ Church (Cardinal College) 14, 47, 54, 218-20, 229, 231

Christ Church Meadow 6, 90

Church Cowley 1, 6, 11, 41, 67-8, 71, 76, 77, 81, 208, 215, 220, 229

Churchill Hospital 10, 86-7

Civil War (English Civil War) 4, 14, 17, 44, 83, 92, 98, 101-3, 111, 117-18, 124, 125, 127, 132-3, 136, 184, 230, 241

Clark, Andrew 4

Clay (Oxford Clay) 5, 10, 22

Clay pipes (tobacco) 132, 136, 174, 183

Clayton, Thomas 141

Coins (Medieval) 126, 134-5, 165, 179
Corallian Limestone 3-4, 10, 30-2, 111, 129, 163
Cornish's Pit 8, 18, 74
Corpus Christi College 203-13
CORS Project 41, 59
Cowley 1, 6, 9, 33, 52, 199-218
Cowley Fathers 220
Cowley Marsh 4, 11, 20, 25, 36, 81, 118, 208, 220, 222, 225, 226
Cowley Road 1, 23, 33, 111-12, 119, 202, 209, 219, 224-5
Crawford, Barbara 28-30
Crescent Road 222
Cricket Road 74, 81, 83

Danes 12, 28-30, 33, 229
De Gomme, Bernard 101-4, 218
Derby, John 186, 231
Detached Parishes Act (1882) 220
Devereux, Robert 184
Dodgson, Charles (Lewis Carroll) 219
Domesday Book 12, 71, 216-17
Donnington 8-9, 16, 36, 45, 50, 62, 67, 68, 74-5, 81, 88, 94-7, 220
Donnington, excavation (2013) 68, 81, 103-10, 228, 240, 243-5
Dorchester-on-Thames 10, 11, 88, 96-7, 205
Dugdale, William 4
Durham, Brian 38, 113

Eastfield House 9, 10
Edward II, King 144, 145
Edward III, King 117
Edward VI, King 140
Elbe, River 27
Enclosure 101, 206-7, 218-22, 227, 229
Evelyn, John 141
Exeter College 136, 189

Fairacres 19, 66, 68, 70, 81, 84, 85, 88, 201, 229
Fairfax, Sir Thomas, General 14
Fingest 147
Fish, Shellfish 130, 172
Floodplains 3, 40
Florence Park 1, 90

Garsington Road 206, 209
Geophysics 41, 43-4, 90-98, 120-1, 228
Gelling, Margaret 145
Gewissae 11
Gilchrist, Roberta 171, 176
Gill, Eric 98
Glass 153, 172
Glisson, Francis 140-1
Godstow Abbey 163, 170, 180, 185, 193
GPS 44, 247
Graham, Malcolm 224

Grandpont 210
Greenshields, Thomas 222
Gregory IX, Pope 116
Grenoble Road 154

Haberly, Loyd 181
Hacklingcroft 214-15
Hamilton, Andrew 41, 55
Harrold Priory 188
Hassall, Tom 6
Happisburgh 8
Harris, Jim 30
Headington 3, 9, 10, 11, 14, 22, 28, 36, 144, 199, 201, 215, 216
Headington Hill Park 2, 218
Henry I, King 14, 116, 144
Henry VIII, King 14
Heritage Lottery Fund 39-40, 50-1
Hewes, Richard 191-3
Highmore, Nathaniel 142
Hockmore Street 6, 77, 81, 215, 217, 220
Horde, Edmund 192-3
Horspath 10, 11, 209, 220
Hospitallers (Knights Hospitaller) 13, 152, 172

Ice Age 8
Iffley 1, 9, 10, 11, 33, 41, 52, 67, 70, 73-4, 79-80, 90, 199-218, 229-30
Iffley Fields 8-9, 18, 70, 74-5, 80-1, 88, 230
Iffley Road 9, 21-2, 36, 201, 209, 229
Innocent IV, Pope 175
Iron Age 9-10, 65
Isotopes 129, 142-3

Jetton, Nuremberg 132, 134-6
Jews 12, 145
Jewitt, Llewellyn 10
John Moore Heritage Services (JMHS) 46, 154-5, 160, 161, 162, 169-70, 175, 176, 186-8, 231
Jope, E.M. 6
Joyliffe, George 141
Julian Housing 47, 238

Kassam Stadium 9, 152-3, 176
Keys 56, 177
'King of Prussia' Public House 9
Kilwinning Abbey 176

Landscape Archaeology 36-7, 40-1
Langdon, Thomas 203-6
Leeds, E.T. 4, 22-5
Leopold Street 30
Leopold Street (Hoard) 9, 16, 22-6, 47, 228, 235
Leprosy 16, 121-7, 138-40, 185, 188, 230
Leper Hospitals 16, 121-5, 137-40
Lewis, Carenza 61
Lewknor, 145

Leviticus, Book of 137, 145
Lidar 44, 93, 95, 99-102, 223
Lincoln, Bishop of 152, 189-93
Lithics 8-9, 18-22, 60, 64-5, 108-9, 134
Little Dissolution 151, 160, 162, 169, 176, 185
Little Marlow 163
Littlemore 9, 33, 41, 75-6, 79, 81, 152, 175, 199-218, 231
Littlemore Book 155, 167, 175, 188-9
Littlemore Brook 4, 68, 70, 76, 152, 202-4, 215
Littlemore Priory 10, 14, 17, 36, 46, 47, 50, 52, 68, 72, 81, 149-197, 230-1, 235, 240, 244
Loggan, David 4, 218
Long Wittenham 232
Lye Valley 10, 202

Magdalen Bridge 1, 6, 11, 13, 14, 26-30, 36, 47, 205, 210, 218-19, 229, 236
Magdalen Wood 10
Manning, Percy 4, 16
Manzil Way 38
Marston 9, 10, 90, 220
Marston Street 220
Matilda, Queen 38, 145, 189, 217
McLaren, Archibald 223
Medieval Period 12-13, 26-32, 60-82, 109, 111-47, 149-82, 186-97, 199-219
Metalworking 25, 175, 178, 179, 209
Mesolithic Period 8-9, 19-20, 64-5, 103, 158-60
Mileways Act, 1576 218
Milham Meadow / Ford 210, 219, 222
Mills 205, 216, 223
Minchery Paddock excavation (2012) 46-8, 149-197, 230-1, 232-3, 234, 240, 242, 245-6, 248
Moore, Sir Norman 139
Morris Motors 33
Museum of Oxford 232, 241
Musical instruments (Medieval) 134-5, 165, 175, 179, 231
Musket balls, lead 132

Neolithic Period 8-9, 19-20, 22, 64-5, 104-7, 110, 134, 153, 183-4
Neolithic Flint Mines 22
Newman, John Henry 188, 195, 196-7, 224
Northfield Brook 4, 9, 155, 203, 215
Northfield School 243-4
Nuneham 22
NVQ 49

OAHS 6, 38
Open fields 2, 203-6, 229
Ordnance Survey 2, 22
Oriel College 13, 45, 47, 54, 117, 128, 132, 139, 145, 147
Oseney (Osney) Abbey 208
Oxen Ford 11, 29

Oxentia (formerly Isis Innovation) 51
Oxford Academy (Peers School) 11, 68
Oxford Archaeological Unit 6
Oxford Archaeology (OA) 6, 38, 53, 118, 240
'Oxford Before the University' 11
Oxford Brookes University 38, 47
Oxford Castle 6, 11, 142, 237
Oxford Improvement Act (1771) 218
Oxford Research Archive 50
Oxford Science Park 6, 9, 11, 68, 70, 88, 152-4, 176, 229
Oxfordshire History Centre 54
'Oxoniensia' 4

Palaeolithic period 3, 8, 18, 157-9
Palstaves 22-6
Pantin, W.A. 6, 154, 173, 169, 175, 231
Peat deposits 9, 155-9, 231
Peppard Common 22
Pitt Rivers Museum 4, 18, 38, 47
Place-names 16, 145, 147, 199-214
Pleistocene 8, 157
PPG16 6
Pollen analysis 68, 156
Port Meadow 8
Postumus (Roman coin of) 55-6, 85
Post-Medieval Period 14-15
Pottery (Prehistoric) 63-5
Pottery (Roman) 63, 65-8, 118, 134, 153, 159-60, 169, 177-80, 228
Pottery (Anglo-Saxon) 63, 68-72, 107-9, 177, 229
Pottery (Medieval) 60-3, 74, 81, 88-90, 108-9, 118-9, 122, 125-6, 134-5, 152, 159, 165, 171, 173, 177, 229-31
Pottery (Post-Medieval) 63, 81-5, 132, 135-6, 173, 177, 179
Poundbury Camp 139
Powder cap 184
Pre-Construct Archaeology 154
Pressed Steel Works, excavation 10

Radford, David 38
Radiocarbon dates 70, 106-7, 127, 130, 132, 137, 158-9, 161, 163, 165, 185
Railway (Oxford to Princes Risborough) 152
Randall McIver, David and Joanna 98
Raunds 176
Rawcliffe, Carole 137
Reading 29
Repton 29
Research Questions 15-17
Restore 40, 42
Reformation 14, 32, 152
Rewley Abbey 180
Rewley House 52-4
Richardson, Andrew 222-3
Ridge and Furrow 1, 98-103

Roberts, Alison 54
Roman Period 9-10, 16, 61, 65-8, 104, 107, 153, 228
Roman Pottery Industry 10, 16, 67-8, 86-8, 152-3, 177, 228
Roman Roads 10-11, 67, 93-5, 228
Romsley 147
Rose Hill 1, 4, 9, 10, 11, 36, 43, 67, 81, 92-3, 202, 226
Rowley, Trevor 6

Salmon, Graeme 15
Sandford 13, 14, 76, 152, 175, 189, 193-4, 202, 205
Sandford, Robert de 189, 193
Sandford, Christine de 189, 194
Shapwick Project 41, 59
Shield boss (Anglo-Saxon) 11, 26-8
Shotover Forest 10, 13, 69, 70, 201-2, 208
Shroud pins (Medieval) 177, 179, 188
Skerne 30
Skinner, Annie 15
Slade, The 202
Smith, Andrew MP xvii, 41
South Park 2, 33, 44, 92, 98-103, 218, 227
Southfield Farm 222
Spoon handle (Medieval) 134-5
Stanley Road 85, 229
St Aldate's 179
St Anselm 188-90
St Bartholomew (cult of) 14, 111, 116-18, 138-9, 144-7
St Brice's Day Massacre 12, 29, 33, 214, 229
St Catherine's College 224
St Chad (dedications to) 194
St Clement (dedications to) 12, 229
St Clements 1, 3, 6, 12, 13, 14, 26-32, 47, 101, 118, 205, 209, 214, 218, 221, 233
St Clement's Church (Old) 12, 14-15, 47, 101, 218-9
St Clement Dane (London) 29
St Ebbe's 6, 225
St Edmund (dedications to) 194-5
St Frideswide's Minster / Priory 11, 193, 201, 214
St George's House, Littlemore 47, 195-7, 231
St John's College (burials) 12, 143
St Mary (dedications to) 193-4
St Mary Magdalen, Partney 125
St Mary Magdalen, Winchester 138, 230
St Nicholas (dedications to) 193-4
Stephen, King 151
Stirrups (Viking) 28-30
Stockmore Street 220
Stonehenge 183
Svein Forkbeard, King of Denmark 12

Tacitus 28
Taunt, Henry 14-15, 117, 121, 133, 222, 224-6
Templars (Knights Templar) 13, 16, 77, 78, 152, 172, 175, 186, 189
Temple Cowley 1, 6, 13, 41, 56, 71, 77-8, 79, 83, 209, 215, 220, 225-6
Temple Farm, Sandford 13
Test pits 16, 41, 59-86, 119-20
Thames Discovery Programme 41
Thames Gravels 3, 9, 18, 40, 95-8, 109,
Thames, River 1, 3, 4, 8, 19, 22, 74, 86, 95, 99, 163, 202-3, 216, 226
'Thames through Time' 8
Third Lateran Council (1179) 138
Tiles, Floor (Medieval) 165, 170, 173, 180-2, 186
Tiles, Roof (Medieval) 165, 172-3, 180-2
Toggle (Medieval) 177, 179
Tolley, Job 223
Tomlins, Richard 141
Torksey 29
Trapham, Thomas 141
Trinity College 142
Tweezers (Medieval) 177, 179

Victoria County History 15

Wallingford 59
Warneford Meadow 90
Watlington 145
Wells, springs 4, 112-13, 137-9, 145, 194, 202-203, 212
Wells, Katherine 152, 188-93
Westgate Centre, excavation 6, 232
Weston, Adam de 117
Whetstones 125, 134-5
Whittlewood Project 41, 59, 61
Whittock, Nathaniel 222-3
Wick Farm 10
Williams, Gwilym 173, 180
Wittenham Clumps 9
Woburn 192
Wolsey, Cardinal Thomas 14, 193, 219, 231
Wolvercote Brick Pit 8, 18
Wood, Anthony 4, 14, 116, 145, 152
Wood Farm 1, 36
Woodland Clearance 8-9, 33
Woolley, Liz 15
Wulfheodenas 47, 236
Wytham Woods 3

Yarnton 70